INTRODUCTION

"What do you do at work Daddy?"

When Alex Osterwalder, the inventor of the Business Model Canvas, tried to answer this question from his children, the Biz4Kids comic was born.

Together with his friend Holger Nils Pohl, a business coach and visual strategist, and Holger's team of illustrators, they invented the stories, created the characters and drew and designed this comic, supported by Alex' and Holger's children and their friends.

The comic is first and foremost made to entertain and engage kids aged 7 and above. And teachers, parents and grandparents will also enjoy reading this book to their kids.

Business and entrepreneurship should not be reserved for adults only. These important topics should be introduced to children as early as possible. Showing kids how business works at an early age allows them to take advantage of the countless opportunities that exist in today's world.

IDEA
ALEX OSTERWALDER AND HOLGER NILS POHL

STORY
ALEX OSTERWALDER, HOLGER NILS POHL,
BENI DAMMEIER, NELE POTTHOFF, LUKAS THUM

LATIF BALDÉ, MALINA OSTERWALDER
ALENA POHL, MIRIAM KUCKHOFF-POHL

COVER
LUKAS THUM

ART DIRECTION
LUKAS THUM

ILLUSTRATIONS
BENI DAMMEIER, LUKAS THUM

COLORS
BENI DAMMEIER, NELE POTTHOFF, LUKAS THUM

DIALOGUE
BENI DAMMEIER, NELE POTTHOFF, LUKAS THUM

EDITING & PROJECTMANAGEMENT
LUCA BERNASCONI, NELE POTTHOFF

SPECIAL THANKS TO
STEVE BLANK,
FRANCK DEBANE, LÉONARD DEBANE,
RICK DWYER, HADLEY DWYER,
SÉBASTIEN TONDEUR, MARYLOU TONDEUR,
REEM ALMAREI, HAMAD ALMAREI,
MARCELO DE ABREU BRANDI

CREDENTIALS
BIZ4KIDS – A BUSINESS MODEL COMIC FOR KIDS
ALEXANDER OSTERWALDER AND HOLGER NILS POHL

CHEMIN DES ABBESSES 21
1027 LONAY
SWITZERLAND

BIZ4KIDS

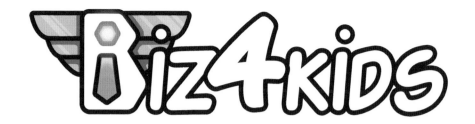

CHAPTER 1: AUSTRALIA

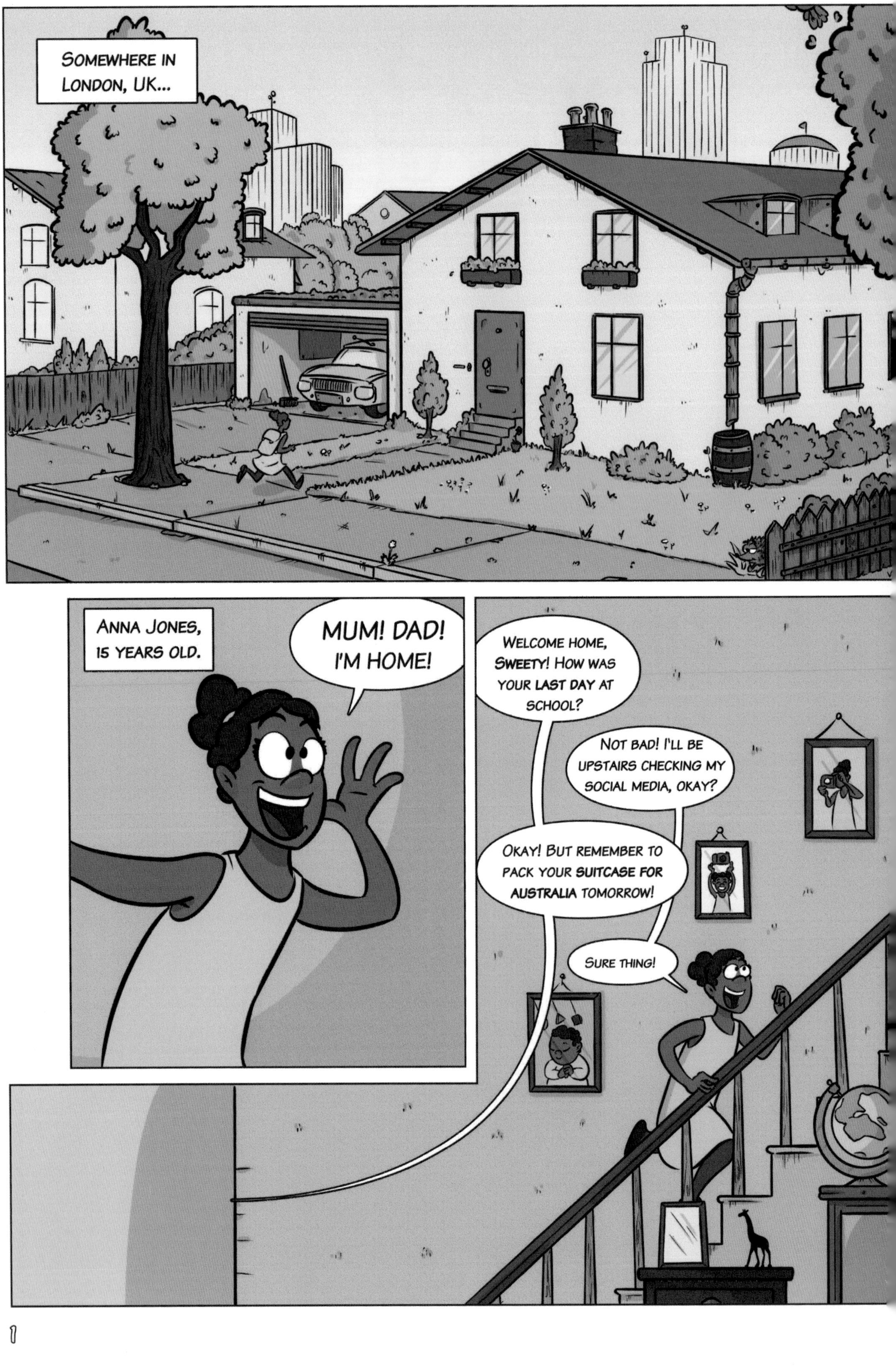

SOMEWHERE IN LONDON, UK...
ANNA JONES, 15 YEARS OLD.
MUM! DAD! I'M HOME!
WELCOME HOME, SWEETY! HOW WAS YOUR LAST DAY AT SCHOOL?
NOT BAD! I'LL BE UPSTAIRS CHECKING MY SOCIAL MEDIA, OKAY?
OKAY! BUT REMEMBER TO PACK YOUR SUITCASE FOR AUSTRALIA TOMORROW!
SURE THING!

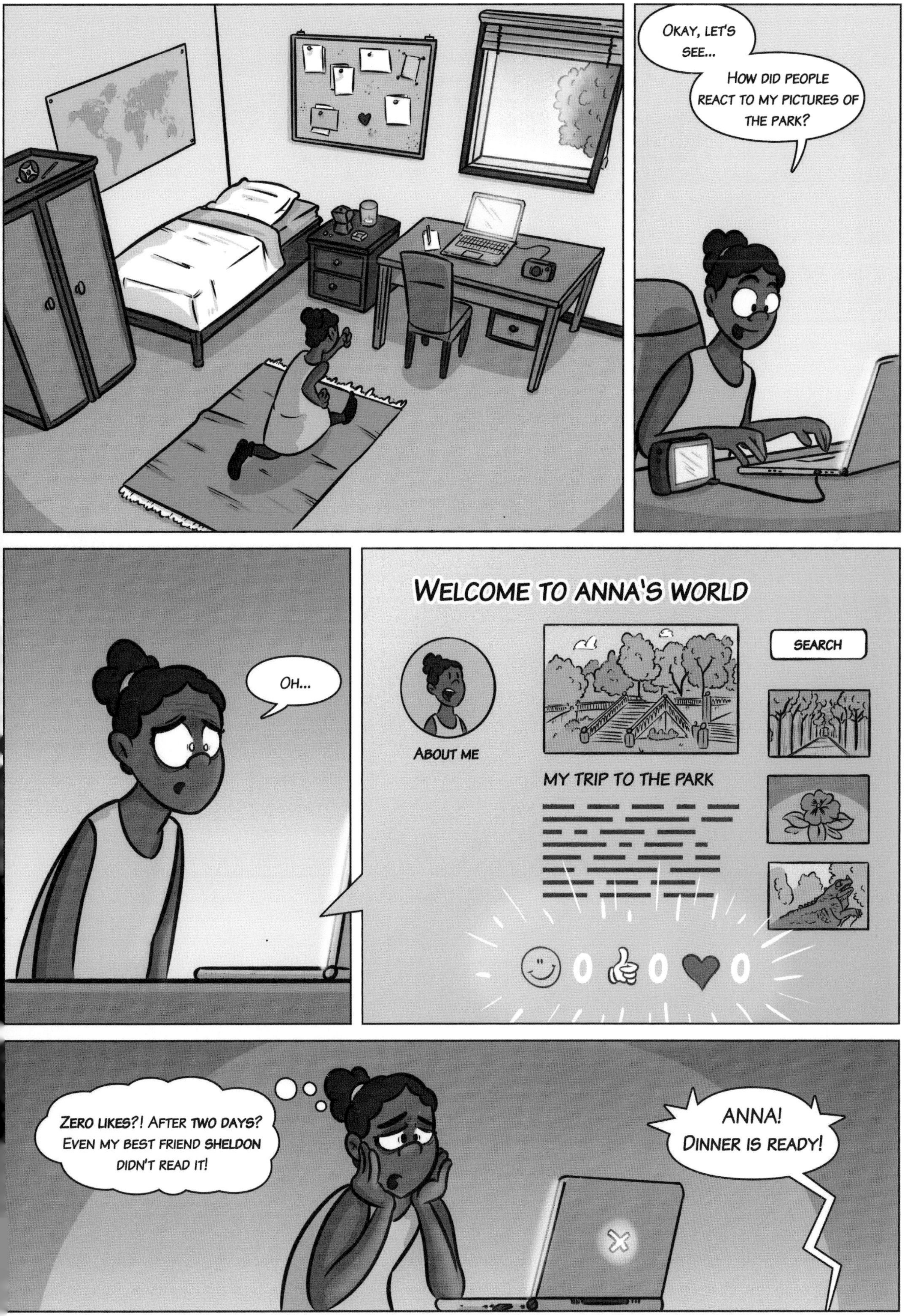

Okay, let's see...
How did people react to my pictures of the park?
Oh...
Welcome to Anna's world
About me
Search
My trip to the park
0 0 0
Zero likes?! After two days? Even my best friend Sheldon didn't read it!
ANNA! Dinner is ready!

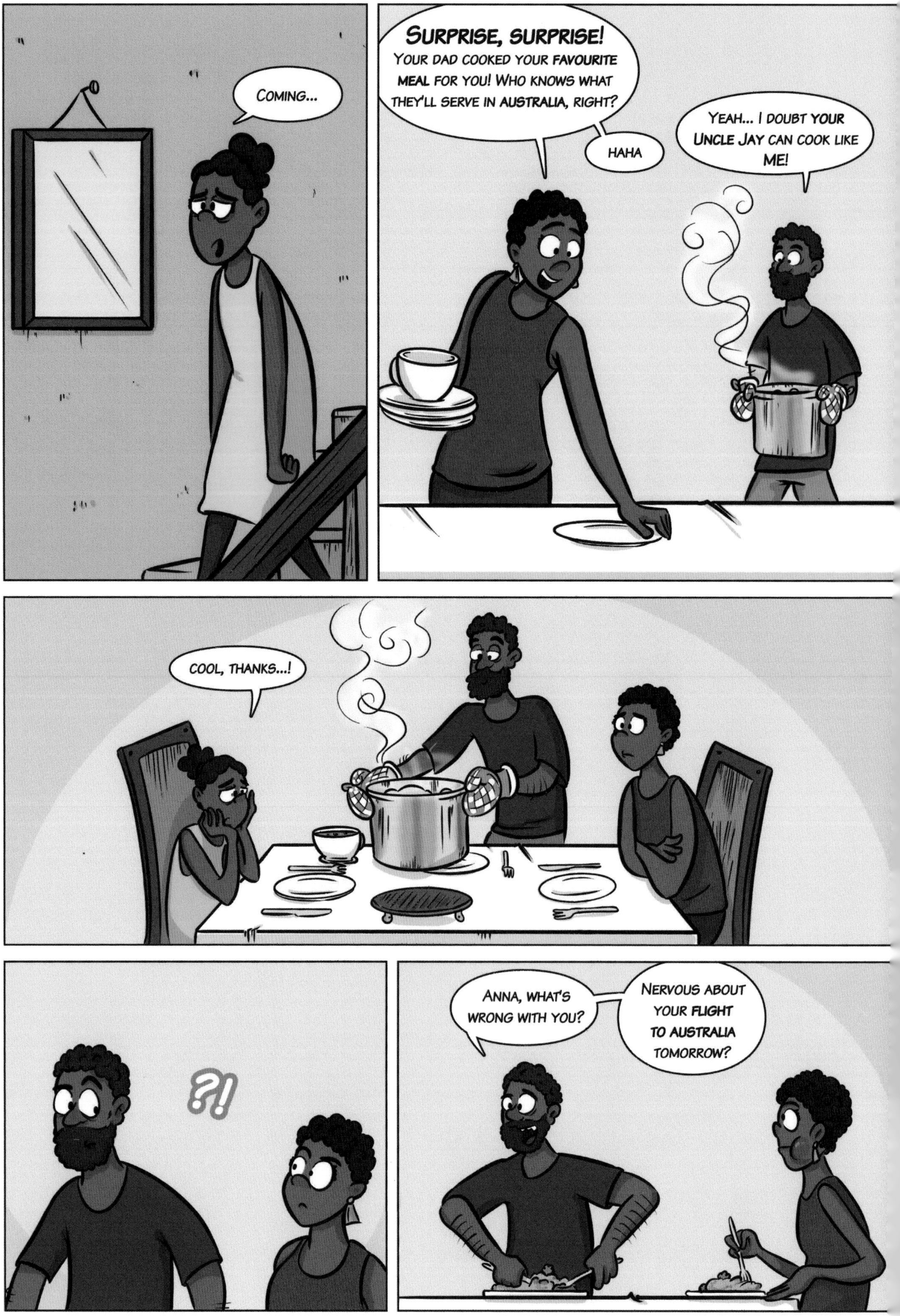
COMING...
SURPRISE, SURPRISE!
YOUR DAD COOKED YOUR FAVOURITE MEAL FOR YOU! WHO KNOWS WHAT THEY'LL SERVE IN AUSTRALIA, RIGHT?
HAHA
YEAH... I DOUBT YOUR UNCLE JAY CAN COOK LIKE ME!
COOL, THANKS...!
?!
ANNA, WHAT'S WRONG WITH YOU?
NERVOUS ABOUT YOUR FLIGHT TO AUSTRALIA TOMORROW?

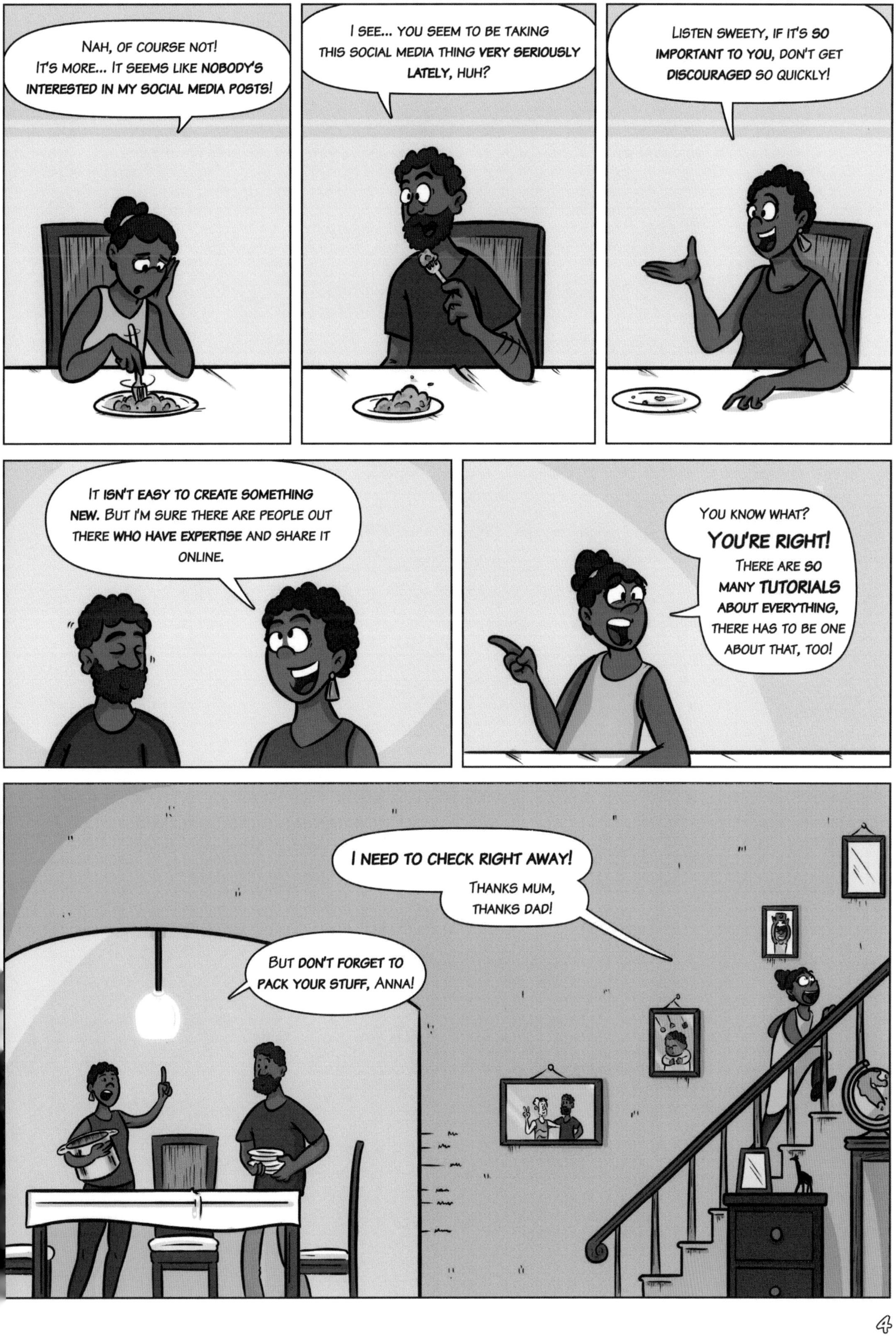
NAH, OF COURSE NOT! IT'S MORE... IT SEEMS LIKE NOBODY'S INTERESTED IN MY SOCIAL MEDIA POSTS!
I SEE... YOU SEEM TO BE TAKING THIS SOCIAL MEDIA THING VERY SERIOUSLY LATELY, HUH?
LISTEN SWEETY, IF IT'S SO IMPORTANT TO YOU, DON'T GET DISCOURAGED SO QUICKLY!
IT ISN'T EASY TO CREATE SOMETHING NEW. BUT I'M SURE THERE ARE PEOPLE OUT THERE WHO HAVE EXPERTISE AND SHARE IT ONLINE.
YOU KNOW WHAT? YOU'RE RIGHT! THERE ARE SO MANY TUTORIALS ABOUT EVERYTHING, THERE HAS TO BE ONE ABOUT THAT, TOO!
I NEED TO CHECK RIGHT AWAY!
THANKS MUM, THANKS DAD!
BUT DON'T FORGET TO PACK YOUR STUFF, ANNA!

AND A FEW SEARCHES LATER...

OH, THIS ONE COULD BE INTERESTING ...

HEY THERE, I'M STEVE. I WANT TO TALK TO YOU ABOUT **THE POSITIVE ASPECTS OF FAILURE.** YES, THE GOOD PART! IT'S OKAY TO FAIL WHEN YOU ARE TRYING SOMETHING NEW THAT YOU ARE **PASSIONATE ABOUT.**

STEVE BLANK, BUSINESS EXPERT

"OF COURSE FAILURE IS ANNOYING. IT'S EMBARRASSING, BUT YOU CAN LEARN FROM YOUR MISTAKES AND ADAPT YOUR IDEAS."

"**BE BRAVE** AND DON'T LOOSE COURAGE BECAUSE OF YOUR MISTAKES. LEARN FROM THEM! THEN ASK YOURSELF WHAT WENT WRONG. WHAT DID YOU LEARN AND **WHAT CAN YOU DO DIFFERENTLY?**

NOW TRY AGAIN! "

"**DON'T GIVE UP** UNTIL YOU FIGURE OUT WHAT WORKS!"

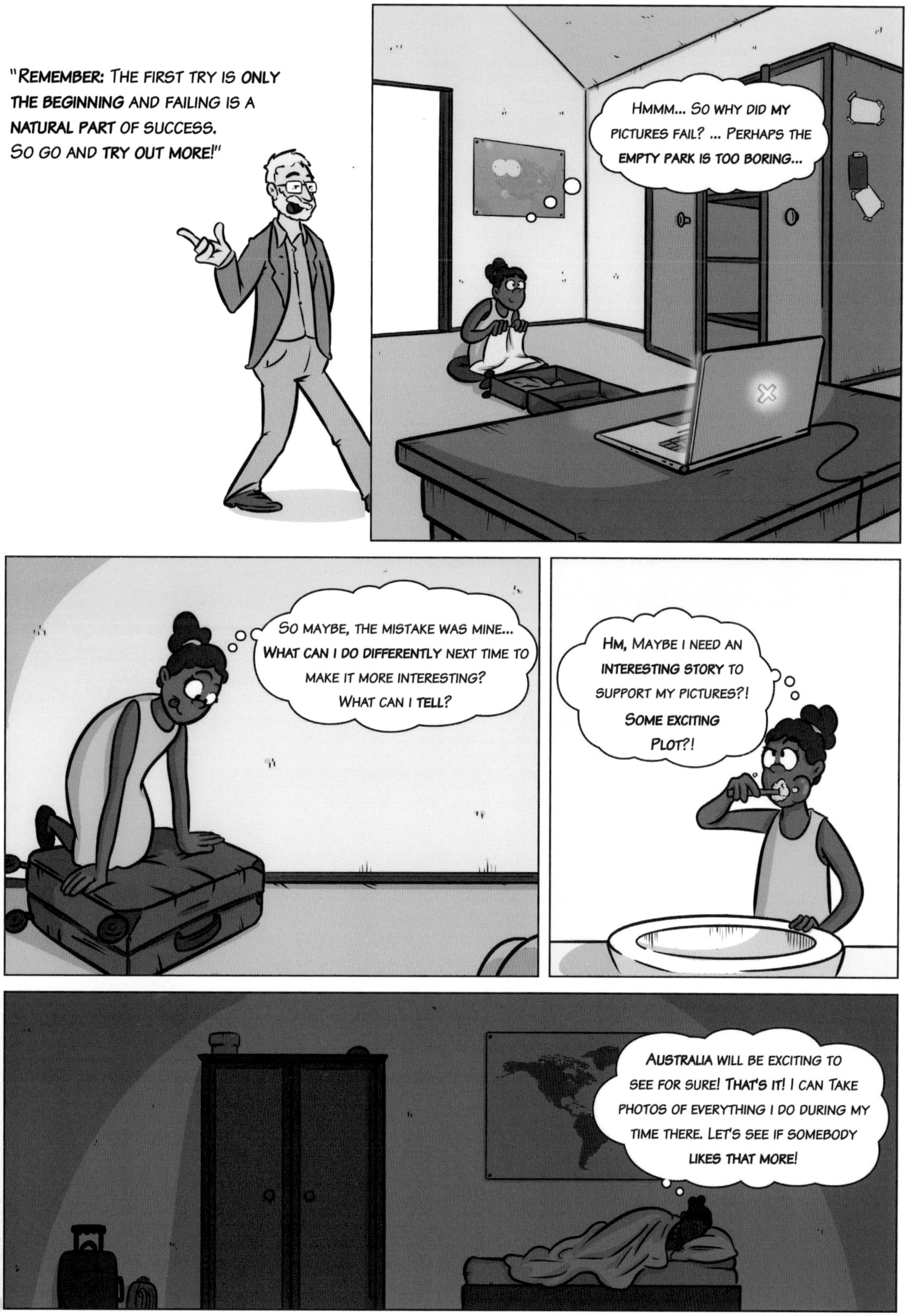
"REMEMBER: THE FIRST TRY IS ONLY THE BEGINNING AND FAILING IS A NATURAL PART OF SUCCESS. SO GO AND TRY OUT MORE!"
HMMM... SO WHY DID MY PICTURES FAIL? ... PERHAPS THE EMPTY PARK IS TOO BORING...
SO MAYBE, THE MISTAKE WAS MINE... WHAT CAN I DO DIFFERENTLY NEXT TIME TO MAKE IT MORE INTERESTING? WHAT CAN I TELL?
HM, MAYBE I NEED AN INTERESTING STORY TO SUPPORT MY PICTURES?! SOME EXCITING PLOT?!
AUSTRALIA WILL BE EXCITING TO SEE FOR SURE! THAT'S IT! I CAN TAKE PHOTOS OF EVERYTHING I DO DURING MY TIME THERE. LET'S SEE IF SOMEBODY LIKES THAT MORE!

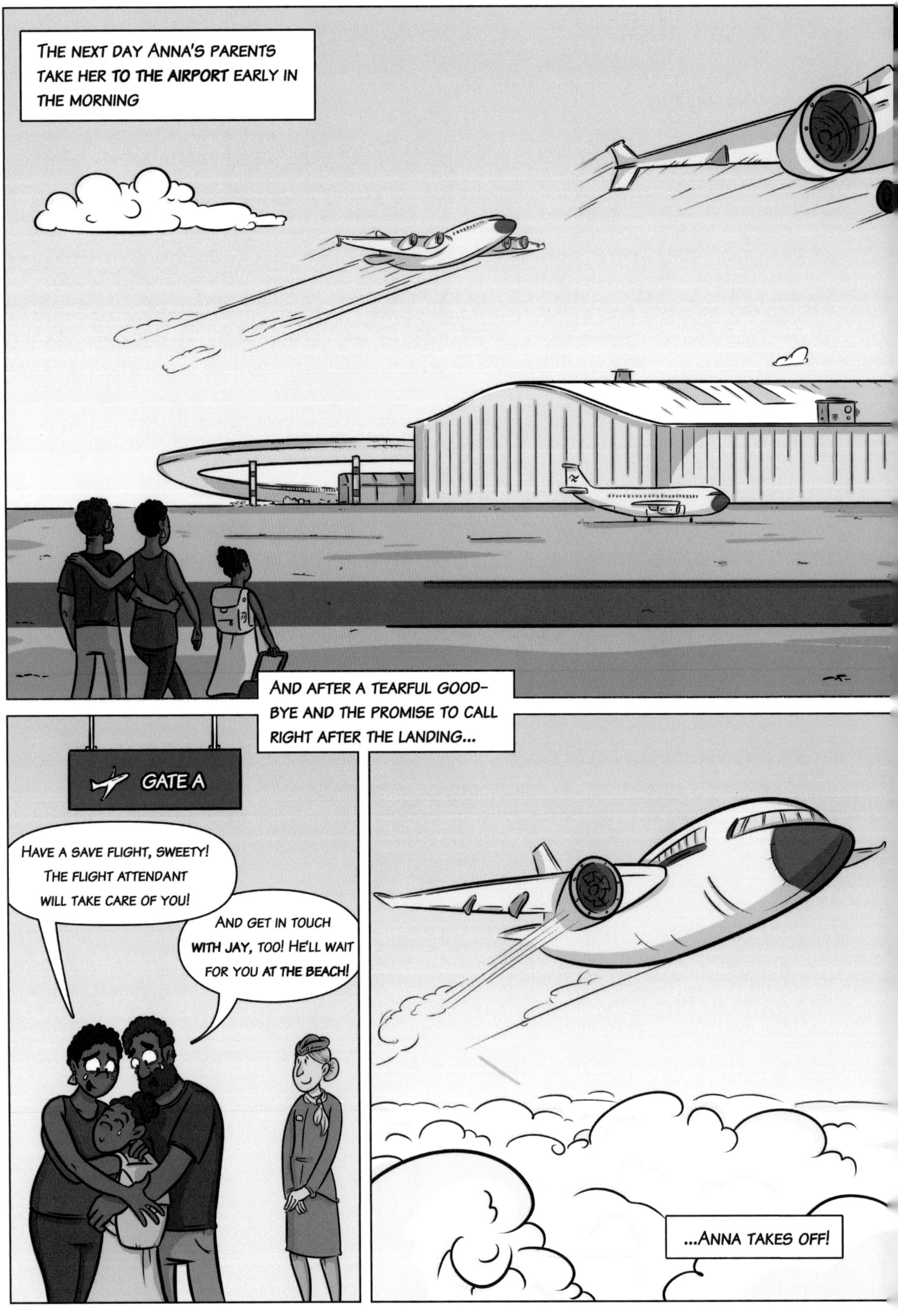
THE NEXT DAY ANNA'S PARENTS TAKE HER TO THE AIRPORT EARLY IN THE MORNING
AND AFTER A TEARFUL GOOD-BYE AND THE PROMISE TO CALL RIGHT AFTER THE LANDING...
GATE A
HAVE A SAVE FLIGHT, SWEETY! THE FLIGHT ATTENDANT WILL TAKE CARE OF YOU!
AND GET IN TOUCH WITH JAY, TOO! HE'LL WAIT FOR YOU AT THE BEACH!
...ANNA TAKES OFF!

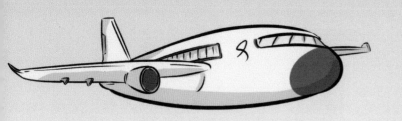

22 LONG HOURS LATER, FINALLY:

AUSTRALIA!

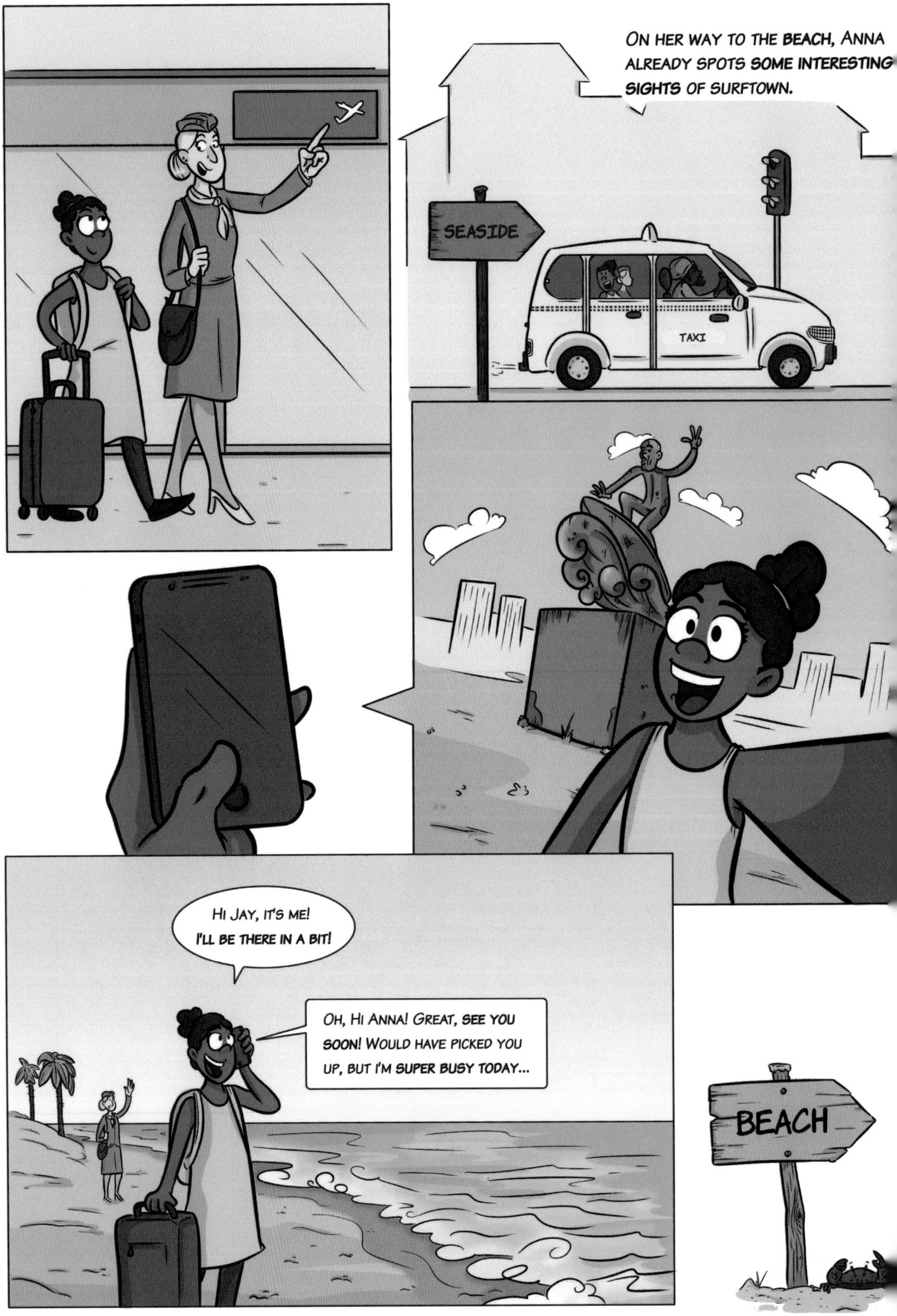
ON HER WAY TO THE BEACH, ANNA ALREADY SPOTS SOME INTERESTING SIGHTS OF SURFTOWN.
SEASIDE
TAXI
HI JAY, IT'S ME! I'LL BE THERE IN A BIT!
OH, HI ANNA! GREAT, SEE YOU SOON! WOULD HAVE PICKED YOU UP, BUT I'M SUPER BUSY TODAY...
BEACH

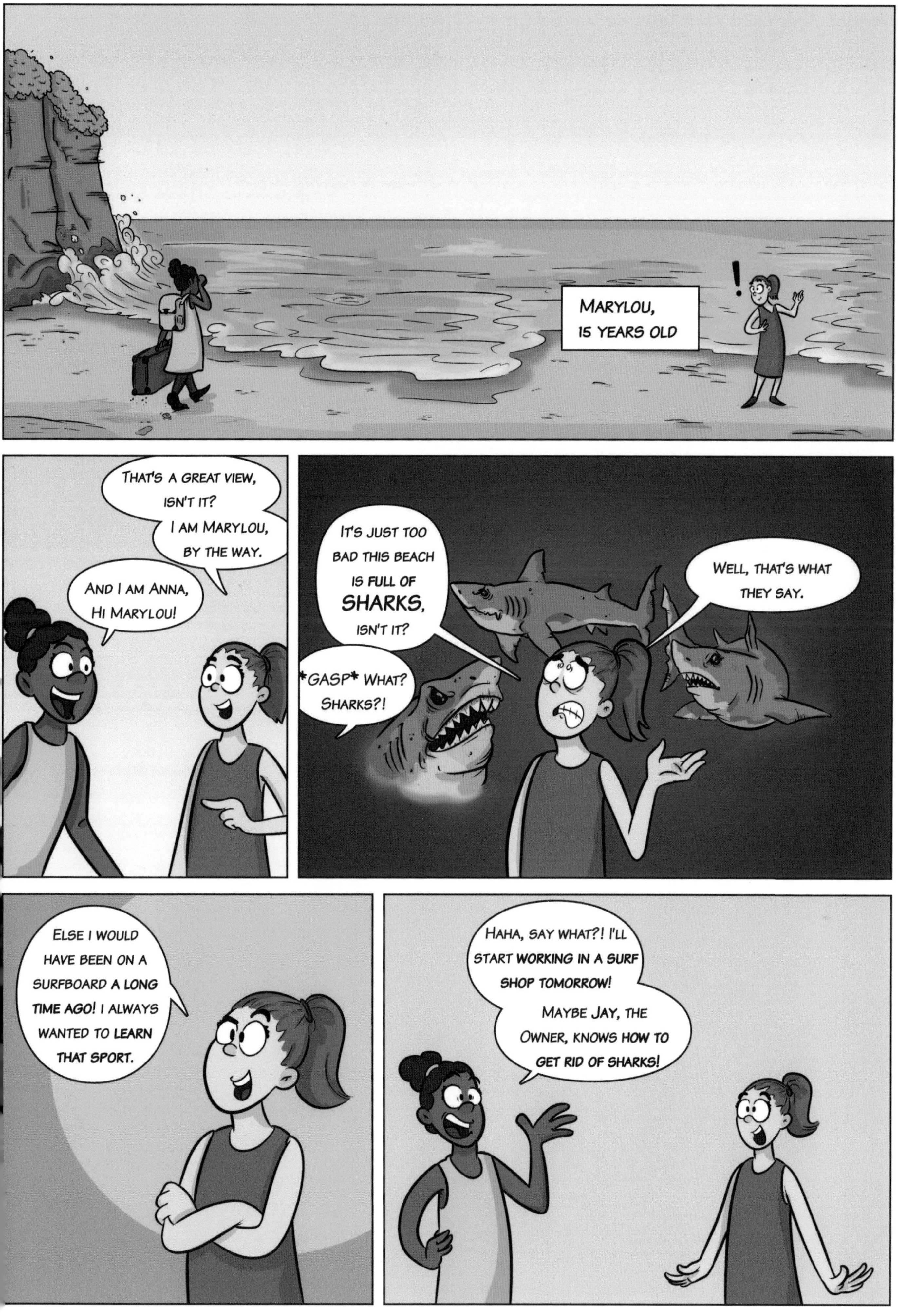
MARYLOU, 15 YEARS OLD
!
THAT'S A GREAT VIEW, ISN'T IT?
I AM MARYLOU, BY THE WAY.
AND I AM ANNA, HI MARYLOU!
IT'S JUST TOO BAD THIS BEACH IS FULL OF SHARKS, ISN'T IT?
GASP WHAT? SHARKS?!
WELL, THAT'S WHAT THEY SAY.
ELSE I WOULD HAVE BEEN ON A SURFBOARD A LONG TIME AGO! I ALWAYS WANTED TO LEARN THAT SPORT.
HAHA, SAY WHAT?! I'LL START WORKING IN A SURF SHOP TOMORROW!
MAYBE JAY, THE OWNER, KNOWS HOW TO GET RID OF SHARKS!

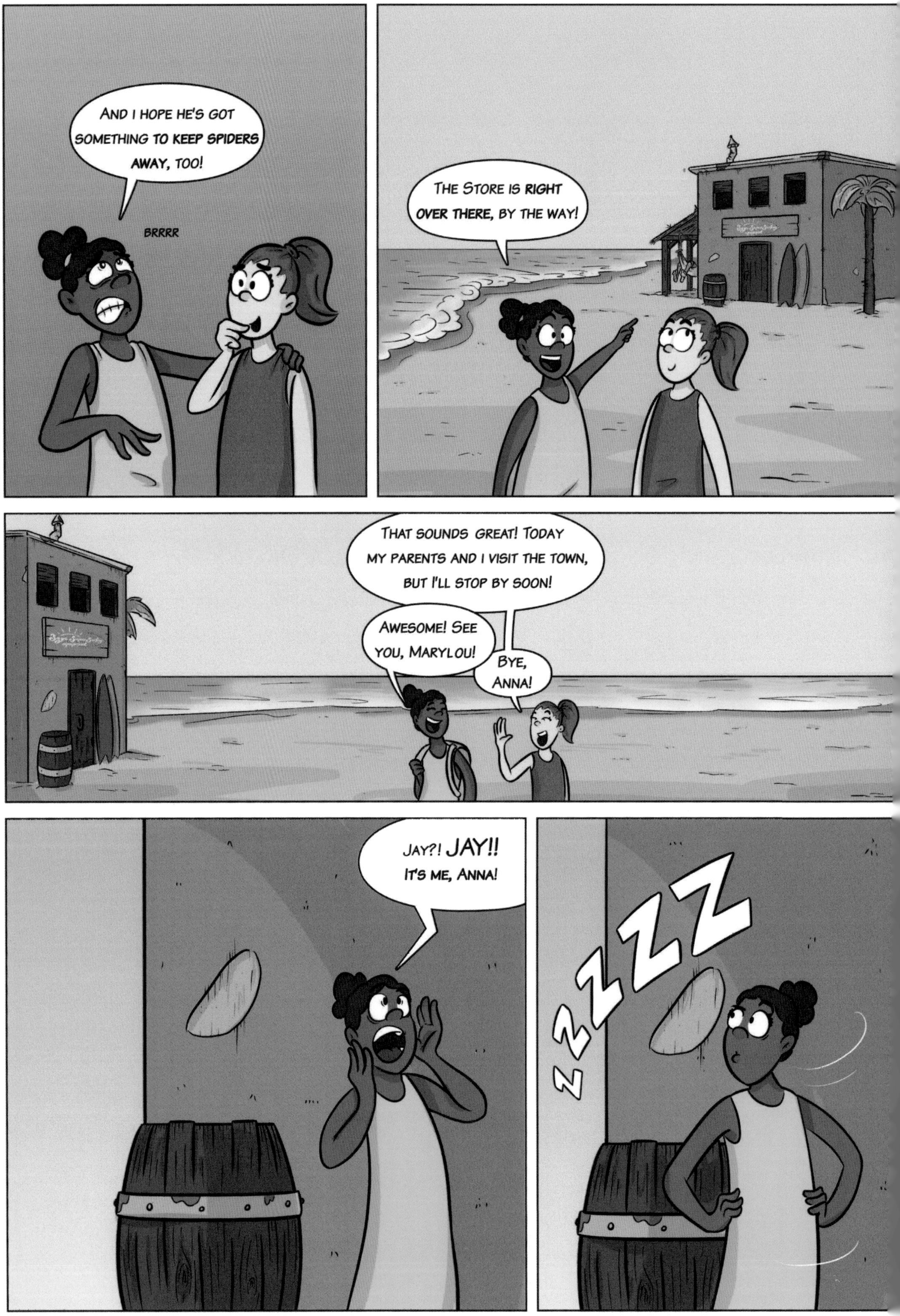

And I hope he's got something to keep spiders away, too!
BRRRR
The Store is right over there, by the way!
That sounds great! Today my parents and I visit the town, but I'll stop by soon!
Awesome! See you, Marylou!
Bye, Anna!
Jay?! JAY!! It's me, Anna!
ZZZZZZ

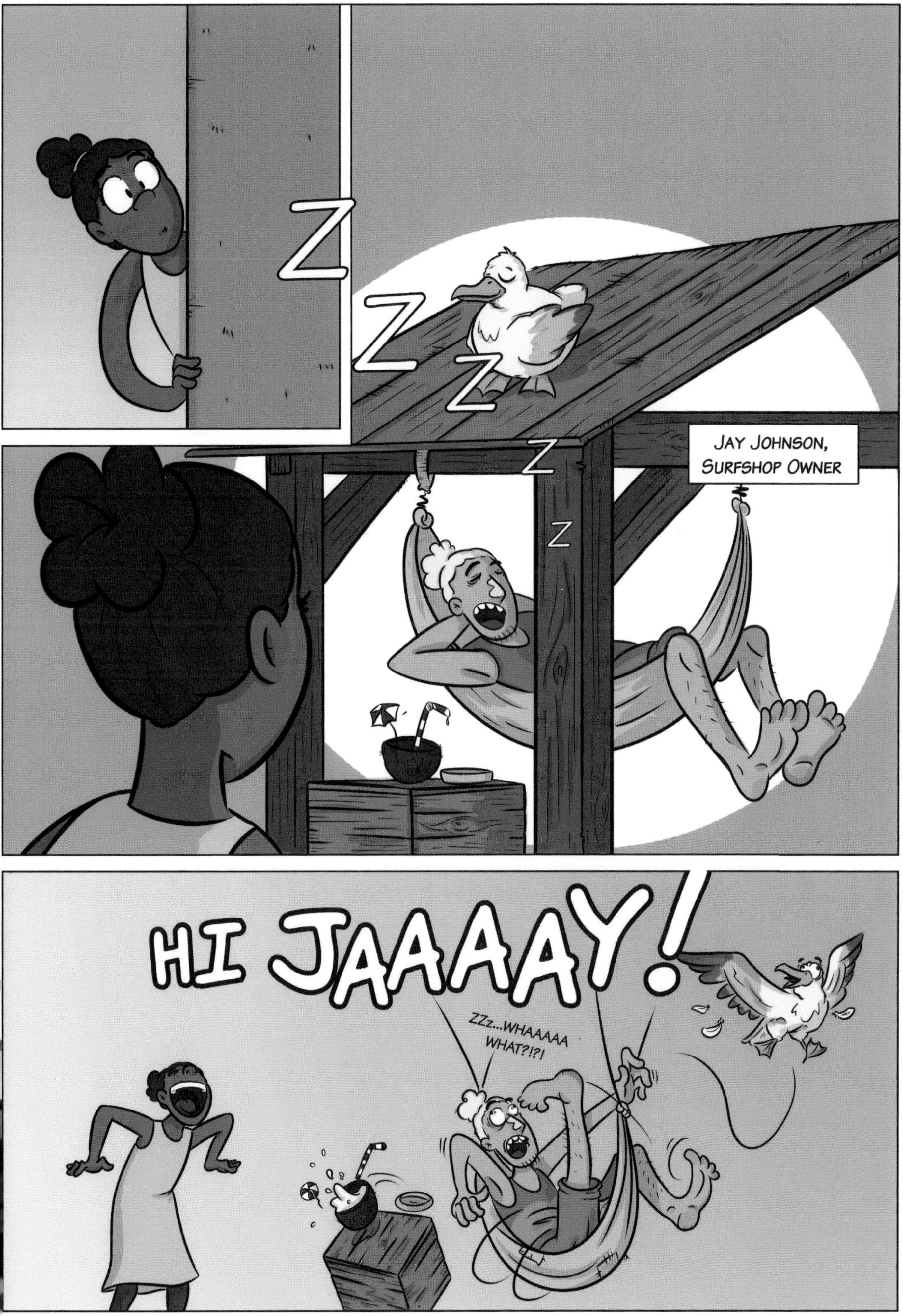
Z
Z
Z
Z
Z
JAY JOHNSON,
SURFSHOP OWNER
HI JAAAAY!
ZZz...WHAAAAA
WHAT?!?!

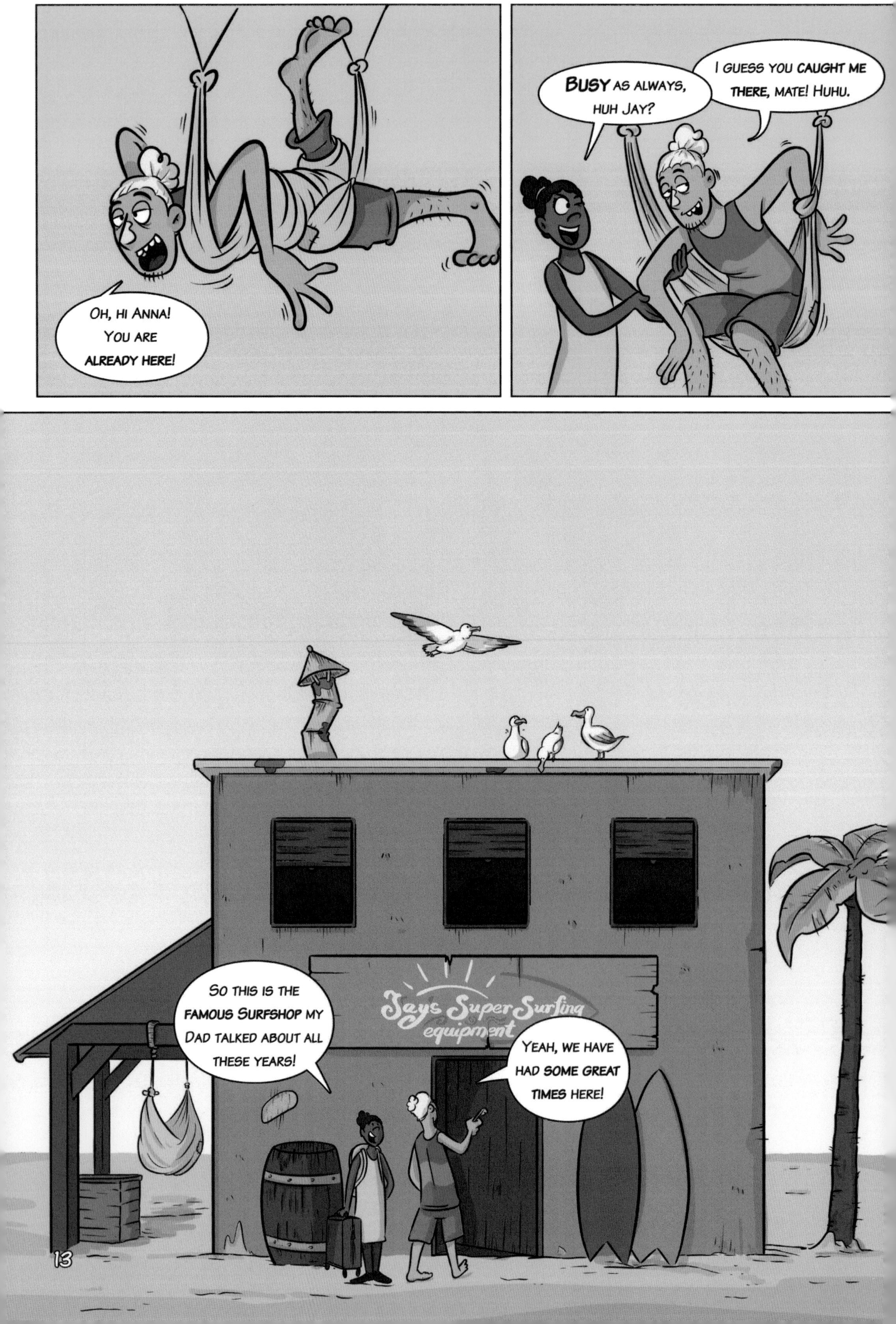
Oh, hi Anna! You are already here!
Busy as always, huh Jay?
I guess you caught me there, mate! Huhu.
Jays Super Surfing equipment
So this is the famous Surfshop my Dad talked about all these years!
Yeah, we have had some great times here!

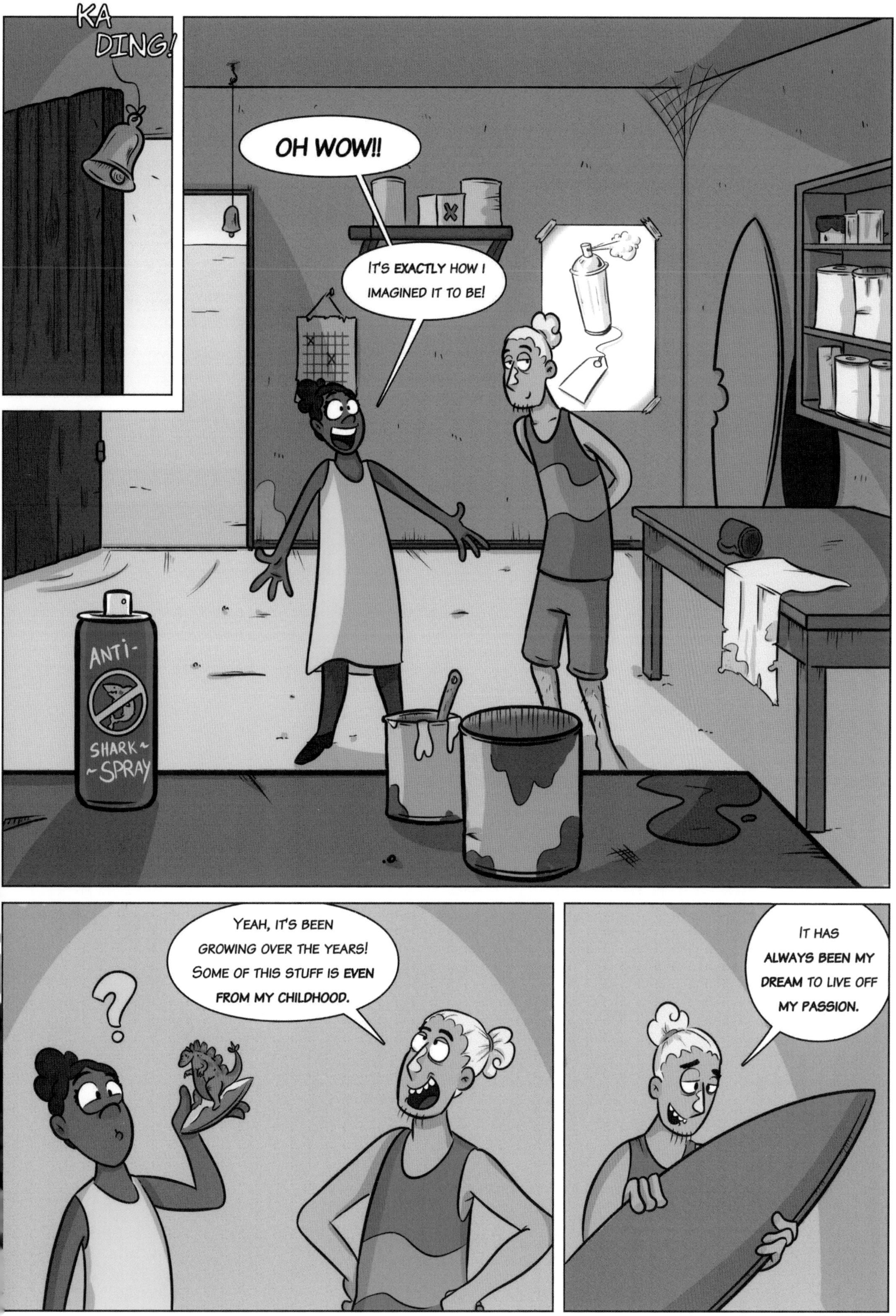
KA DING!
OH WOW!!
IT'S EXACTLY HOW I IMAGINED IT TO BE!
ANTI- SHARK ~SPRAY
?
YEAH, IT'S BEEN GROWING OVER THE YEARS! SOME OF THIS STUFF IS EVEN FROM MY CHILDHOOD.
IT HAS ALWAYS BEEN MY DREAM TO LIVE OFF MY PASSION.

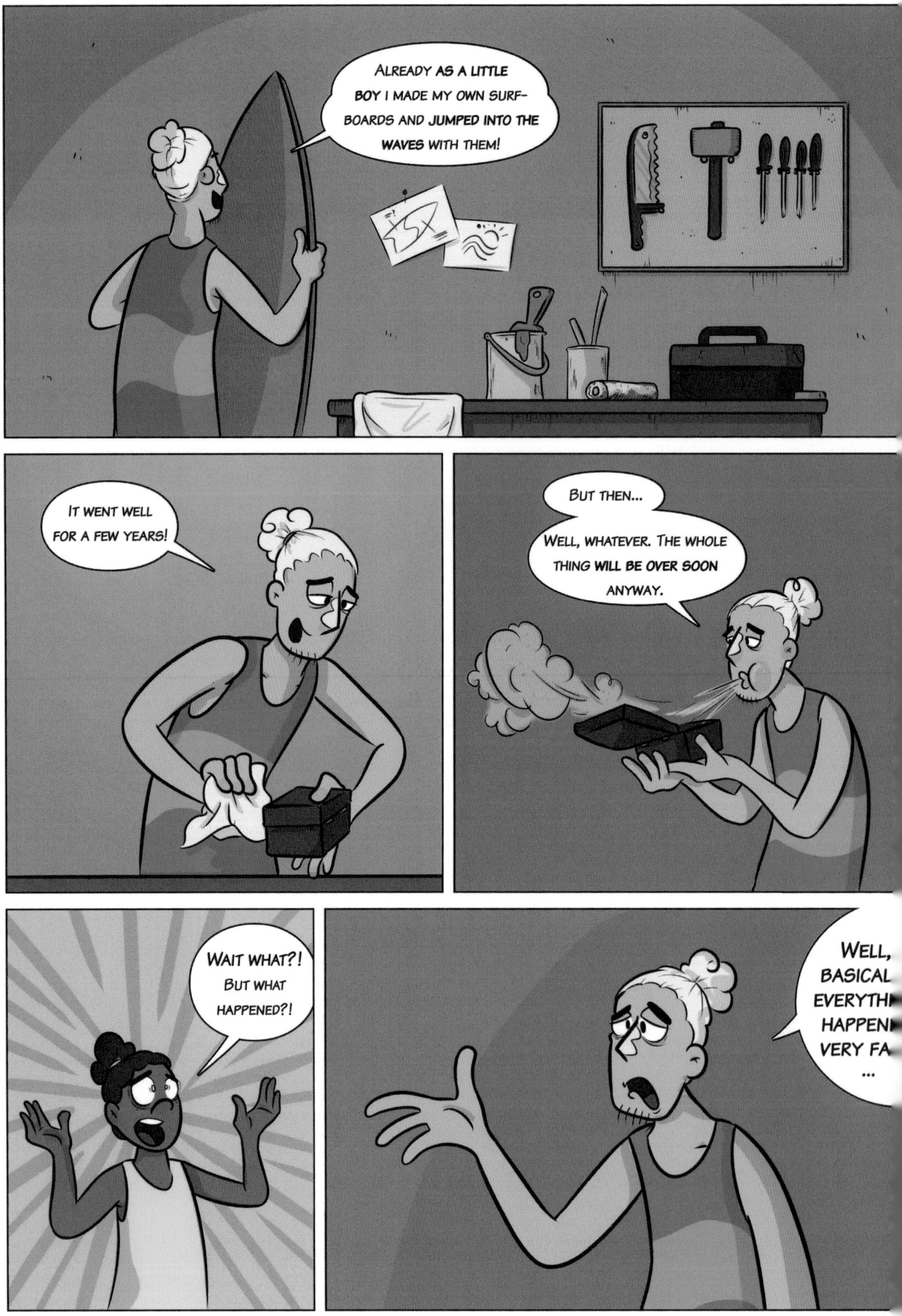

Already as a little boy I made my own surf-boards and jumped into the waves with them!
It went well for a few years!
But then...
Well, whatever. The whole thing will be over soon anyway.
Wait what?! But what happened?!

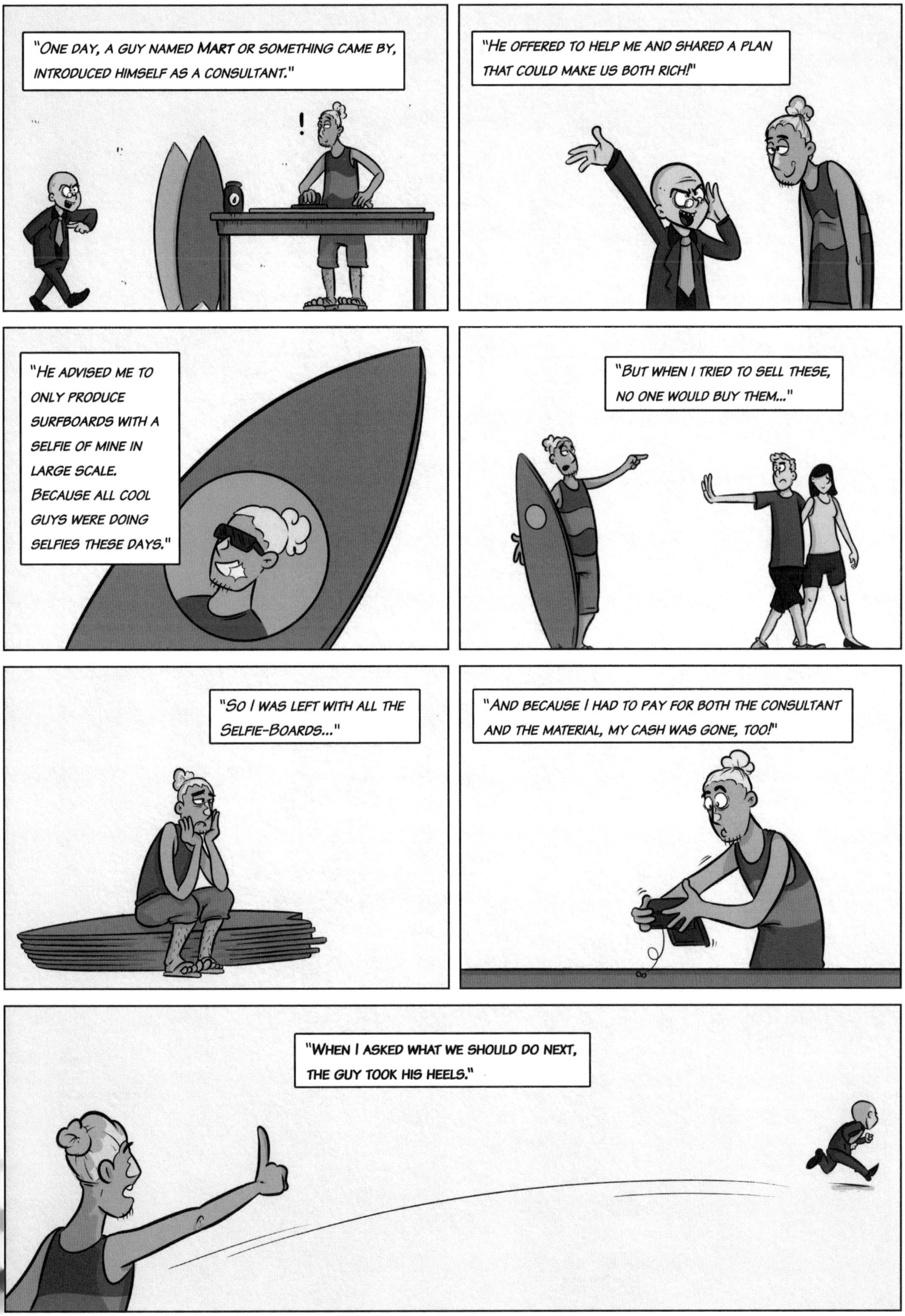
"One day, a guy named Mart or something came by, introduced himself as a consultant."
!
"He offered to help me and shared a plan that could make us both rich!"
"He advised me to only produce surfboards with a selfie of mine in large scale. Because all cool guys were doing selfies these days."
"But when I tried to sell these, no one would buy them..."
"So I was left with all the Selfie-Boards..."
"And because I had to pay for both the consultant and the material, my cash was gone, too!"
"When I asked what we should do next, the guy took his heels."

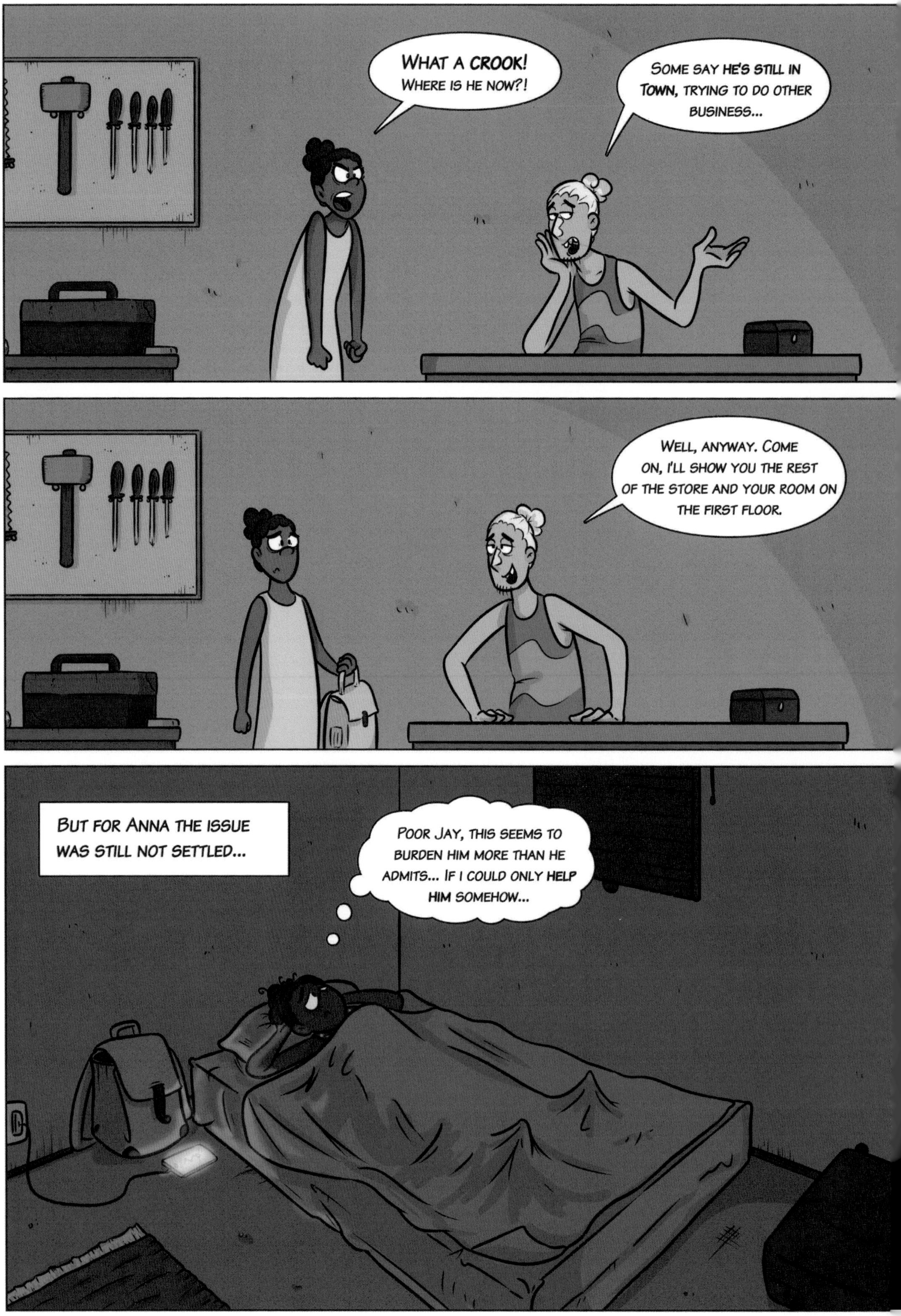
WHAT A CROOK! WHERE IS HE NOW?!
SOME SAY HE'S STILL IN TOWN, TRYING TO DO OTHER BUSINESS...
WELL, ANYWAY. COME ON, I'LL SHOW YOU THE REST OF THE STORE AND YOUR ROOM ON THE FIRST FLOOR.
BUT FOR ANNA THE ISSUE WAS STILL NOT SETTLED...
POOR JAY, THIS SEEMS TO BURDEN HIM MORE THAN HE ADMITS... IF I COULD ONLY HELP HIM SOMEHOW...

THE NEXT MORNING, ANNA IS UP EARLY

FIRST OF ALL, I NEED TO EXPLORE THIS PLACE!

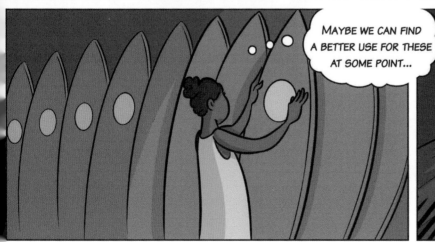

MAYBE WE CAN FIND A BETTER USE FOR THESE AT SOME POINT...

18

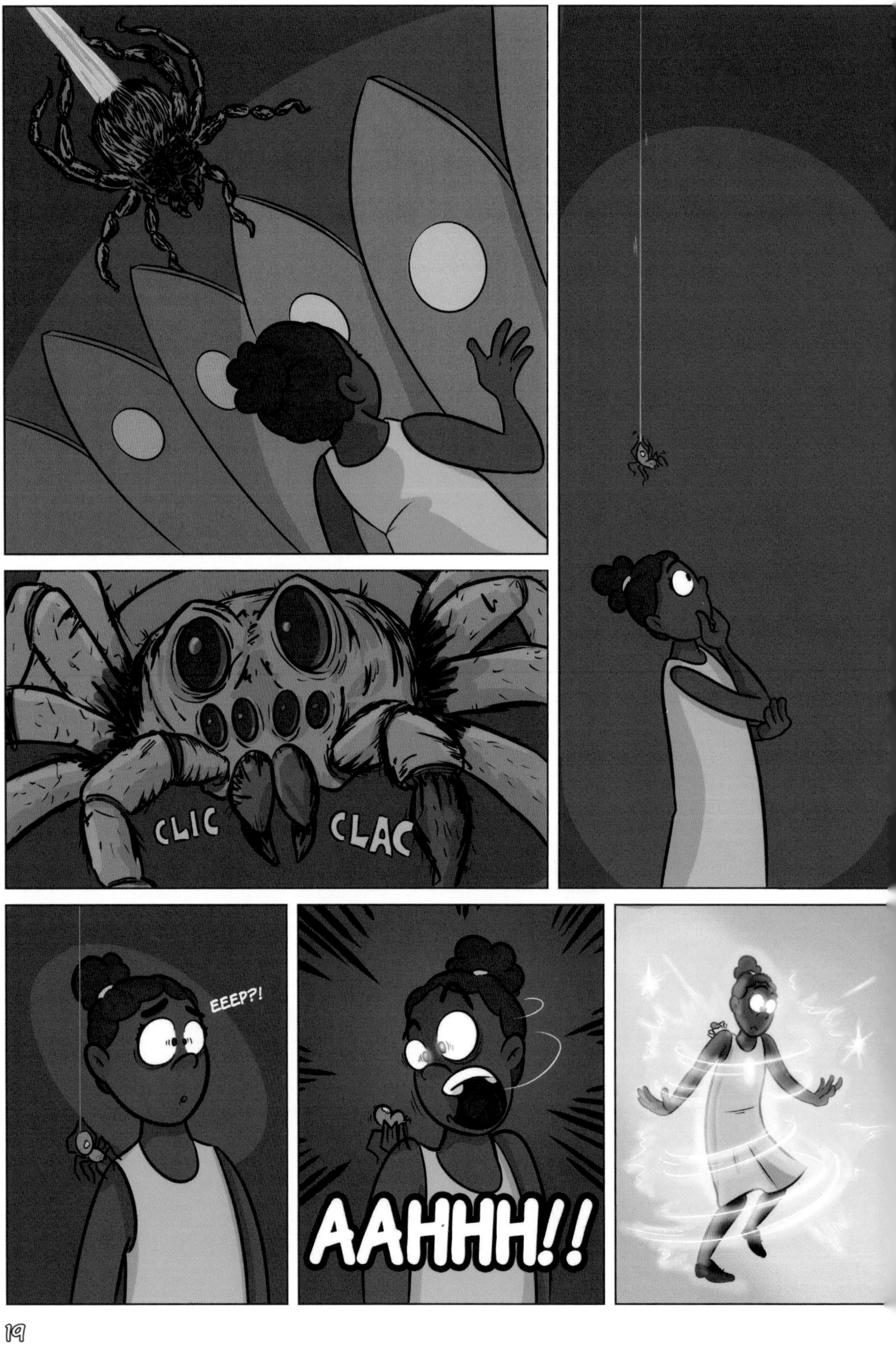
CLIC
CLAC
EEEP?!
AAHHH!!

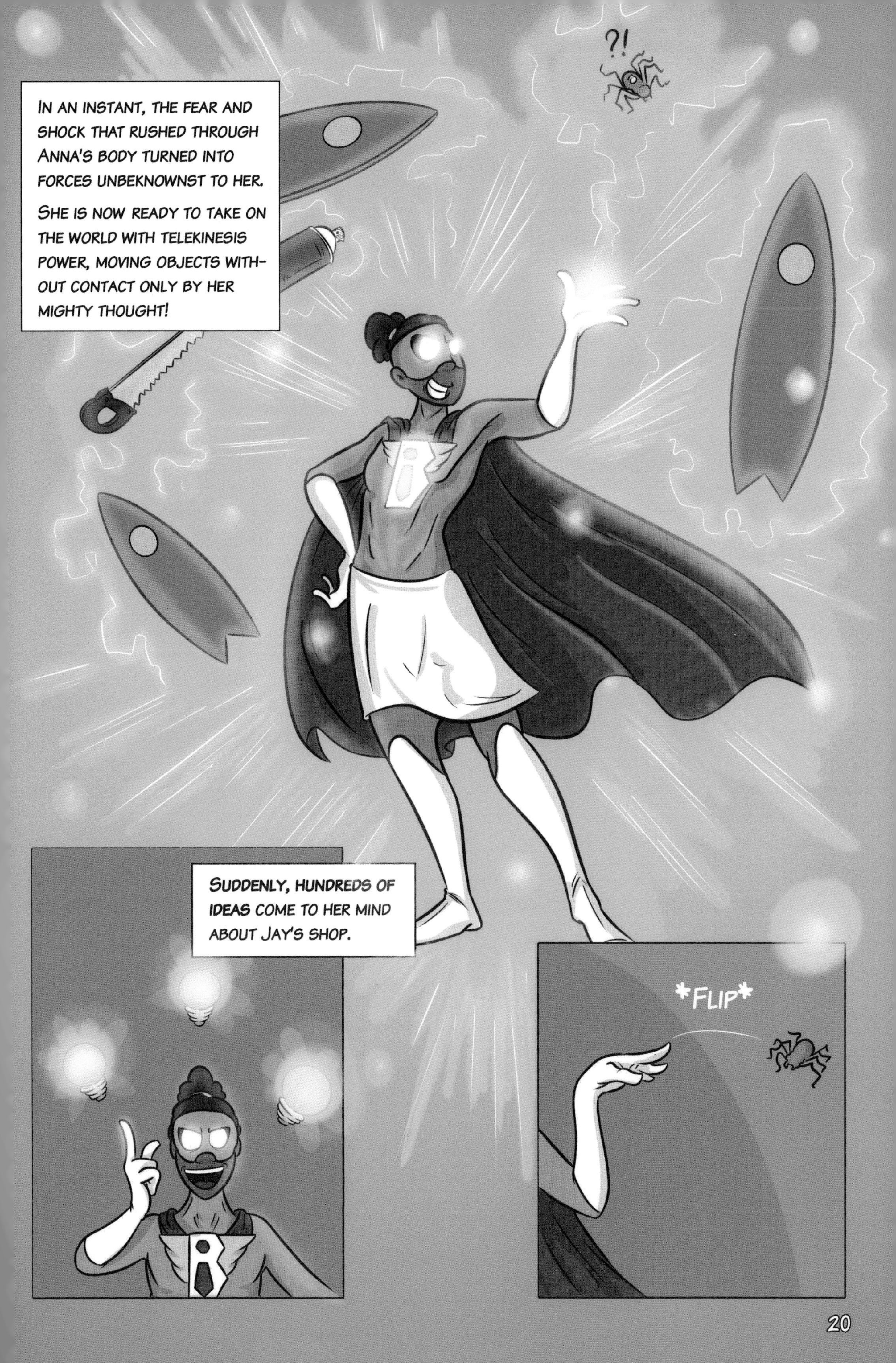
IN AN INSTANT, THE FEAR AND SHOCK THAT RUSHED THROUGH ANNA'S BODY TURNED INTO FORCES UNBEKNOWNST TO HER.
SHE IS NOW READY TO TAKE ON THE WORLD WITH TELEKINESIS POWER, MOVING OBJECTS WITHOUT CONTACT ONLY BY HER MIGHTY THOUGHT!
?!
SUDDENLY, HUNDREDS OF IDEAS COME TO HER MIND ABOUT JAY'S SHOP.
FLIP

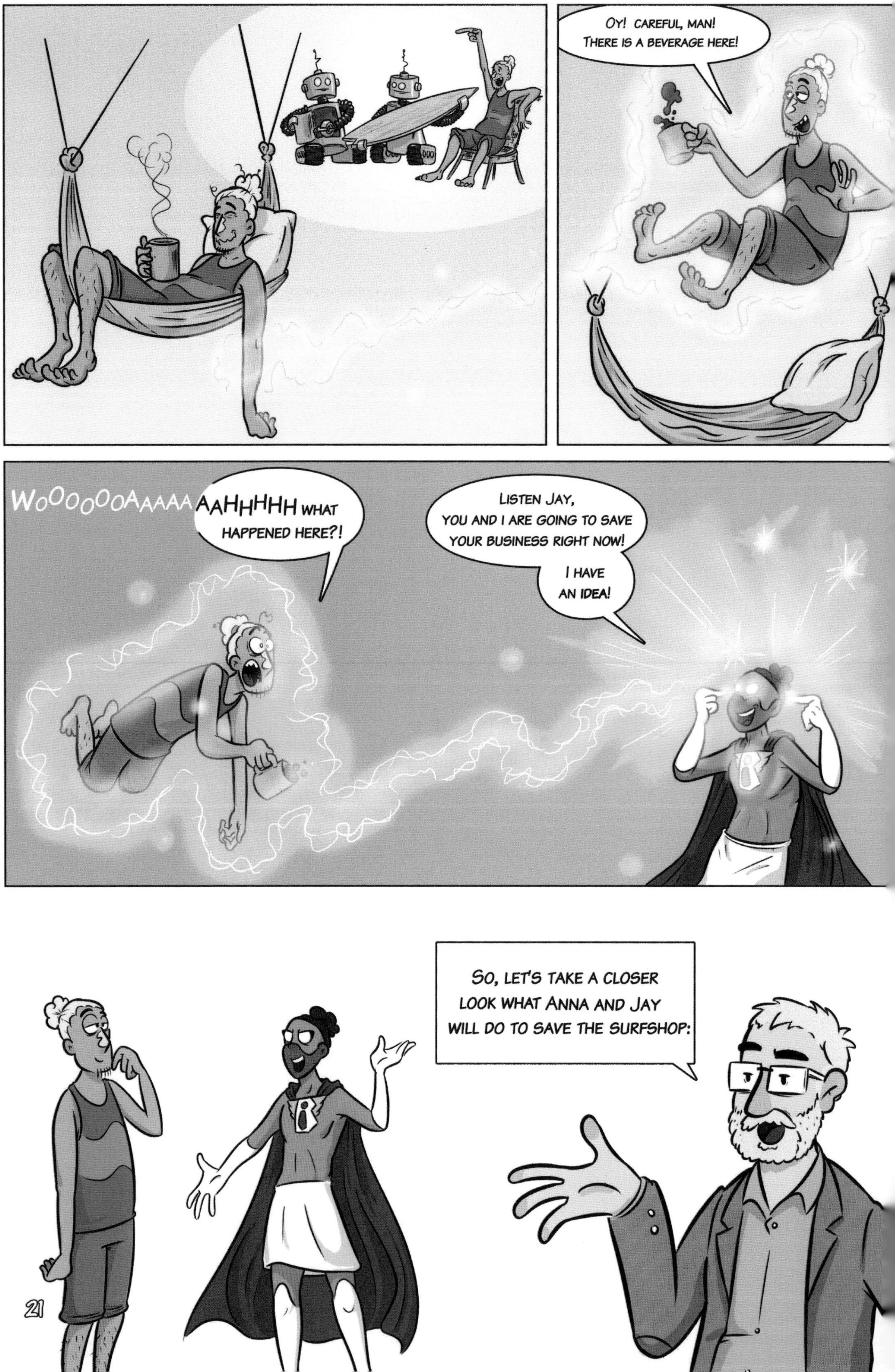

OY! CAREFUL, MAN!
THERE IS A BEVERAGE HERE!
WOOOOOOAAAAAAAHHHHHH WHAT HAPPENED HERE?!
LISTEN JAY, YOU AND I ARE GOING TO SAVE YOUR BUSINESS RIGHT NOW!
I HAVE AN IDEA!
SO, LET'S TAKE A CLOSER LOOK WHAT ANNA AND JAY WILL DO TO SAVE THE SURFSHOP:

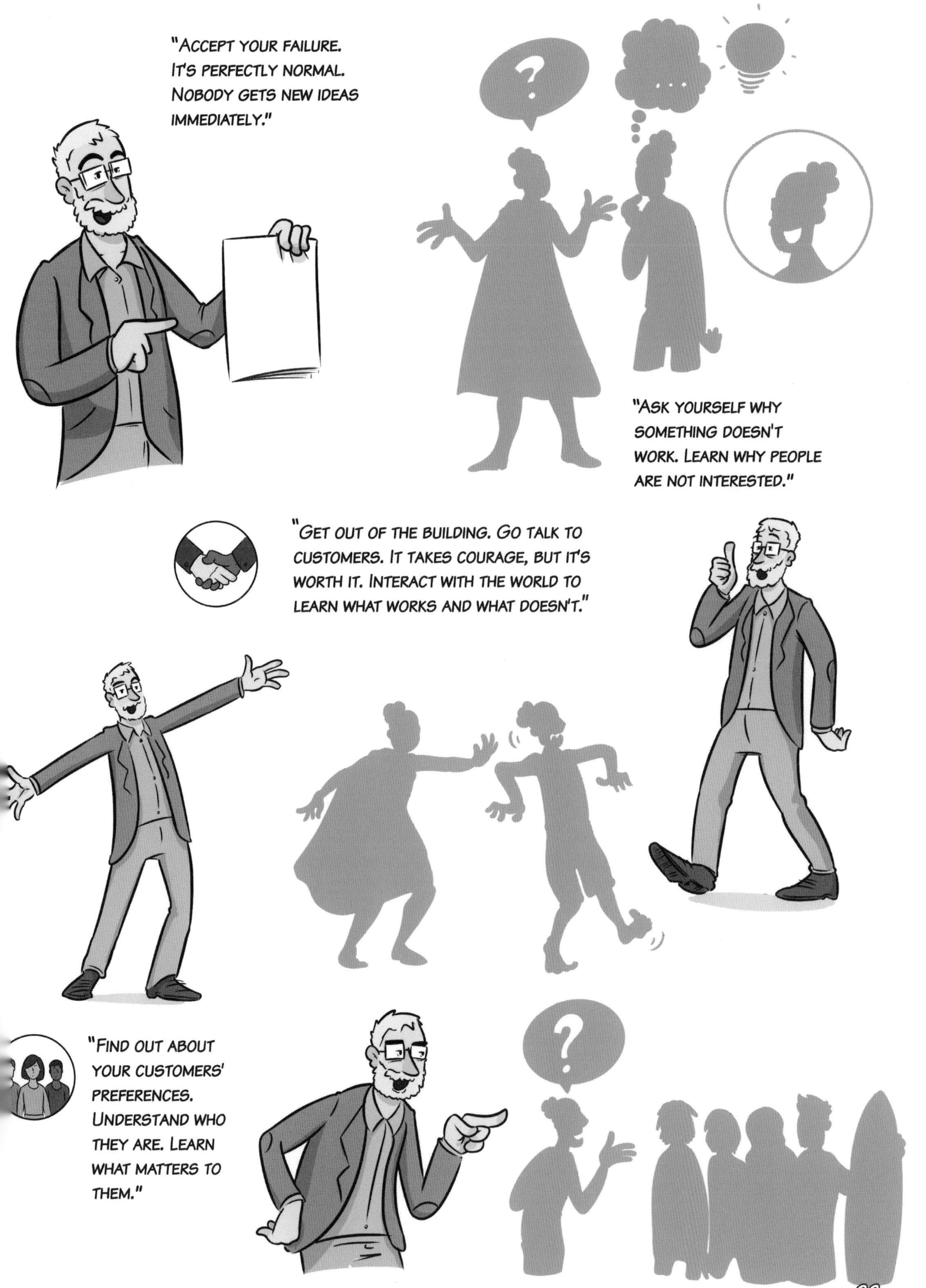
"ACCEPT YOUR FAILURE. IT'S PERFECTLY NORMAL. NOBODY GETS NEW IDEAS IMMEDIATELY."
"ASK YOURSELF WHY SOMETHING DOESN'T WORK. LEARN WHY PEOPLE ARE NOT INTERESTED."
"GET OUT OF THE BUILDING. GO TALK TO CUSTOMERS. IT TAKES COURAGE, BUT IT'S WORTH IT. INTERACT WITH THE WORLD TO LEARN WHAT WORKS AND WHAT DOESN'T."
"FIND OUT ABOUT YOUR CUSTOMERS' PREFERENCES. UNDERSTAND WHO THEY ARE. LEARN WHAT MATTERS TO THEM."

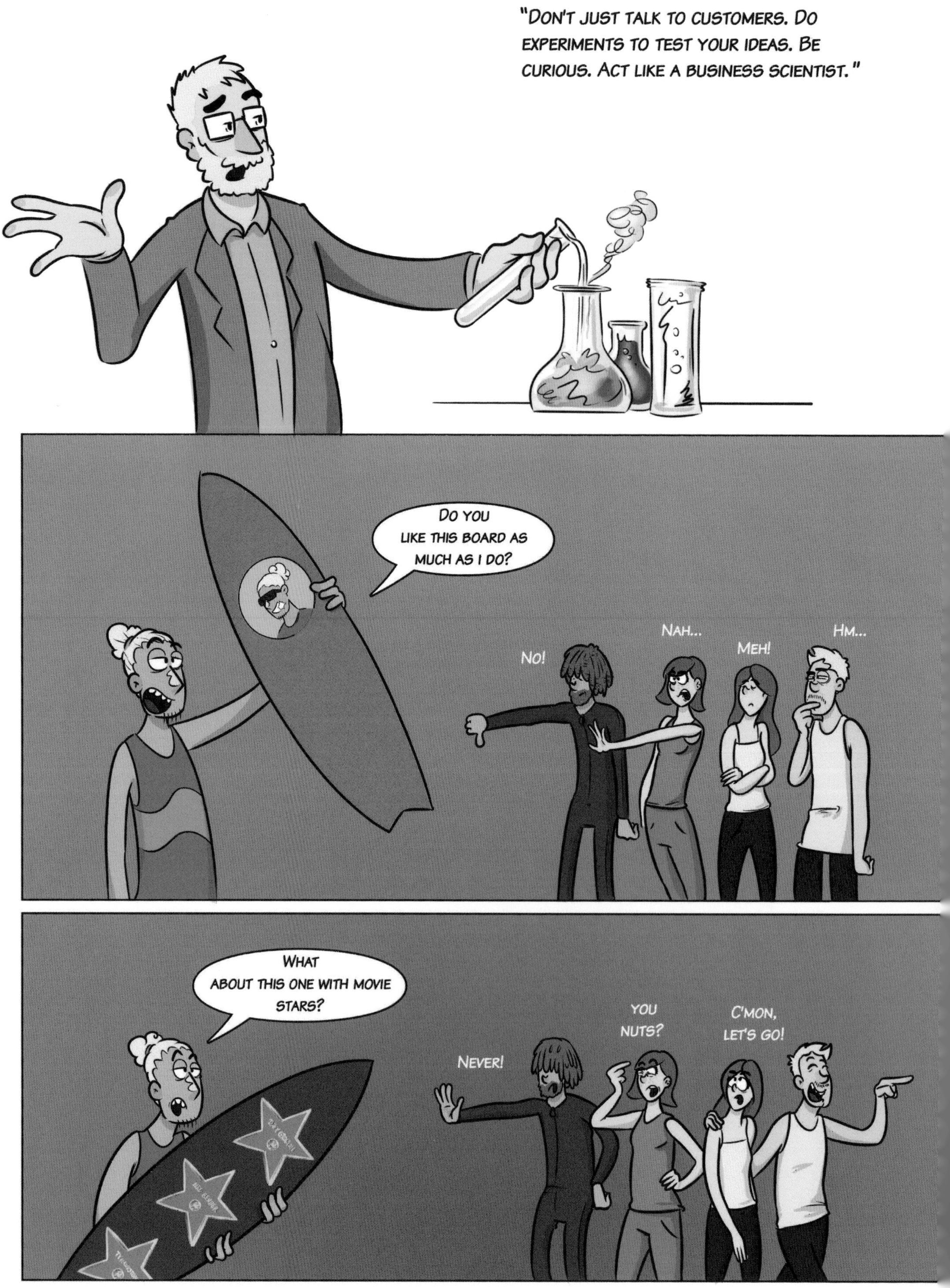
"DON'T JUST TALK TO CUSTOMERS. DO EXPERIMENTS TO TEST YOUR IDEAS. BE CURIOUS. ACT LIKE A BUSINESS SCIENTIST."
DO YOU LIKE THIS BOARD AS MUCH AS I DO?
NO!
NAH...
MEH!
HM...
WHAT ABOUT THIS ONE WITH MOVIE STARS?
NEVER!
YOU NUTS?
C'MON, LET'S GO!

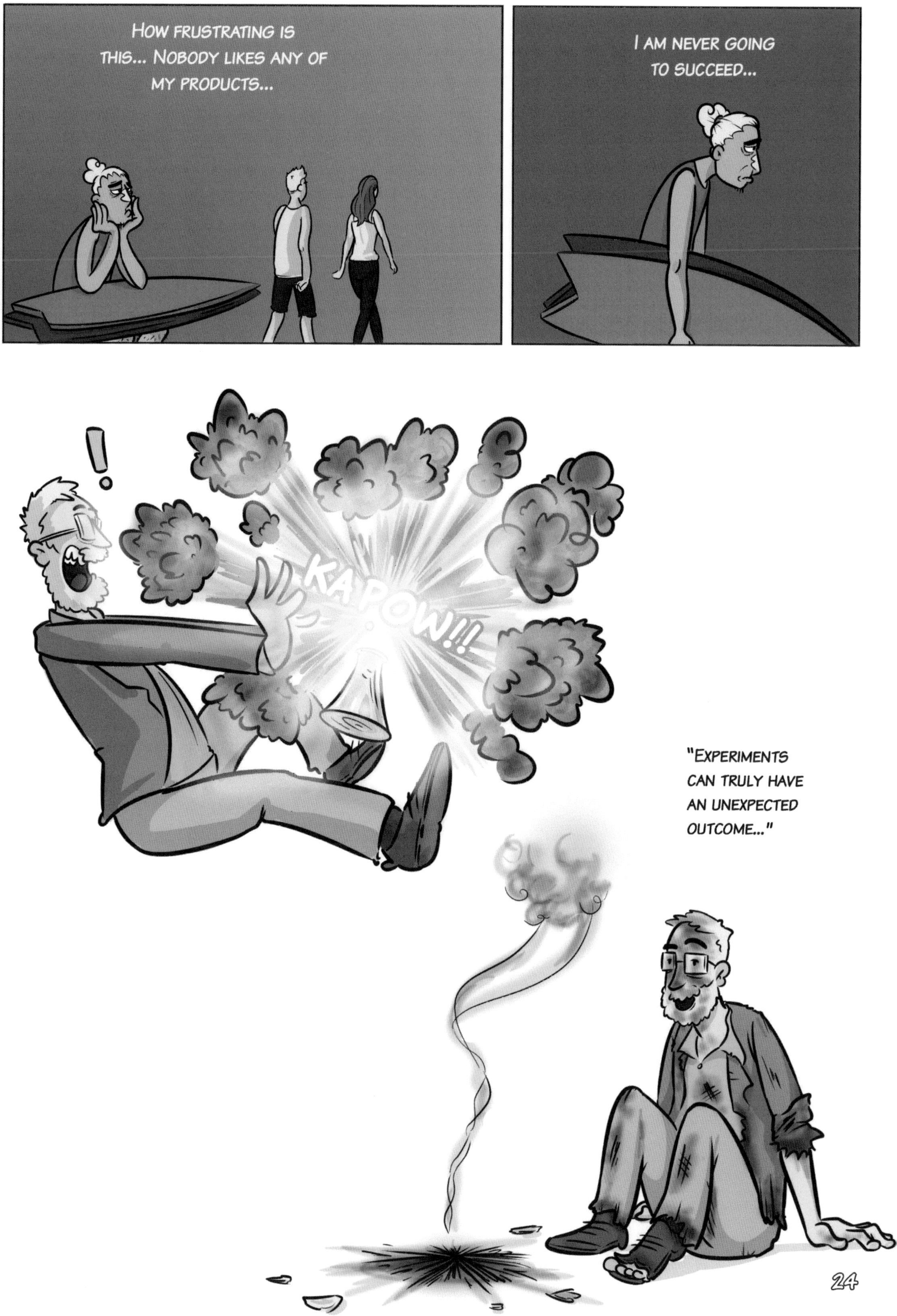
HOW FRUSTRATING IS THIS... NOBODY LIKES ANY OF MY PRODUCTS...
I AM NEVER GOING TO SUCCEED...
!
KAPOW!!
"EXPERIMENTS CAN TRULY HAVE AN UNEXPECTED OUTCOME..."

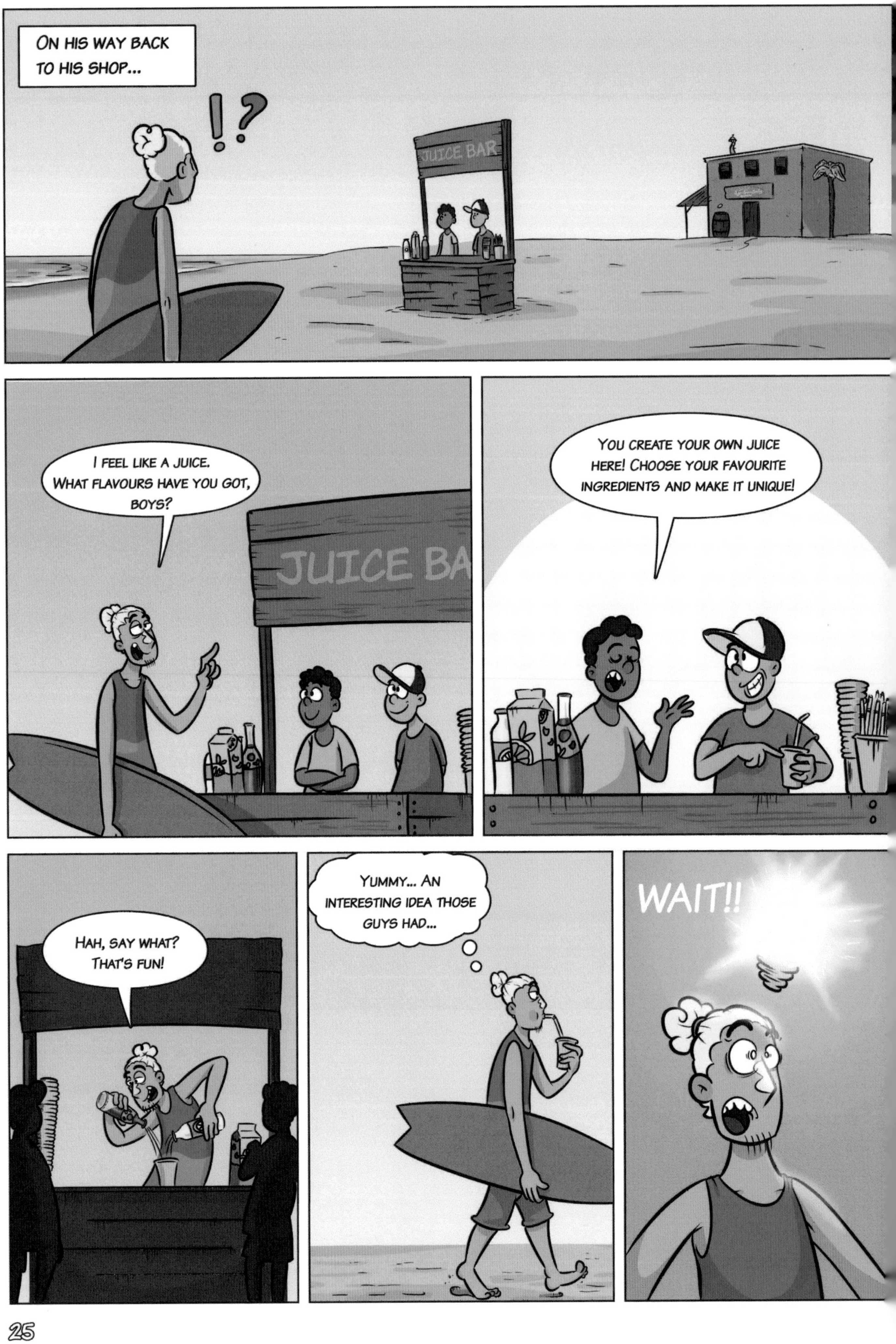
ON HIS WAY BACK TO HIS SHOP...
!?
JUICE BAR
I FEEL LIKE A JUICE. WHAT FLAVOURS HAVE YOU GOT, BOYS?
YOU CREATE YOUR OWN JUICE HERE! CHOOSE YOUR FAVOURITE INGREDIENTS AND MAKE IT UNIQUE!
HAH, SAY WHAT? THAT'S FUN!
YUMMY... AN INTERESTING IDEA THOSE GUYS HAD...
WAIT!!

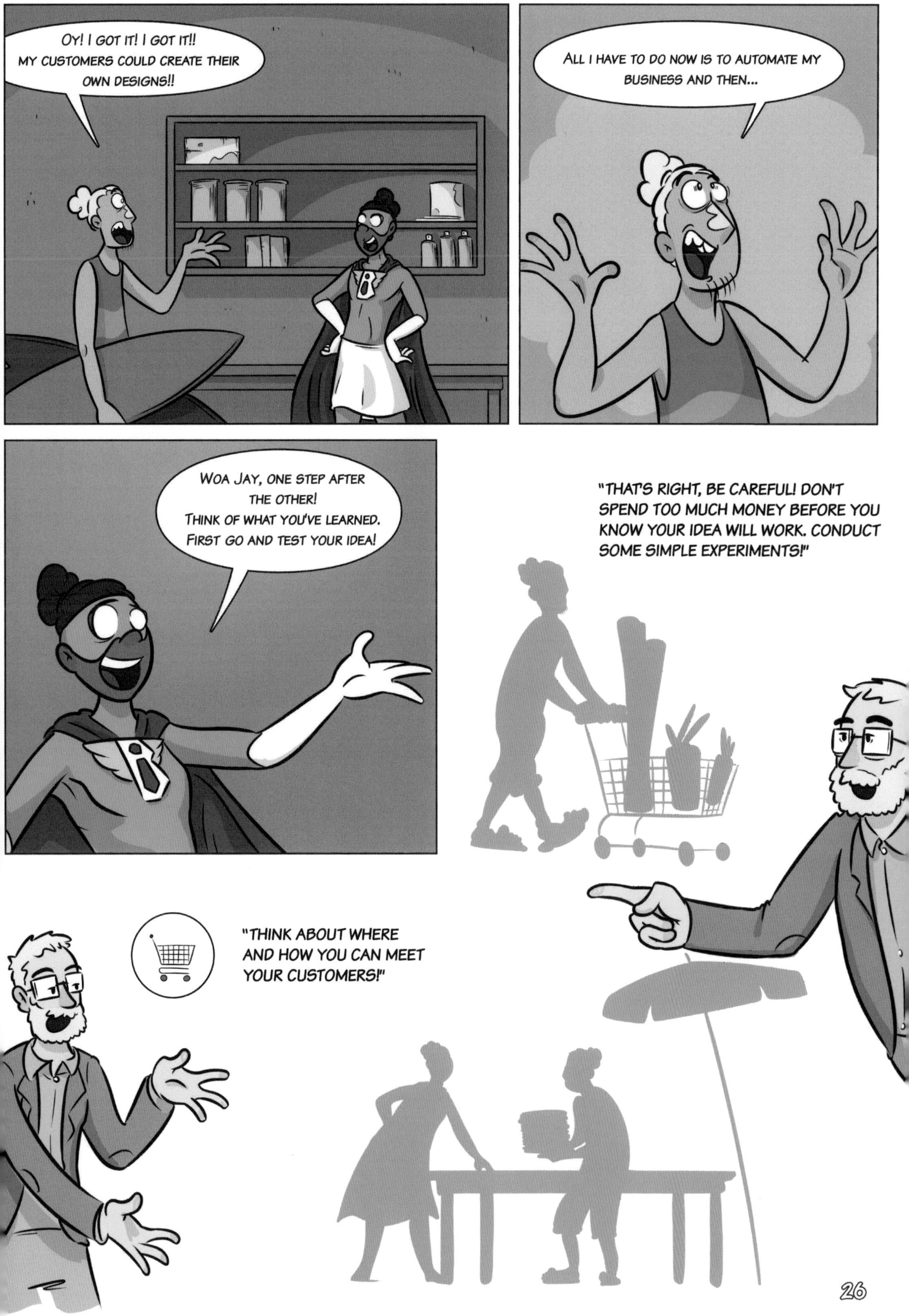
OY! I GOT IT! I GOT IT!! MY CUSTOMERS COULD CREATE THEIR OWN DESIGNS!!
ALL I HAVE TO DO NOW IS TO AUTOMATE MY BUSINESS AND THEN...
WOA JAY, ONE STEP AFTER THE OTHER! THINK OF WHAT YOU'VE LEARNED. FIRST GO AND TEST YOUR IDEA!
"THAT'S RIGHT, BE CAREFUL! DON'T SPEND TOO MUCH MONEY BEFORE YOU KNOW YOUR IDEA WILL WORK. CONDUCT SOME SIMPLE EXPERIMENTS!"
"THINK ABOUT WHERE AND HOW YOU CAN MEET YOUR CUSTOMERS!"

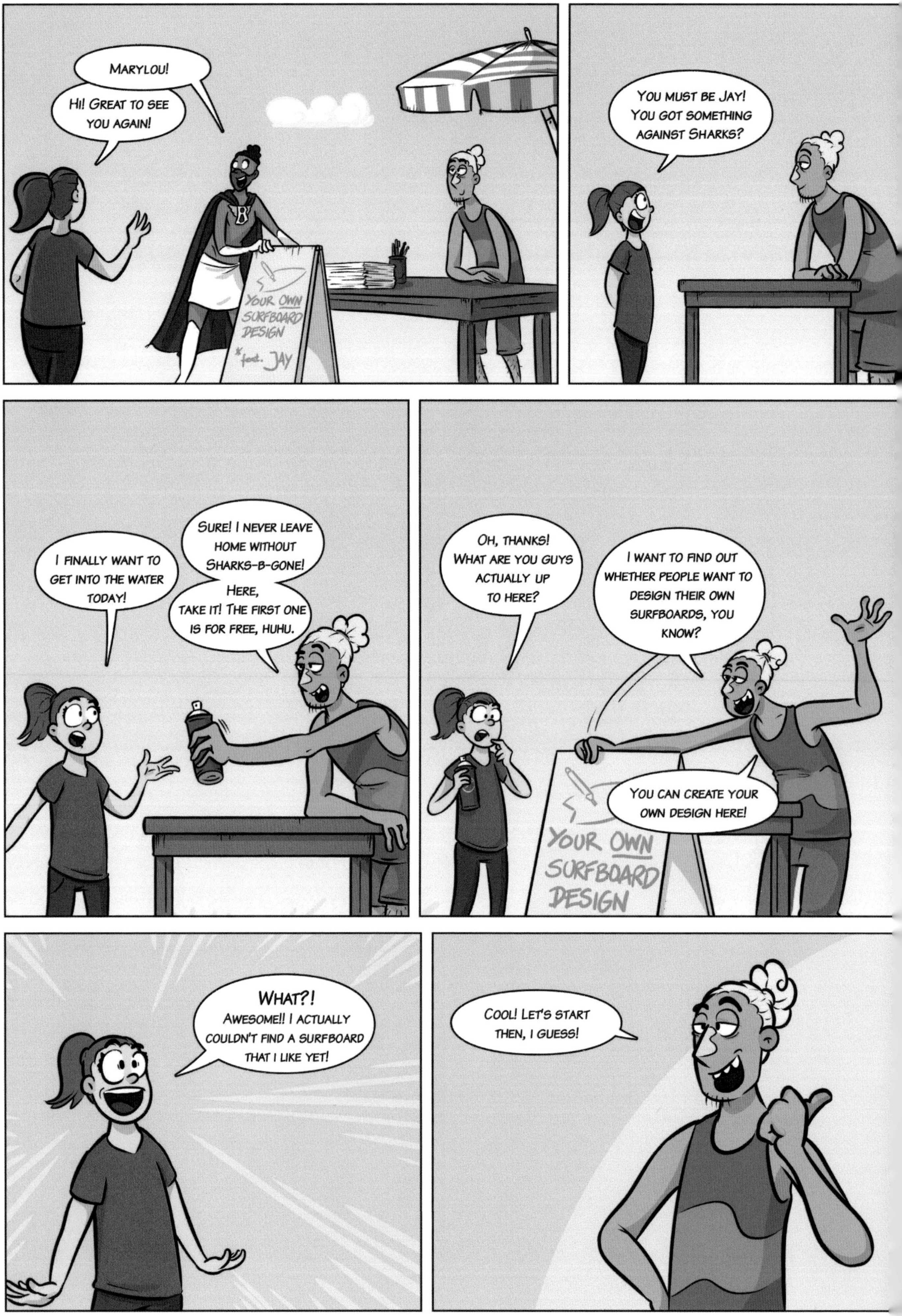
MARYLOU!
HI! GREAT TO SEE YOU AGAIN!
YOUR OWN SURFBOARD DESIGN *feat. JAY
YOU MUST BE JAY! YOU GOT SOMETHING AGAINST SHARKS?
I FINALLY WANT TO GET INTO THE WATER TODAY!
SURE! I NEVER LEAVE HOME WITHOUT SHARKS-B-GONE!
HERE, TAKE IT! THE FIRST ONE IS FOR FREE, HUHU.
OH, THANKS! WHAT ARE YOU GUYS ACTUALLY UP TO HERE?
I WANT TO FIND OUT WHETHER PEOPLE WANT TO DESIGN THEIR OWN SURFBOARDS, YOU KNOW?
YOU CAN CREATE YOUR OWN DESIGN HERE!
YOUR OWN SURFBOARD DESIGN
WHAT?!
AWESOME!! I ACTUALLY COULDN'T FIND A SURFBOARD THAT I LIKE YET!
COOL! LET'S START THEN, I GUESS!

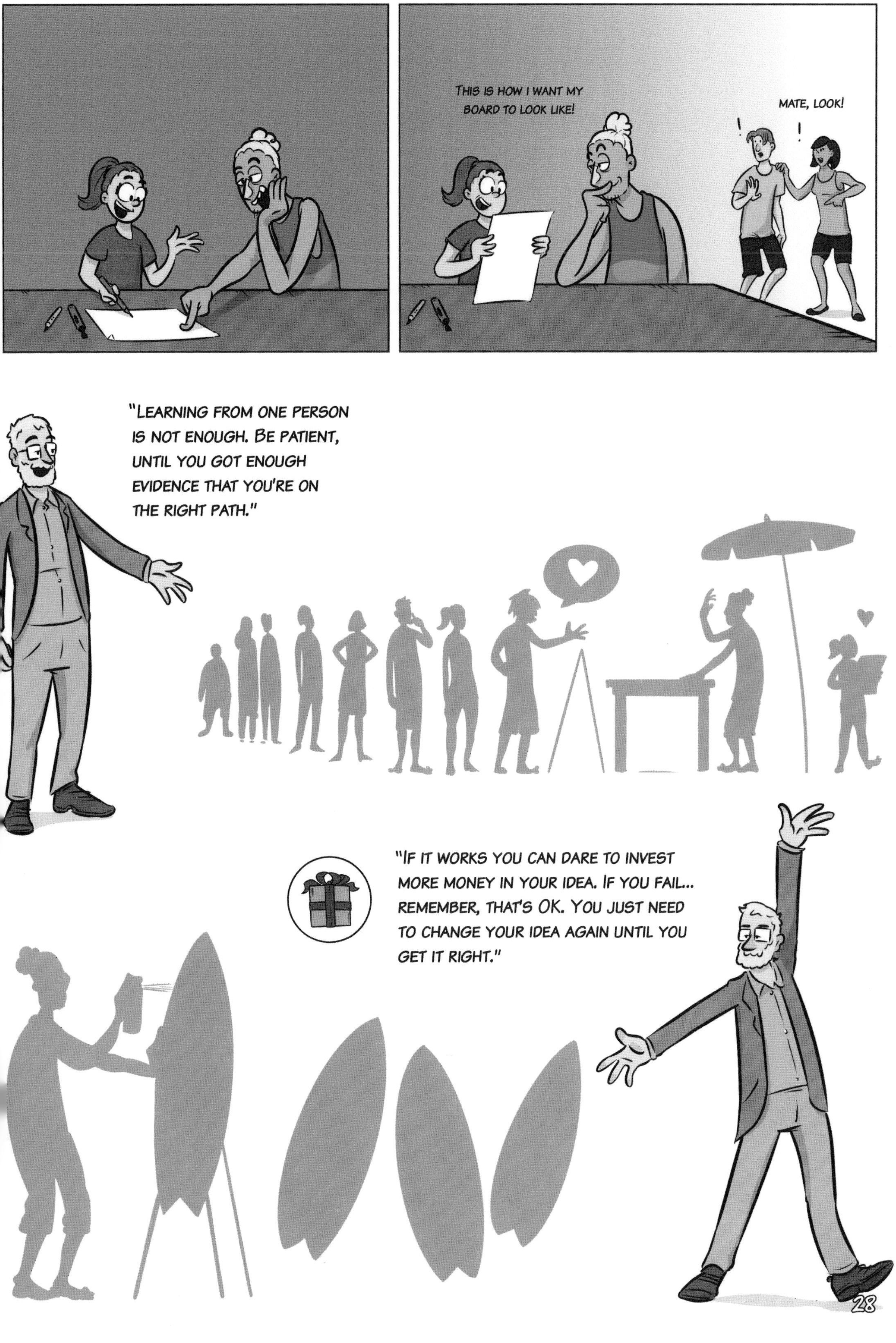
THIS IS HOW I WANT MY BOARD TO LOOK LIKE!
MATE, LOOK!
"LEARNING FROM ONE PERSON IS NOT ENOUGH. BE PATIENT, UNTIL YOU GOT ENOUGH EVIDENCE THAT YOU'RE ON THE RIGHT PATH."
"IF IT WORKS YOU CAN DARE TO INVEST MORE MONEY IN YOUR IDEA. IF YOU FAIL... REMEMBER, THAT'S OK. YOU JUST NEED TO CHANGE YOUR IDEA AGAIN UNTIL YOU GET IT RIGHT."

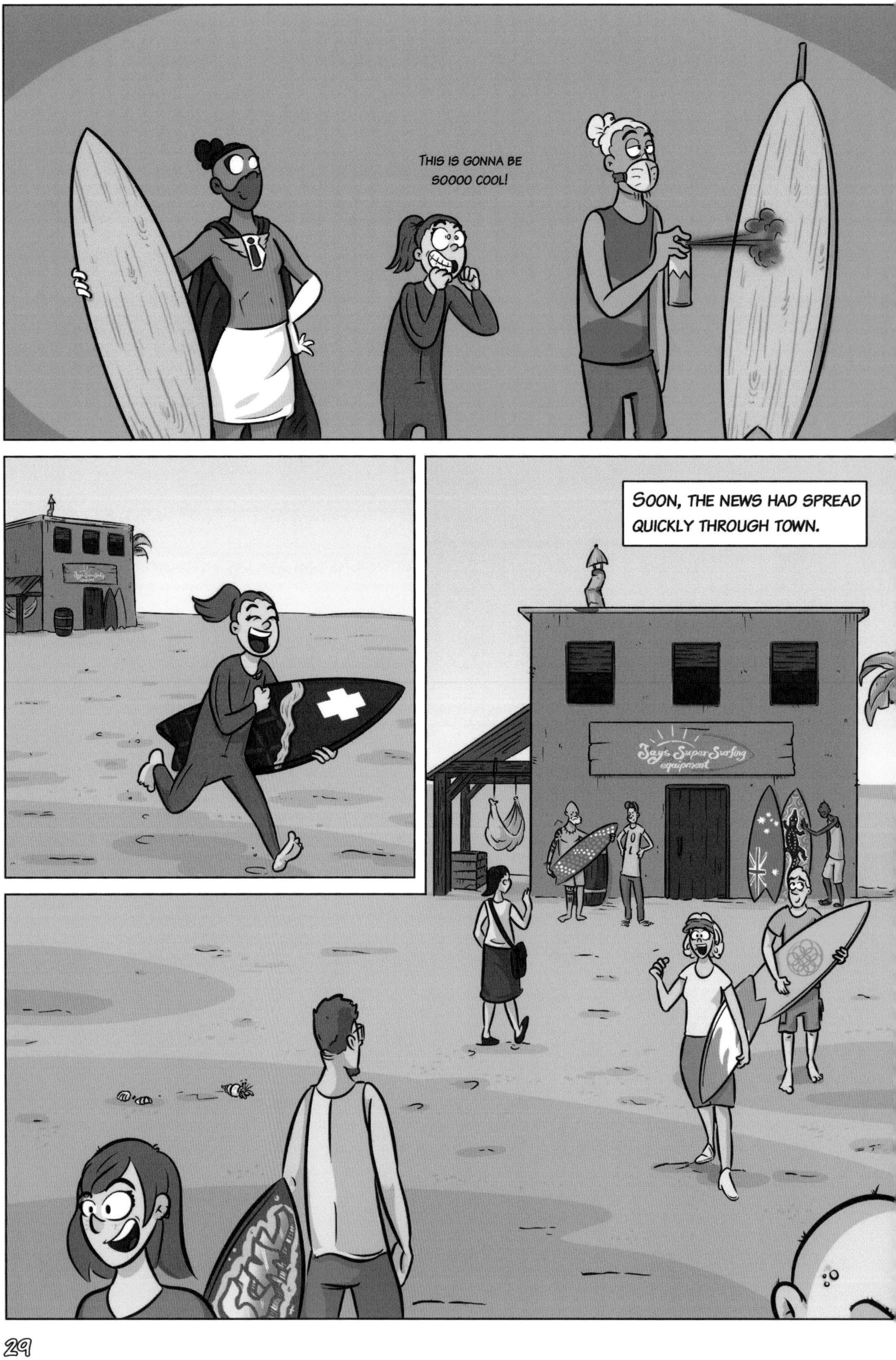
THIS IS GONNA BE SOOOO COOL!
SOON, THE NEWS HAD SPREAD QUICKLY THROUGH TOWN.
Jays Super Surfing equipment

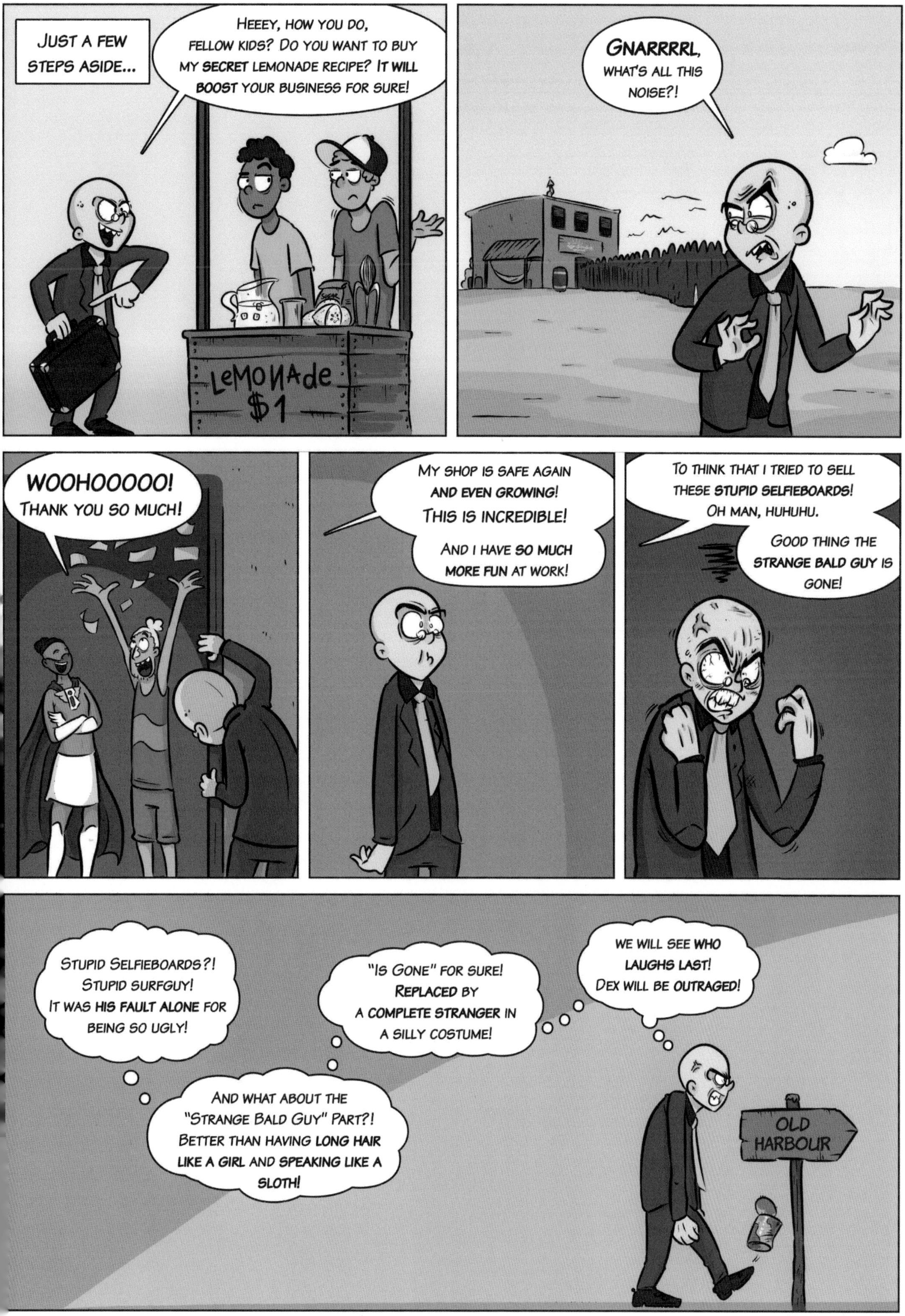
JUST A FEW STEPS ASIDE...
HEEEY, HOW YOU DO, FELLOW KIDS? DO YOU WANT TO BUY MY SECRET LEMONADE RECIPE? IT WILL BOOST YOUR BUSINESS FOR SURE!
LEMONADE $1
GNARRRRL, WHAT'S ALL THIS NOISE?!
WOOHOOOOO! THANK YOU SO MUCH!
MY SHOP IS SAFE AGAIN AND EVEN GROWING! THIS IS INCREDIBLE!
AND I HAVE SO MUCH MORE FUN AT WORK!
TO THINK THAT I TRIED TO SELL THESE STUPID SELFIEBOARDS! OH MAN, HUHUHU.
GOOD THING THE STRANGE BALD GUY IS GONE!
STUPID SELFIEBOARDS?! STUPID SURFGUY! IT WAS HIS FAULT ALONE FOR BEING SO UGLY!
AND WHAT ABOUT THE "STRANGE BALD GUY" PART?! BETTER THAN HAVING LONG HAIR LIKE A GIRL AND SPEAKING LIKE A SLOTH!
"IS GONE" FOR SURE! REPLACED BY A COMPLETE STRANGER IN A SILLY COSTUME!
WE WILL SEE WHO LAUGHS LAST! DEX WILL BE OUTRAGED!
OLD HARBOUR

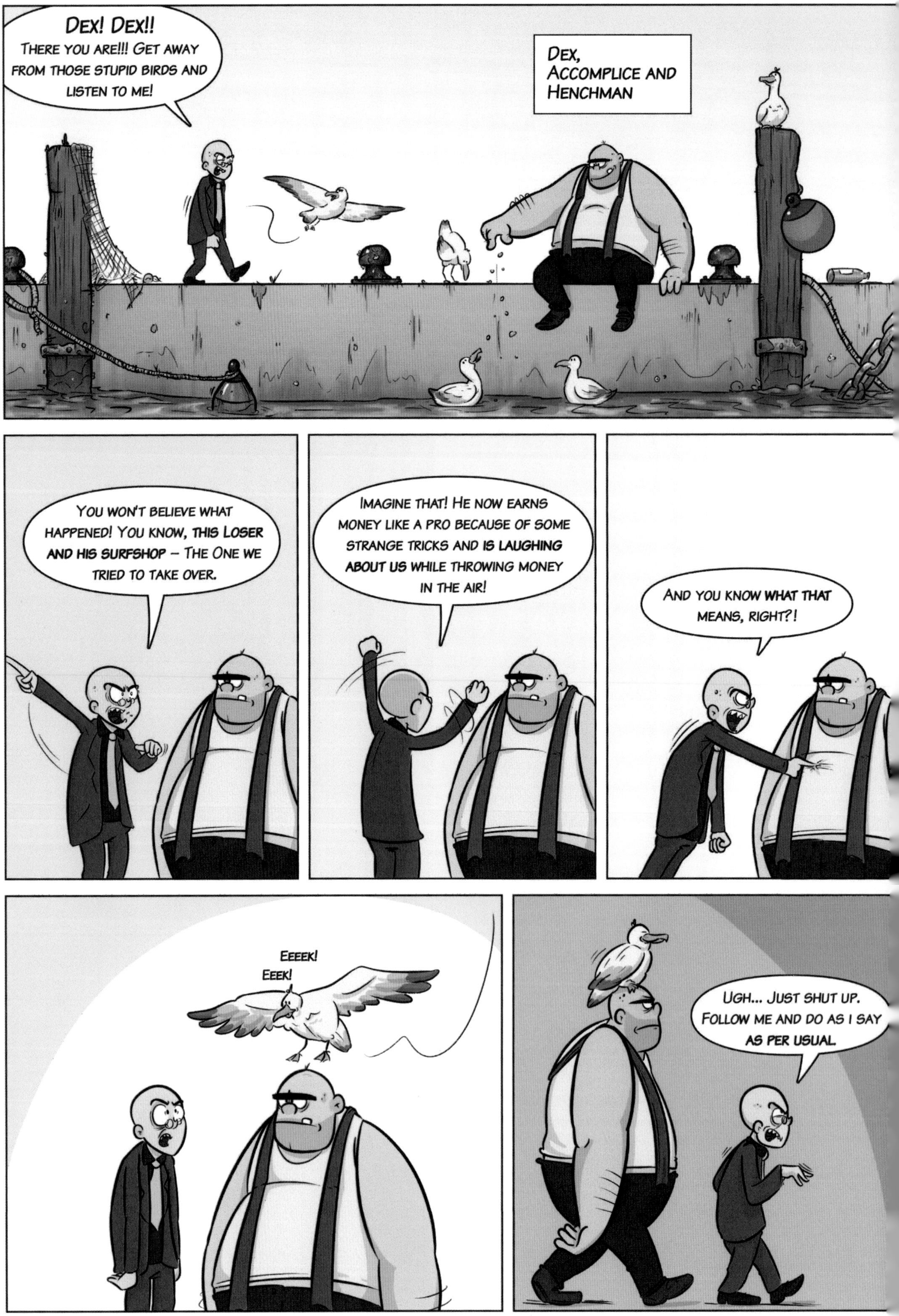
DEX! DEX!! THERE YOU ARE!!! GET AWAY FROM THOSE STUPID BIRDS AND LISTEN TO ME!
DEX, ACCOMPLICE AND HENCHMAN
YOU WON'T BELIEVE WHAT HAPPENED! YOU KNOW, THIS LOSER AND HIS SURFSHOP – THE ONE WE TRIED TO TAKE OVER.
IMAGINE THAT! HE NOW EARNS MONEY LIKE A PRO BECAUSE OF SOME STRANGE TRICKS AND IS LAUGHING ABOUT US WHILE THROWING MONEY IN THE AIR!
AND YOU KNOW WHAT THAT MEANS, RIGHT?!
EEEEK!
EEEK!
UGH... JUST SHUT UP. FOLLOW ME AND DO AS I SAY AS PER USUAL.

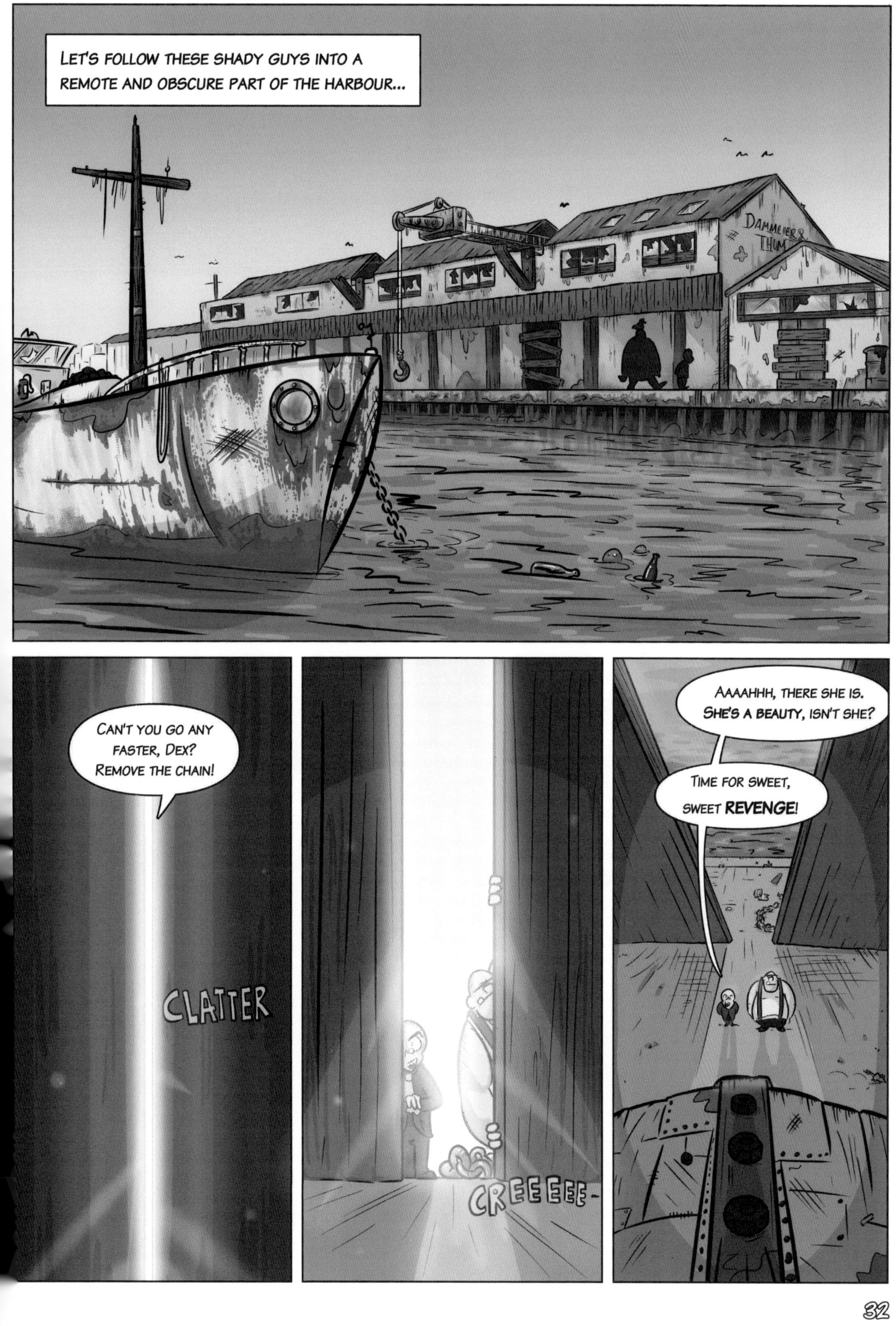
LET'S FOLLOW THESE SHADY GUYS INTO A REMOTE AND OBSCURE PART OF THE HARBOUR...
DAMMEIER & THUM
CAN'T YOU GO ANY FASTER, DEX? REMOVE THE CHAIN!
CLATTER
CREEEEE-
AAAAHHH, THERE SHE IS. SHE'S A BEAUTY, ISN'T SHE?
TIME FOR SWEET, SWEET REVENGE!

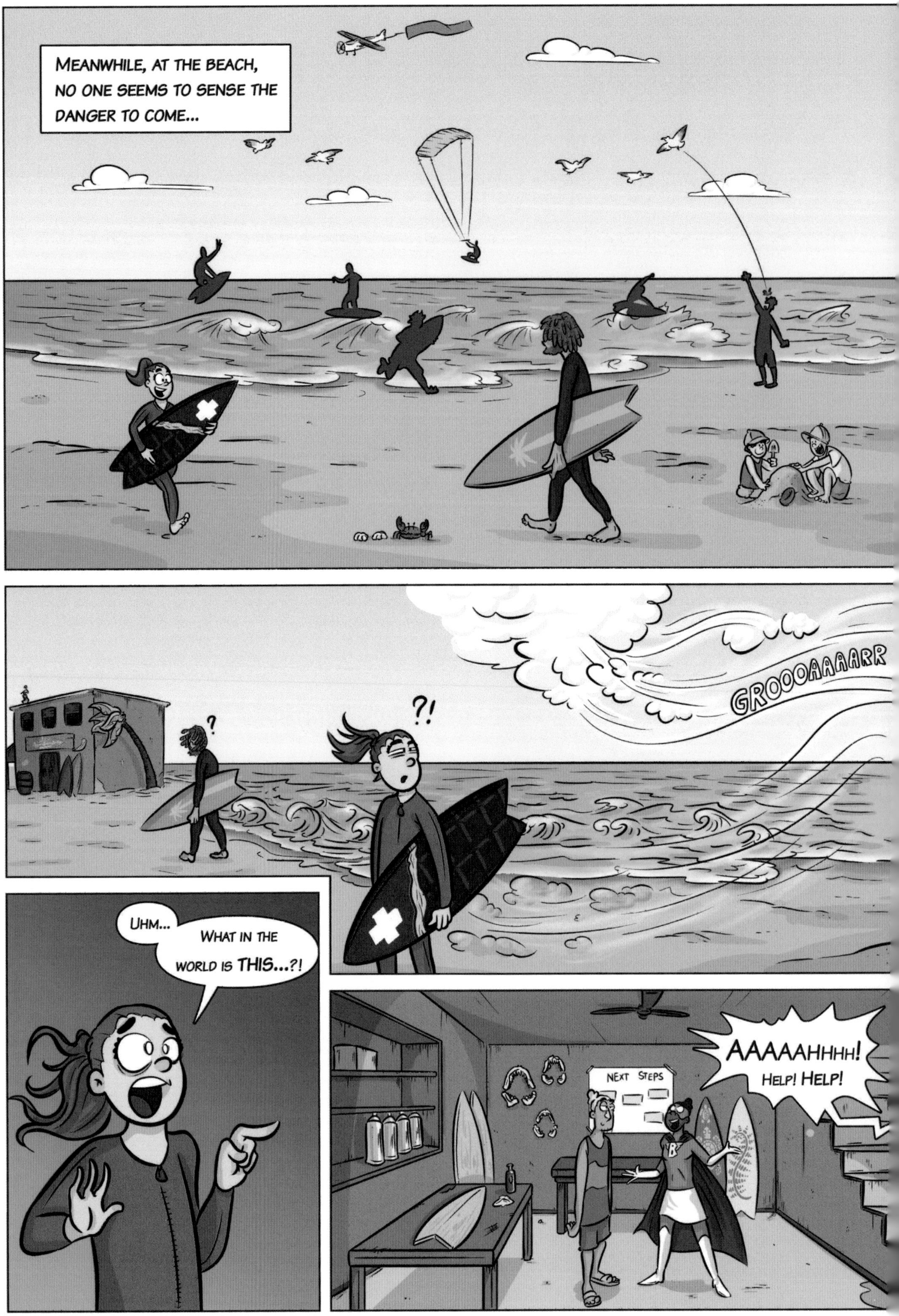
MEANWHILE, AT THE BEACH, NO ONE SEEMS TO SENSE THE DANGER TO COME...
?
?!
GROOOAAAARR
UHM...
WHAT IN THE WORLD IS THIS...?!
NEXT STEPS
AAAAAHHHH!
HELP! HELP!

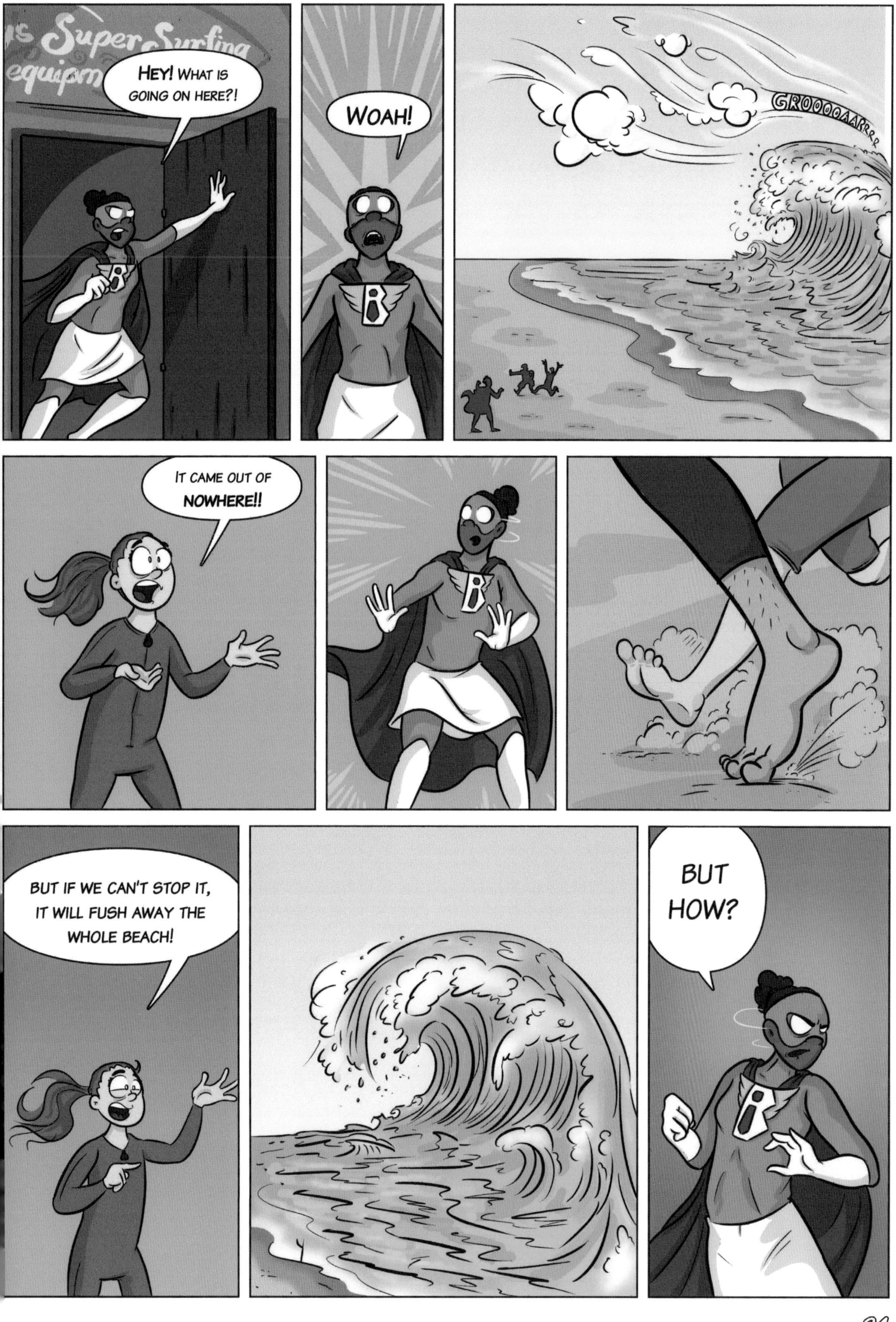
Super Surfing equipm
HEY! WHAT IS GOING ON HERE?!
WOAH!
GROOOOAARRRR
IT CAME OUT OF NOWHERE!!
BUT IF WE CAN'T STOP IT, IT WILL FUSH AWAY THE WHOLE BEACH!
BUT HOW?

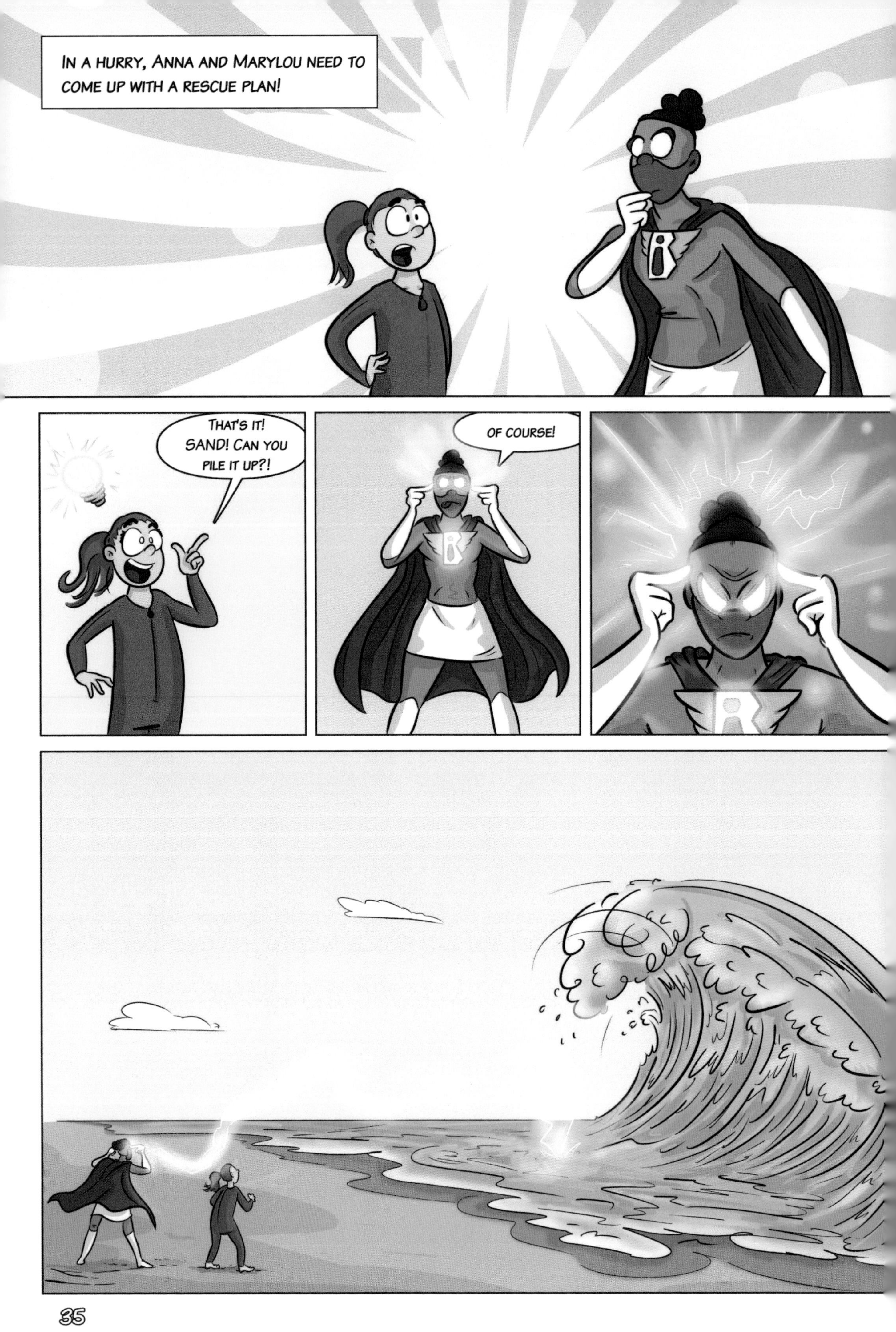
In a hurry, Anna and Marylou need to come up with a rescue plan!
That's it! SAND! Can you pile it up?!
Of course!

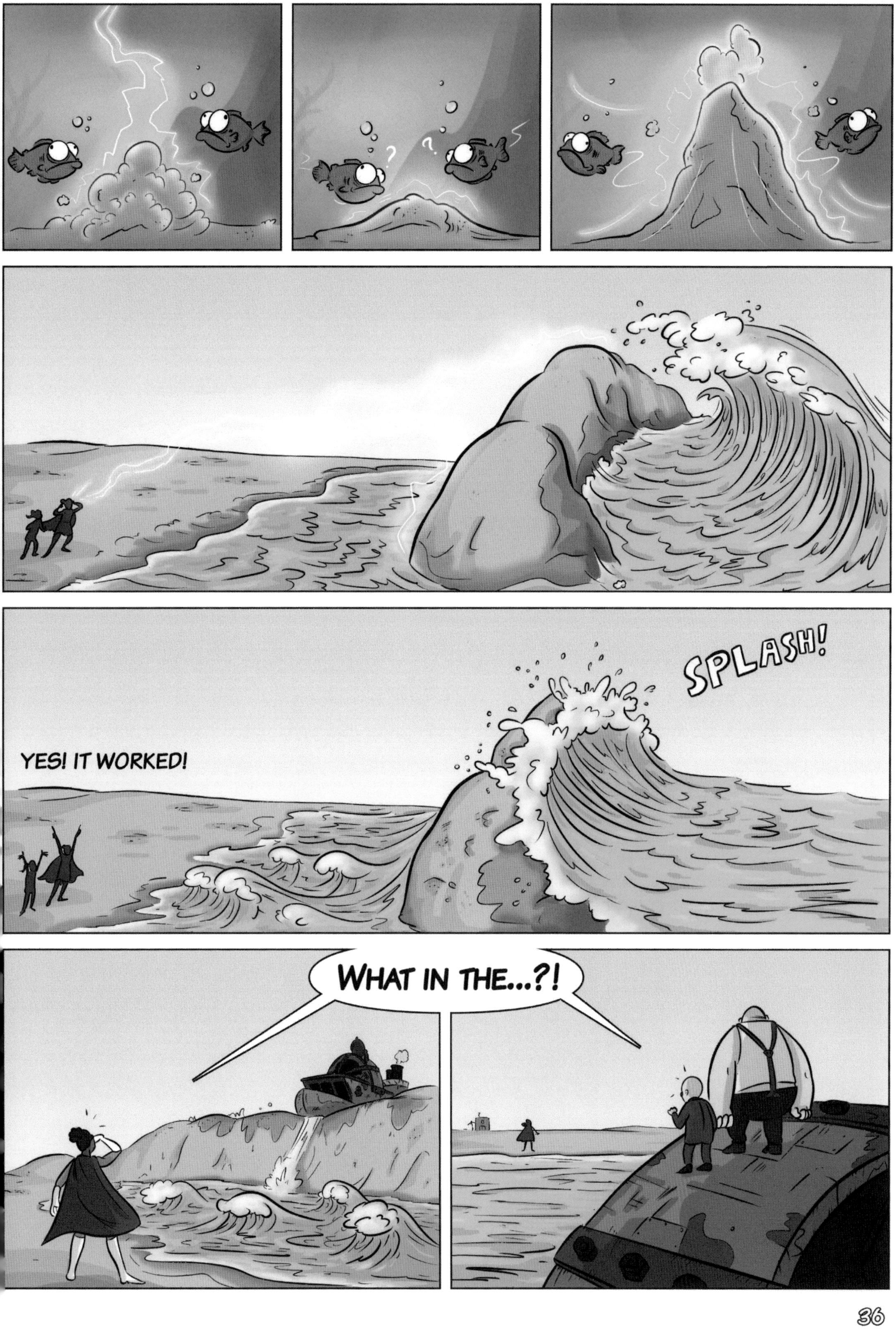
SPLASH!
YES! IT WORKED!
WHAT IN THE...?!

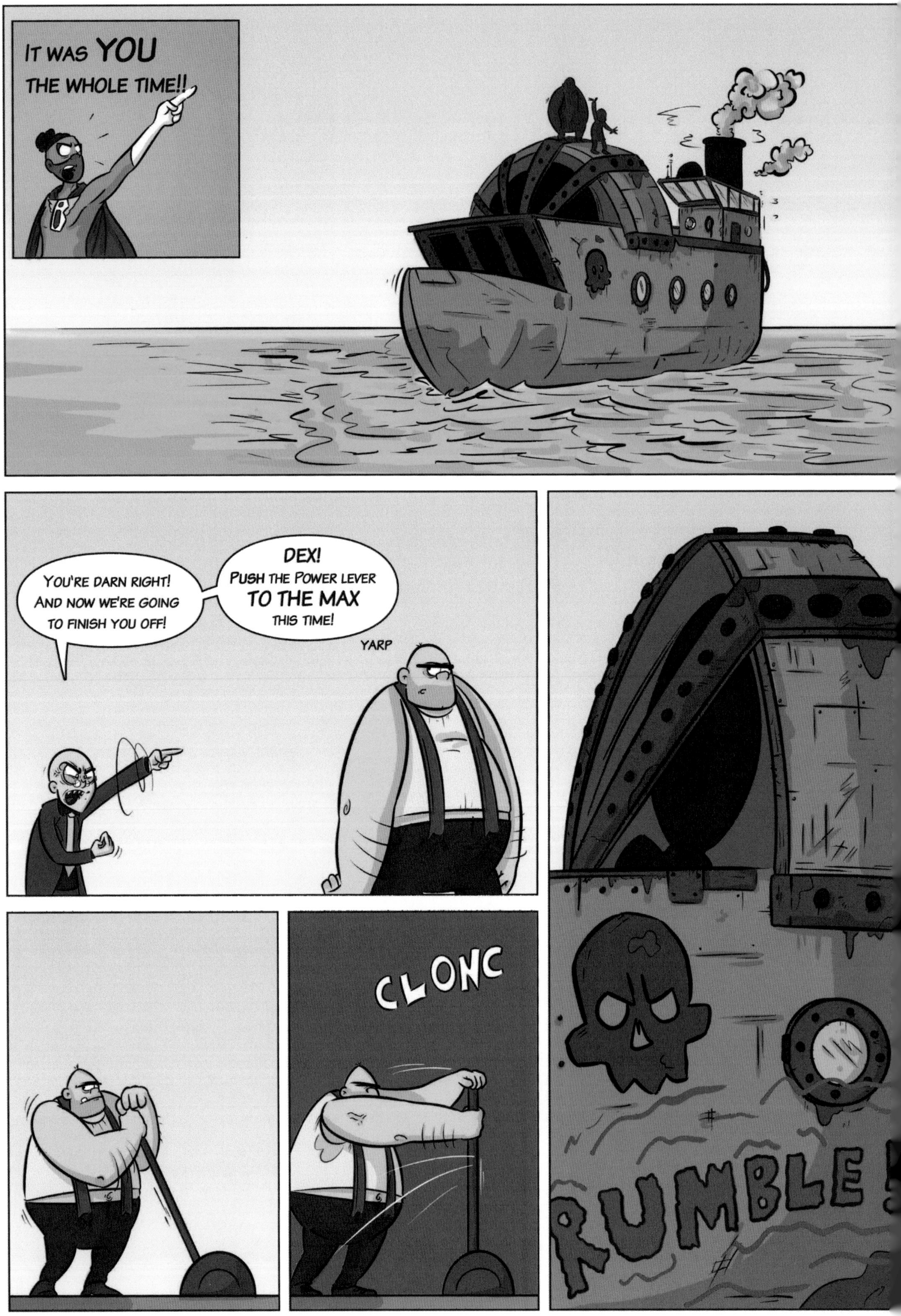

IT WAS YOU THE WHOLE TIME!!
YOU'RE DARN RIGHT! AND NOW WE'RE GOING TO FINISH YOU OFF!
DEX! PUSH THE POWER LEVER TO THE MAX THIS TIME!
YARP
CLONC
RUMBLE

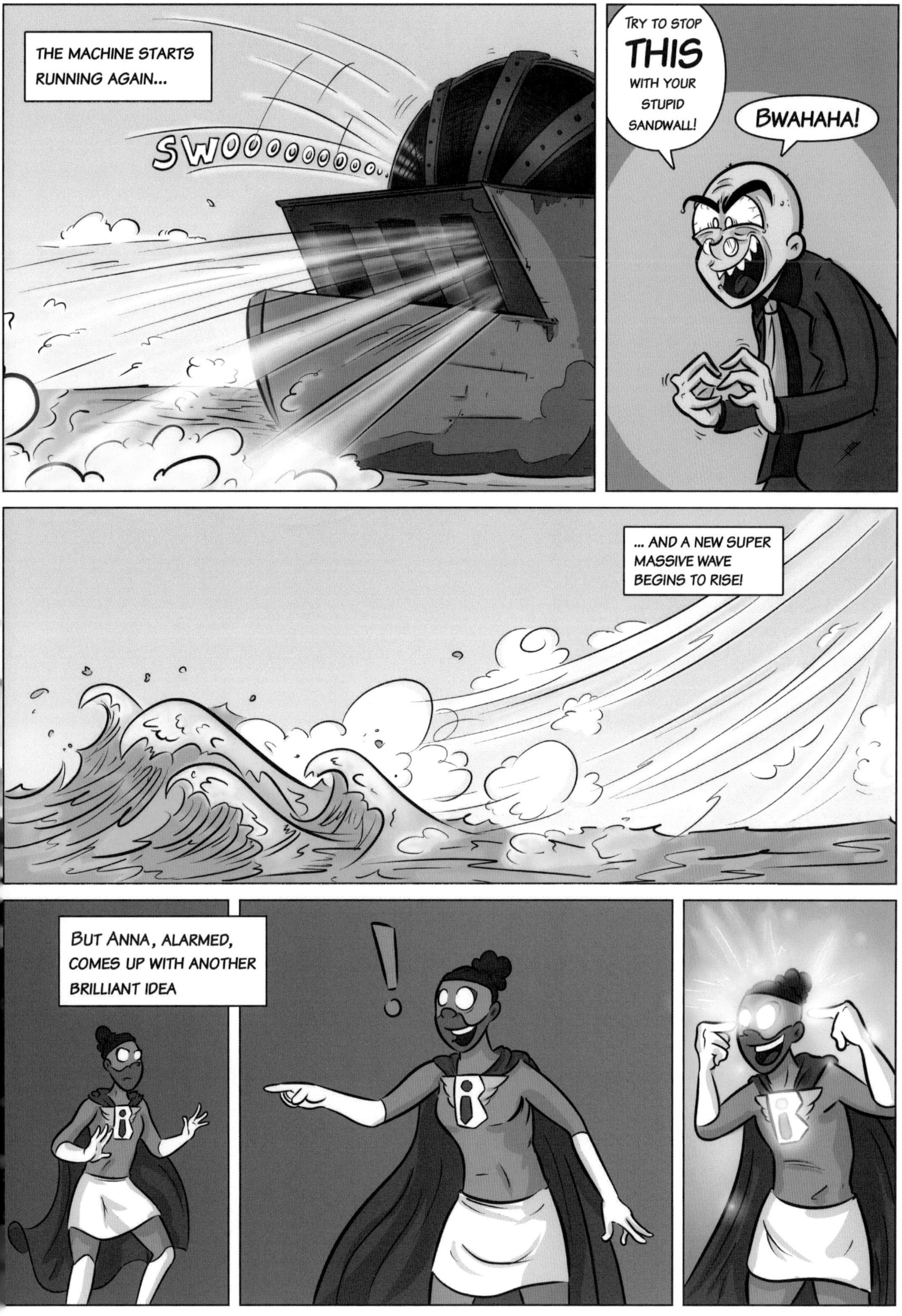
THE MACHINE STARTS RUNNING AGAIN...
SWOOOOOOOOOO...
TRY TO STOP THIS WITH YOUR STUPID SANDWALL!
BWAHAHA!
... AND A NEW SUPER MASSIVE WAVE BEGINS TO RISE!
BUT ANNA, ALARMED, COMES UP WITH ANOTHER BRILLIANT IDEA
!

"I NEED TO FIGHT THE SOURCE ..."

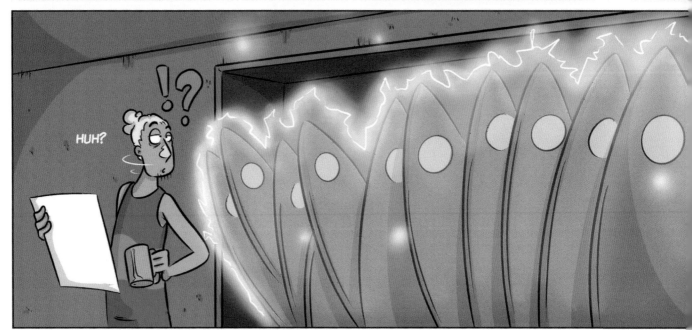

HUH?

Jays Super Surfing equipment

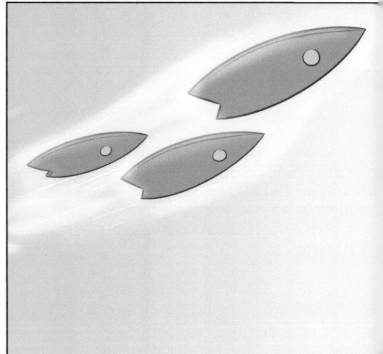

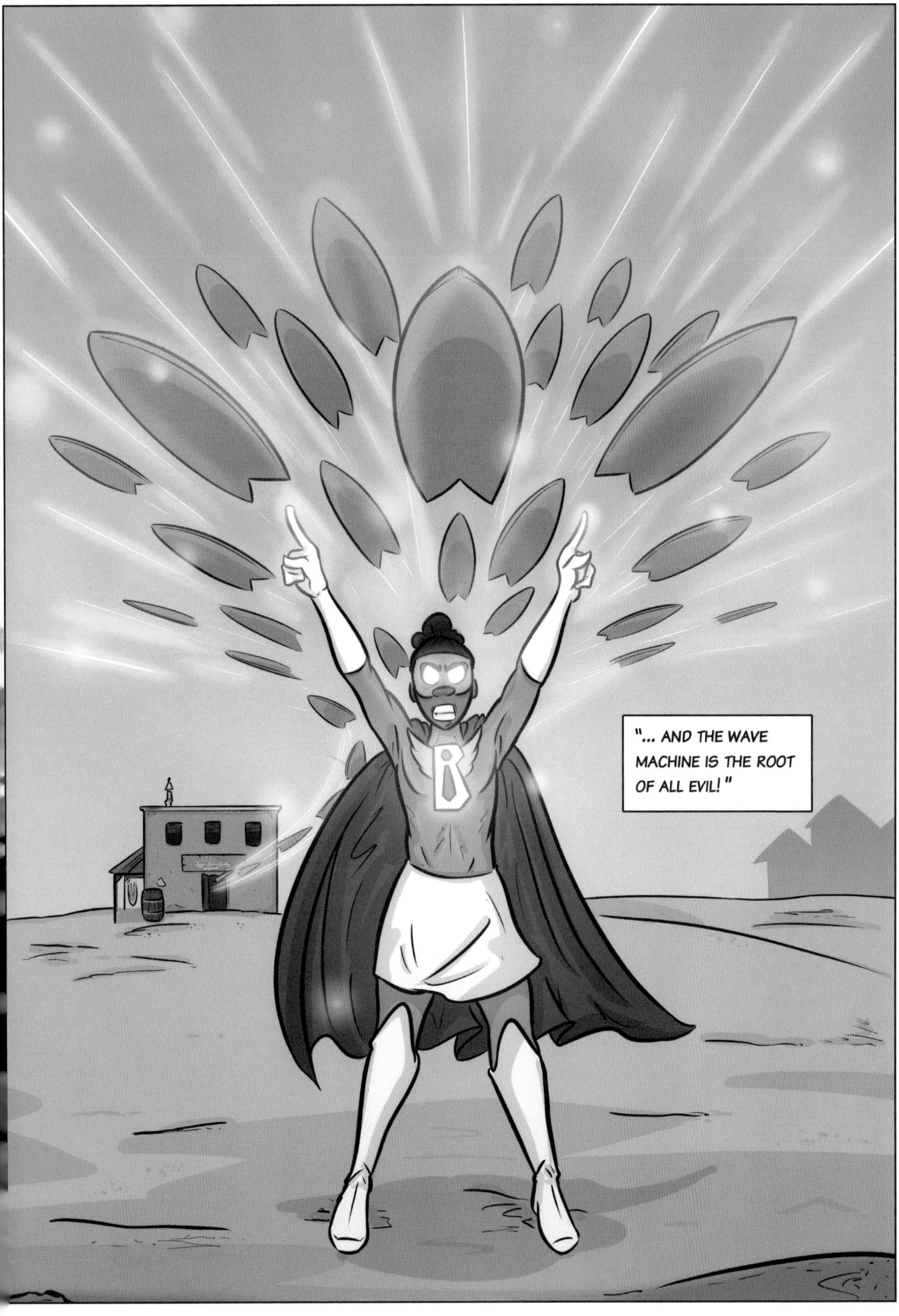
"... AND THE WAVE MACHINE IS THE ROOT OF ALL EVIL!"

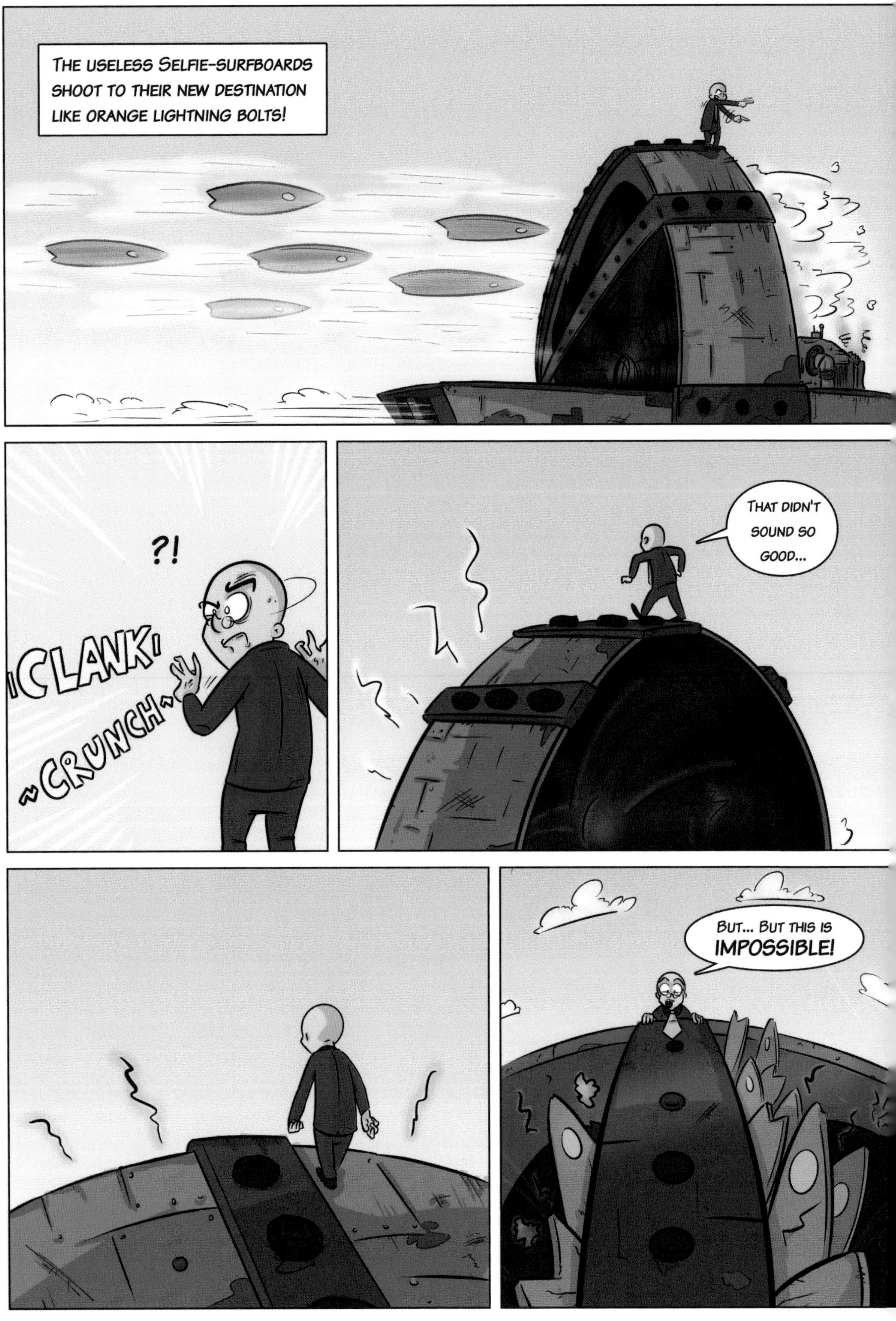
THE USELESS SELFIE-SURFBOARDS SHOOT TO THEIR NEW DESTINATION LIKE ORANGE LIGHTNING BOLTS!
?!
CLANK
CRUNCH
THAT DIDN'T SOUND SO GOOD...
BUT... BUT THIS IS IMPOSSIBLE!

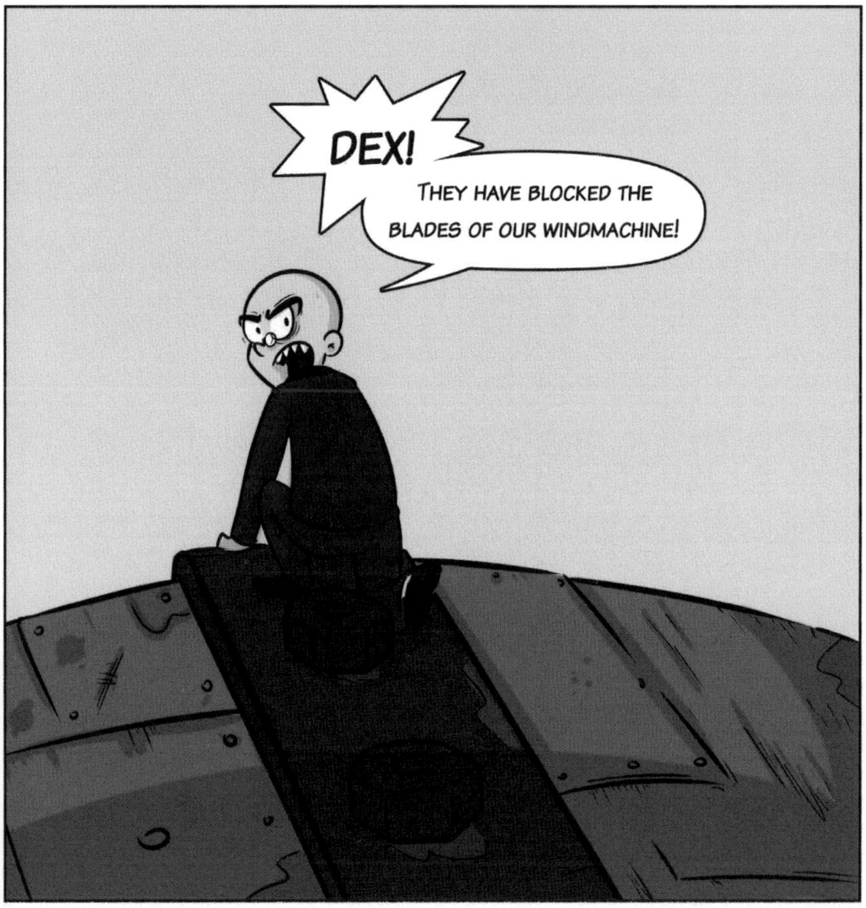
DEX!
THEY HAVE BLOCKED THE BLADES OF OUR WINDMACHINE!

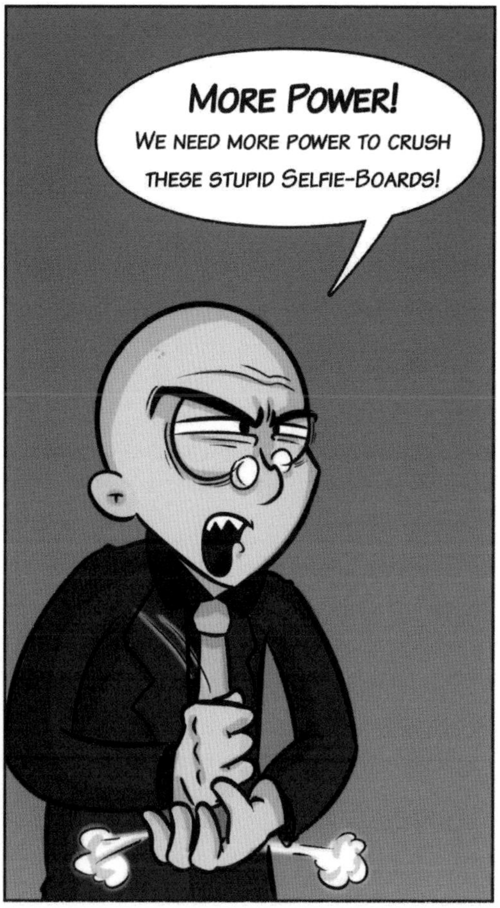
MORE POWER!
WE NEED MORE POWER TO CRUSH THESE STUPID SELFIE-BOARDS!

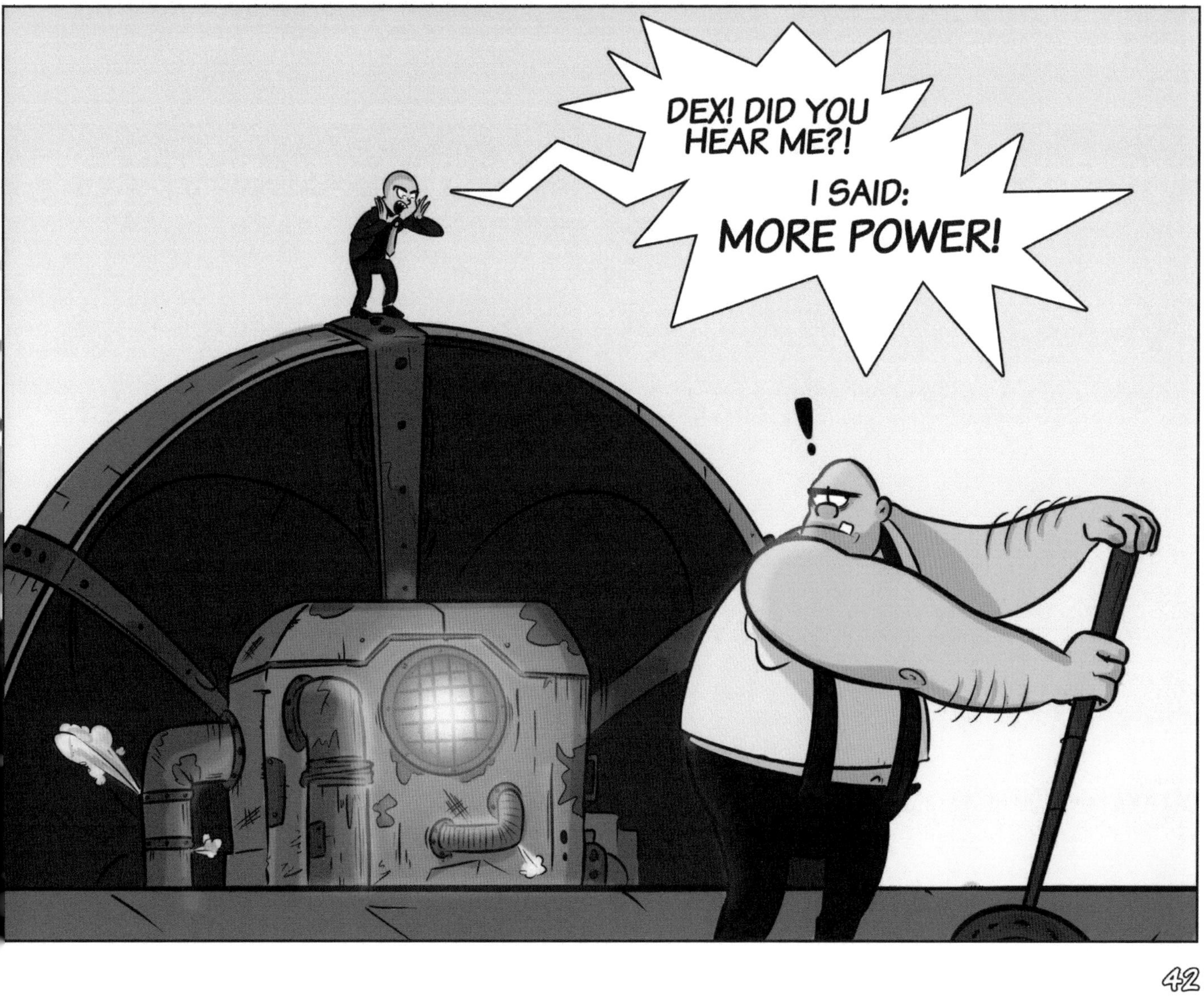
DEX! DID YOU HEAR ME?!
I SAID: MORE POWER!
!

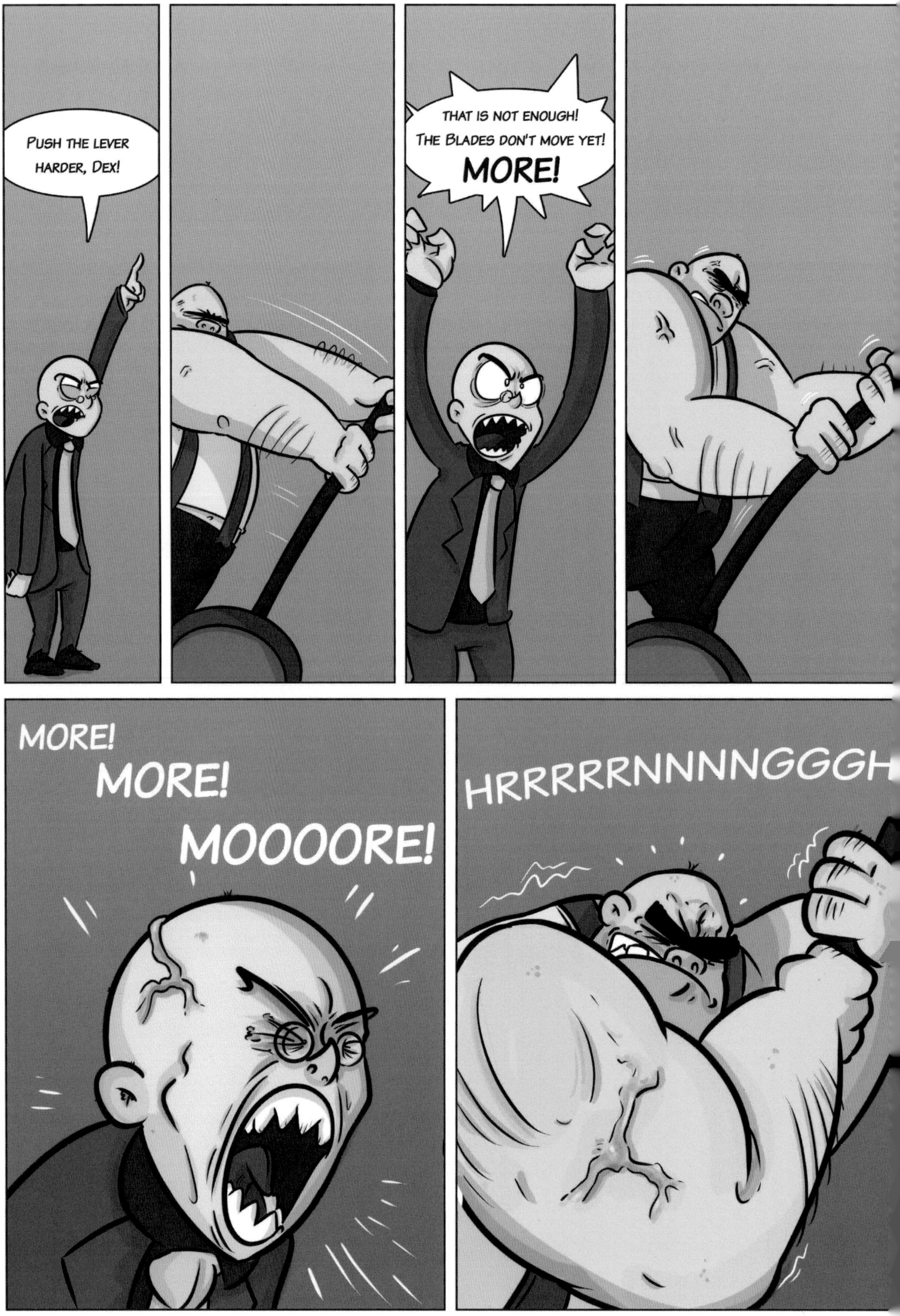

PUSH THE LEVER HARDER, DEX!
THAT IS NOT ENOUGH! THE BLADES DON'T MOVE YET! MORE!
MORE!
MORE!
MOOOORE!
HRRRRRNNNNGGGH

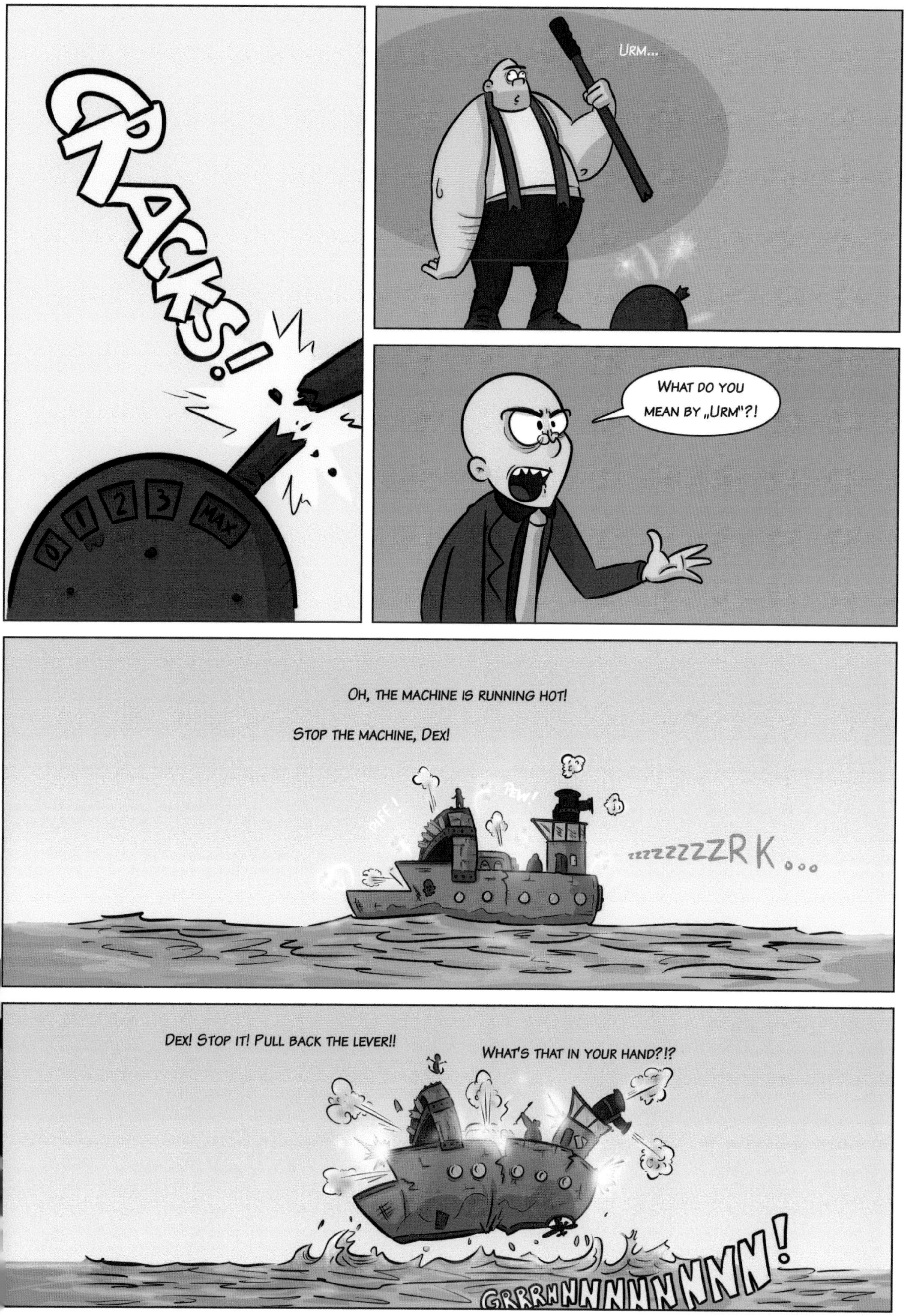
CRACKS!
0
1
2
3
MAX
URM...
WHAT DO YOU MEAN BY „URM"?!
OH, THE MACHINE IS RUNNING HOT!
STOP THE MACHINE, DEX!
PFF!
PEW!
zzzzZZZRK ...
DEX! STOP IT! PULL BACK THE LEVER!!
WHAT'S THAT IN YOUR HAND?!?
GRRRHNNNNNNNNN!

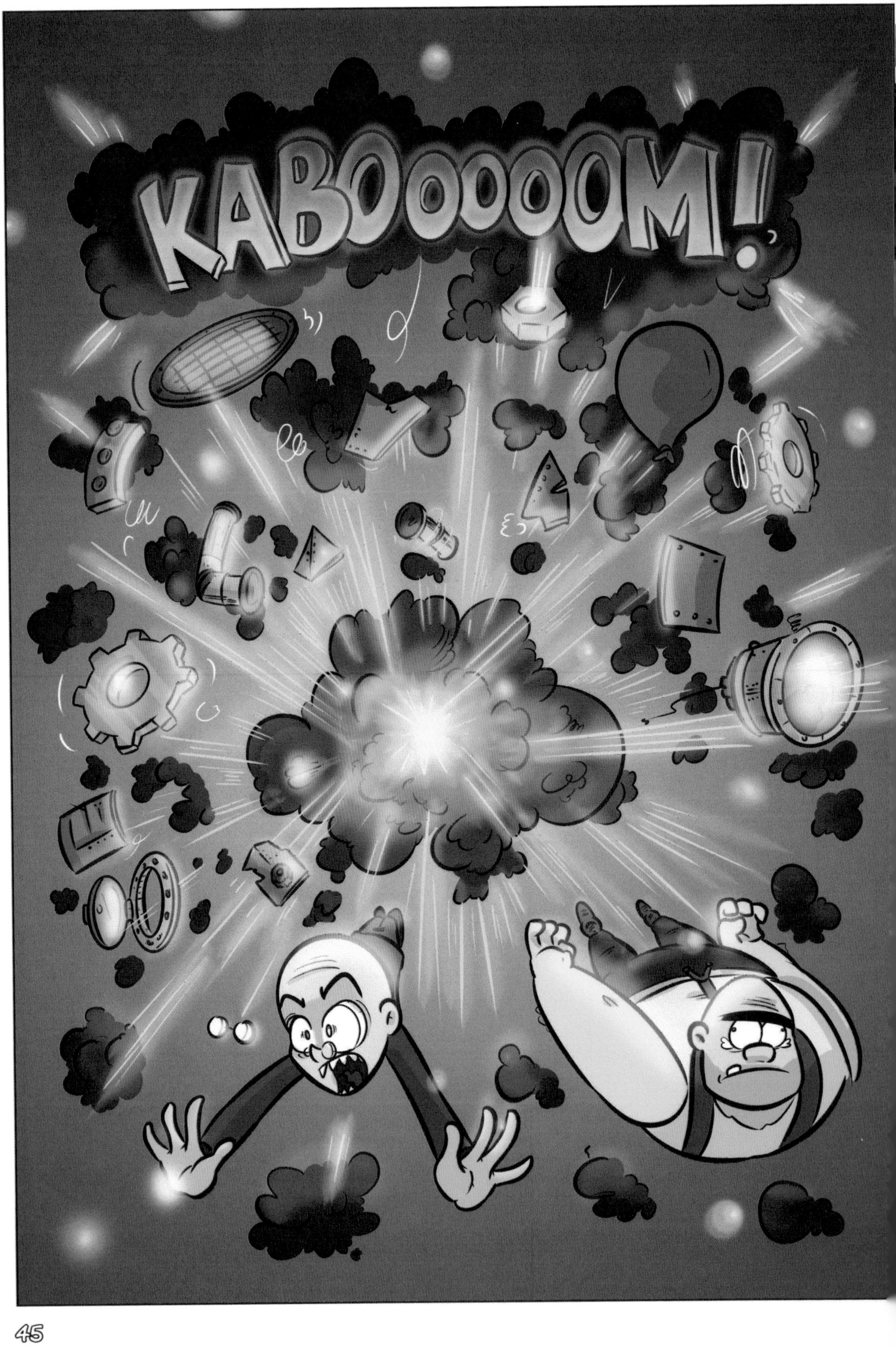
KABOOOOOM!

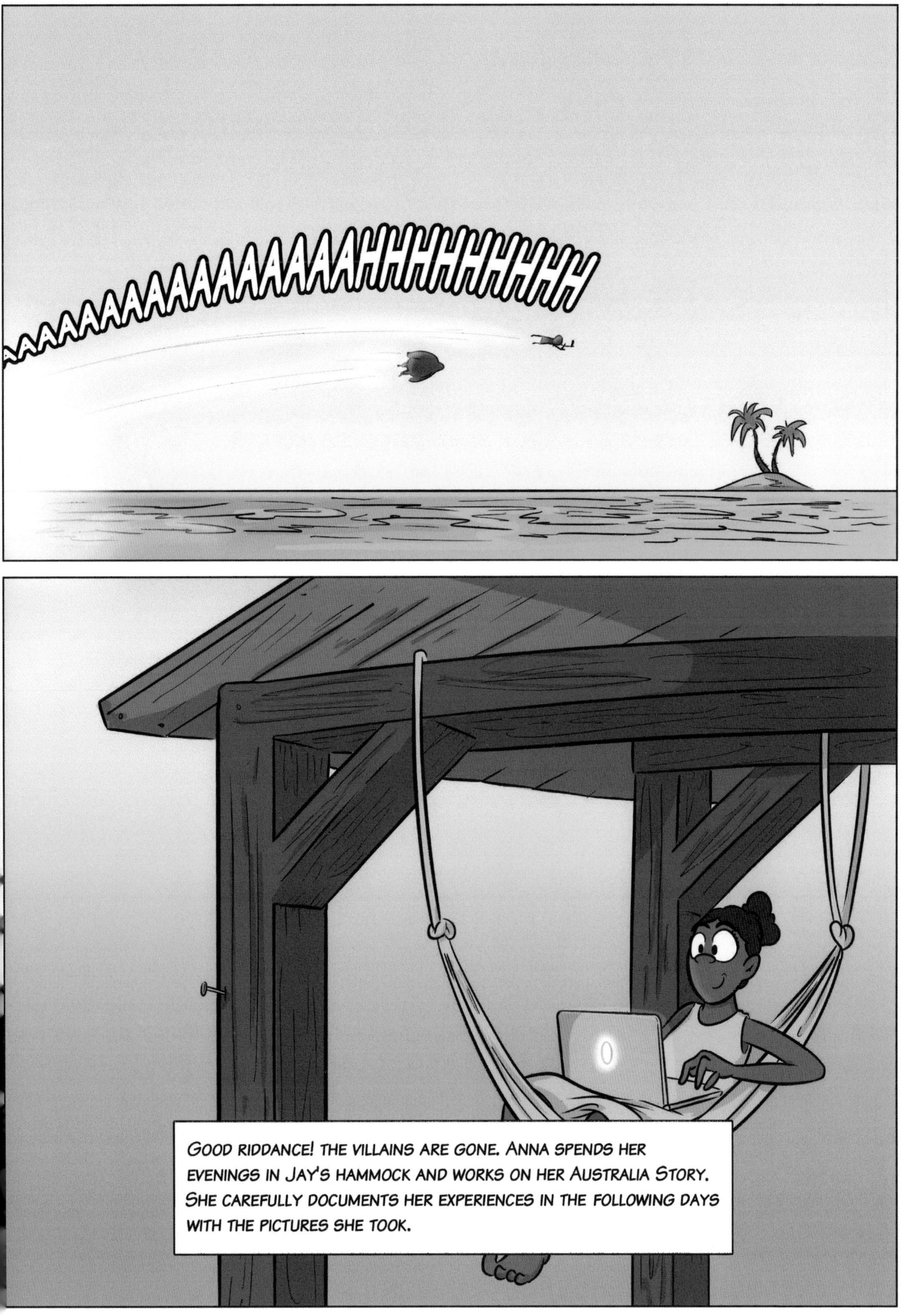
AAAAAAAAAAAAAAAAAAAAAHHHHHHHHHH
Good riddance! The villains are gone. Anna spends her evenings in Jay's hammock and works on her Australia Story. She carefully documents her experiences in the following days with the pictures she took.

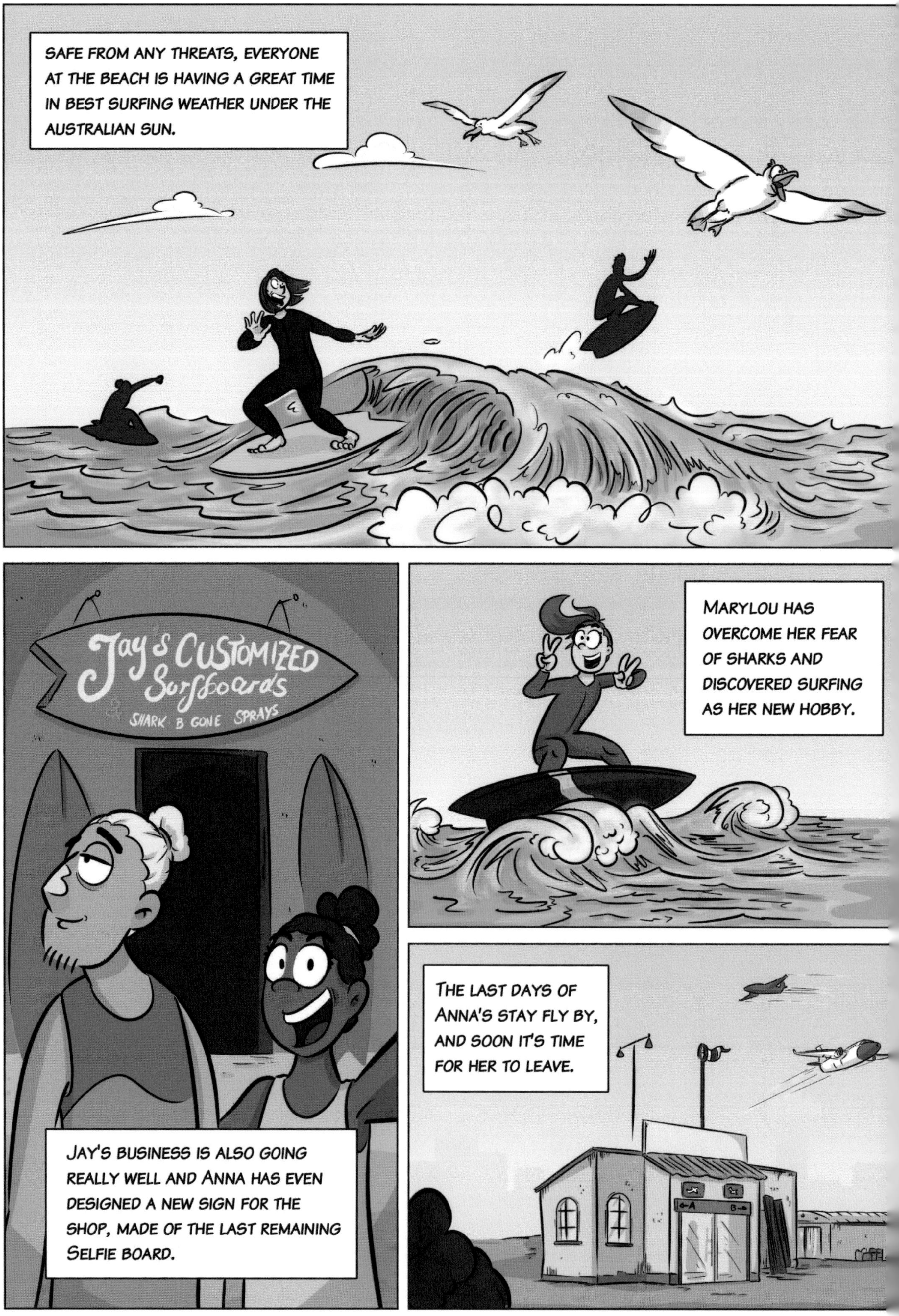
SAFE FROM ANY THREATS, EVERYONE AT THE BEACH IS HAVING A GREAT TIME IN BEST SURFING WEATHER UNDER THE AUSTRALIAN SUN.
Jay's CUSTOMIZED Surfboards
& SHARK B GONE SPRAYS
JAY'S BUSINESS IS ALSO GOING REALLY WELL AND ANNA HAS EVEN DESIGNED A NEW SIGN FOR THE SHOP, MADE OF THE LAST REMAINING SELFIE BOARD.
MARYLOU HAS OVERCOME HER FEAR OF SHARKS AND DISCOVERED SURFING AS HER NEW HOBBY.
THE LAST DAYS OF ANNA'S STAY FLY BY, AND SOON IT'S TIME FOR HER TO LEAVE.

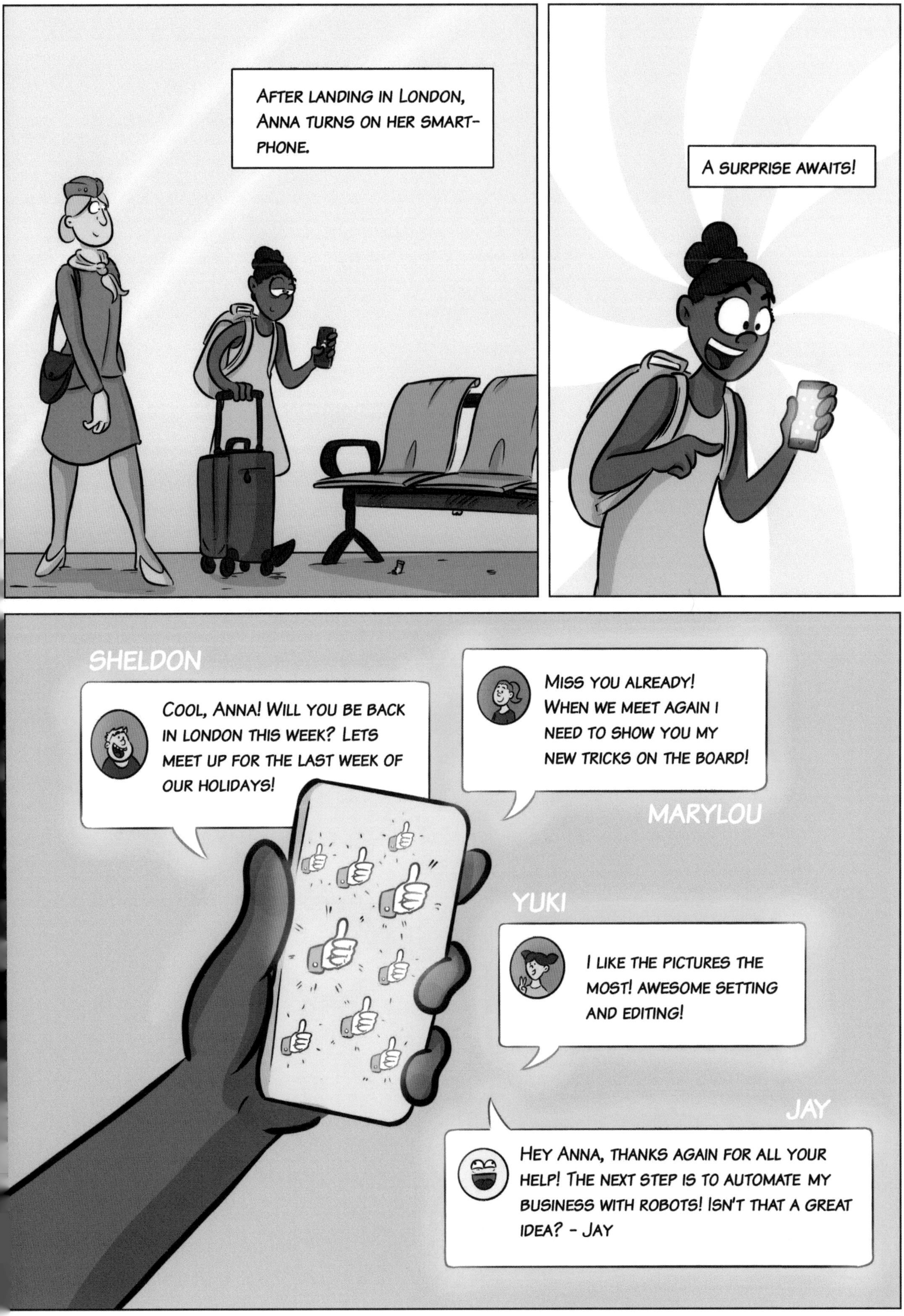
AFTER LANDING IN LONDON, ANNA TURNS ON HER SMART-PHONE.
A SURPRISE AWAITS!
SHELDON
COOL, ANNA! WILL YOU BE BACK IN LONDON THIS WEEK? LETS MEET UP FOR THE LAST WEEK OF OUR HOLIDAYS!
MISS YOU ALREADY! WHEN WE MEET AGAIN I NEED TO SHOW YOU MY NEW TRICKS ON THE BOARD!
MARYLOU
YUKI
I LIKE THE PICTURES THE MOST! AWESOME SETTING AND EDITING!
JAY
HEY ANNA, THANKS AGAIN FOR ALL YOUR HELP! THE NEXT STEP IS TO AUTOMATE MY BUSINESS WITH ROBOTS! ISN'T THAT A GREAT IDEA? - JAY

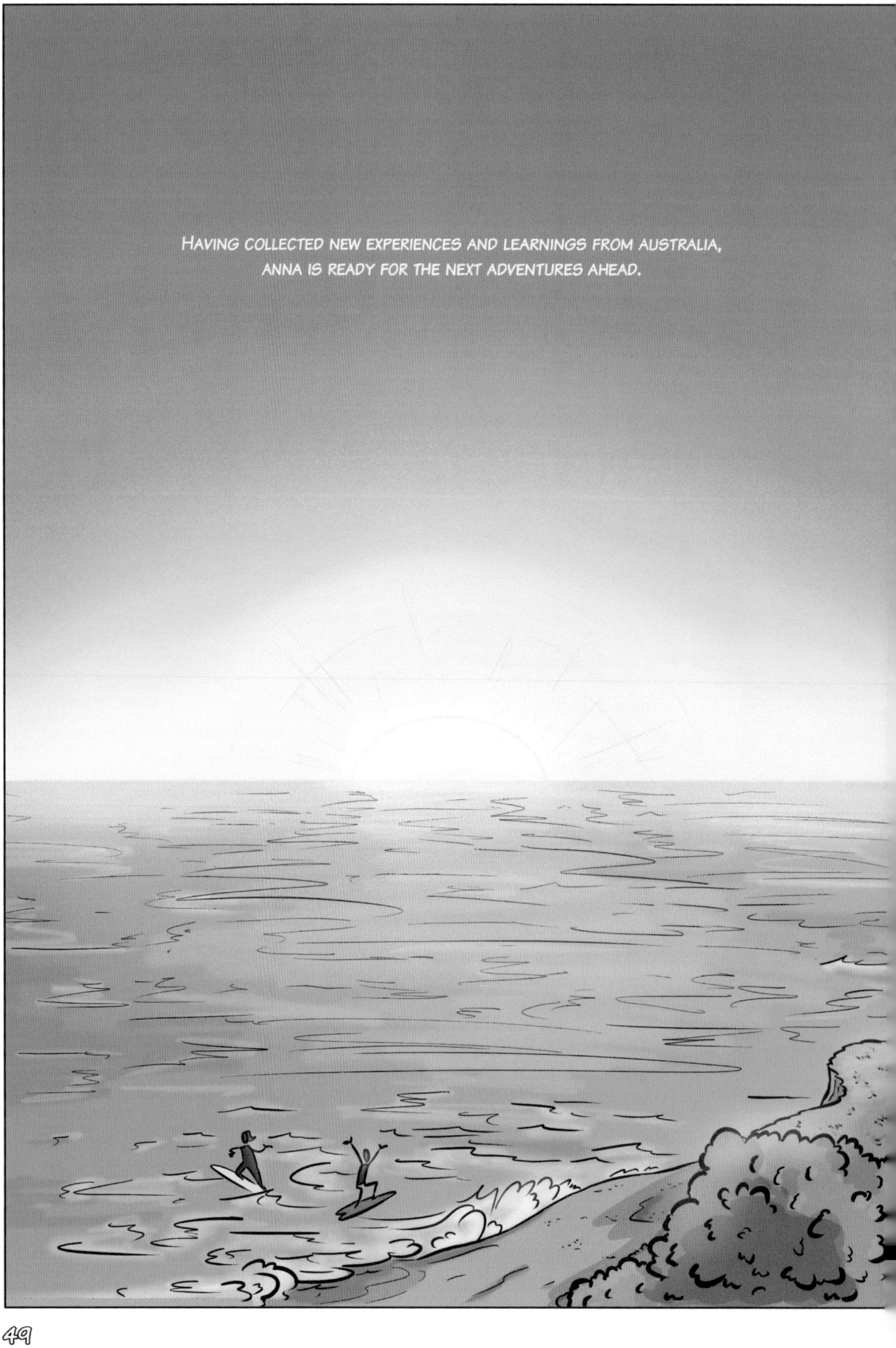
HAVING COLLECTED NEW EXPERIENCES AND LEARNINGS FROM AUSTRALIA,
ANNA IS READY FOR THE NEXT ADVENTURES AHEAD.

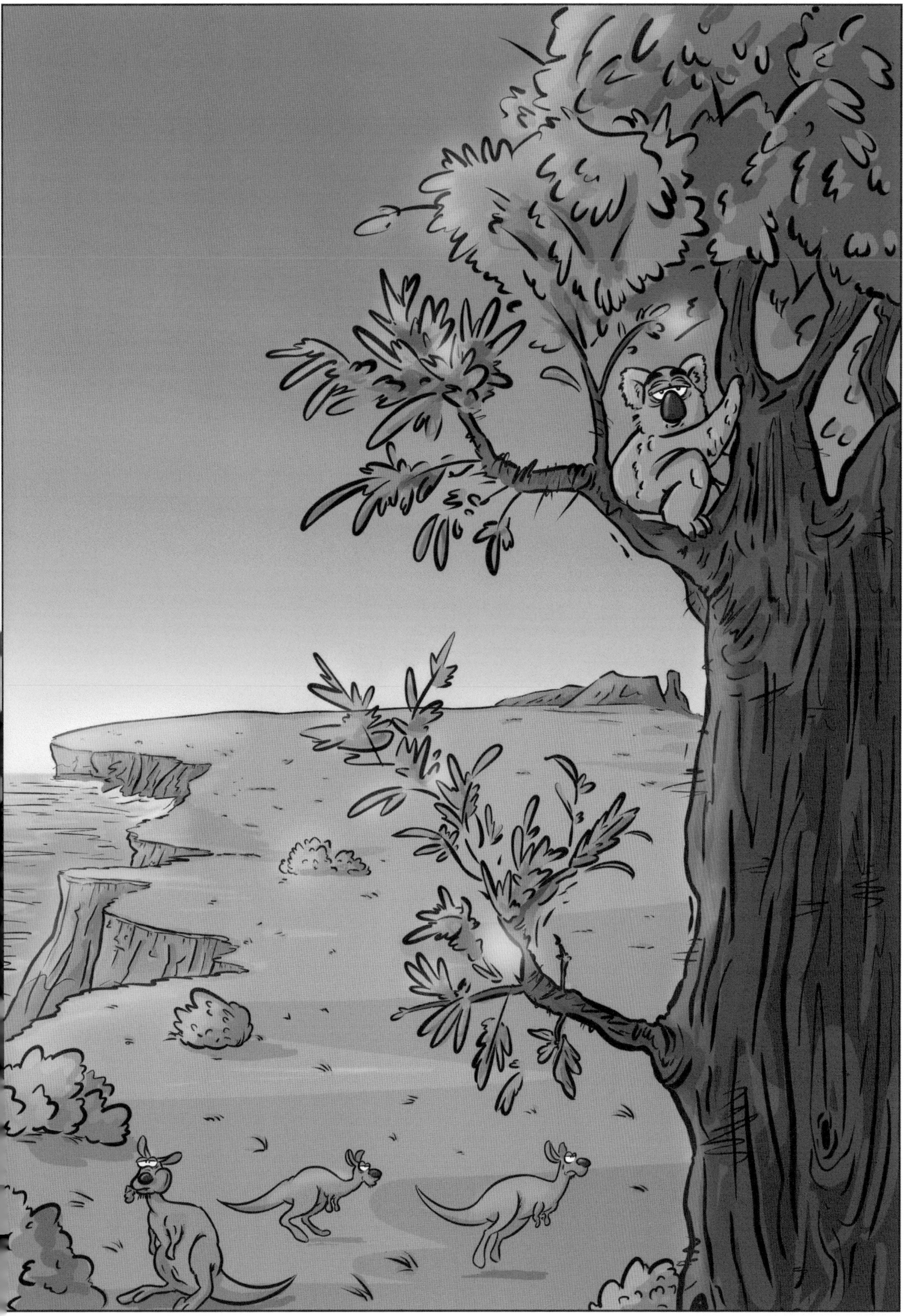

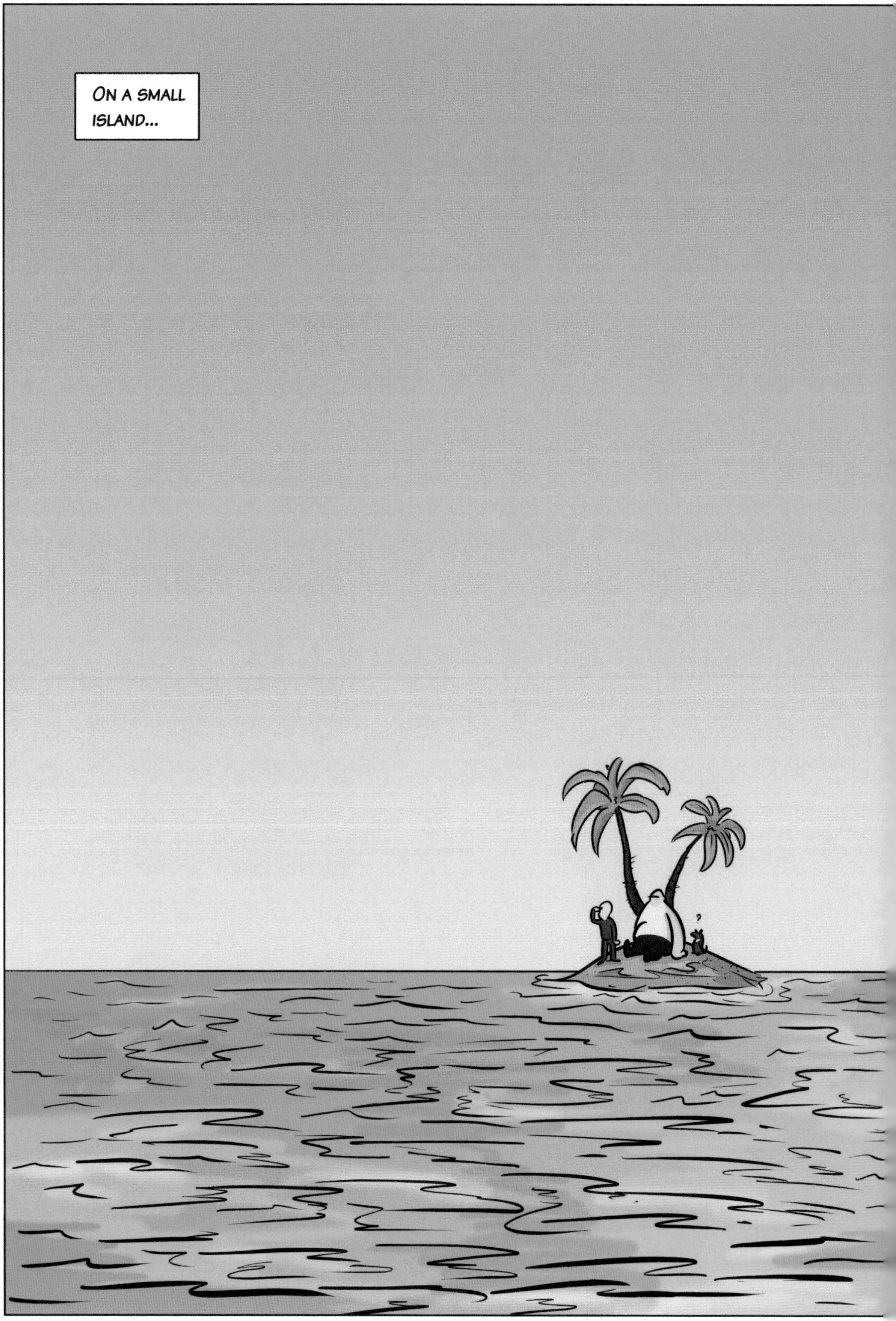
ON A SMALL ISLAND...
?

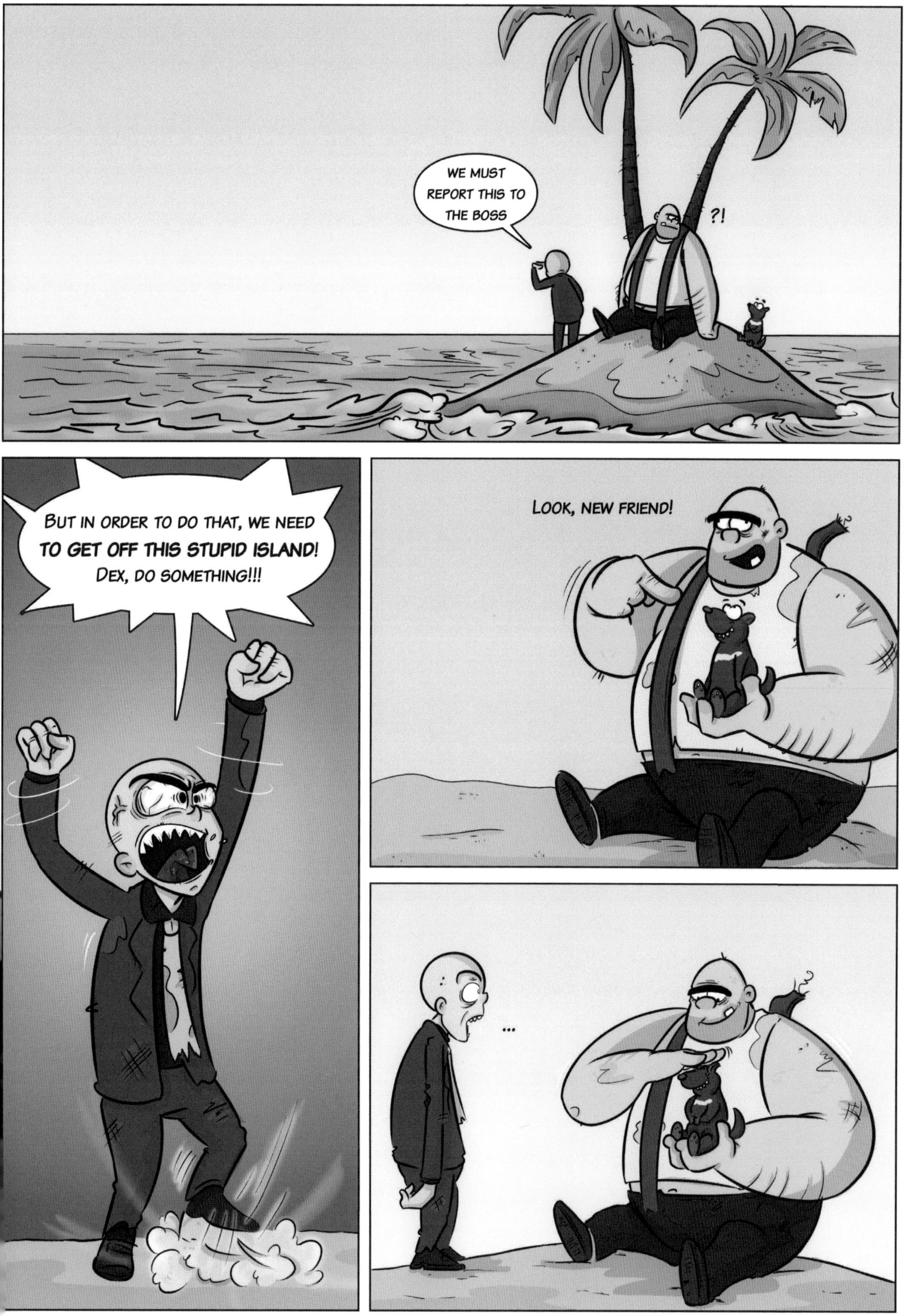
WE MUST REPORT THIS TO THE BOSS
?!
BUT IN ORDER TO DO THAT, WE NEED TO GET OFF THIS STUPID ISLAND! DEX, DO SOMETHING!!!
LOOK, NEW FRIEND!
...

CHAPTER 2: LONDON

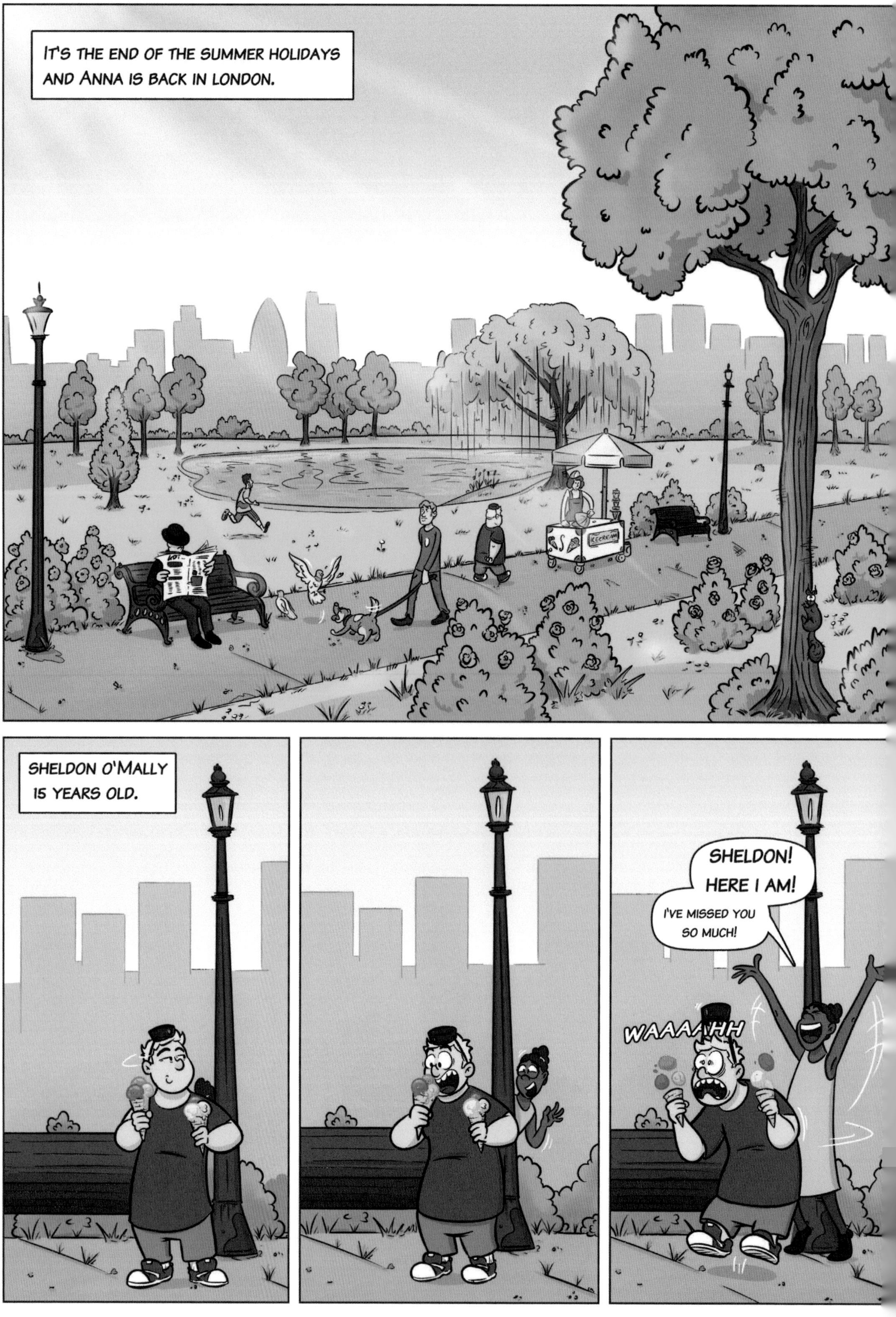
IT'S THE END OF THE SUMMER HOLIDAYS AND ANNA IS BACK IN LONDON.
ICECREAM
SHELDON O'MALLY 15 YEARS OLD.
WAAAAHH
SHELDON! HERE I AM!
I'VE MISSED YOU SO MUCH!

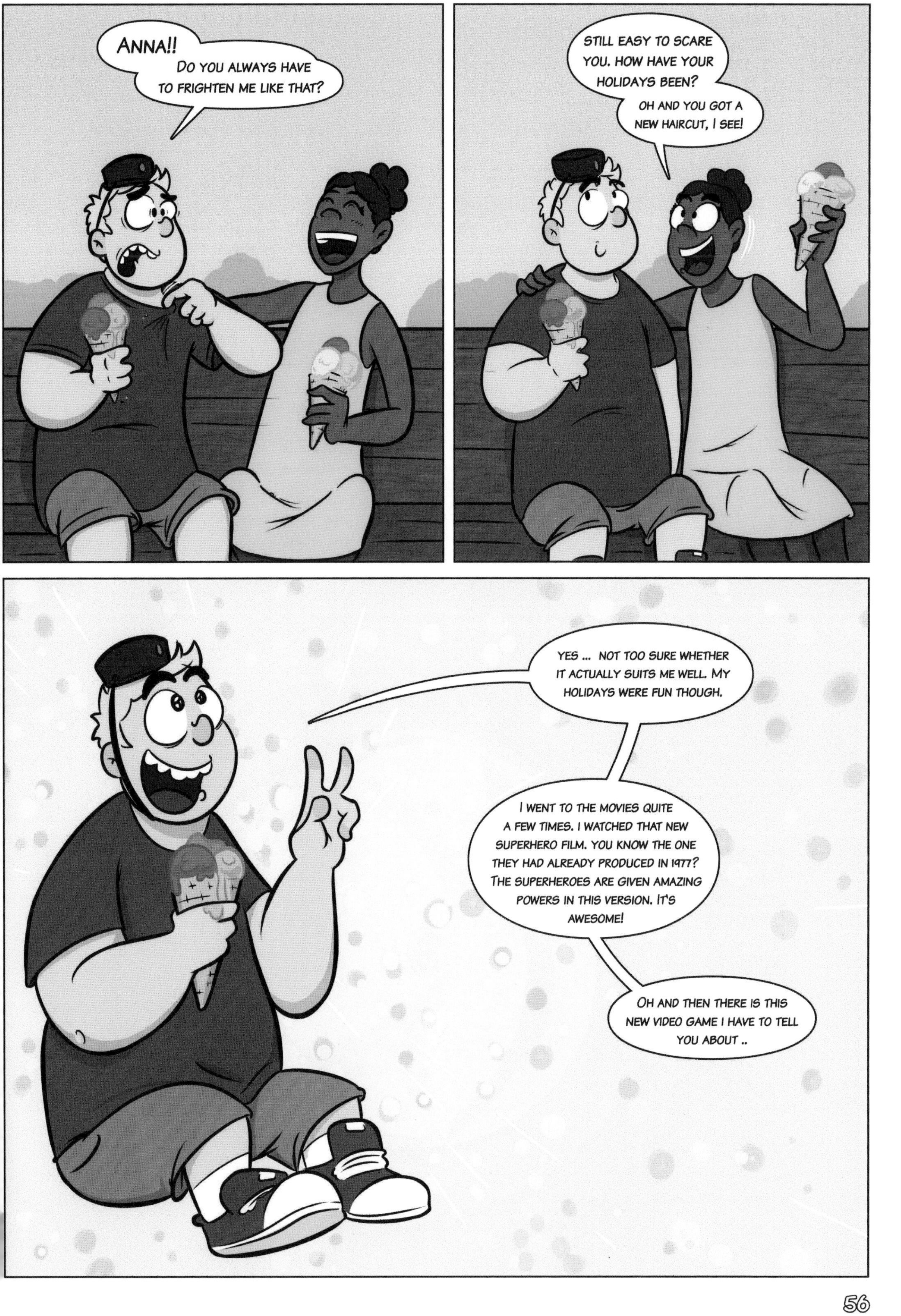
ANNA!!
DO YOU ALWAYS HAVE TO FRIGHTEN ME LIKE THAT?
STILL EASY TO SCARE YOU. HOW HAVE YOUR HOLIDAYS BEEN?
OH AND YOU GOT A NEW HAIRCUT, I SEE!
YES ... NOT TOO SURE WHETHER IT ACTUALLY SUITS ME WELL. MY HOLIDAYS WERE FUN THOUGH.
I WENT TO THE MOVIES QUITE A FEW TIMES. I WATCHED THAT NEW SUPERHERO FILM. YOU KNOW THE ONE THEY HAD ALREADY PRODUCED IN 1977? THE SUPERHEROES ARE GIVEN AMAZING POWERS IN THIS VERSION. IT'S AWESOME!
OH AND THEN THERE IS THIS NEW VIDEO GAME I HAVE TO TELL YOU ABOUT ..

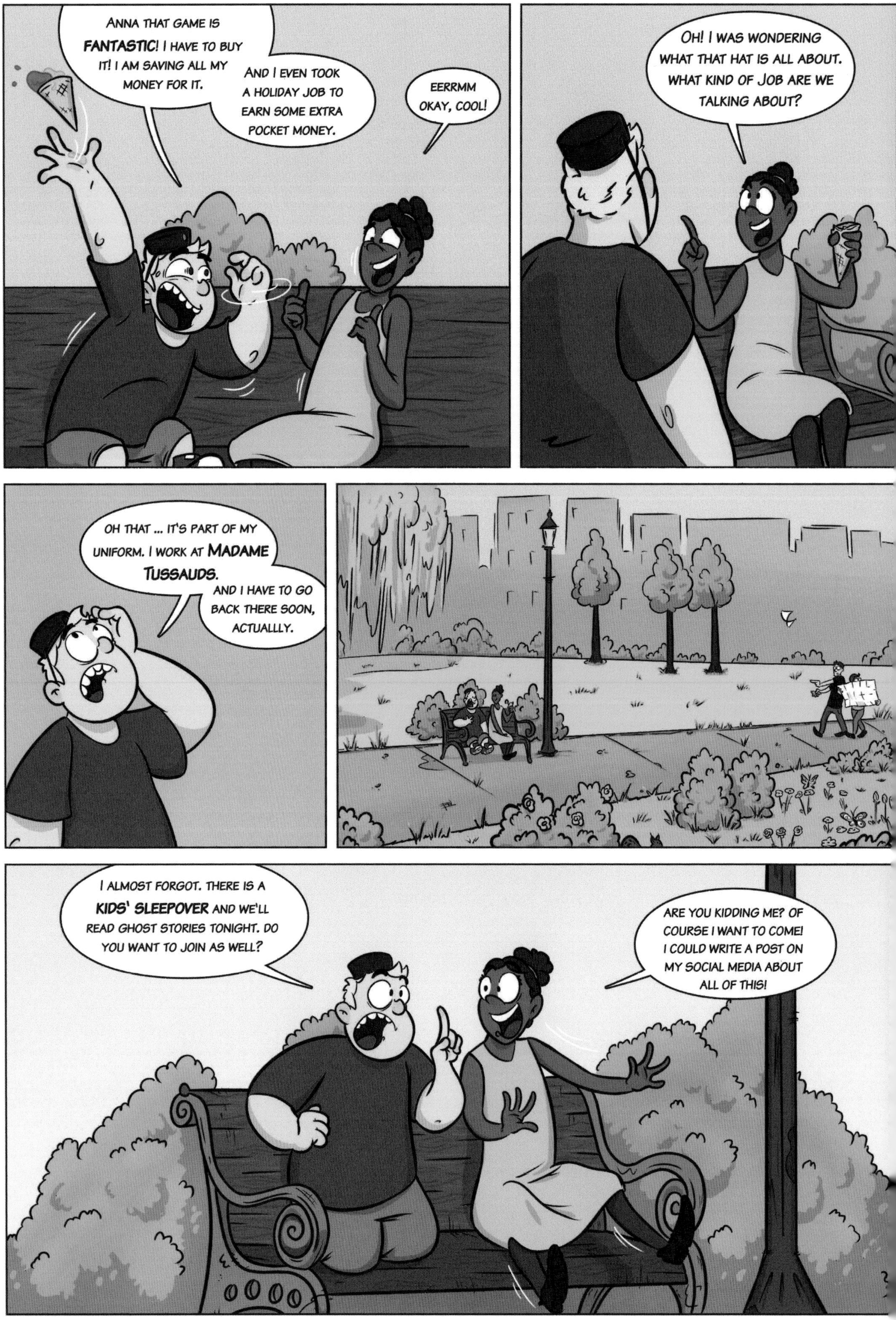
ANNA THAT GAME IS **FANTASTIC**! I HAVE TO BUY IT! I AM SAVING ALL MY MONEY FOR IT.
AND I EVEN TOOK A HOLIDAY JOB TO EARN SOME EXTRA POCKET MONEY.
EERRMM OKAY, COOL!
OH! I WAS WONDERING WHAT THAT HAT IS ALL ABOUT. WHAT KIND OF JOB ARE WE TALKING ABOUT?
OH THAT ... IT'S PART OF MY UNIFORM. I WORK AT **MADAME TUSSAUDS**.
AND I HAVE TO GO BACK THERE SOON, ACTUALLLY.
I ALMOST FORGOT. THERE IS A **KIDS' SLEEPOVER** AND WE'LL READ GHOST STORIES TONIGHT. DO YOU WANT TO JOIN AS WELL?
ARE YOU KIDDING ME? OF COURSE I WANT TO COME! I COULD WRITE A POST ON MY SOCIAL MEDIA ABOUT ALL OF THIS!

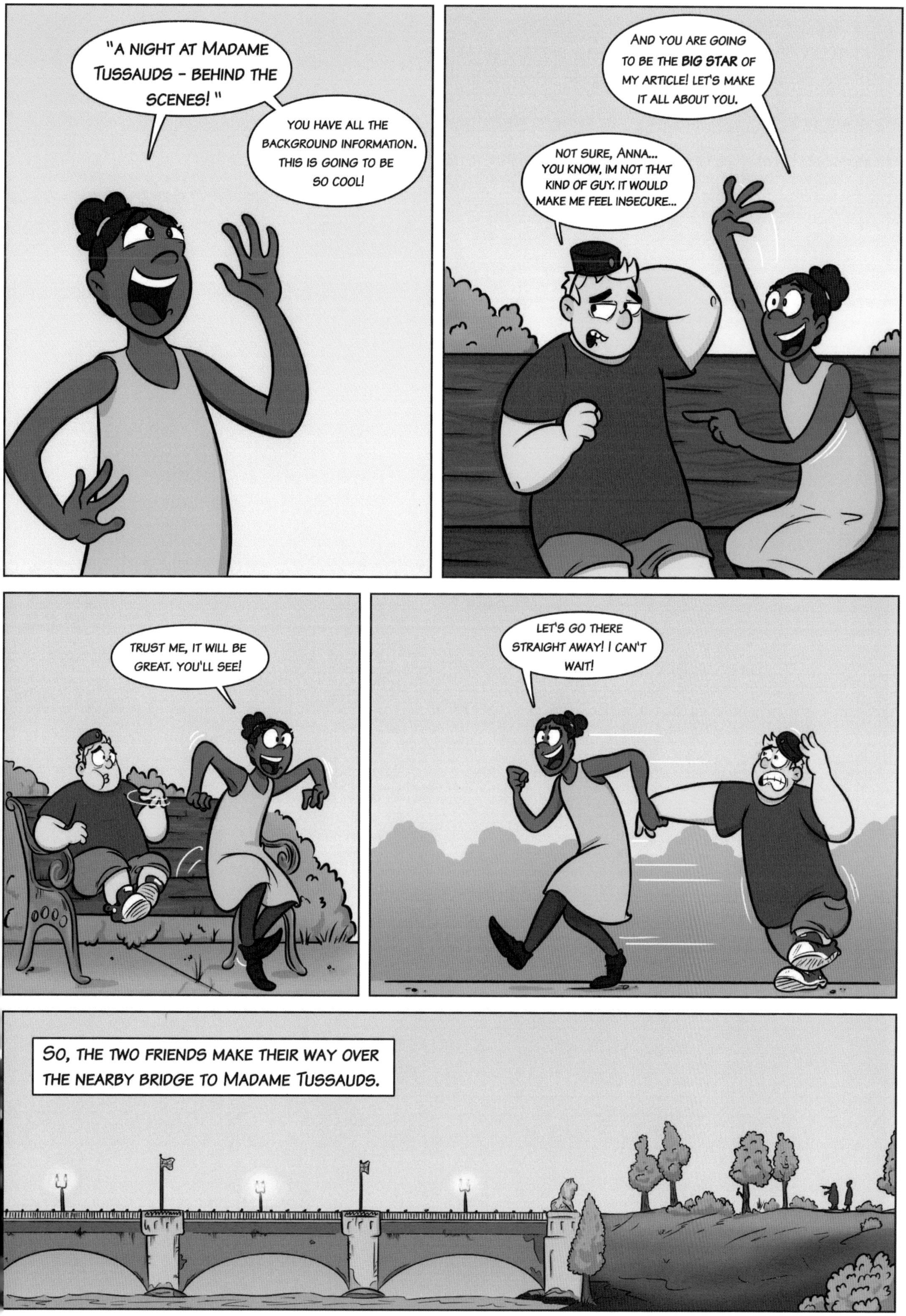

"A NIGHT AT MADAME TUSSAUDS - BEHIND THE SCENES!"
YOU HAVE ALL THE BACKGROUND INFORMATION. THIS IS GOING TO BE SO COOL!
AND YOU ARE GOING TO BE THE BIG STAR OF MY ARTICLE! LET'S MAKE IT ALL ABOUT YOU.
NOT SURE, ANNA... YOU KNOW, IM NOT THAT KIND OF GUY. IT WOULD MAKE ME FEEL INSECURE...
TRUST ME, IT WILL BE GREAT. YOU'LL SEE!
LET'S GO THERE STRAIGHT AWAY! I CAN'T WAIT!
SO, THE TWO FRIENDS MAKE THEIR WAY OVER THE NEARBY BRIDGE TO MADAME TUSSAUDS.

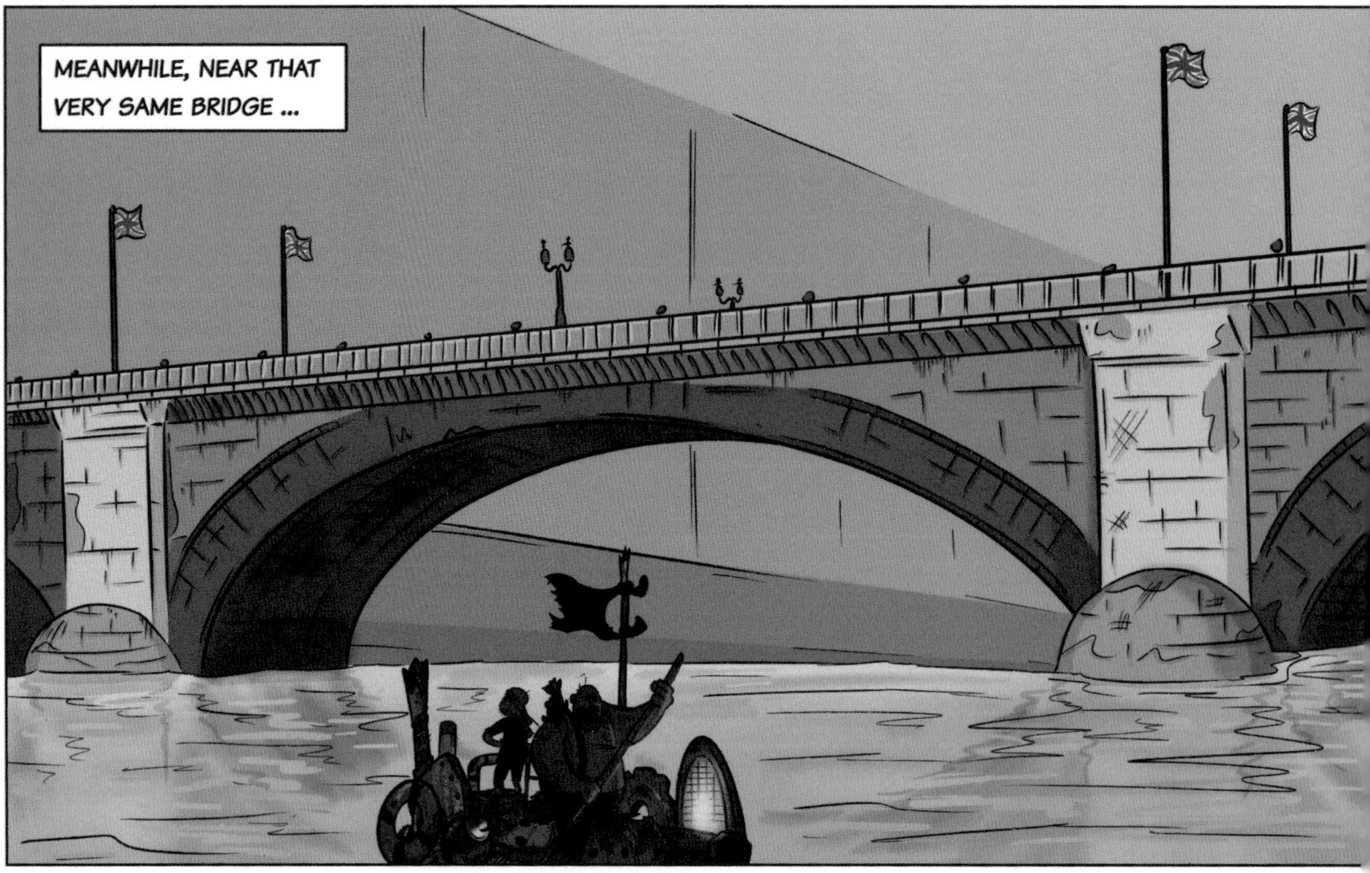
MEANWHILE, NEAR THAT VERY SAME BRIDGE ...

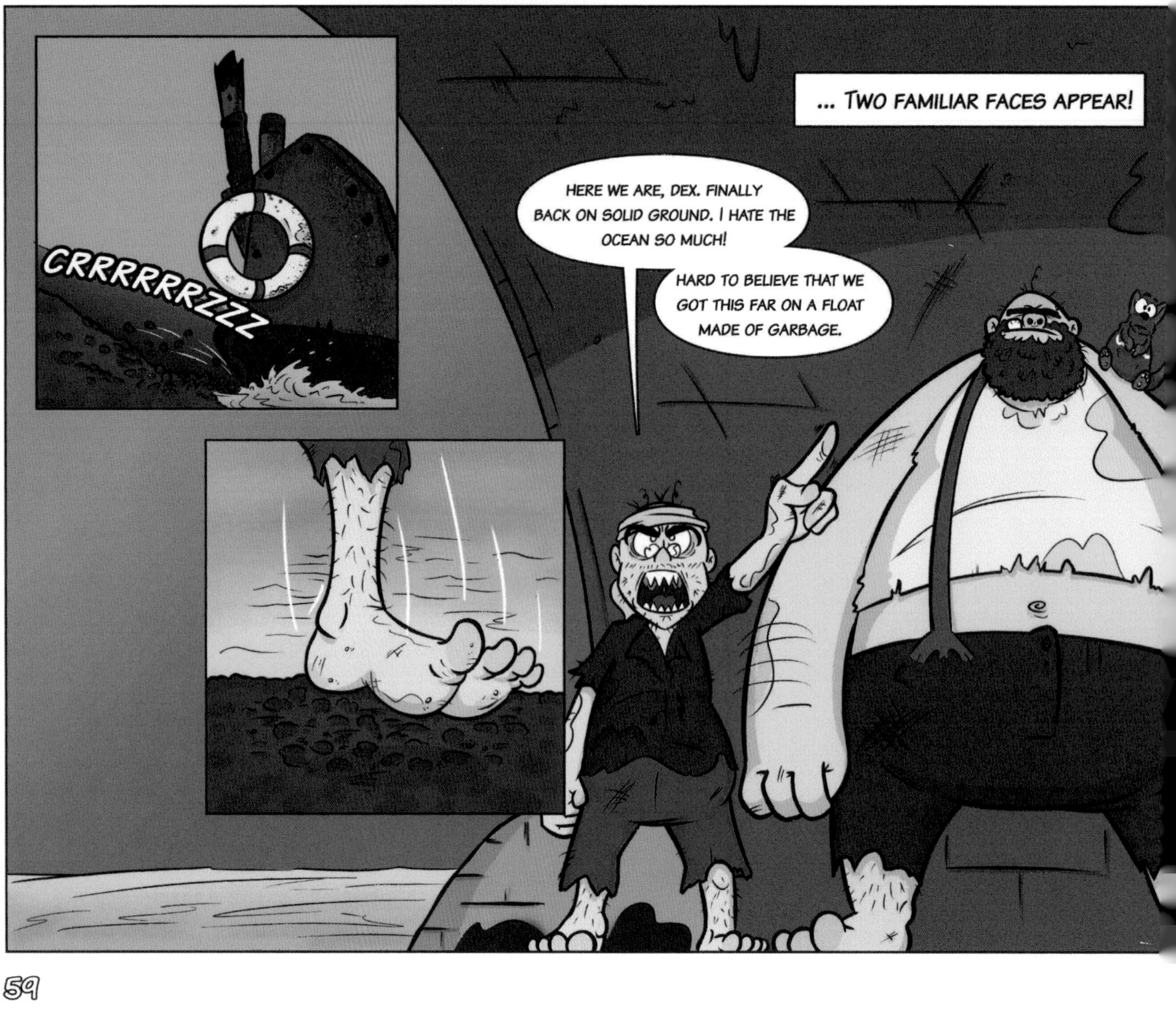
... TWO FAMILIAR FACES APPEAR!
CRRRRRRZZZZ
HERE WE ARE, DEX. FINALLY BACK ON SOLID GROUND. I HATE THE OCEAN SO MUCH!
HARD TO BELIEVE THAT WE GOT THIS FAR ON A FLOAT MADE OF GARBAGE.

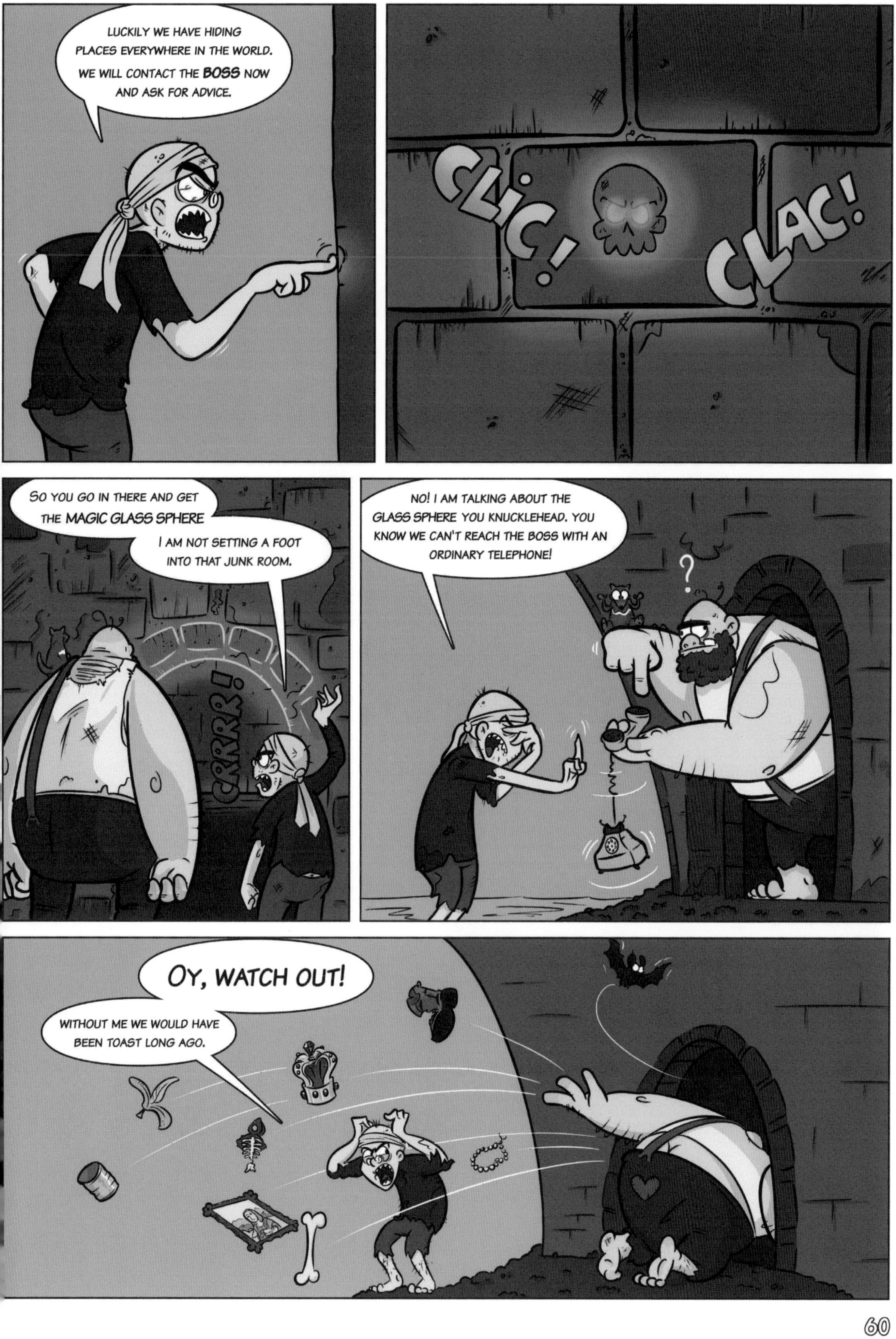
LUCKILY WE HAVE HIDING PLACES EVERYWHERE IN THE WORLD. WE WILL CONTACT THE BOSS NOW AND ASK FOR ADVICE.
CLIC!
CLAC!
SO YOU GO IN THERE AND GET THE MAGIC GLASS SPHERE
I AM NOT SETTING A FOOT INTO THAT JUNK ROOM.
CRRRR!
NO! I AM TALKING ABOUT THE GLASS SPHERE YOU KNUCKLEHEAD. YOU KNOW WE CAN'T REACH THE BOSS WITH AN ORDINARY TELEPHONE!
?
OY, WATCH OUT!
WITHOUT ME WE WOULD HAVE BEEN TOAST LONG AGO.

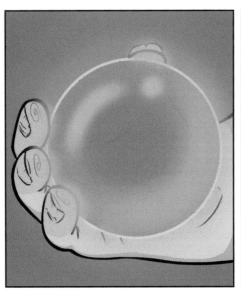

AHHH THERE IT IS! CAREFUL WITH IT, IT'S A FRAGILE MAGICAL OBJECT! FINALLY WE CAN...

HOLD ON! THEY TRIED TO DESTROY JAY'S SURFSHOP WITH A GIANT WAVE-WHAT?! ROFL!

IN FACT, IT WAS VERY DANGEROUS! I BLOCKED THE ROTORBLADES WITH THE USELESS OLD SELFIE-BOARDS.

THE MACHINE BLEW UP AND MART AND THE BIG ONE WERE OUT OF THE PICTURE!

WOAH, WHAT AN INCREDIBLE STORY! SOUNDS LIKE YOU HAD SUPER EXCITING HOLIDAYS.

PSSST DEX! GUESS WHAT MY MASTERMIND JUST COMPUTED! THIS GIRL UP THERE IS OUR ARCH-ENEMY IN DISGUISE!

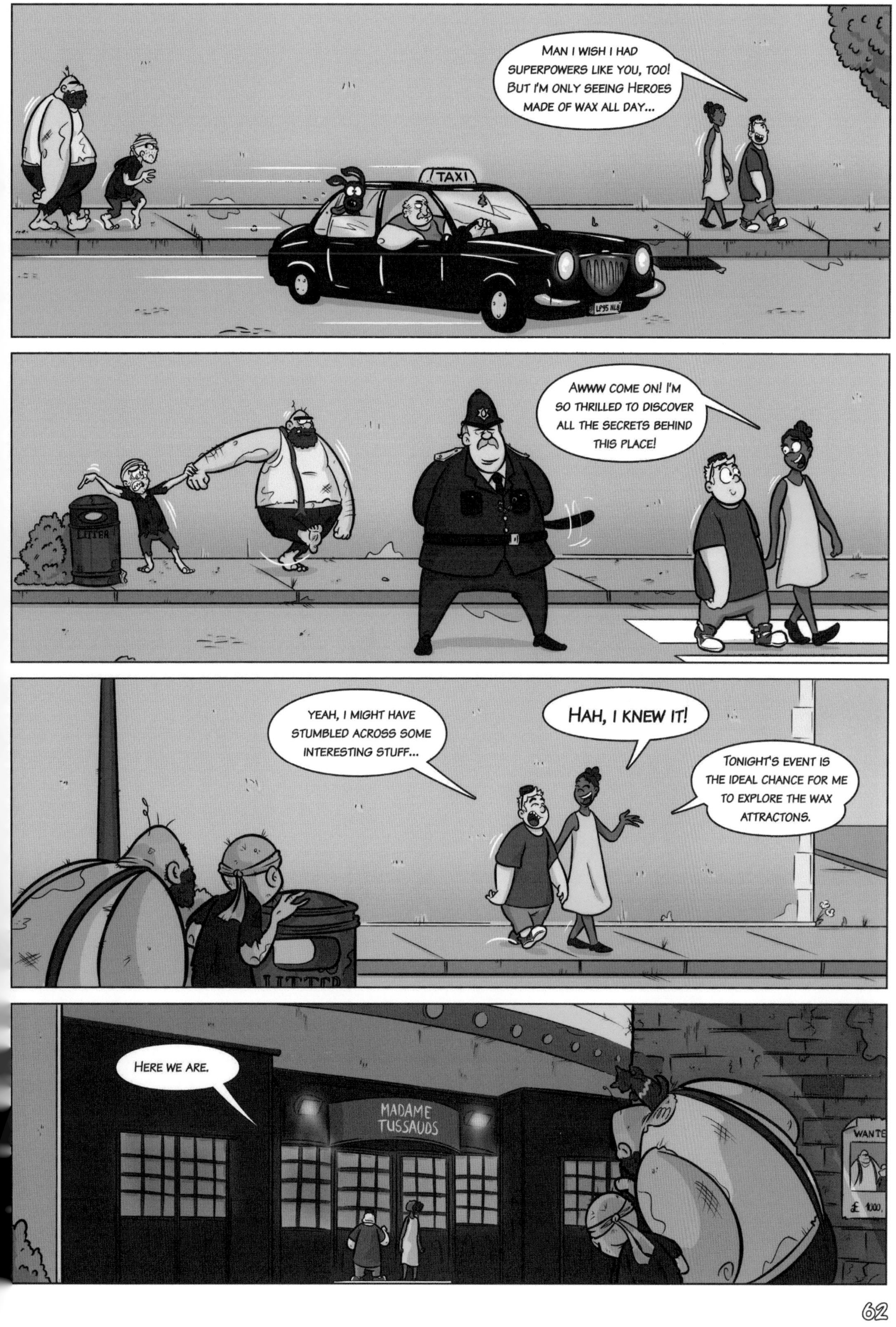
MAN I WISH I HAD SUPERPOWERS LIKE YOU, TOO! BUT I'M ONLY SEEING HEROES MADE OF WAX ALL DAY...
TAXI
AWWW COME ON! I'M SO THRILLED TO DISCOVER ALL THE SECRETS BEHIND THIS PLACE!
LITTER
YEAH, I MIGHT HAVE STUMBLED ACROSS SOME INTERESTING STUFF...
HAH, I KNEW IT!
TONIGHT'S EVENT IS THE IDEAL CHANCE FOR ME TO EXPLORE THE WAX ATTRACTONS.
HERE WE ARE.
MADAME TUSSAUDS
WANTE
£ 1000,

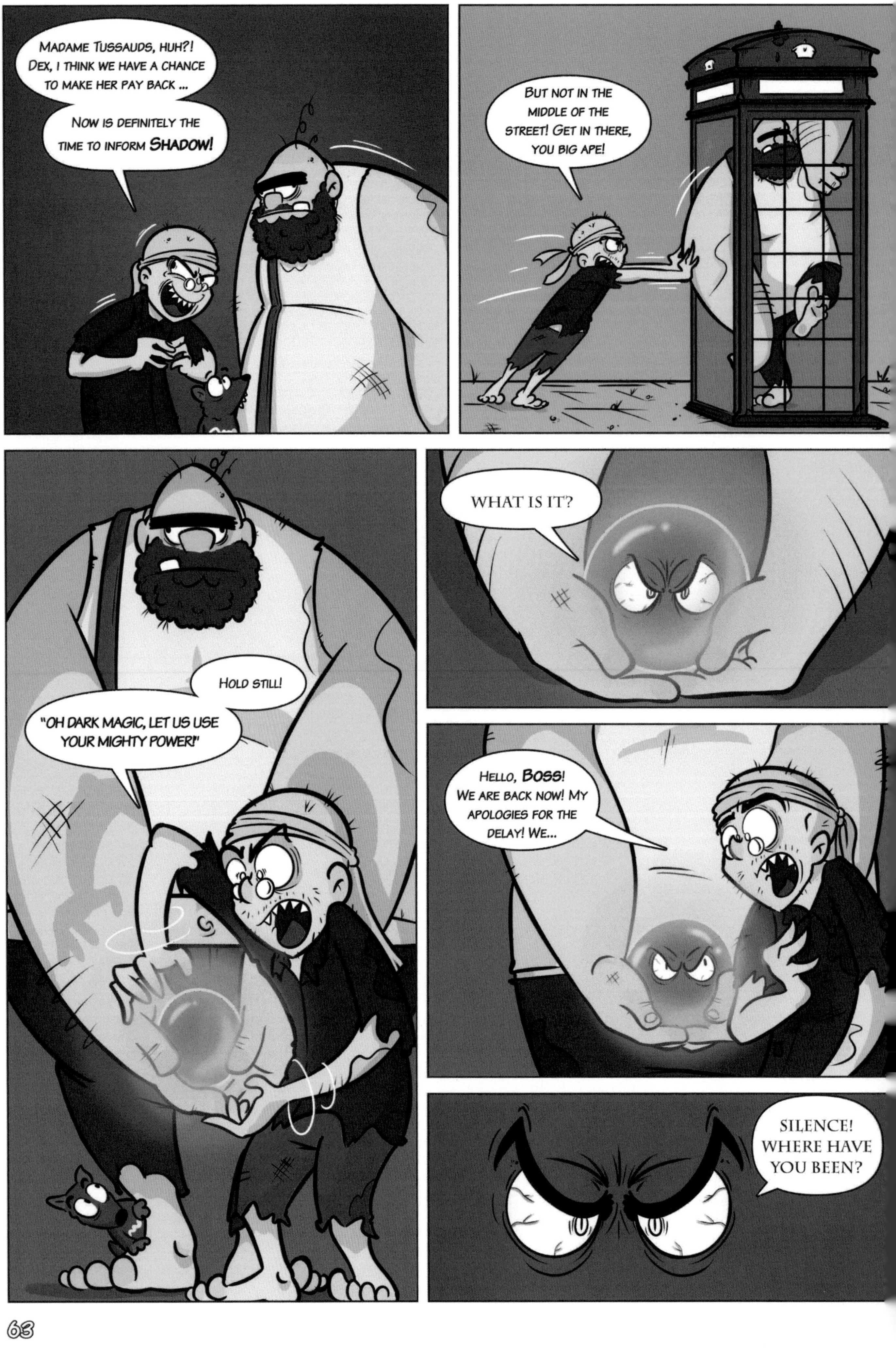
MADAME TUSSAUDS, HUH?! DEX, I THINK WE HAVE A CHANCE TO MAKE HER PAY BACK ...
NOW IS DEFINITELY THE TIME TO INFORM SHADOW!
BUT NOT IN THE MIDDLE OF THE STREET! GET IN THERE, YOU BIG APE!
HOLD STILL!
"OH DARK MAGIC, LET US USE YOUR MIGHTY POWER!"
WHAT IS IT?
HELLO, BOSS! WE ARE BACK NOW! MY APOLOGIES FOR THE DELAY! WE...
SILENCE! WHERE HAVE YOU BEEN?

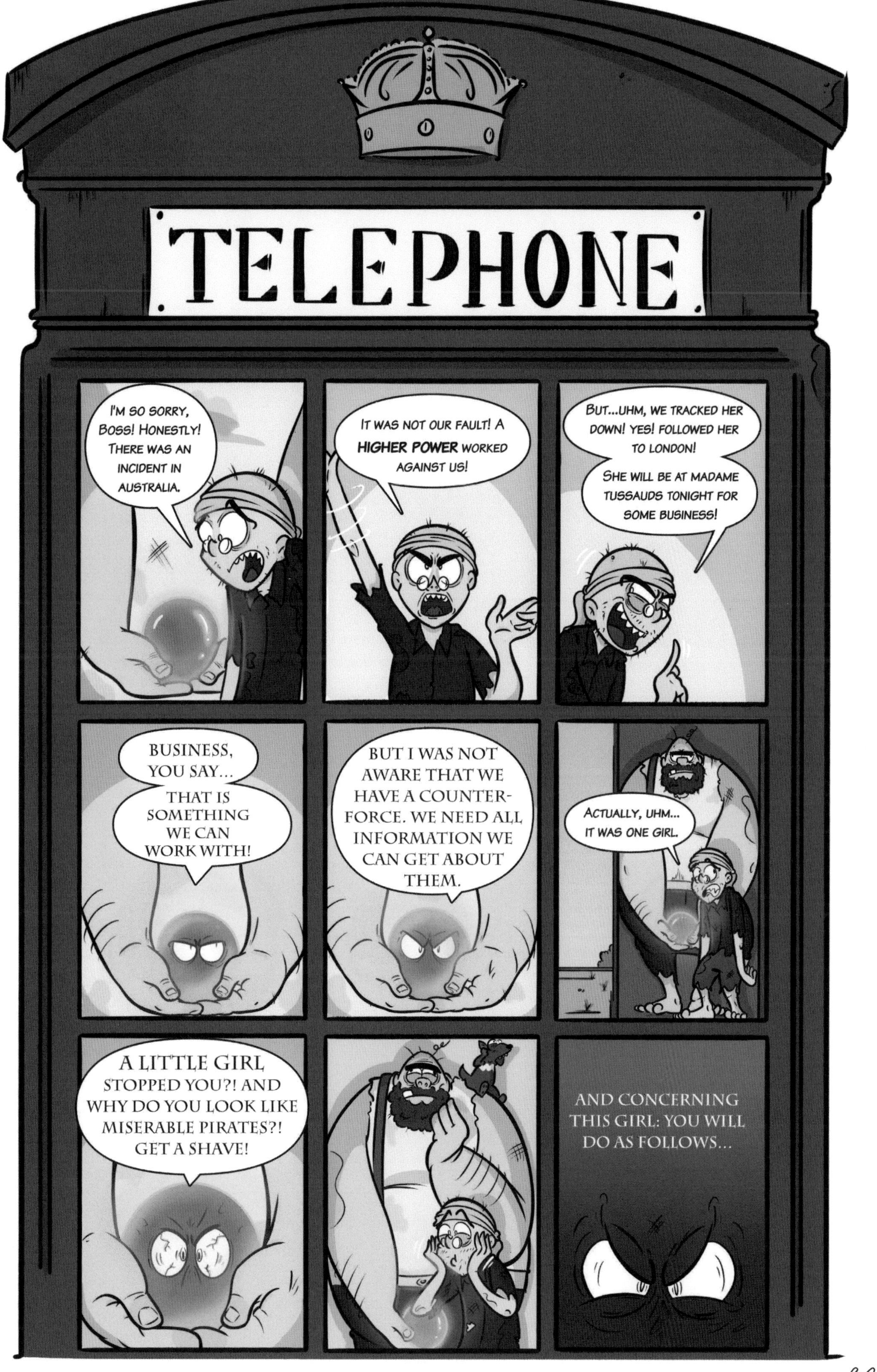
TELEPHONE
I'M SO SORRY, BOSS! HONESTLY! THERE WAS AN INCIDENT IN AUSTRALIA.
IT WAS NOT OUR FAULT! A HIGHER POWER WORKED AGAINST US!
BUT...UHM, WE TRACKED HER DOWN! YES! FOLLOWED HER TO LONDON!
SHE WILL BE AT MADAME TUSSAUDS TONIGHT FOR SOME BUSINESS!
BUSINESS, YOU SAY...
THAT IS SOMETHING WE CAN WORK WITH!
BUT I WAS NOT AWARE THAT WE HAVE A COUNTER-FORCE. WE NEED ALL INFORMATION WE CAN GET ABOUT THEM.
ACTUALLY, UHM... IT WAS ONE GIRL.
A LITTLE GIRL STOPPED YOU?! AND WHY DO YOU LOOK LIKE MISERABLE PIRATES?! GET A SHAVE!
AND CONCERNING THIS GIRL: YOU WILL DO AS FOLLOWS...

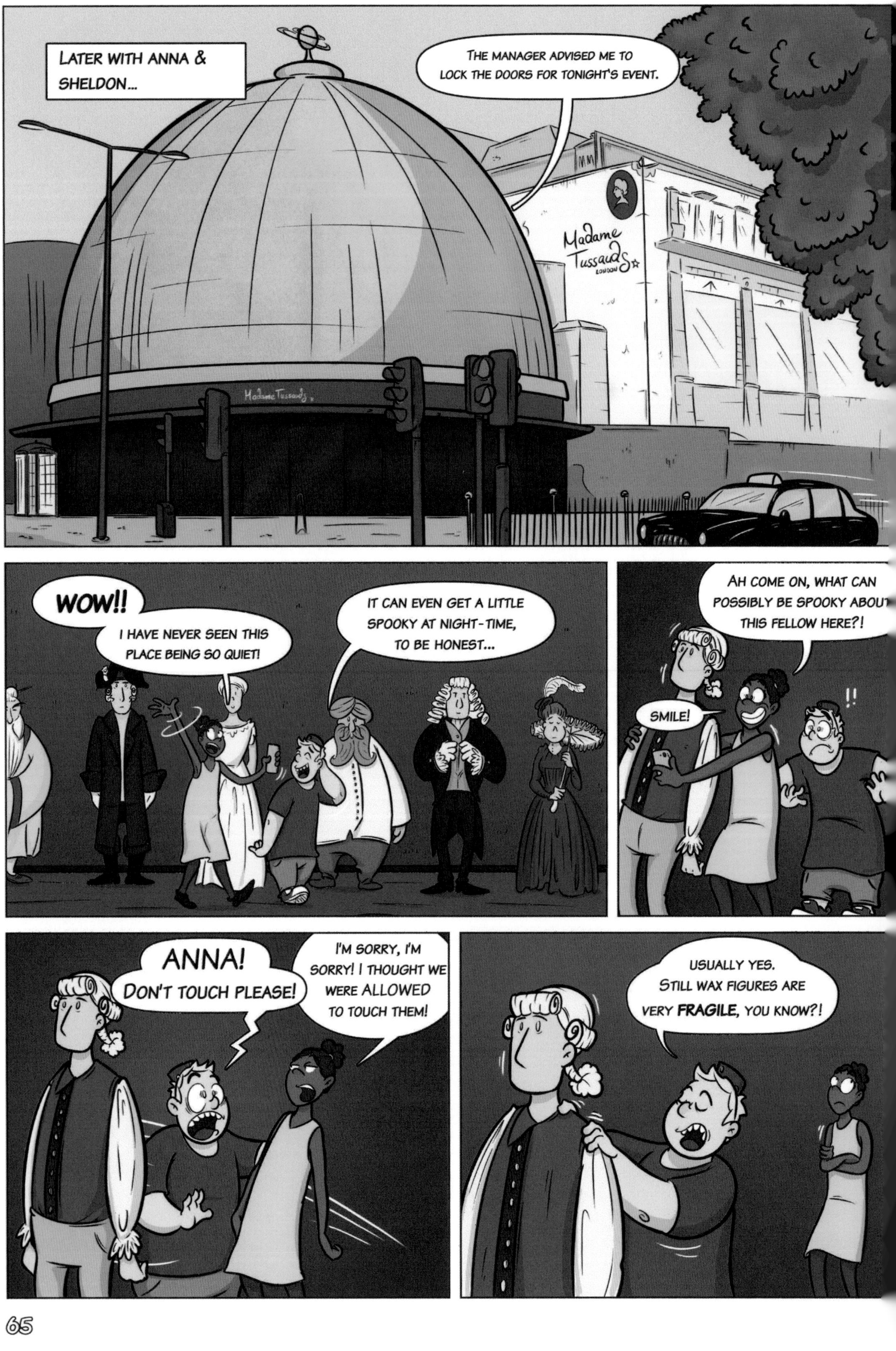
LATER WITH ANNA & SHELDON...
THE MANAGER ADVISED ME TO LOCK THE DOORS FOR TONIGHT'S EVENT.
Madame Tussauds LONDON
Madame Tussauds
WOW!! I HAVE NEVER SEEN THIS PLACE BEING SO QUIET!
IT CAN EVEN GET A LITTLE SPOOKY AT NIGHT-TIME, TO BE HONEST...
AH COME ON, WHAT CAN POSSIBLY BE SPOOKY ABOUT THIS FELLOW HERE?!
SMILE!
!!
ANNA! DON'T TOUCH PLEASE!
I'M SORRY, I'M SORRY! I THOUGHT WE WERE ALLOWED TO TOUCH THEM!
USUALLY YES. STILL WAX FIGURES ARE VERY **FRAGILE**, YOU KNOW?!

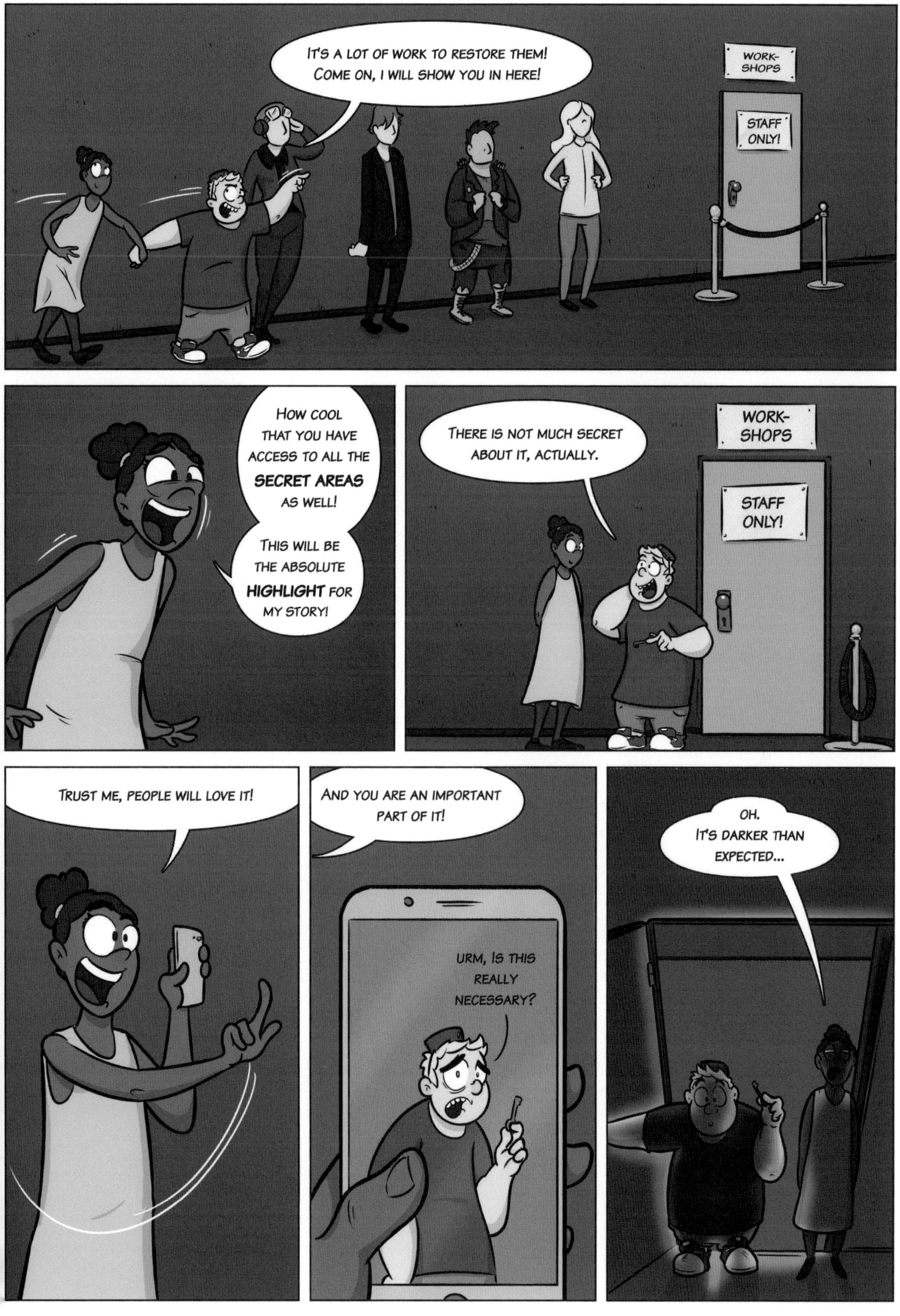

IT'S A LOT OF WORK TO RESTORE THEM! COME ON, I WILL SHOW YOU IN HERE!
WORK-SHOPS
STAFF ONLY!
HOW COOL THAT YOU HAVE ACCESS TO ALL THE SECRET AREAS AS WELL!
THIS WILL BE THE ABSOLUTE HIGHLIGHT FOR MY STORY!
THERE IS NOT MUCH SECRET ABOUT IT, ACTUALLY.
WORK-SHOPS
STAFF ONLY!
TRUST ME, PEOPLE WILL LOVE IT!
AND YOU ARE AN IMPORTANT PART OF IT!
URM, IS THIS REALLY NECESSARY?
OH. IT'S DARKER THAN EXPECTED...

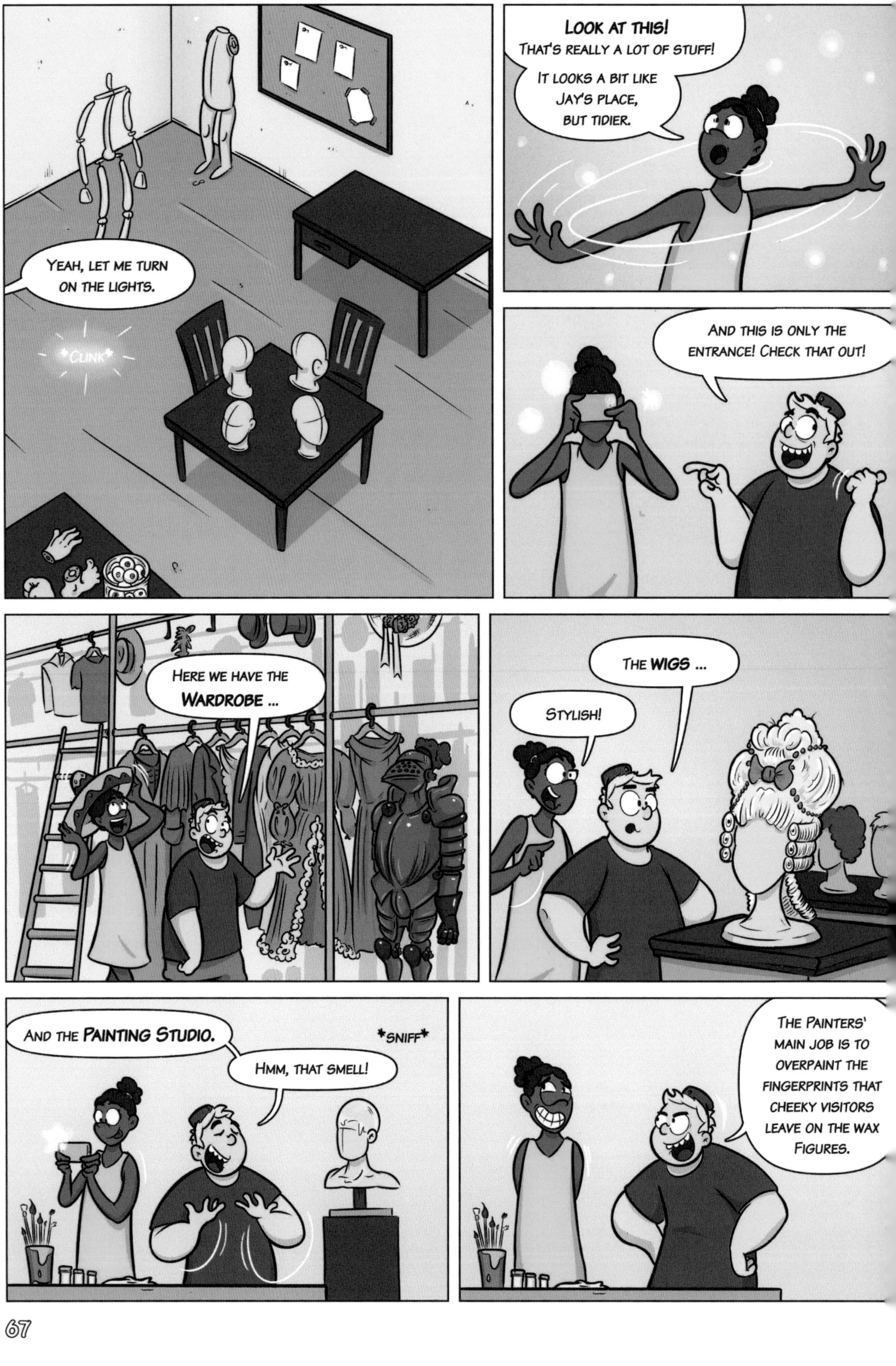
YEAH, LET ME TURN ON THE LIGHTS.
CLINK
LOOK AT THIS!
THAT'S REALLY A LOT OF STUFF!
IT LOOKS A BIT LIKE JAY'S PLACE, BUT TIDIER.
AND THIS IS ONLY THE ENTRANCE! CHECK THAT OUT!
HERE WE HAVE THE WARDROBE ...
THE WIGS ...
STYLISH!
AND THE PAINTING STUDIO.
SNIFF
HMM, THAT SMELL!
THE PAINTERS' MAIN JOB IS TO OVERPAINT THE FINGERPRINTS THAT CHEEKY VISITORS LEAVE ON THE WAX FIGURES.

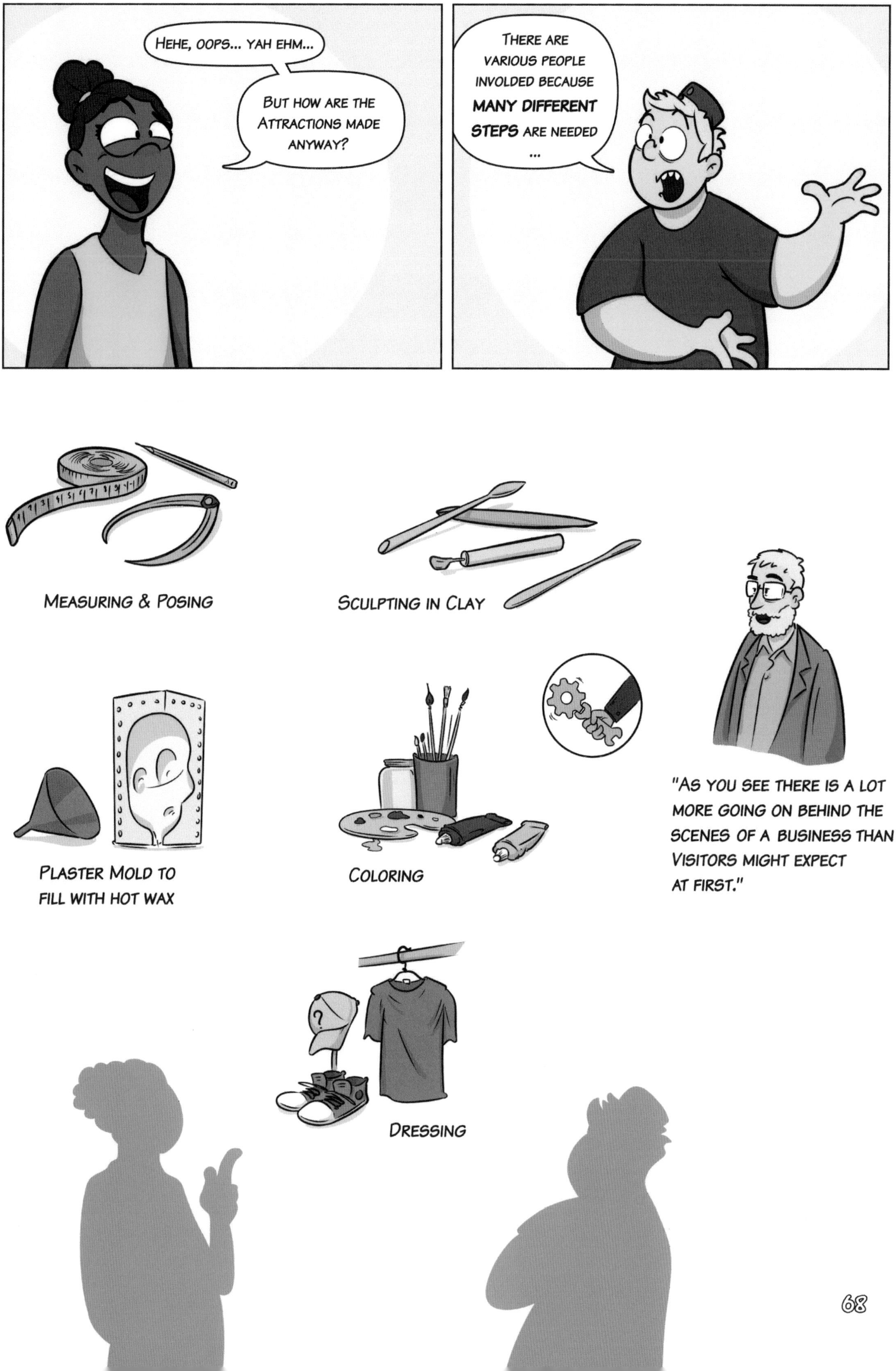

HEHE, OOPS... YAH EHM...
BUT HOW ARE THE ATTRACTIONS MADE ANYWAY?
THERE ARE VARIOUS PEOPLE INVOLDED BECAUSE **MANY DIFFERENT STEPS** ARE NEEDED ...
MEASURING & POSING
SCULPTING IN CLAY
PLASTER MOLD TO FILL WITH HOT WAX
COLORING
"AS YOU SEE THERE IS A LOT MORE GOING ON BEHIND THE SCENES OF A BUSINESS THAN VISITORS MIGHT EXPECT AT FIRST."
DRESSING

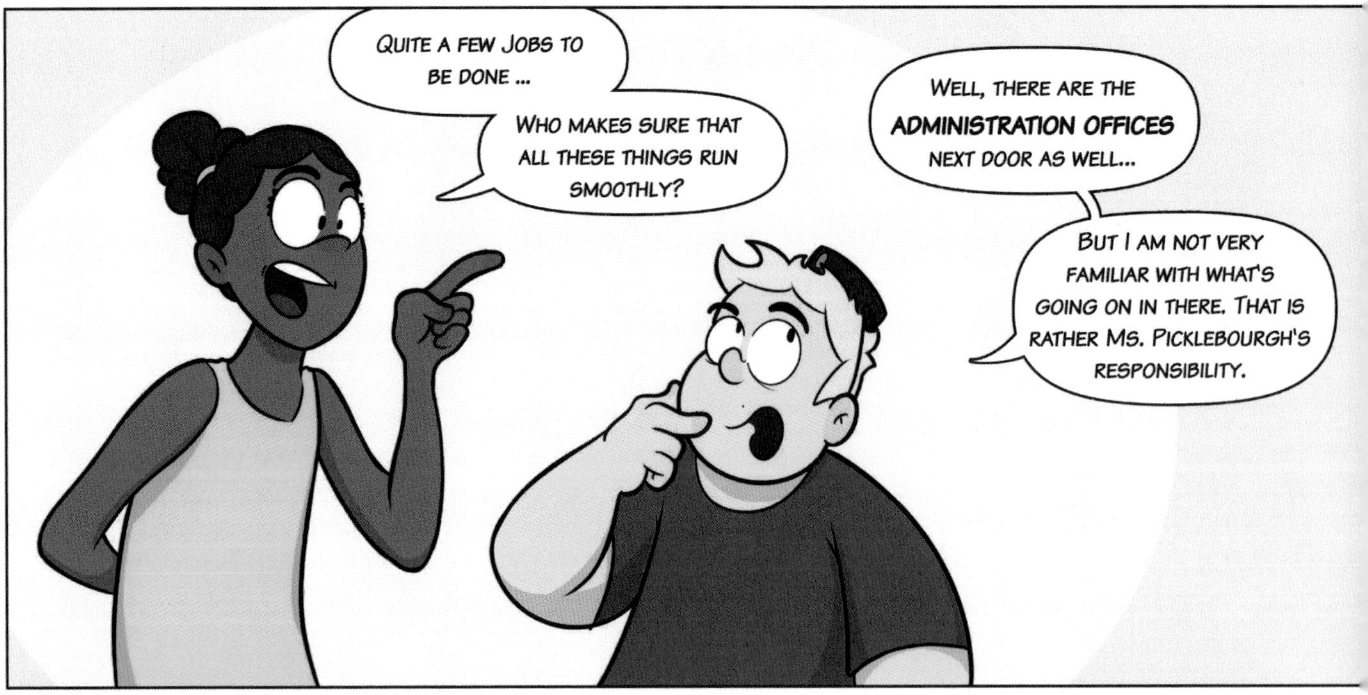
QUITE A FEW JOBS TO BE DONE ...
WHO MAKES SURE THAT ALL THESE THINGS RUN SMOOTHLY?
WELL, THERE ARE THE **ADMINISTRATION OFFICES** NEXT DOOR AS WELL...
BUT I AM NOT VERY FAMILIAR WITH WHAT'S GOING ON IN THERE. THAT IS RATHER MS. PICKLEBOURGH'S RESPONSIBILITY.

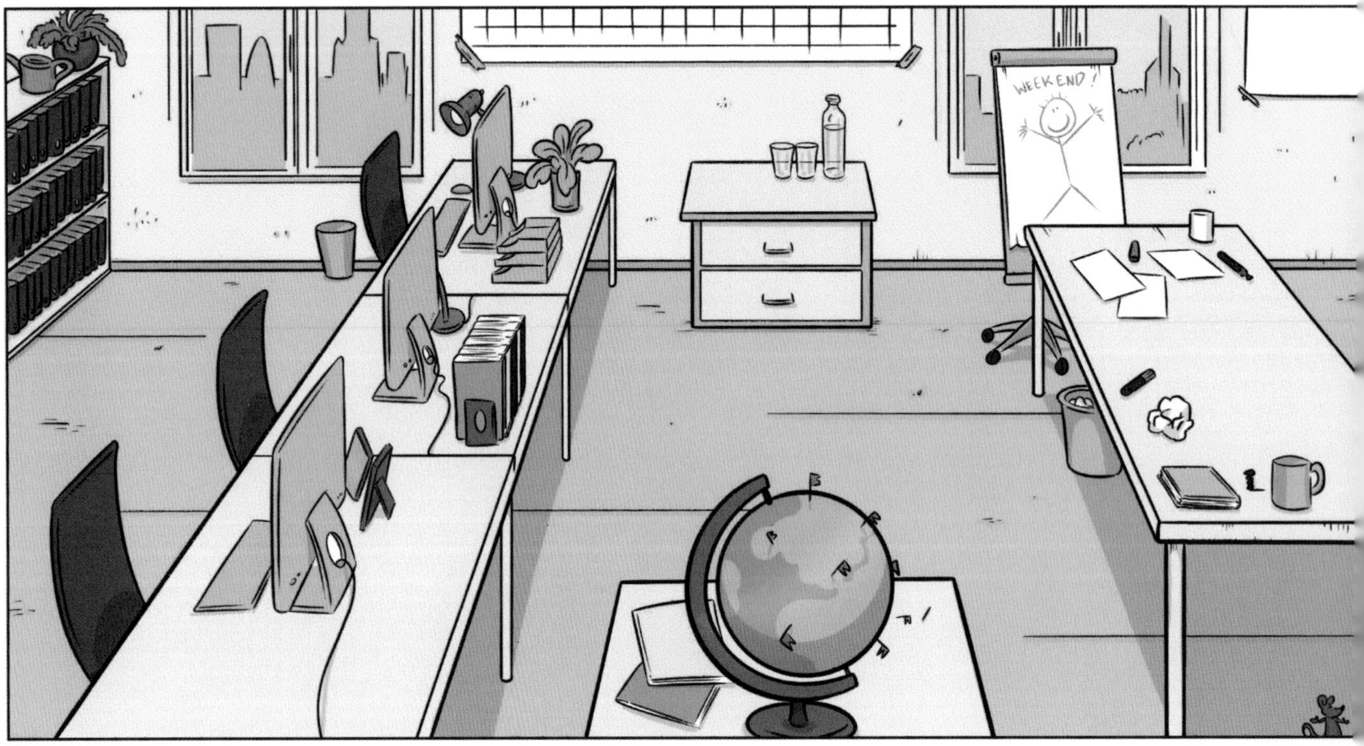
WEEKEND!

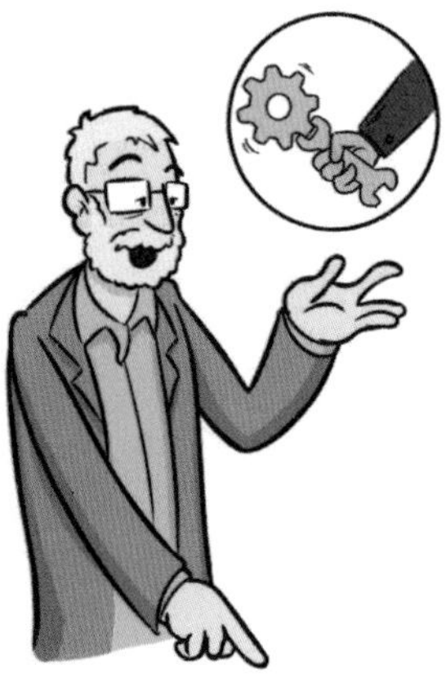

"MANY INTERESTING THINGS GO ON IN THE ADMINISTRATION OFFICES. MOST OF THESE ACTIVITIES ARE NOT CLEARLY VISIBLE FROM THE OUTSIDE. SUCH AS:"

"MARKETING ACTIVITIES: ORGANIZING MAGAZINE ADS, SOCIAL MEDIA ADS, OR EVEN BILLBOARDS..."

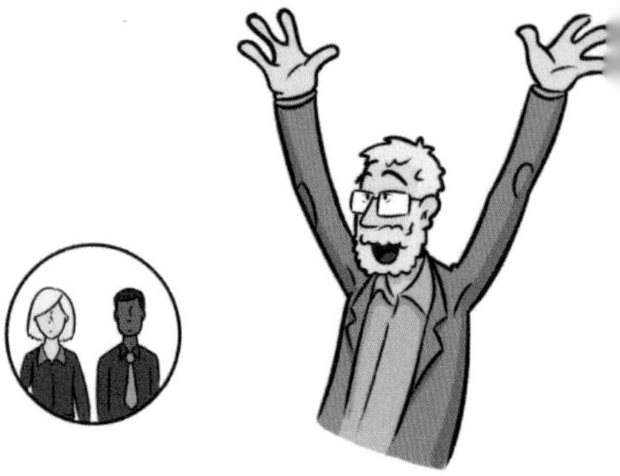

"... OR CALLING CELEBRITIES TO ASK WHETHER THEY WOULD LIKE TO HAVE A FIGURE OF THEMSELVES AT MADAME TUSSAUDS."

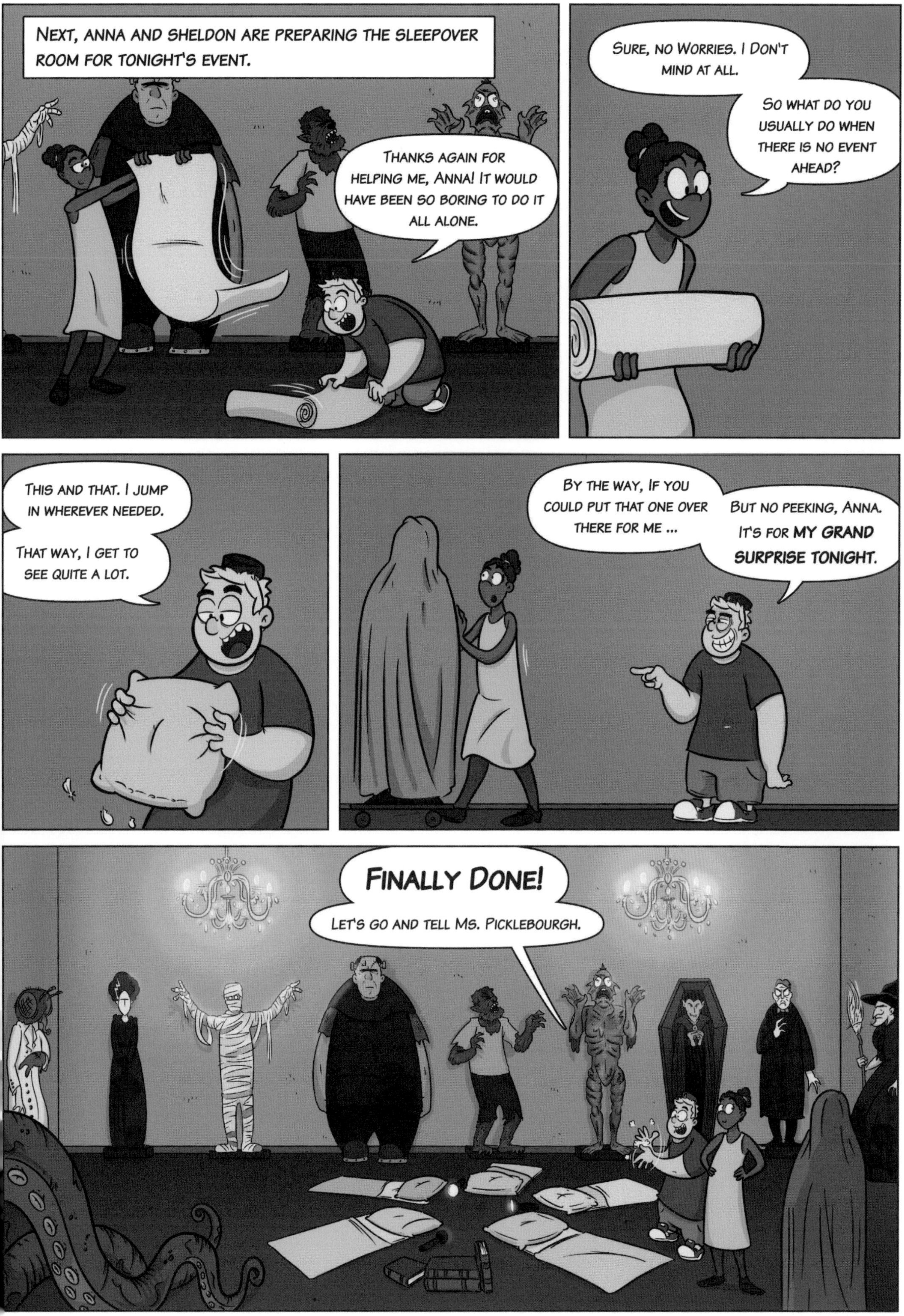

NEXT, ANNA AND SHELDON ARE PREPARING THE SLEEPOVER ROOM FOR TONIGHT'S EVENT.
THANKS AGAIN FOR HELPING ME, ANNA! IT WOULD HAVE BEEN SO BORING TO DO IT ALL ALONE.
SURE, NO WORRIES. I DON'T MIND AT ALL.
SO WHAT DO YOU USUALLY DO WHEN THERE IS NO EVENT AHEAD?
THIS AND THAT. I JUMP IN WHEREVER NEEDED.
THAT WAY, I GET TO SEE QUITE A LOT.
BY THE WAY, IF YOU COULD PUT THAT ONE OVER THERE FOR ME ...
BUT NO PEEKING, ANNA. IT'S FOR MY GRAND SURPRISE TONIGHT.
FINALLY DONE!
LET'S GO AND TELL MS. PICKLEBOURGH.

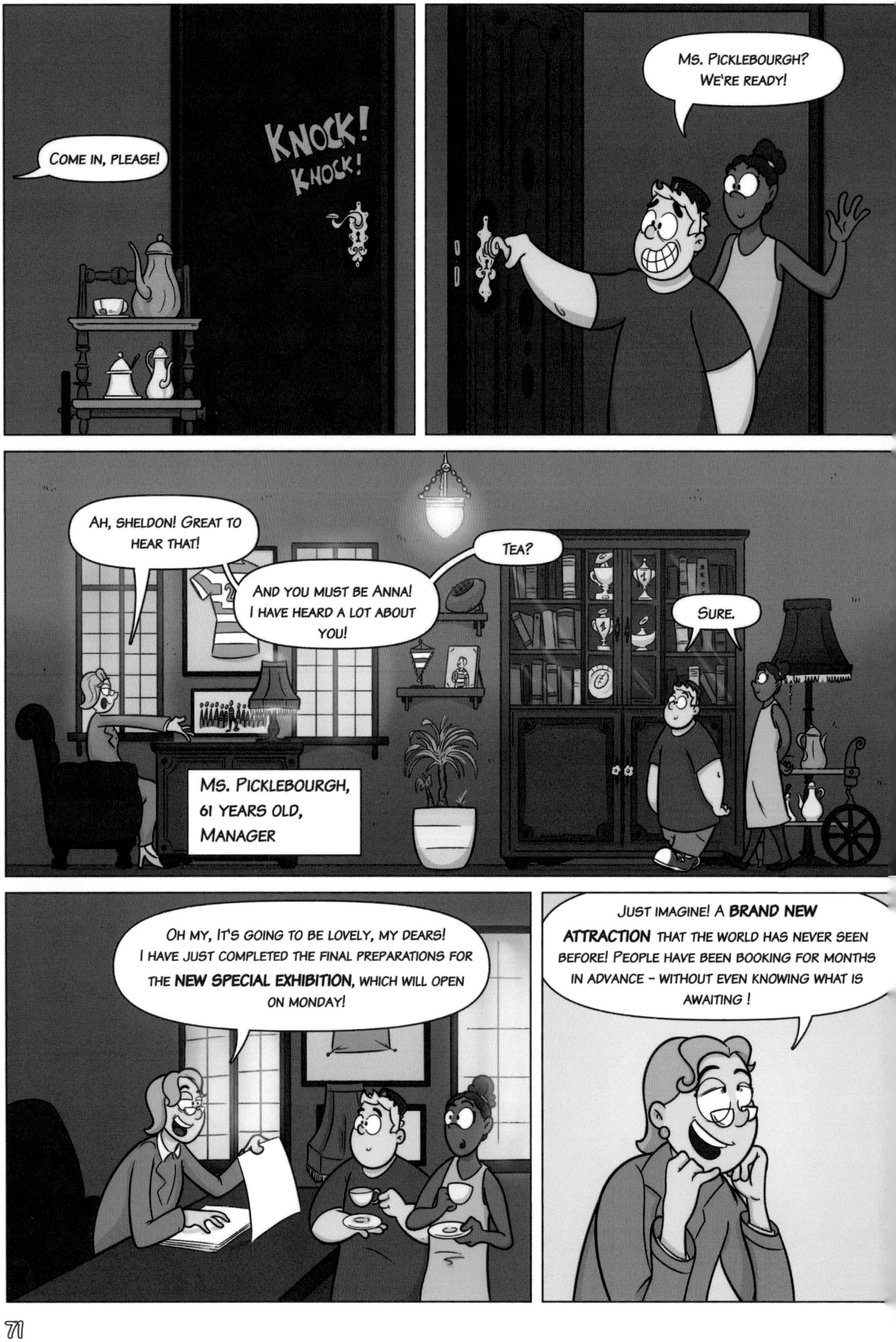
KNOCK! KNOCK!
COME IN, PLEASE!
MS. PICKLEBOURGH? WE'RE READY!
AH, SHELDON! GREAT TO HEAR THAT!
AND YOU MUST BE ANNA! I HAVE HEARD A LOT ABOUT YOU!
TEA?
SURE.
MS. PICKLEBOURGH, 61 YEARS OLD, MANAGER
OH MY, IT'S GOING TO BE LOVELY, MY DEARS! I HAVE JUST COMPLETED THE FINAL PREPARATIONS FOR THE **NEW SPECIAL EXHIBITION**, WHICH WILL OPEN ON MONDAY!
JUST IMAGINE! A **BRAND NEW ATTRACTION** THAT THE WORLD HAS NEVER SEEN BEFORE! PEOPLE HAVE BEEN BOOKING FOR MONTHS IN ADVANCE - WITHOUT EVEN KNOWING WHAT IS AWAITING !

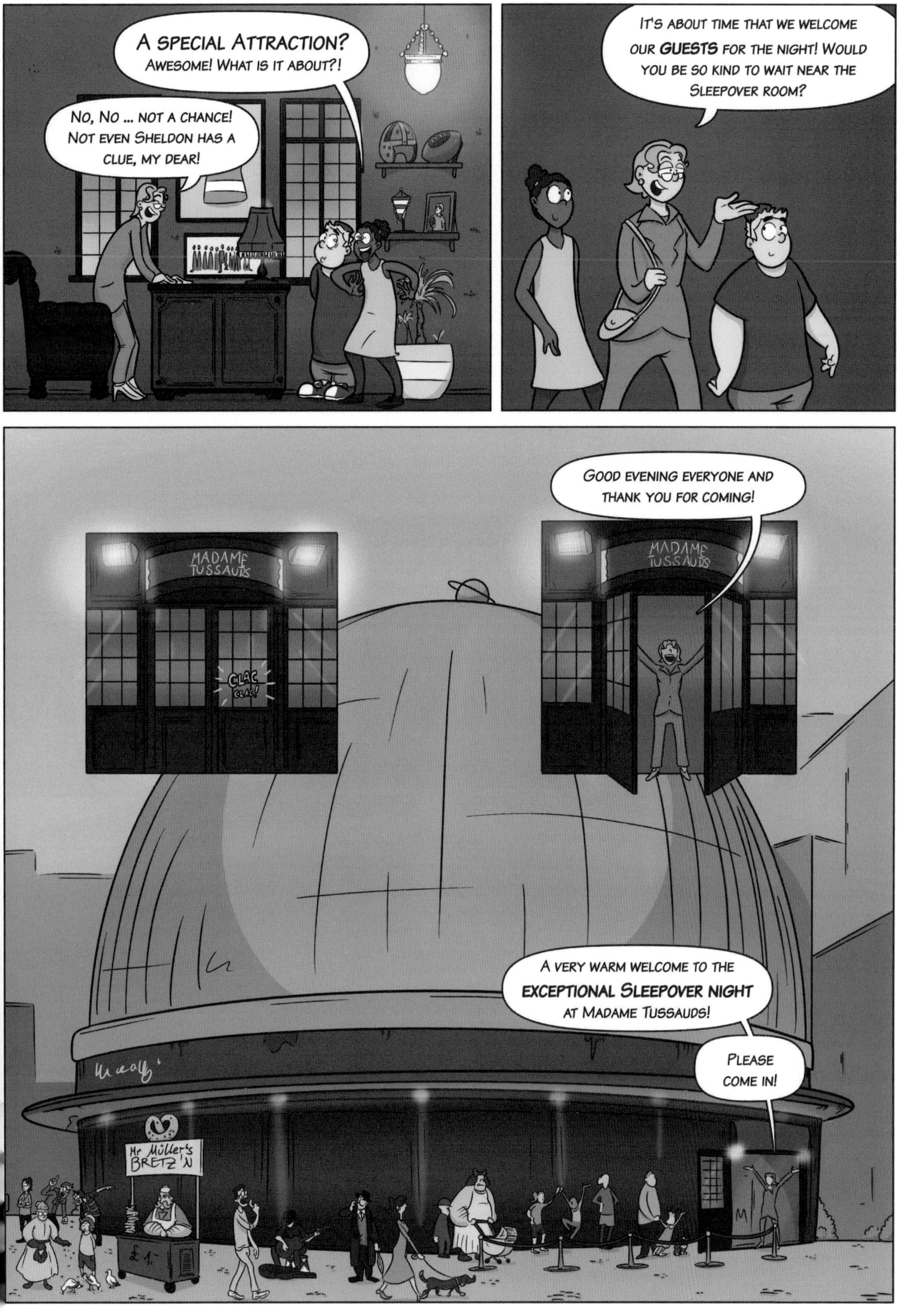
A SPECIAL ATTRACTION? AWESOME! WHAT IS IT ABOUT?!
NO, NO ... NOT A CHANCE! NOT EVEN SHELDON HAS A CLUE, MY DEAR!
IT'S ABOUT TIME THAT WE WELCOME OUR **GUESTS** FOR THE NIGHT! WOULD YOU BE SO KIND TO WAIT NEAR THE SLEEPOVER ROOM?
MADAME TUSSAUDS
CLAC CLAC!
MADAME TUSSAUDS
GOOD EVENING EVERYONE AND THANK YOU FOR COMING!
A VERY WARM WELCOME TO THE **EXCEPTIONAL SLEEPOVER NIGHT** AT MADAME TUSSAUDS!
PLEASE COME IN!
Mr Müller's BRETZ'N
£1.-

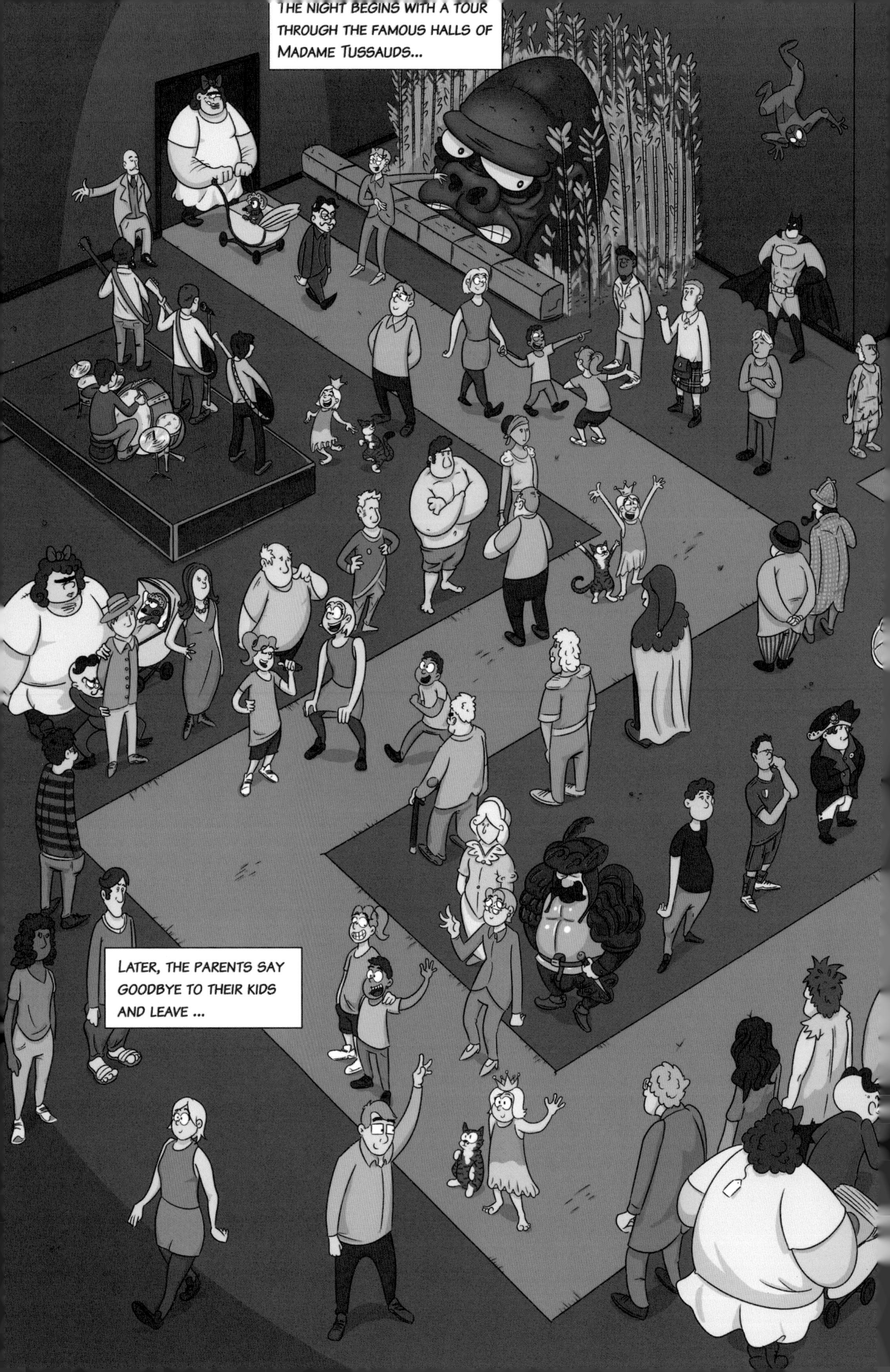

THE NIGHT BEGINS WITH A TOUR THROUGH THE FAMOUS HALLS OF MADAME TUSSAUDS...
LATER, THE PARENTS SAY GOODBYE TO THEIR KIDS AND LEAVE ...

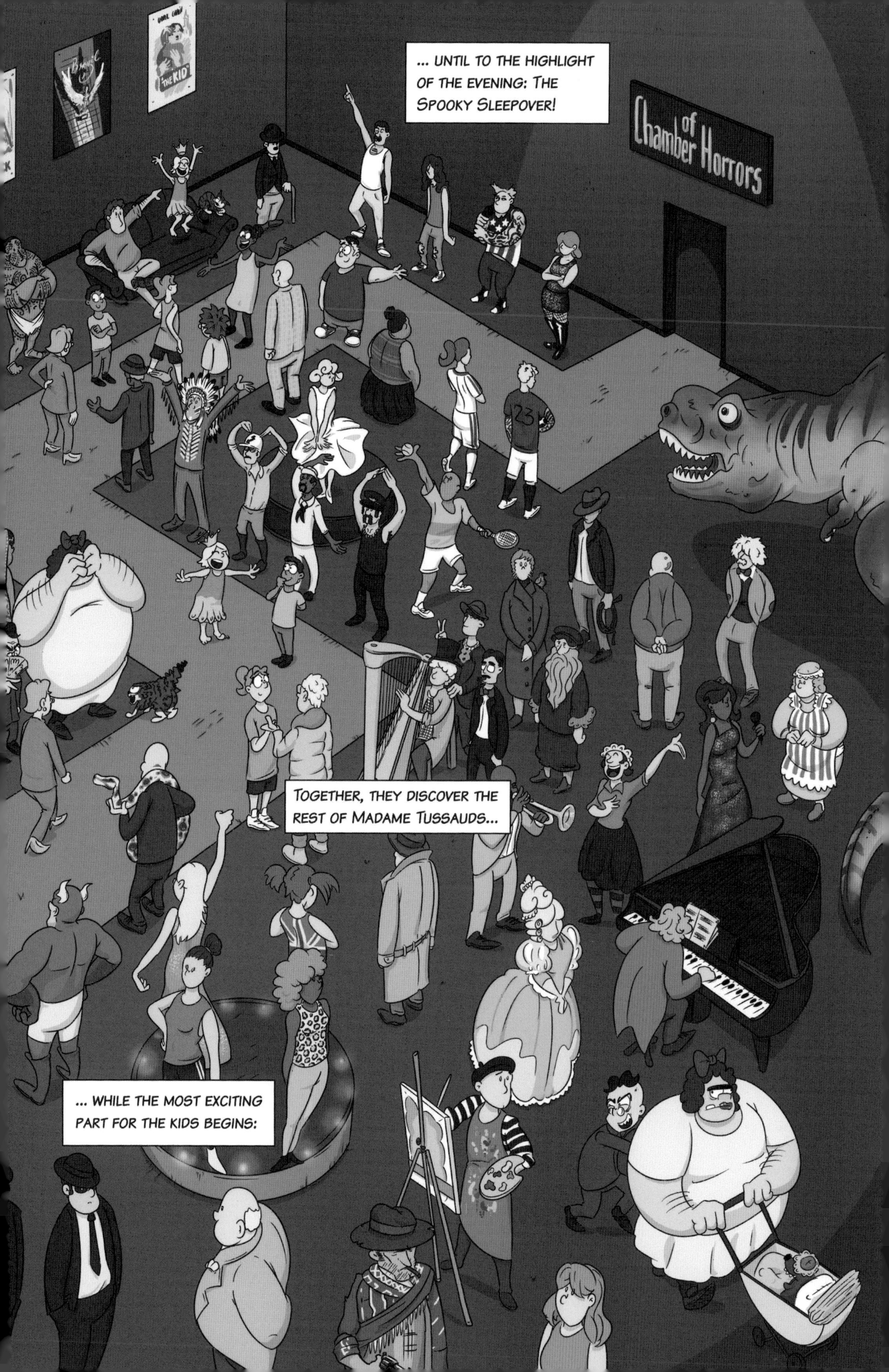

... UNTIL TO THE HIGHLIGHT OF THE EVENING: THE SPOOKY SLEEPOVER!
Chamber of Horrors
THE KID
TOGETHER, THEY DISCOVER THE REST OF MADAME TUSSAUDS...
... WHILE THE MOST EXCITING PART FOR THE KIDS BEGINS:

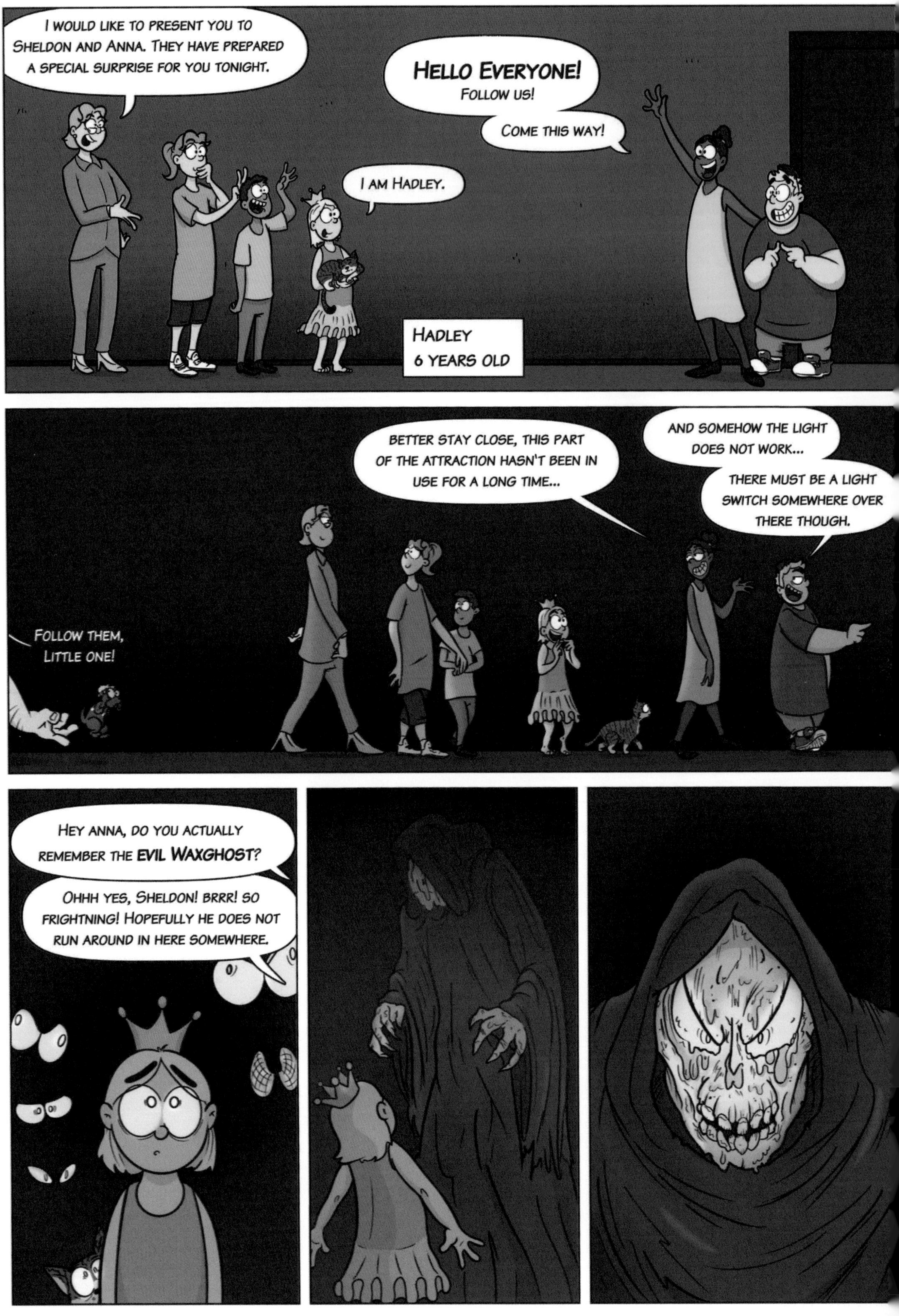

I WOULD LIKE TO PRESENT YOU TO SHELDON AND ANNA. THEY HAVE PREPARED A SPECIAL SURPRISE FOR YOU TONIGHT.
HELLO EVERYONE! FOLLOW US!
COME THIS WAY!
I AM HADLEY.
HADLEY 6 YEARS OLD
BETTER STAY CLOSE, THIS PART OF THE ATTRACTION HASN'T BEEN IN USE FOR A LONG TIME...
AND SOMEHOW THE LIGHT DOES NOT WORK...
THERE MUST BE A LIGHT SWITCH SOMEWHERE OVER THERE THOUGH.
FOLLOW THEM, LITTLE ONE!
HEY ANNA, DO YOU ACTUALLY REMEMBER THE EVIL WAXGHOST?
OHHH YES, SHELDON! BRRR! SO FRIGHTNING! HOPEFULLY HE DOES NOT RUN AROUND IN HERE SOMEWHERE.

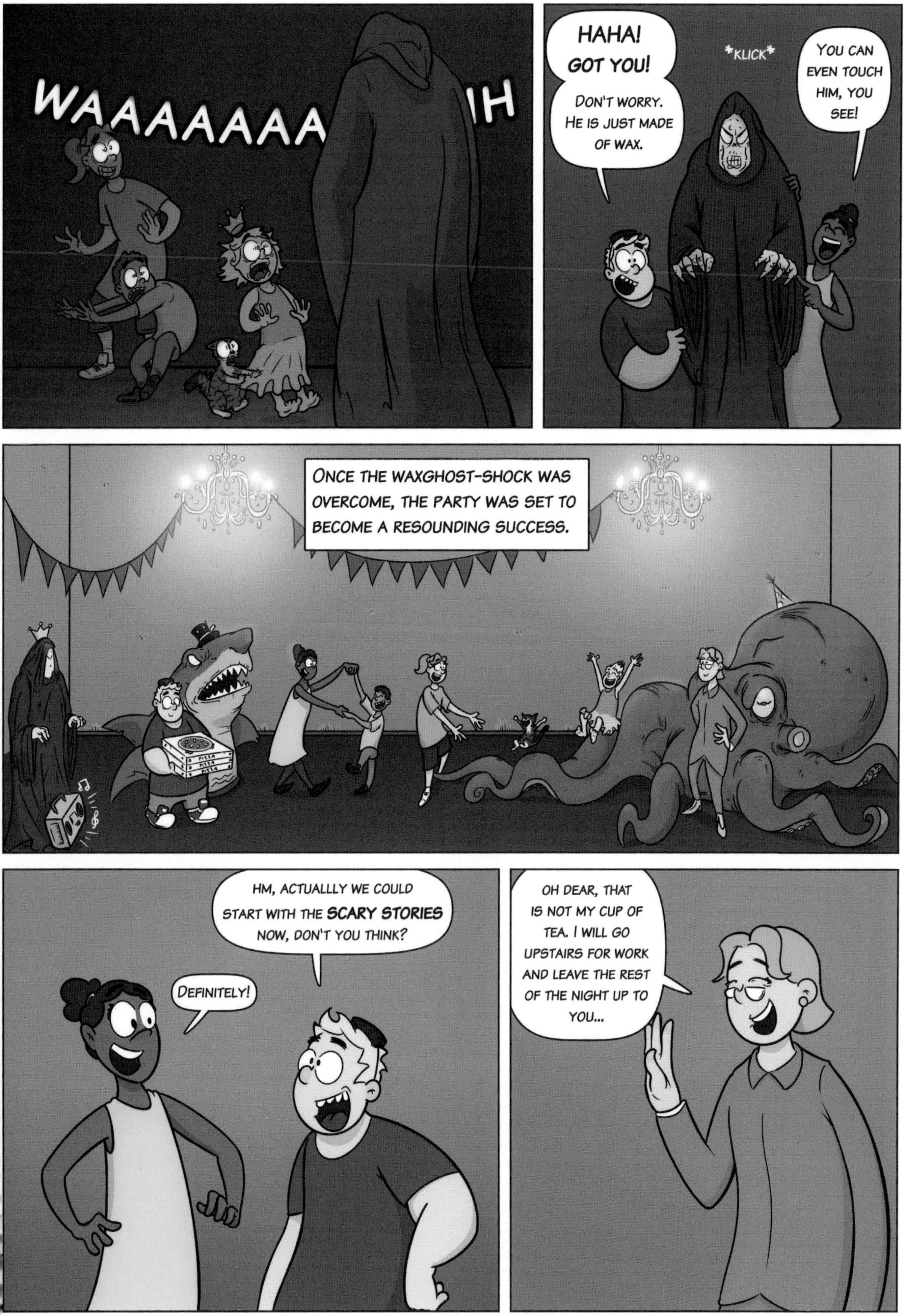
WAAAAAAAAAAAAH
HAHA! GOT YOU!
DON'T WORRY. HE IS JUST MADE OF WAX.
KLICK
YOU CAN EVEN TOUCH HIM, YOU SEE!
ONCE THE WAXGHOST-SHOCK WAS OVERCOME, THE PARTY WAS SET TO BECOME A RESOUNDING SUCCESS.
HM, ACTUALLLY WE COULD START WITH THE **SCARY STORIES** NOW, DON'T YOU THINK?
DEFINITELY!
OH DEAR, THAT IS NOT MY CUP OF TEA. I WILL GO UPSTAIRS FOR WORK AND LEAVE THE REST OF THE NIGHT UP TO YOU...

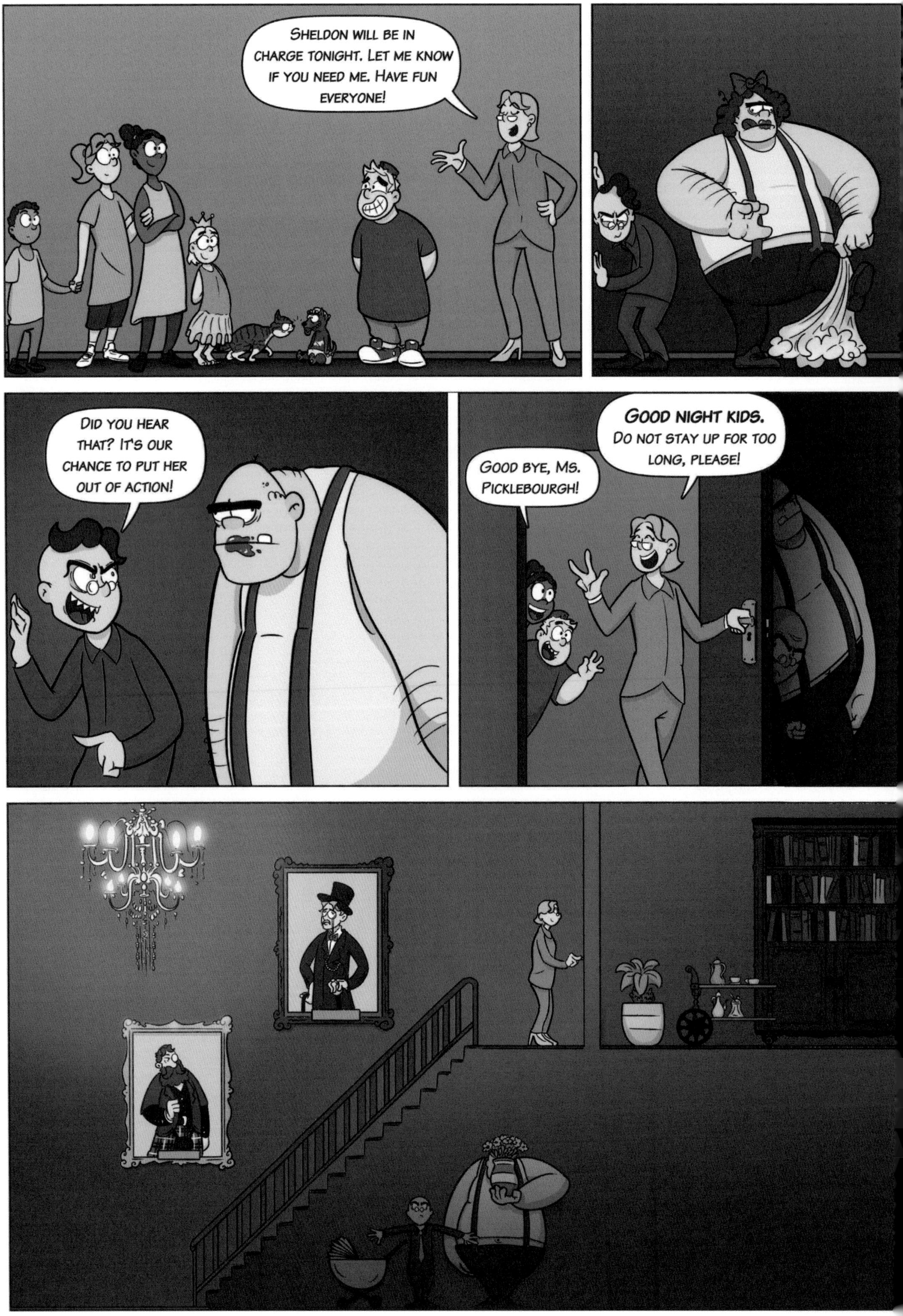

SHELDON WILL BE IN CHARGE TONIGHT. LET ME KNOW IF YOU NEED ME. HAVE FUN EVERYONE!
DID YOU HEAR THAT? IT'S OUR CHANCE TO PUT HER OUT OF ACTION!
GOOD BYE, MS. PICKLEBOURGH!
GOOD NIGHT KIDS. DO NOT STAY UP FOR TOO LONG, PLEASE!

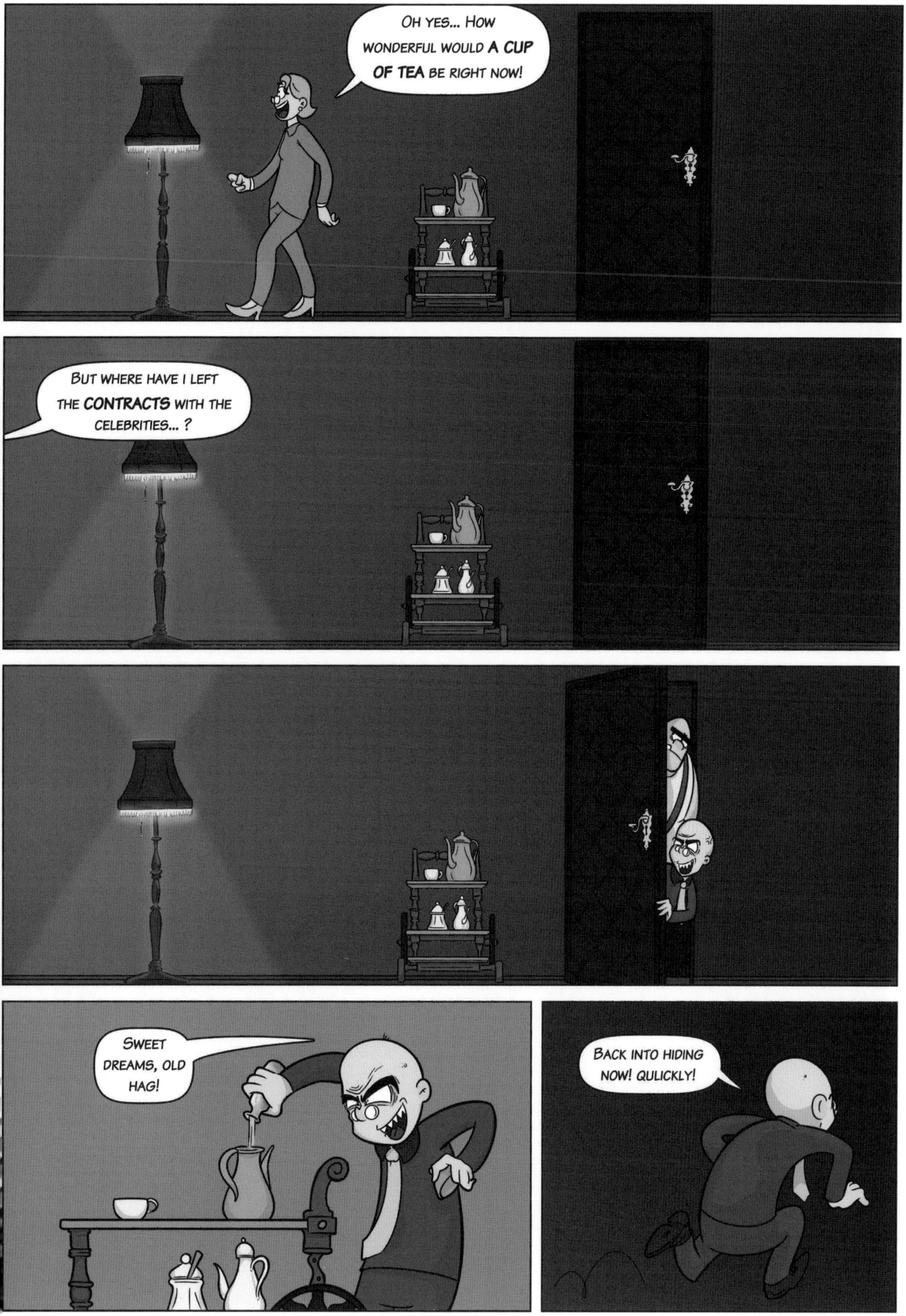

OH YES... HOW WONDERFUL WOULD A CUP OF TEA BE RIGHT NOW!
BUT WHERE HAVE I LEFT THE CONTRACTS WITH THE CELEBRITIES... ?
SWEET DREAMS, OLD HAG!
BACK INTO HIDING NOW! QULICKLY!

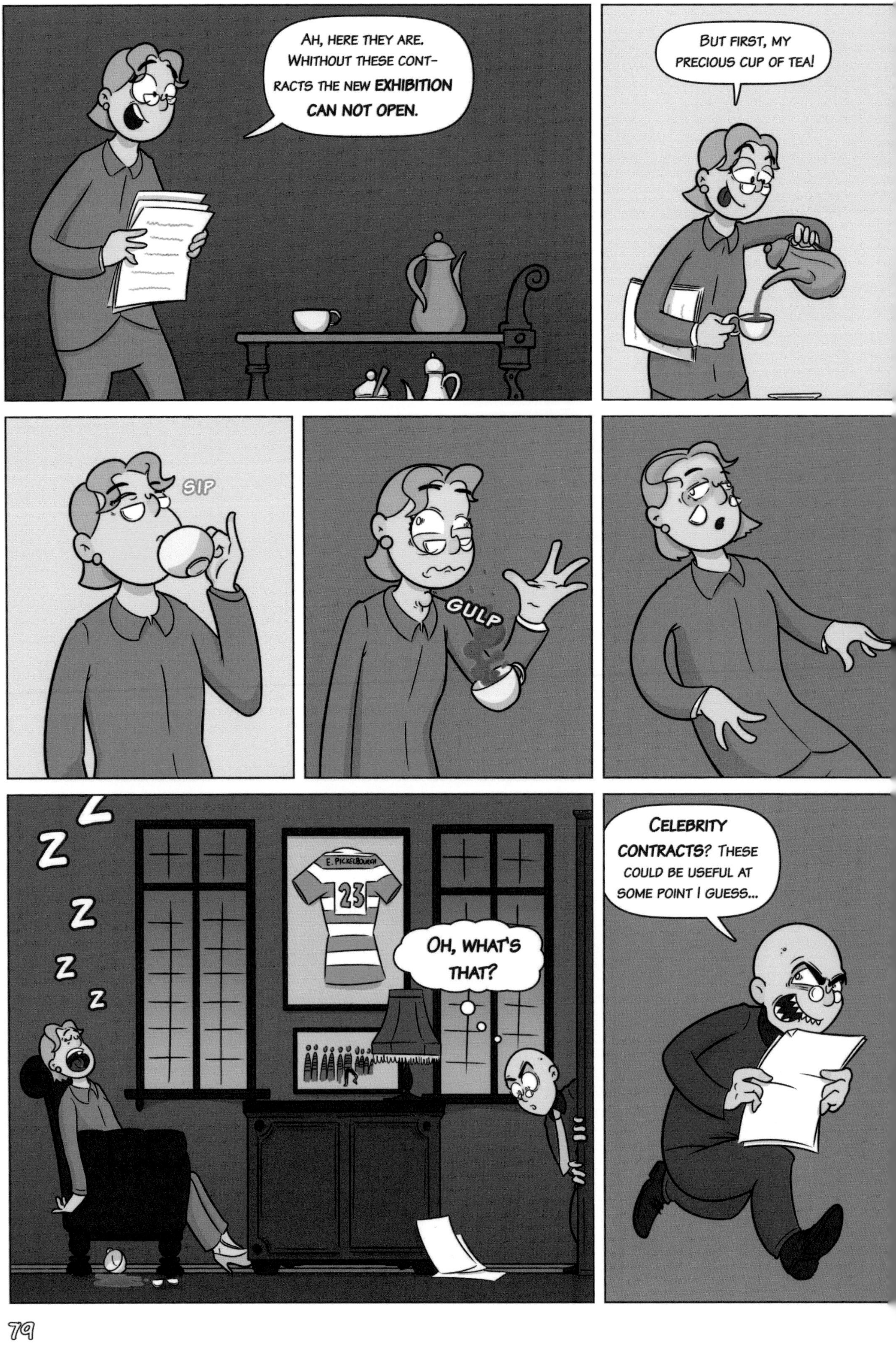

AH, HERE THEY ARE. WHITHOUT THESE CONT-RACTS THE NEW EXHIBITION CAN NOT OPEN.
BUT FIRST, MY PRECIOUS CUP OF TEA!
SIP
GULP
Z Z Z Z Z Z
E. PICKELBOUGH
23
OH, WHAT'S THAT?
CELEBRITY CONTRACTS? THESE COULD BE USEFUL AT SOME POINT I GUESS...

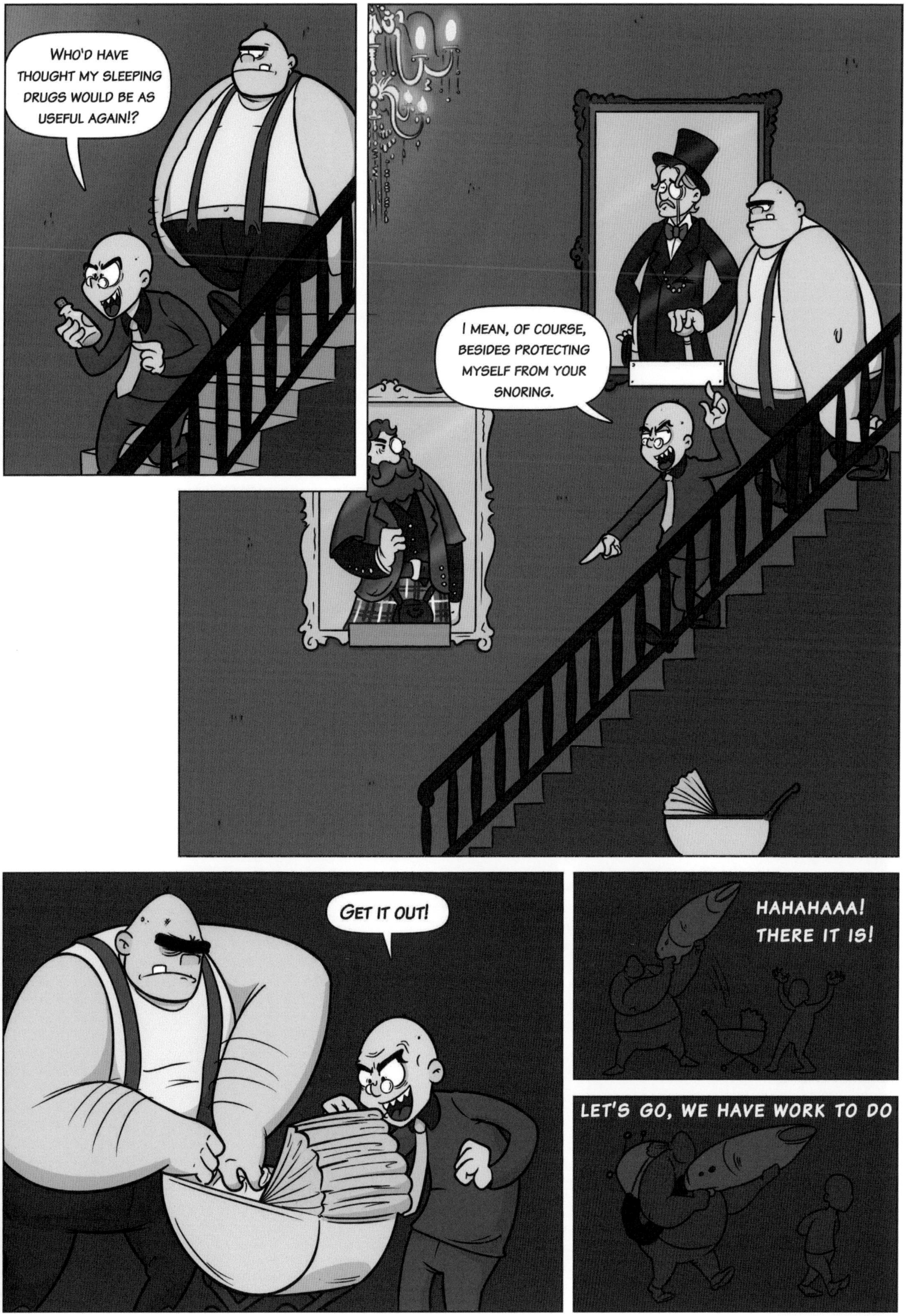

WHO'D HAVE THOUGHT MY SLEEPING DRUGS WOULD BE AS USEFUL AGAIN!?
I MEAN, OF COURSE, BESIDES PROTECTING MYSELF FROM YOUR SNORING.
GET IT OUT!
HAHAHAAA! THERE IT IS!
LET'S GO, WE HAVE WORK TO DO

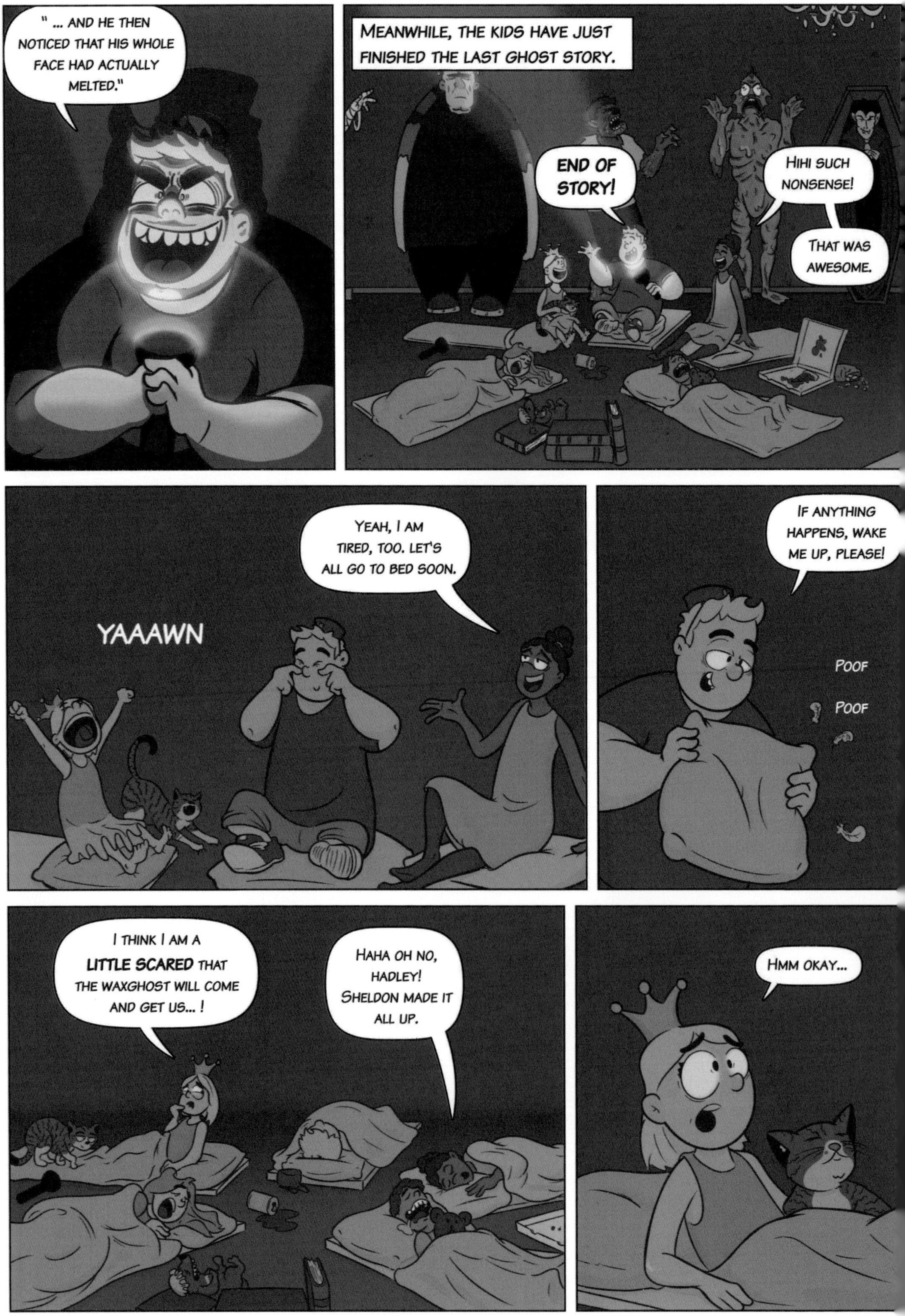
" ... AND HE THEN NOTICED THAT HIS WHOLE FACE HAD ACTUALLY MELTED."
MEANWHILE, THE KIDS HAVE JUST FINISHED THE LAST GHOST STORY.
END OF STORY!
HIHI SUCH NONSENSE!
THAT WAS AWESOME.
YAAAWN
YEAH, I AM TIRED, TOO. LET'S ALL GO TO BED SOON.
IF ANYTHING HAPPENS, WAKE ME UP, PLEASE!
POOF
POOF
I THINK I AM A LITTLE SCARED THAT THE WAXGHOST WILL COME AND GET US... !
HAHA OH NO, HADLEY! SHELDON MADE IT ALL UP.
HMM OKAY...

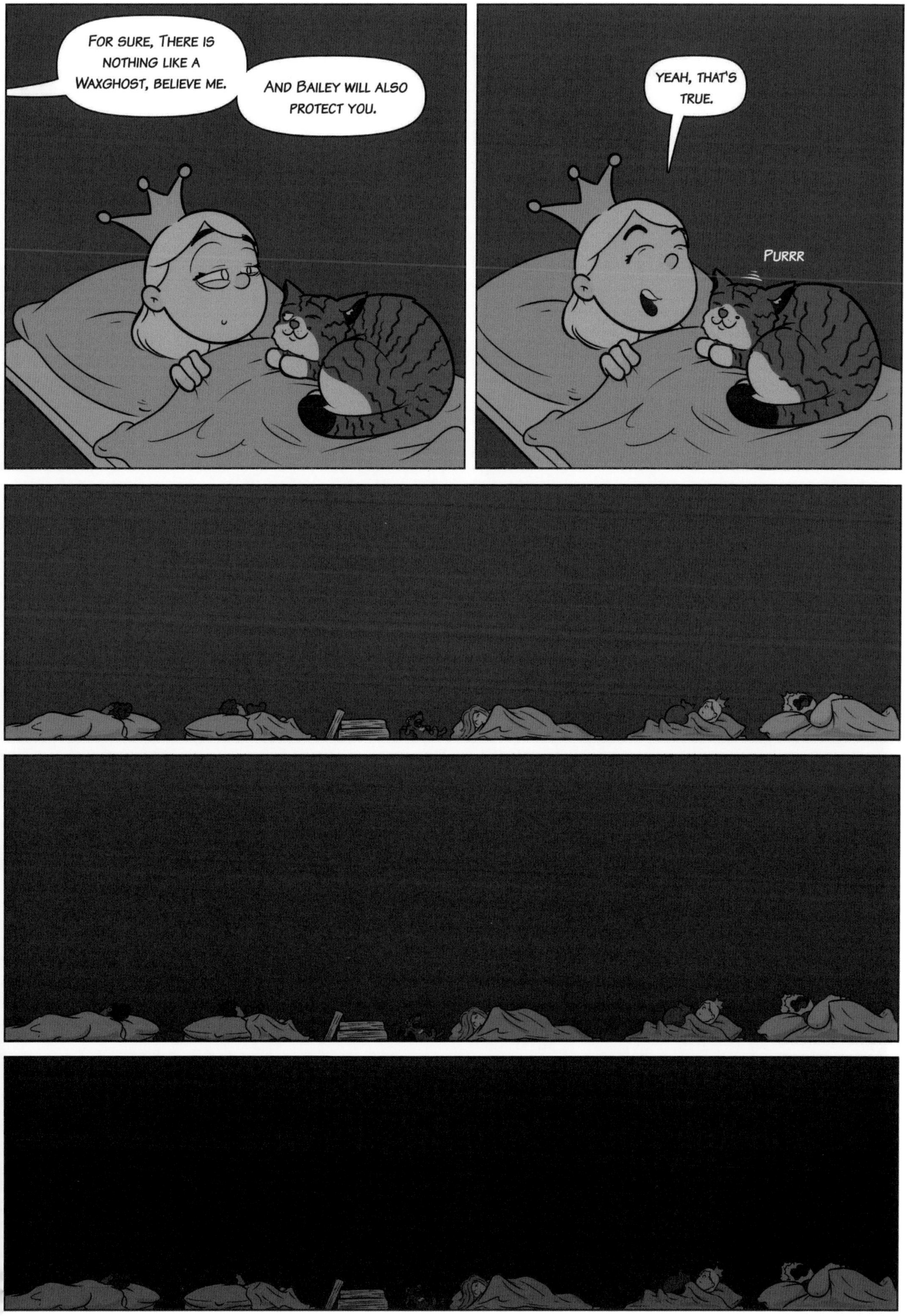
FOR SURE, THERE IS NOTHING LIKE A WAXGHOST, BELIEVE ME.
AND BAILEY WILL ALSO PROTECT YOU.
YEAH, THAT'S TRUE.
PURRR

A LITTLE LATER ...

CLONK

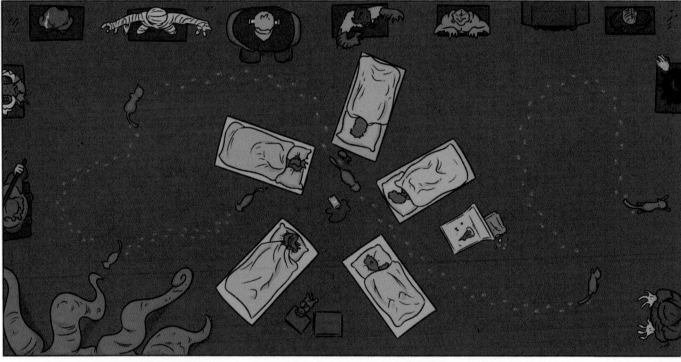

HMM?

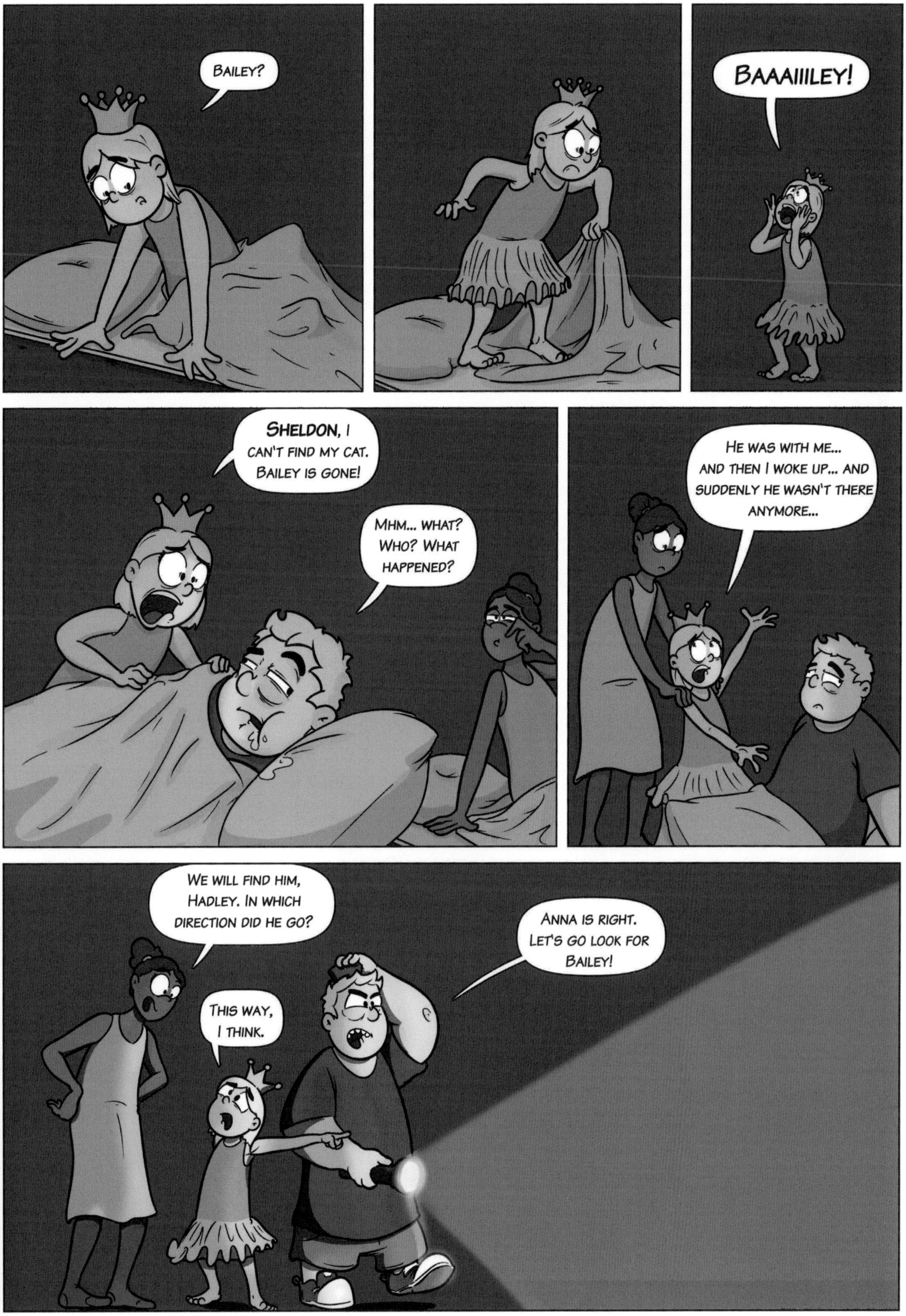
Bailey?
Baaaiiiley!
Sheldon, I can't find my cat. Bailey is gone!
Mhm... what? Who? What happened?
He was with me... and then I woke up... and suddenly he wasn't there anymore...
We will find him, Hadley. In which direction did he go?
This way, I think.
Anna is right. Let's go look for Bailey!

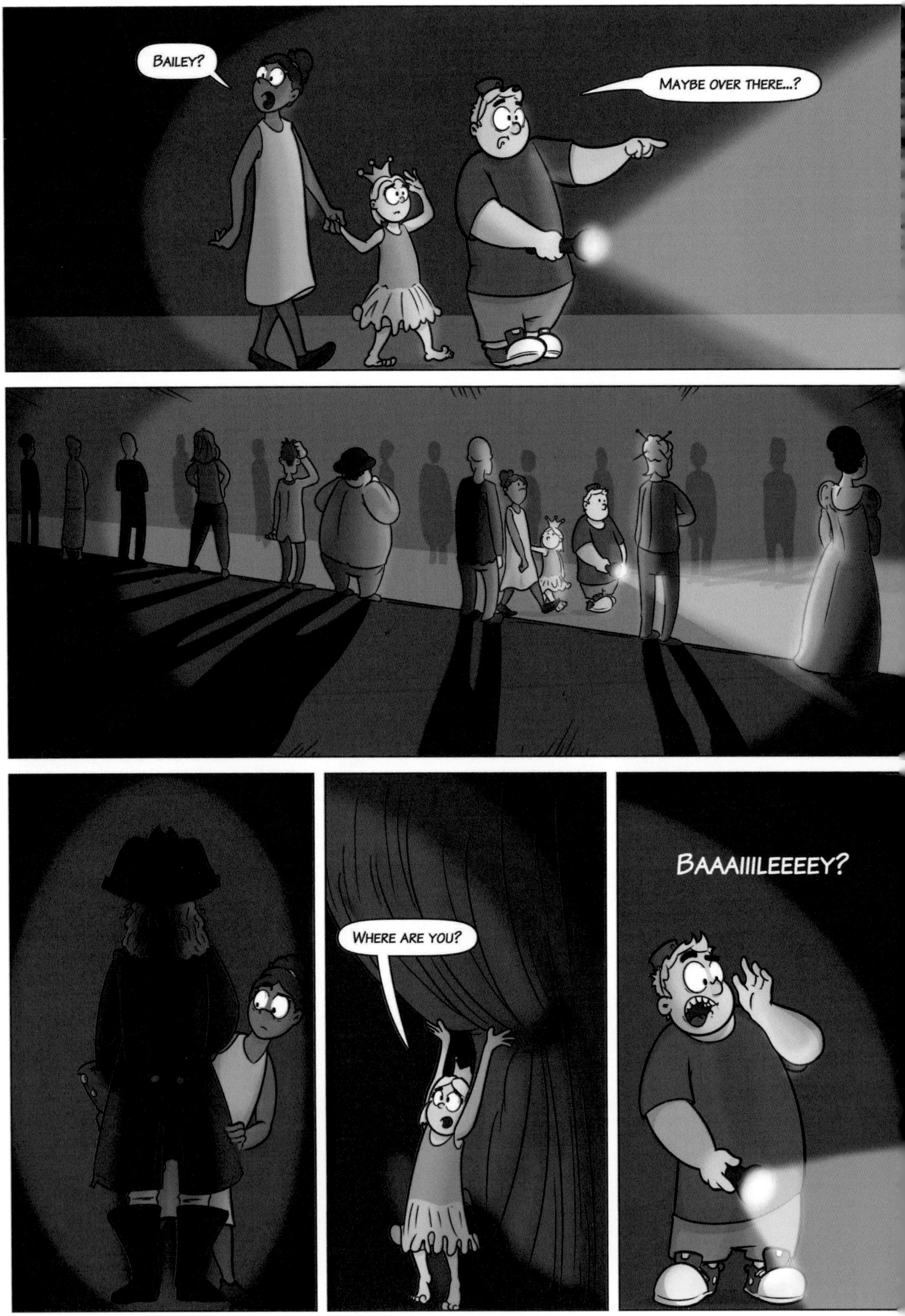
BAILEY?
MAYBE OVER THERE...?
WHERE ARE YOU?
BAAAIIIILEEEEY?

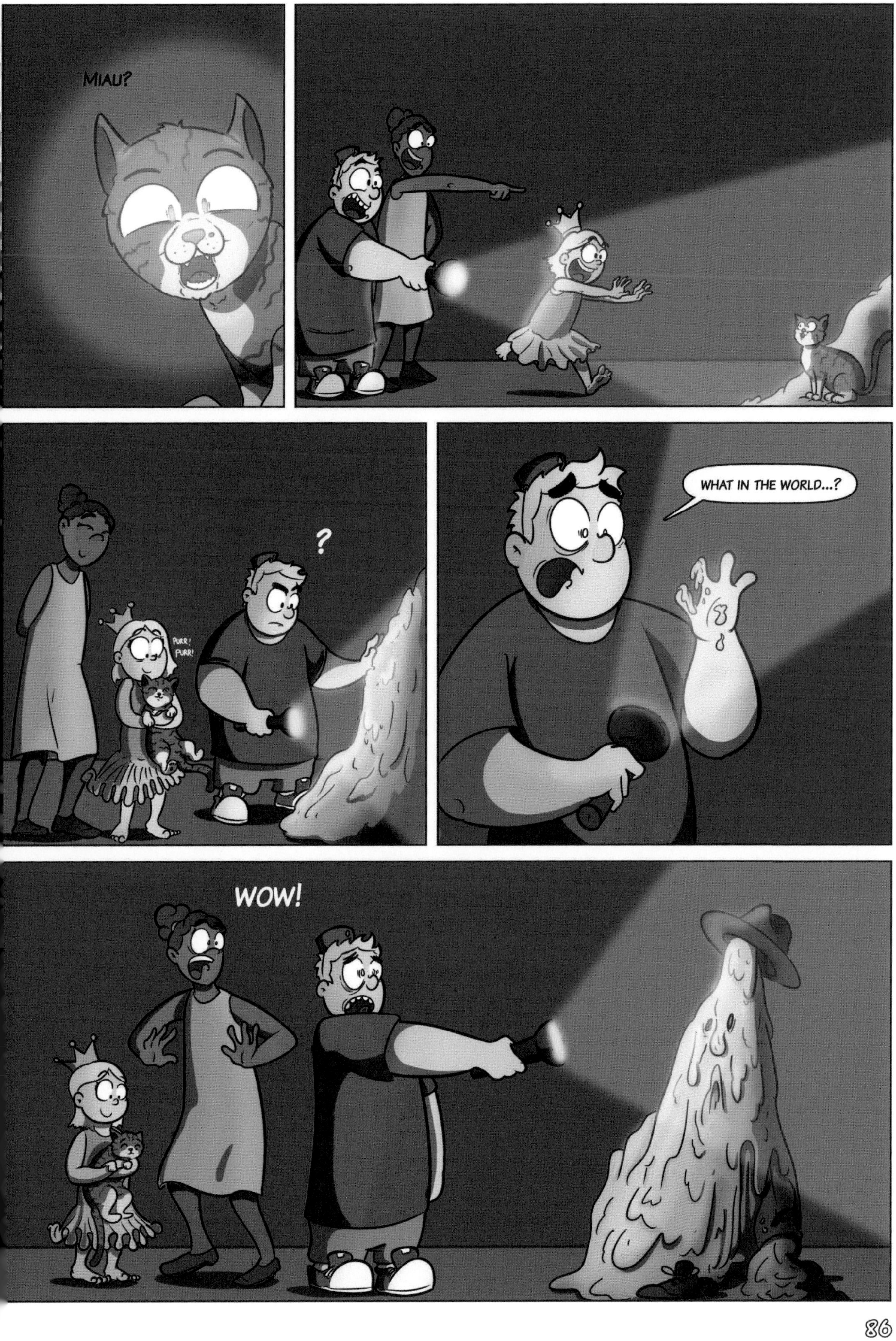
MIAU?
PURR! PURR!
?
WHAT IN THE WORLD...?
WOW!

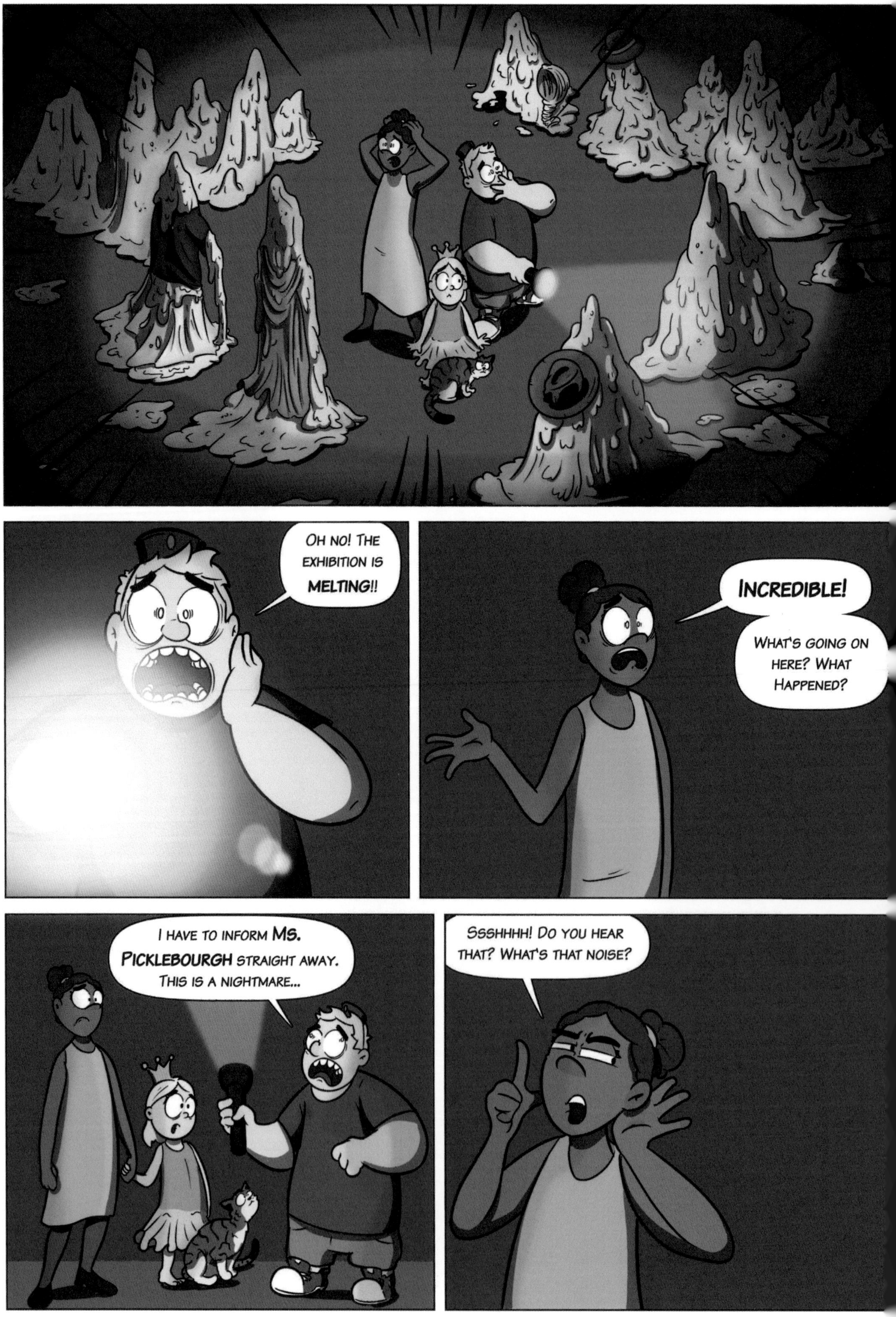
OH NO! THE EXHIBITION IS MELTING!!
INCREDIBLE!
WHAT'S GOING ON HERE? WHAT HAPPENED?
I HAVE TO INFORM MS. PICKLEBOURGH STRAIGHT AWAY. THIS IS A NIGHTMARE...
SSSHHHH! DO YOU HEAR THAT? WHAT'S THAT NOISE?

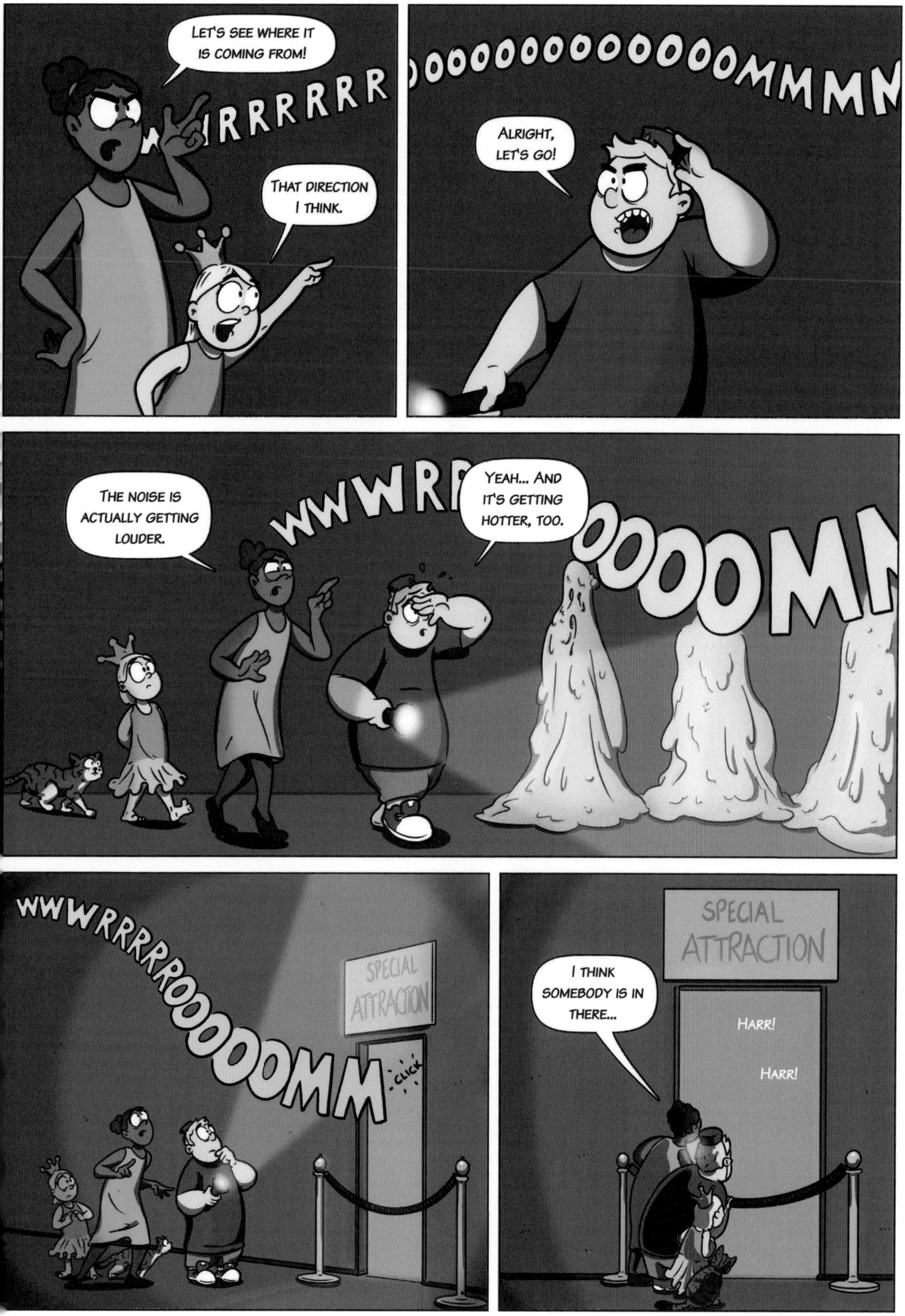
LET'S SEE WHERE IT IS COMING FROM!
WRRRRRRR
THAT DIRECTION I THINK.
OOOOOOOOOOOOOOOMMMM
ALRIGHT, LET'S GO!
THE NOISE IS ACTUALLY GETTING LOUDER.
WWWRR
YEAH... AND IT'S GETTING HOTTER, TOO.
OOOOMM
WWWRRRRROOOOOOMM
SPECIAL ATTRACTION
CLICK
SPECIAL ATTRACTION
I THINK SOMEBODY IS IN THERE...
HARR!
HARR!

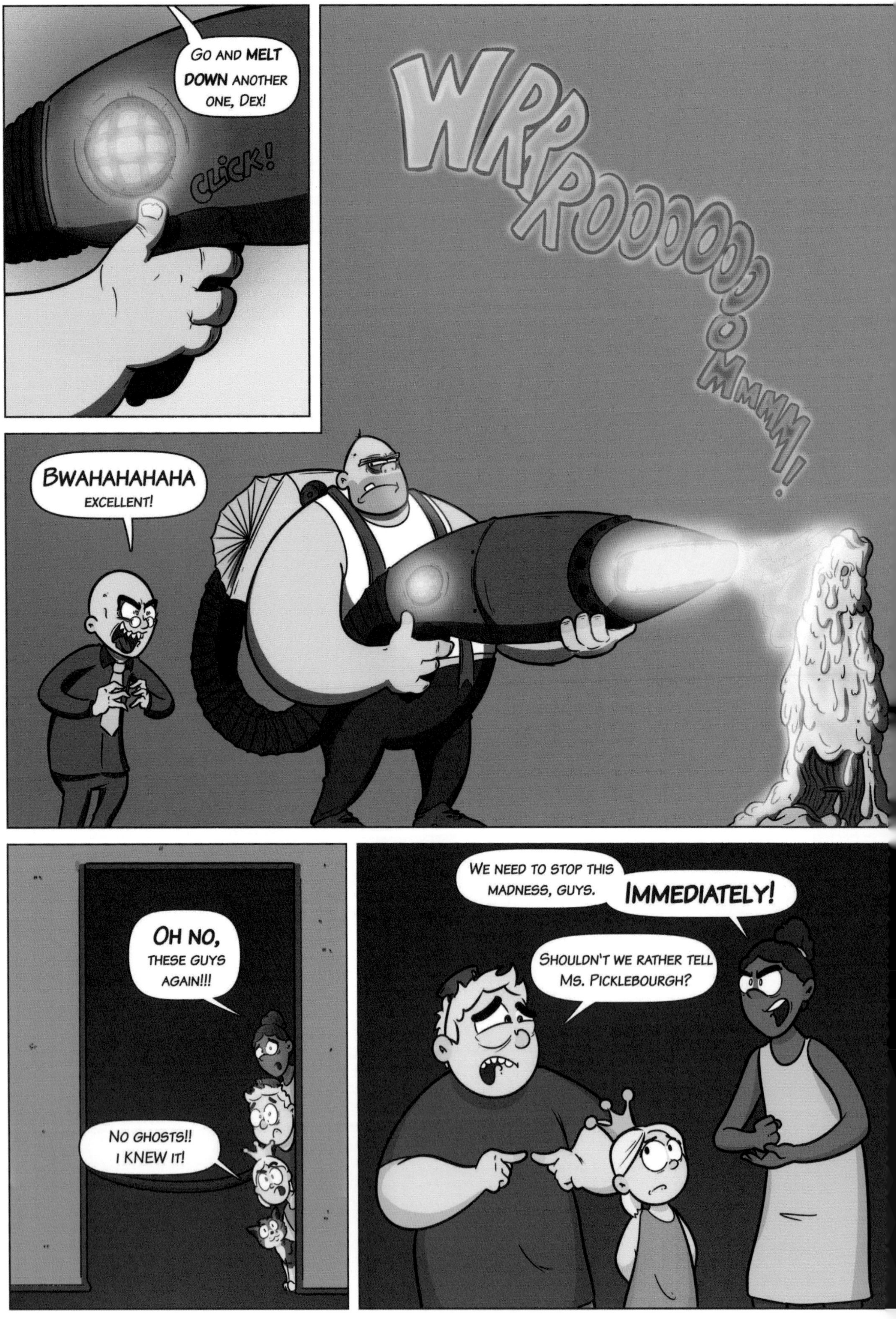
GO AND MELT DOWN ANOTHER ONE, DEX!
CLICK!
WRRROOOOOOOOOMMMMM!
BWAHAHAHAHA EXCELLENT!
OH NO, THESE GUYS AGAIN!!!
NO GHOSTS!! I KNEW IT!
WE NEED TO STOP THIS MADNESS, GUYS.
IMMEDIATELY!
SHOULDN'T WE RATHER TELL MS. PICKLEBOURGH?

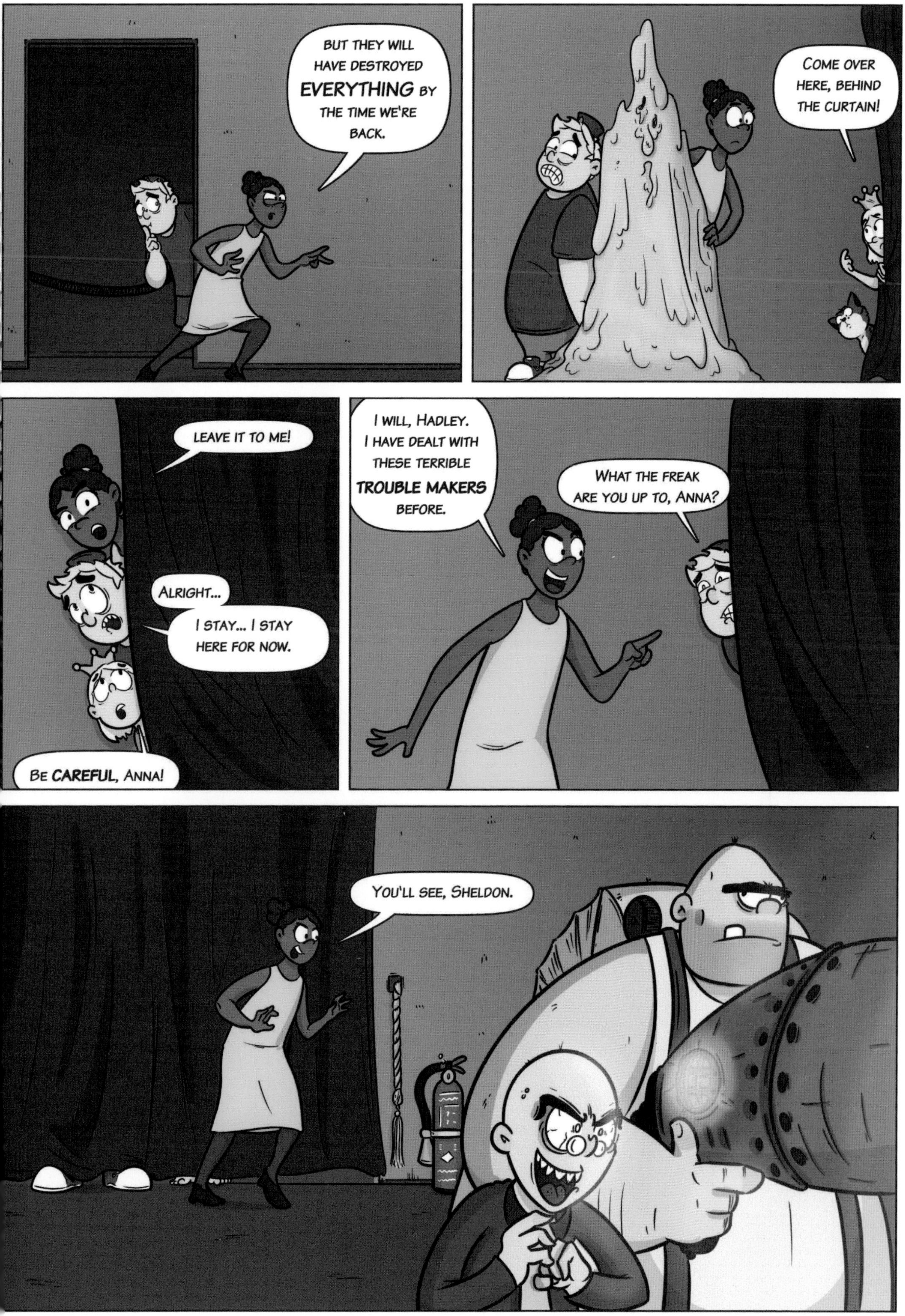
BUT THEY WILL HAVE DESTROYED EVERYTHING BY THE TIME WE'RE BACK.
COME OVER HERE, BEHIND THE CURTAIN!
LEAVE IT TO ME!
ALRIGHT...
I STAY... I STAY HERE FOR NOW.
BE CAREFUL, ANNA!
I WILL, HADLEY. I HAVE DEALT WITH THESE TERRIBLE TROUBLE MAKERS BEFORE.
WHAT THE FREAK ARE YOU UP TO, ANNA?
YOU'LL SEE, SHELDON.

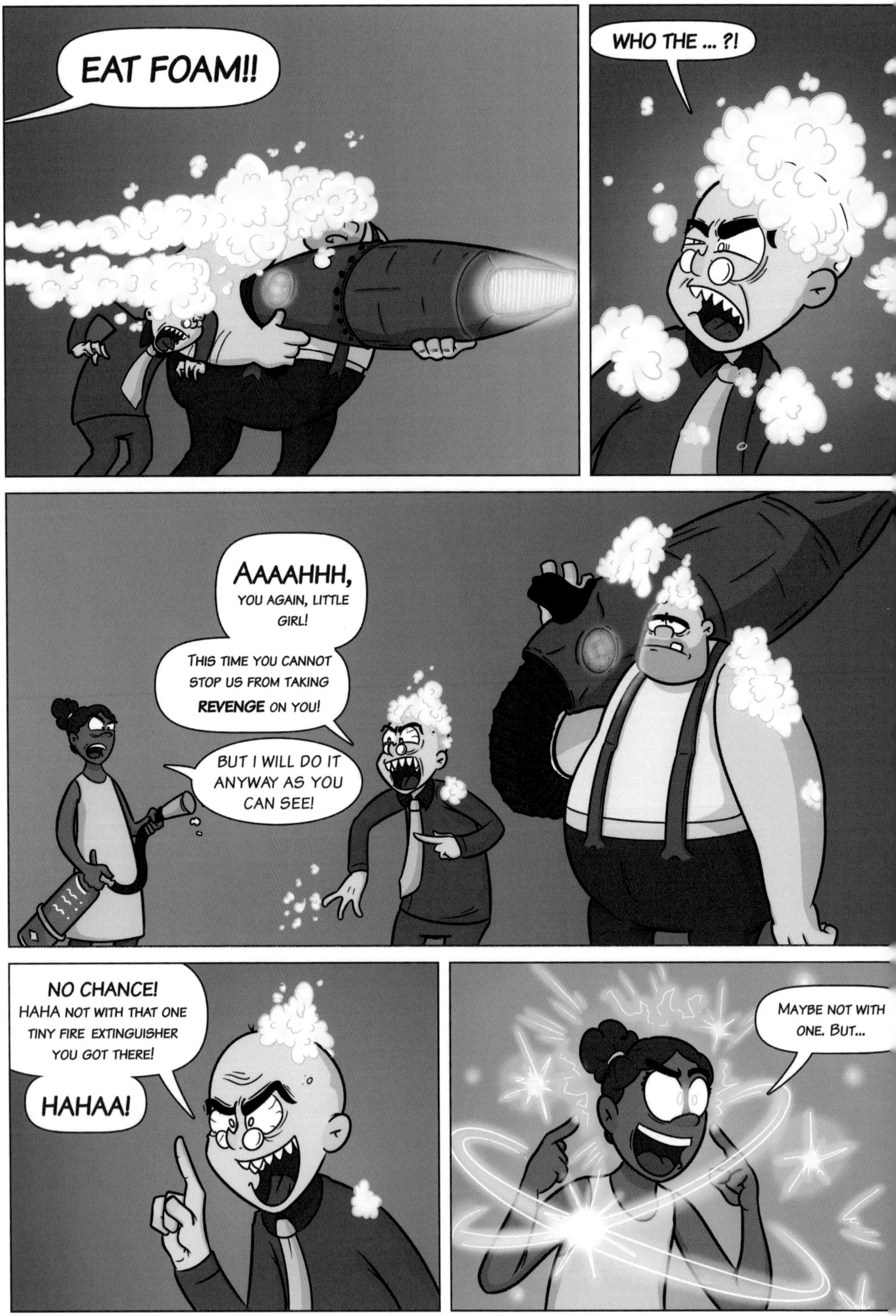
EAT FOAM!!
WHO THE ... ?!
AAAAHHH, YOU AGAIN, LITTLE GIRL!
THIS TIME YOU CANNOT STOP US FROM TAKING REVENGE ON YOU!
BUT I WILL DO IT ANYWAY AS YOU CAN SEE!
NO CHANCE! HAHA NOT WITH THAT ONE TINY FIRE EXTINGUISHER YOU GOT THERE!
HAHAA!
MAYBE NOT WITH ONE. BUT...

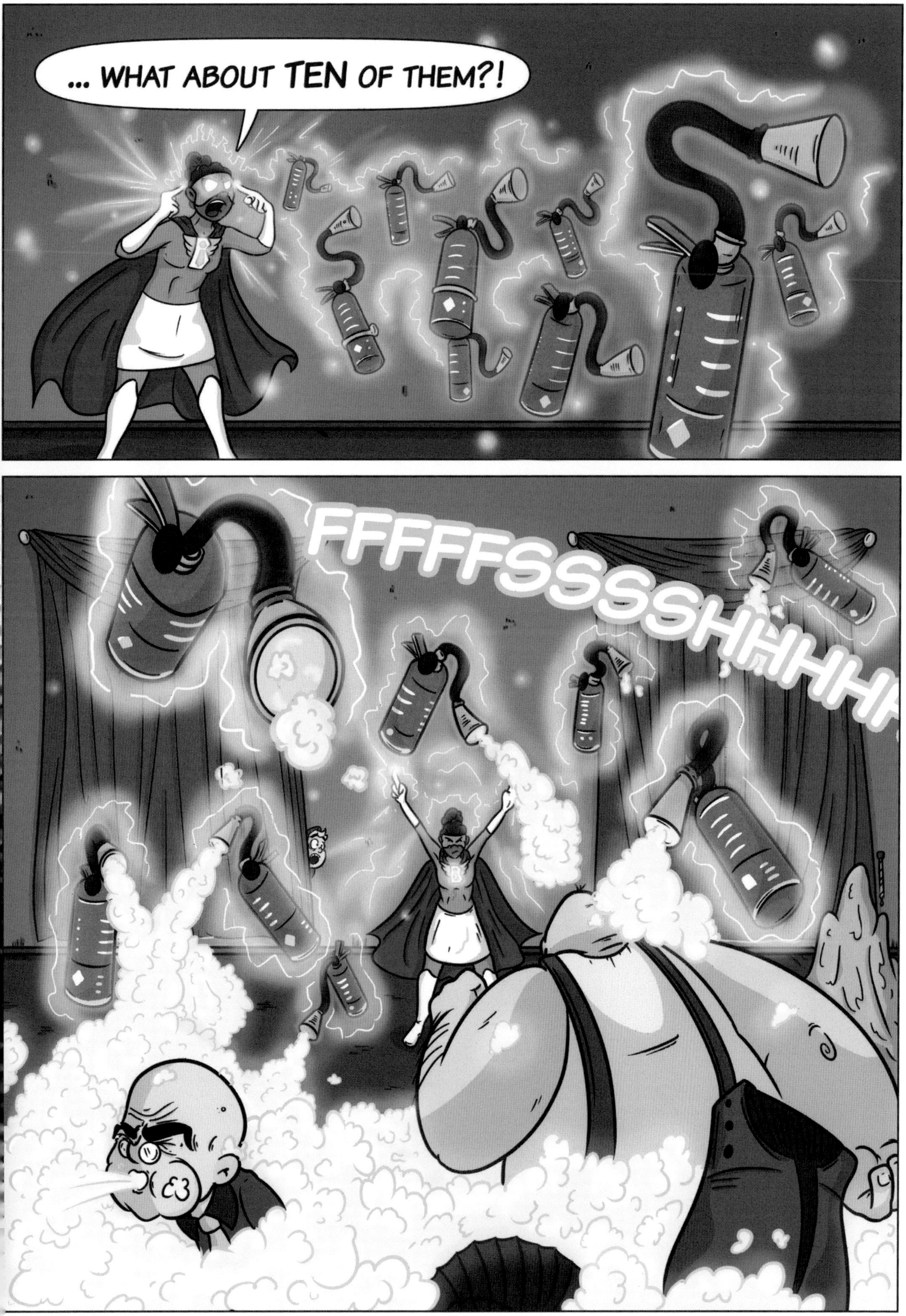
... WHAT ABOUT TEN OF THEM?!
FFFFFSSSSSHHHHH

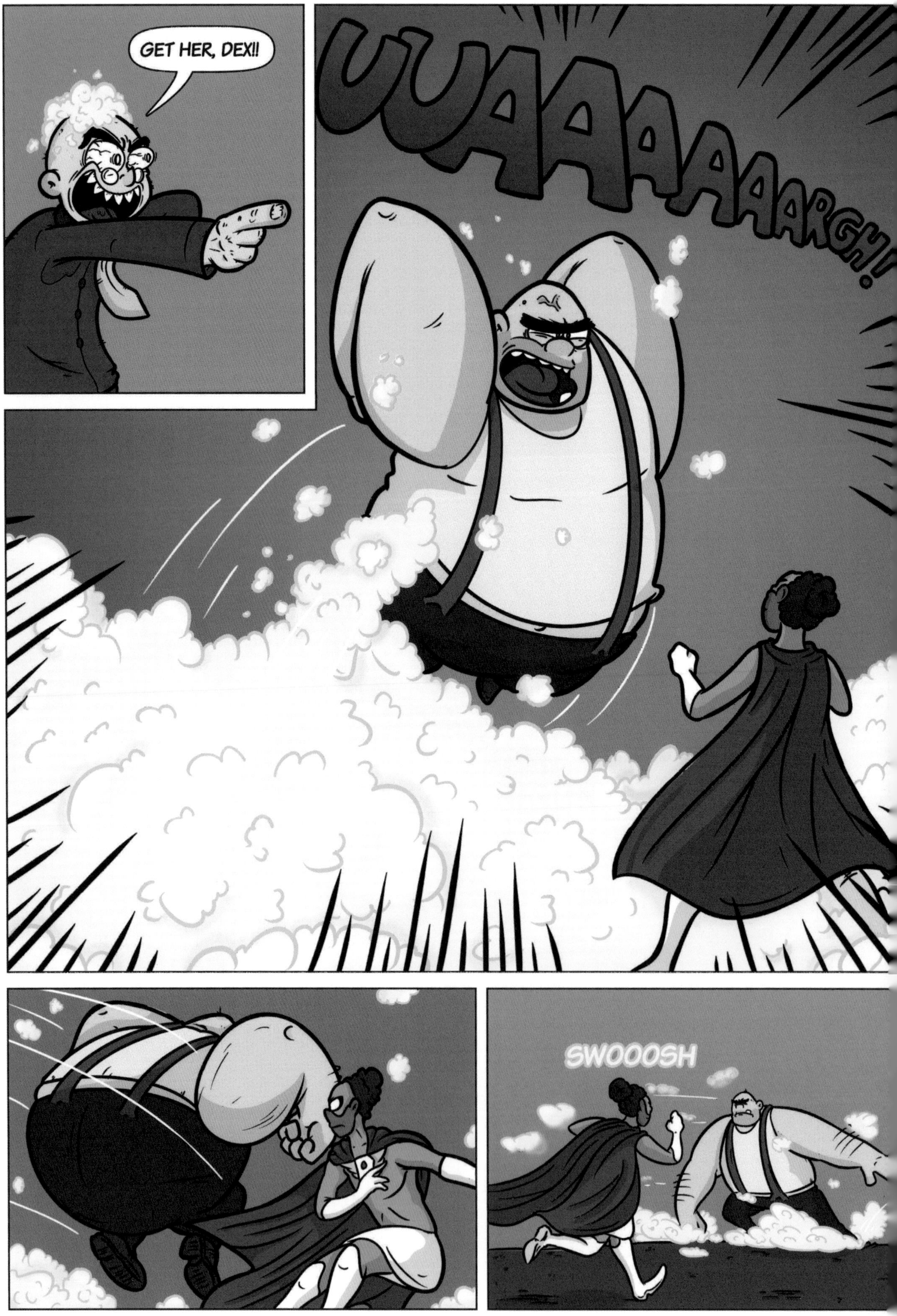
GET HER, DEX!!
UUAAAAAAAARGH!!
SWOOOSH

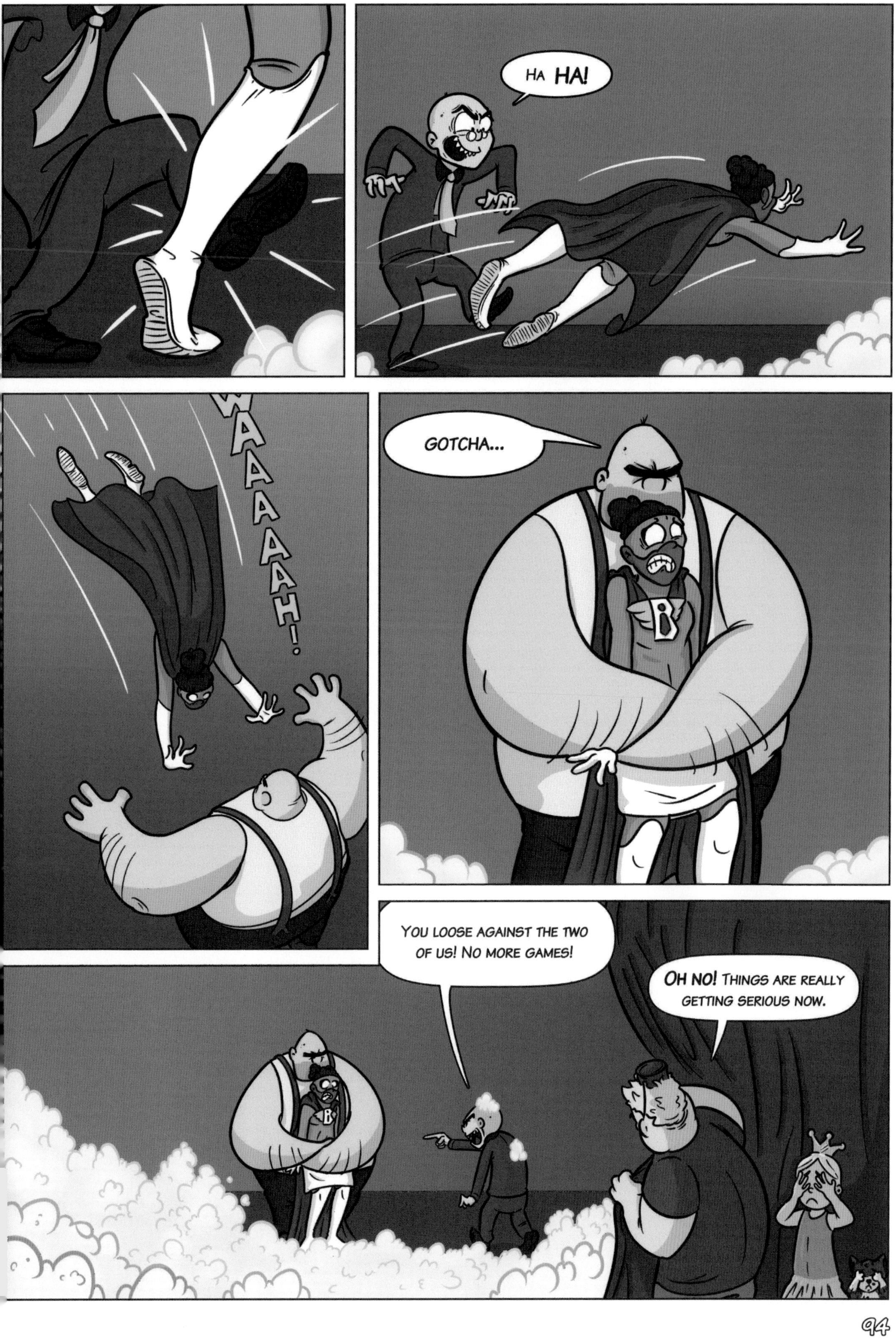
HA HA!
WAAAAAAAAH!
GOTCHA...
YOU LOOSE AGAINST THE TWO OF US! NO MORE GAMES!
OH NO! THINGS ARE REALLY GETTING SERIOUS NOW.

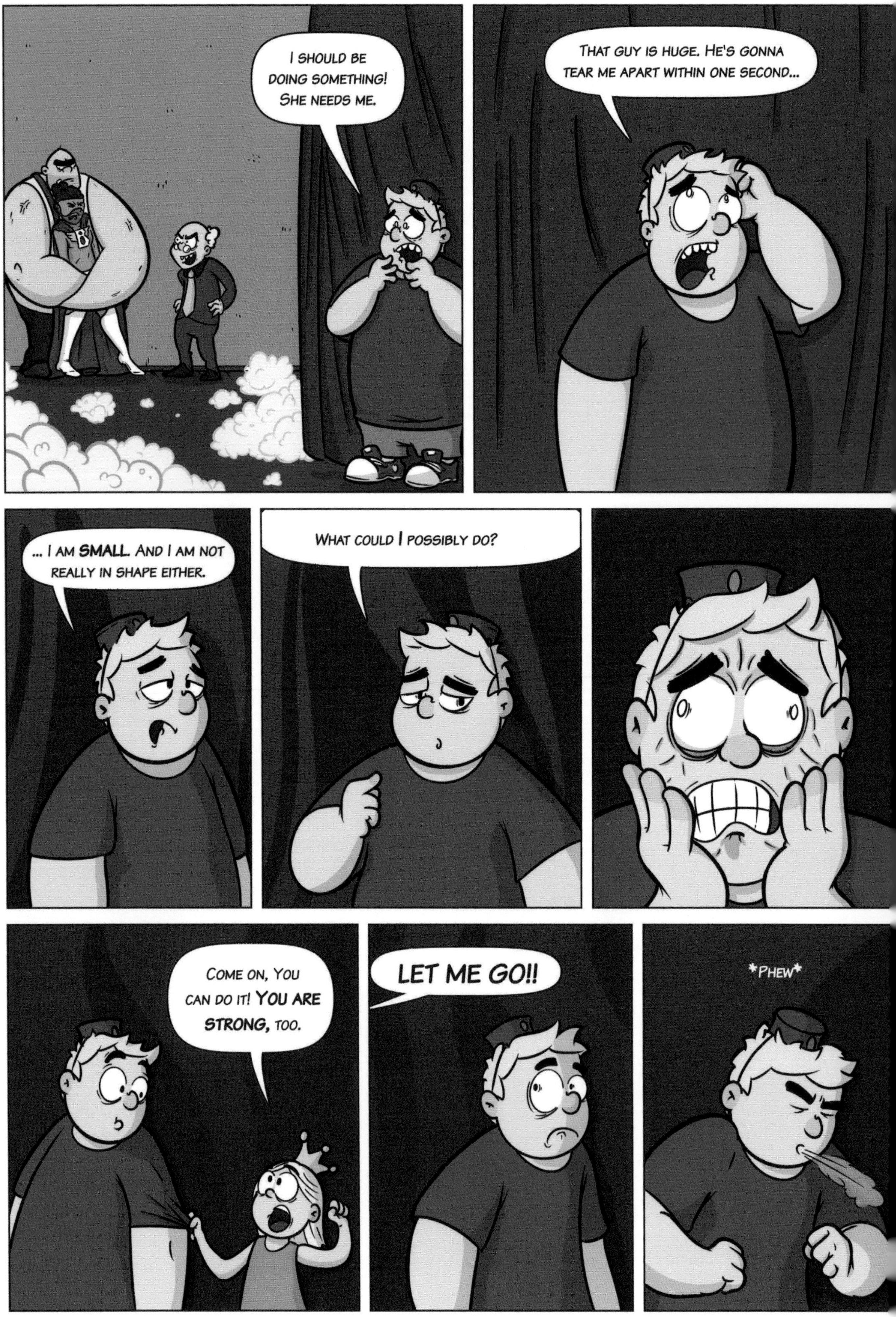
I SHOULD BE DOING SOMETHING! SHE NEEDS ME.
THAT GUY IS HUGE. HE'S GONNA TEAR ME APART WITHIN ONE SECOND...
... I AM **SMALL**. AND I AM NOT REALLY IN SHAPE EITHER.
WHAT COULD I POSSIBLY DO?
COME ON, YOU CAN DO IT! **YOU ARE STRONG,** TOO.
LET ME GO!!
PHEW

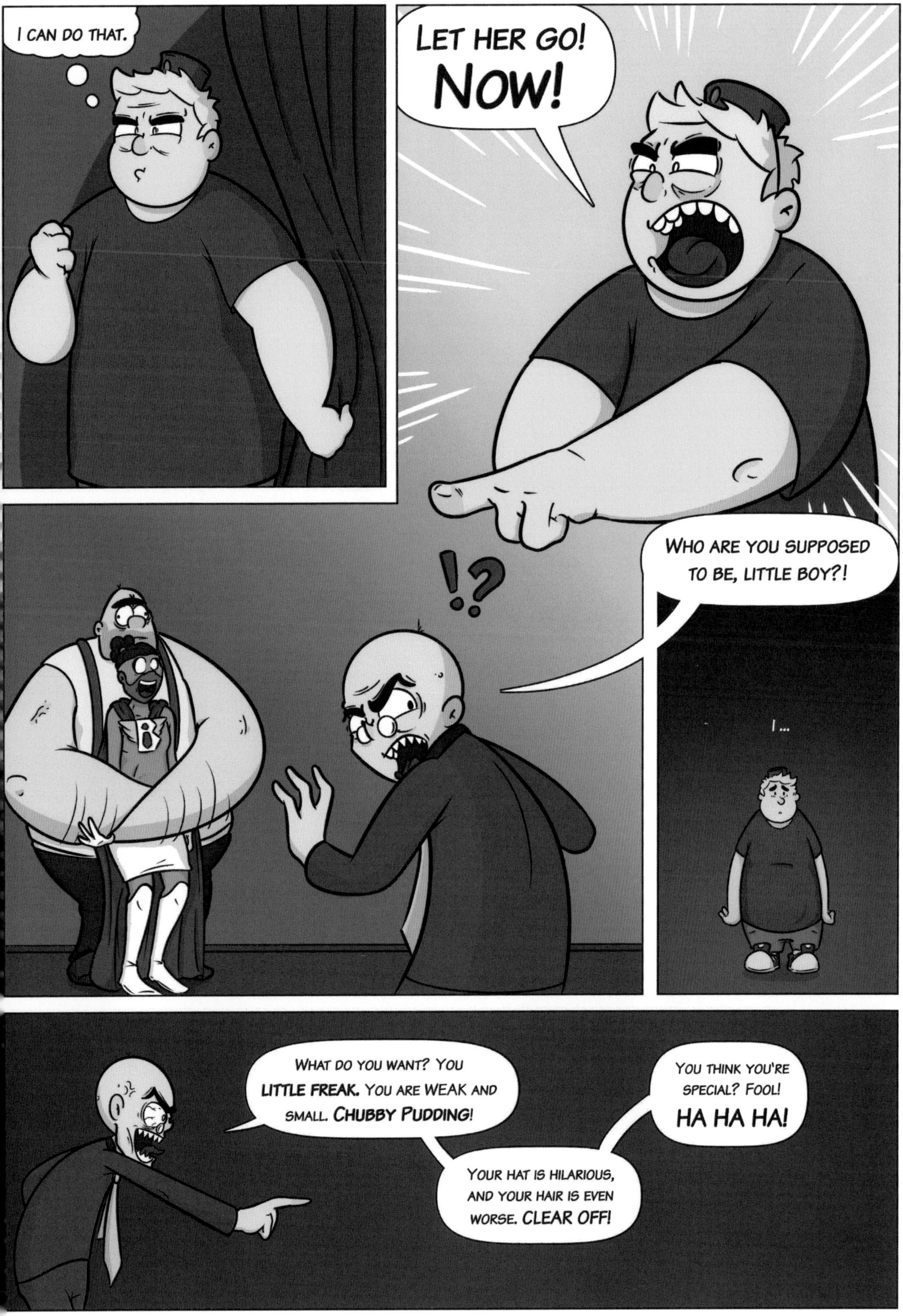
I CAN DO THAT.
LET HER GO! NOW!
!?
WHO ARE YOU SUPPOSED TO BE, LITTLE BOY?!
I...
WHAT DO YOU WANT? YOU LITTLE FREAK. YOU ARE WEAK AND SMALL. CHUBBY PUDDING!
YOUR HAT IS HILARIOUS, AND YOUR HAIR IS EVEN WORSE. CLEAR OFF!
YOU THINK YOU'RE SPECIAL? FOOL! HA HA HA!

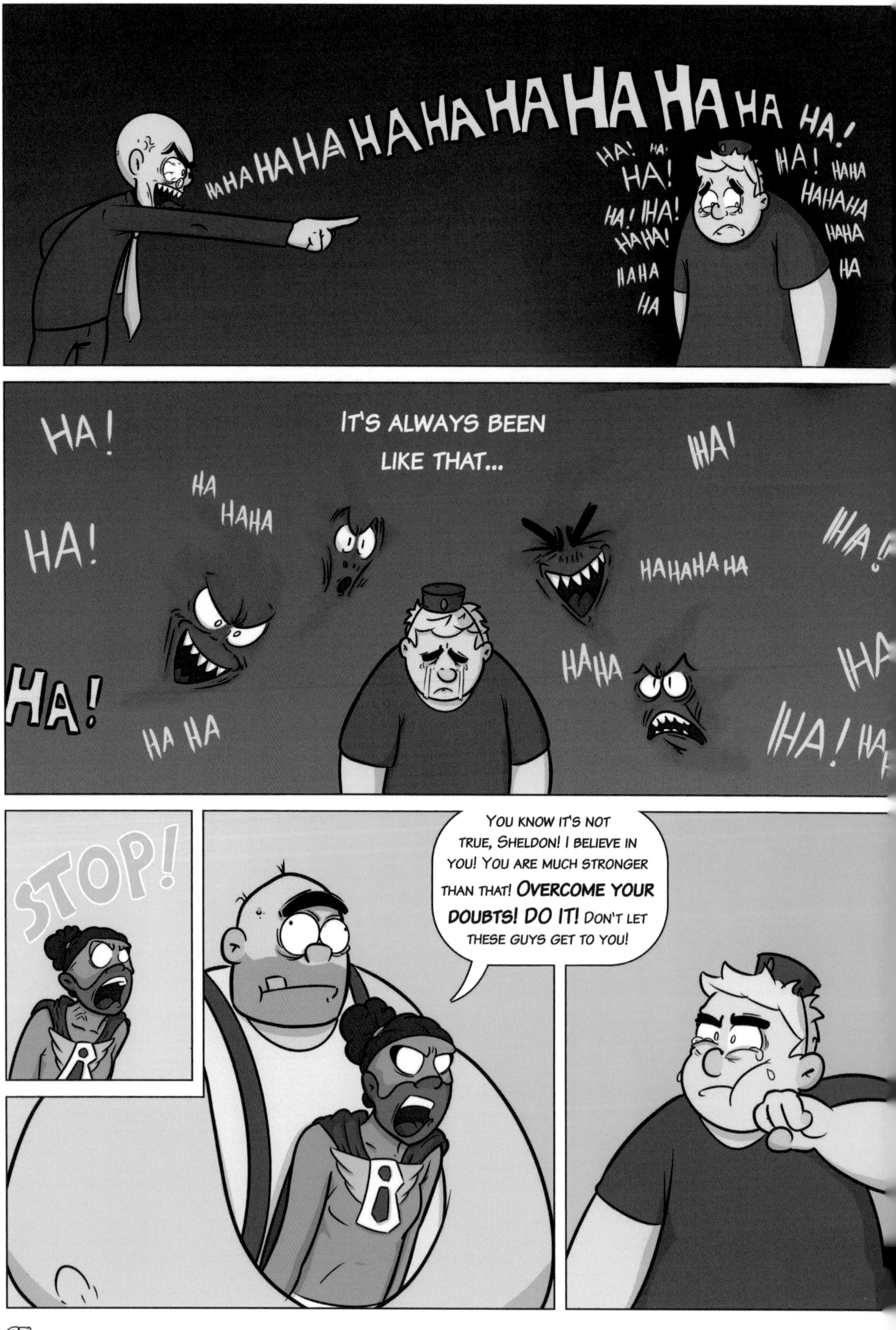
HAHAHAHAHAHAHAHAHAHAHAHAHA HA HA!
HA! HA! HA! HA! HA! HA! HAHA! HAHA HA
HA! HAHA HAHAHA HAHA HA
HA! HA HAHA HA! HA! HA HA
IT'S ALWAYS BEEN LIKE THAT...
HA! HA! HAHAHAHA HA HAHA HA!
STOP!
YOU KNOW IT'S NOT TRUE, SHELDON! I BELIEVE IN YOU! YOU ARE MUCH STRONGER THAN THAT! OVERCOME YOUR DOUBTS! DO IT! DON'T LET THESE GUYS GET TO YOU!

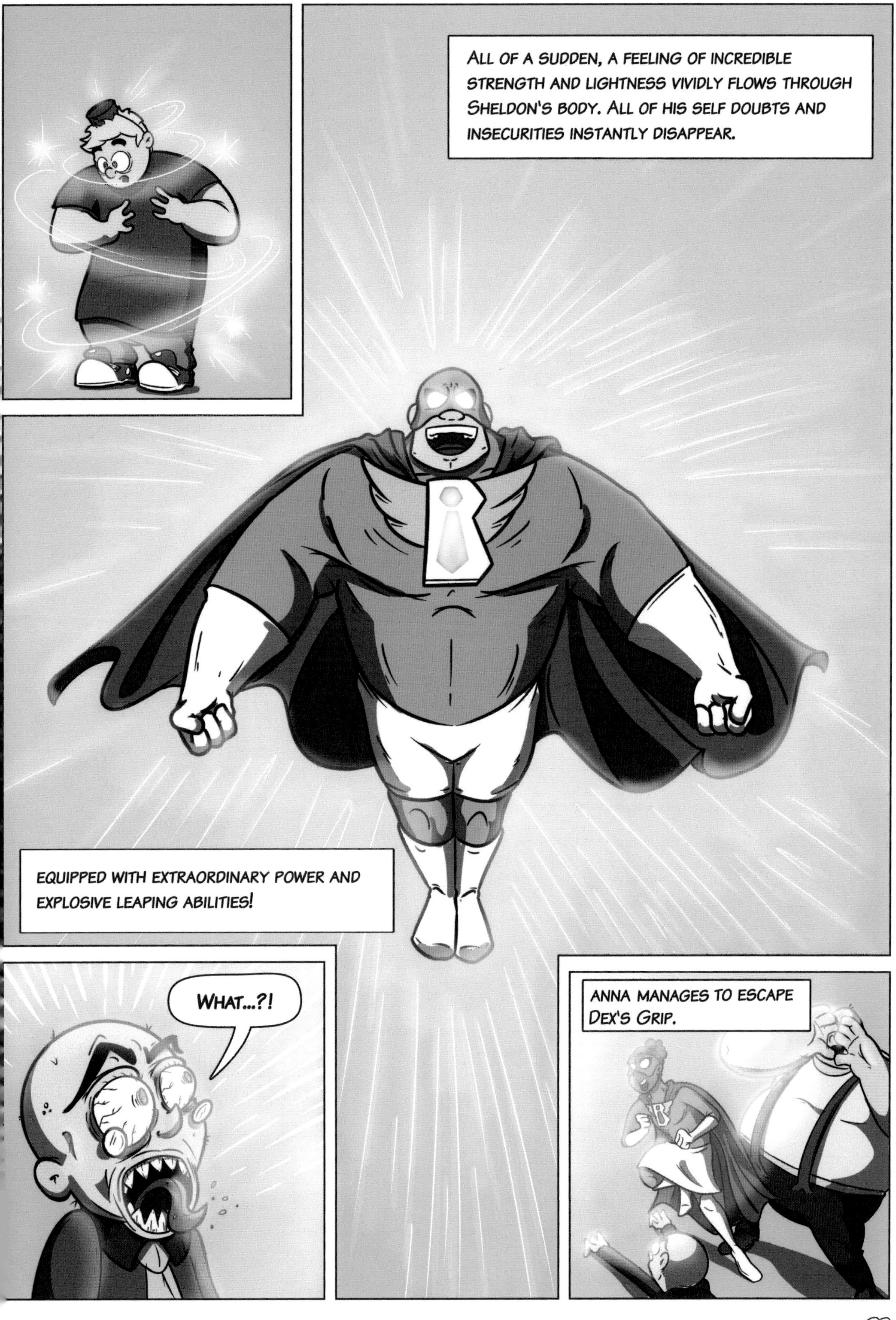
ALL OF A SUDDEN, A FEELING OF INCREDIBLE STRENGTH AND LIGHTNESS VIVIDLY FLOWS THROUGH SHELDON'S BODY. ALL OF HIS SELF DOUBTS AND INSECURITIES INSTANTLY DISAPPEAR.
EQUIPPED WITH EXTRAORDINARY POWER AND EXPLOSIVE LEAPING ABILITIES!
WHAT...?!
ANNA MANAGES TO ESCAPE DEX'S GRIP.

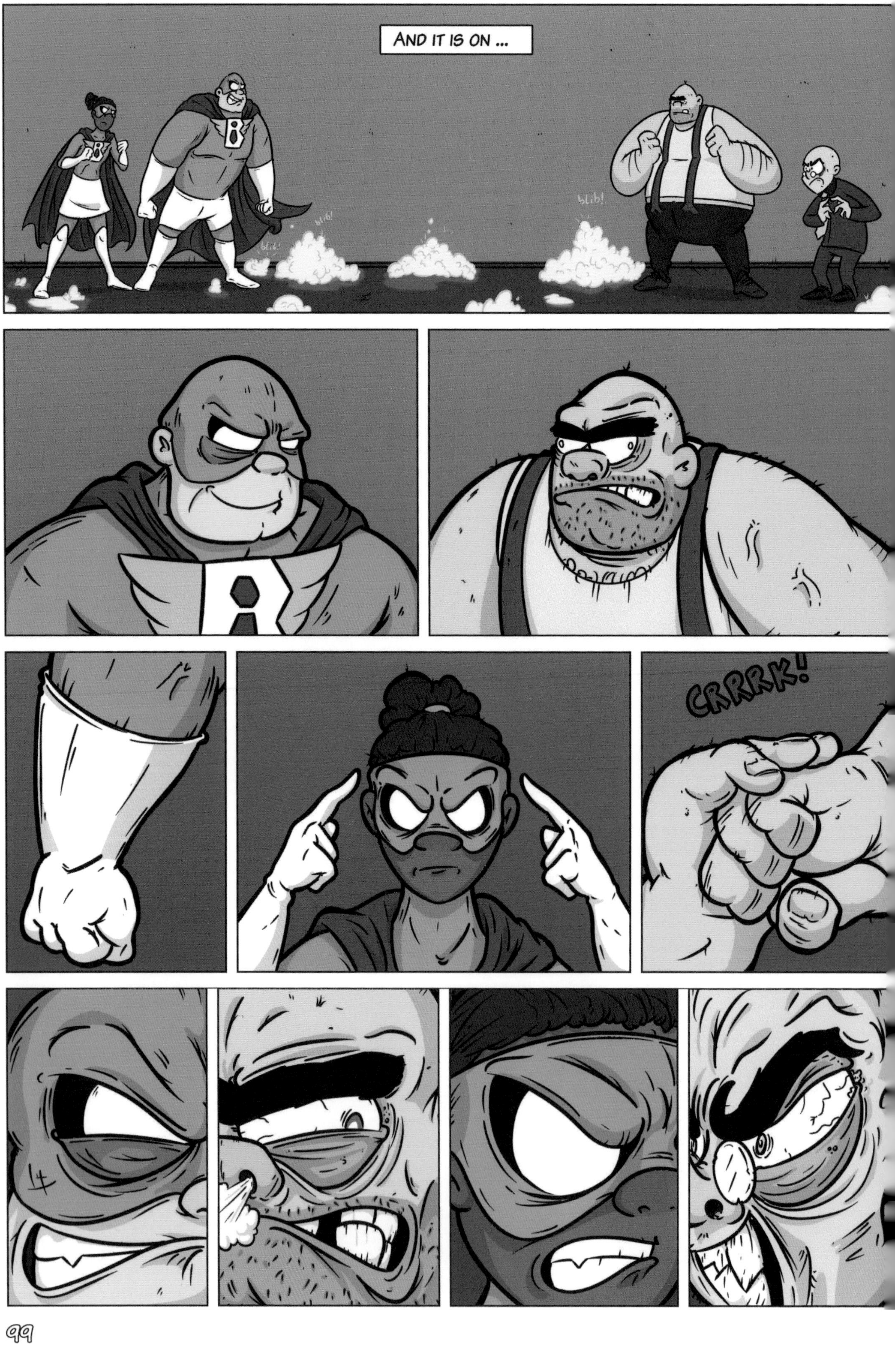
AND IT IS ON ...
blib!
blib!
blib!
CRRRK!

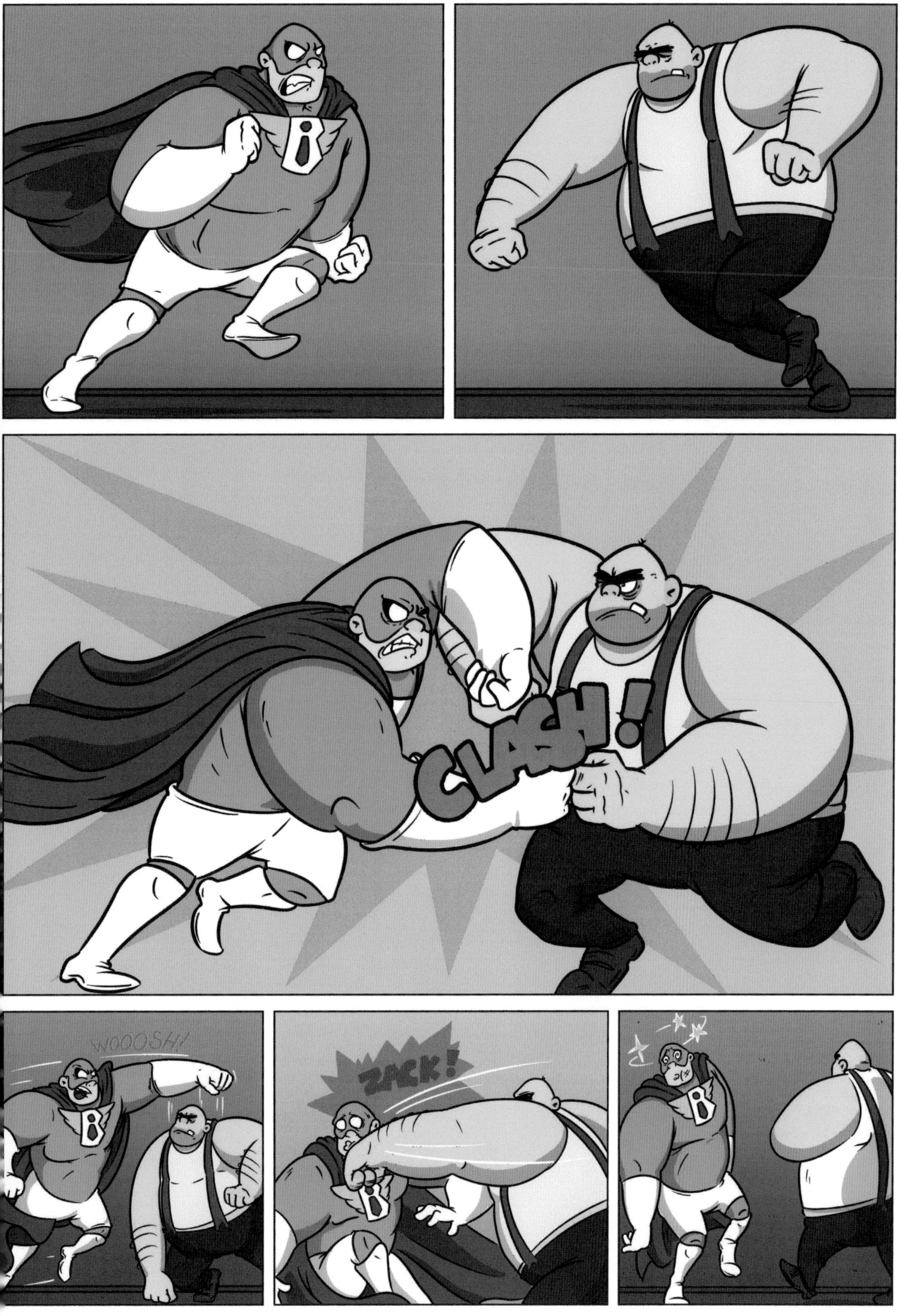
CLASH!
WOOOSH!
ZACK!

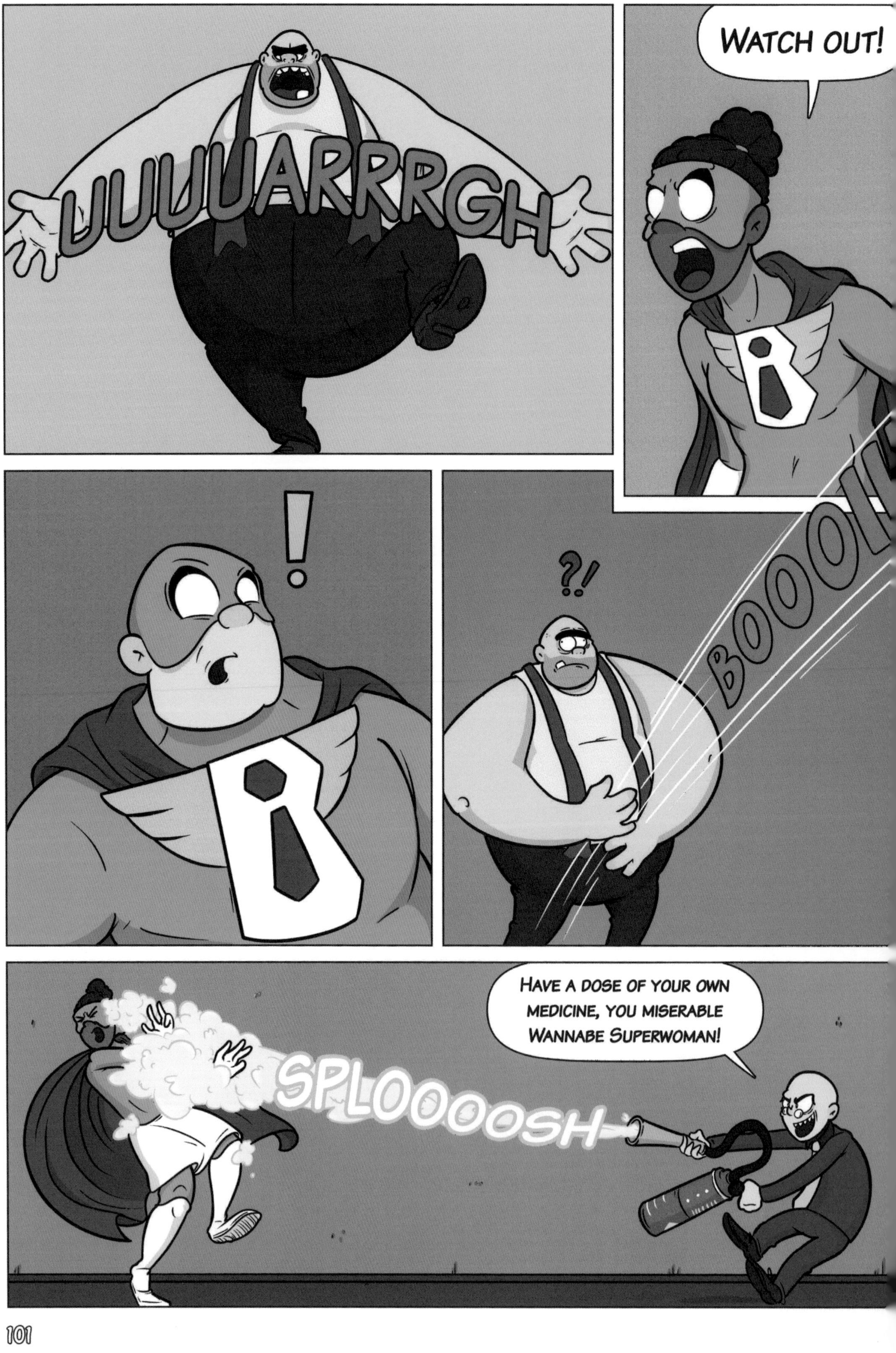
UUUUARRRGH
WATCH OUT!
!
?!
BOOOI
HAVE A DOSE OF YOUR OWN MEDICINE, YOU MISERABLE WANNABE SUPERWOMAN!
SPLOOOOOSH

COME AND TRY TO CATCH ME, BIG BOY!
HAAAA-HA!
AAAAAND TOO SLOW AGAIN!
HUFF ...

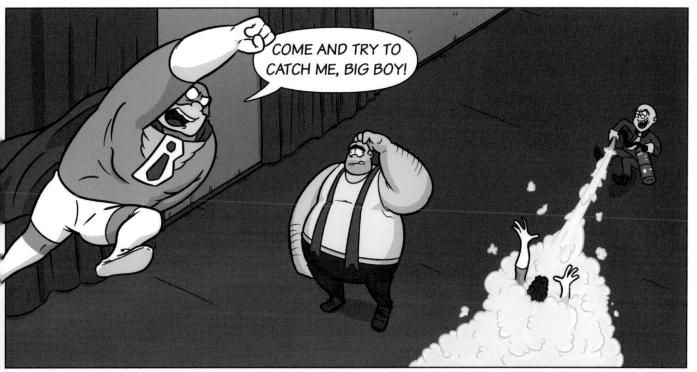

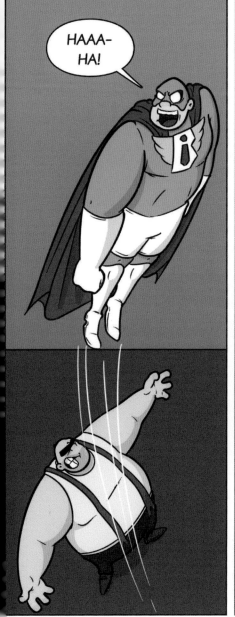

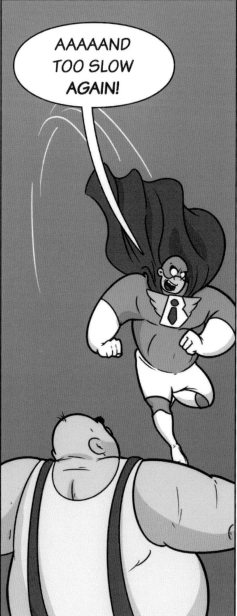

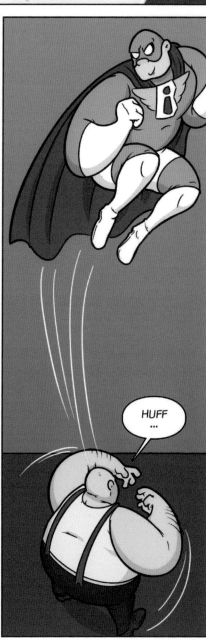

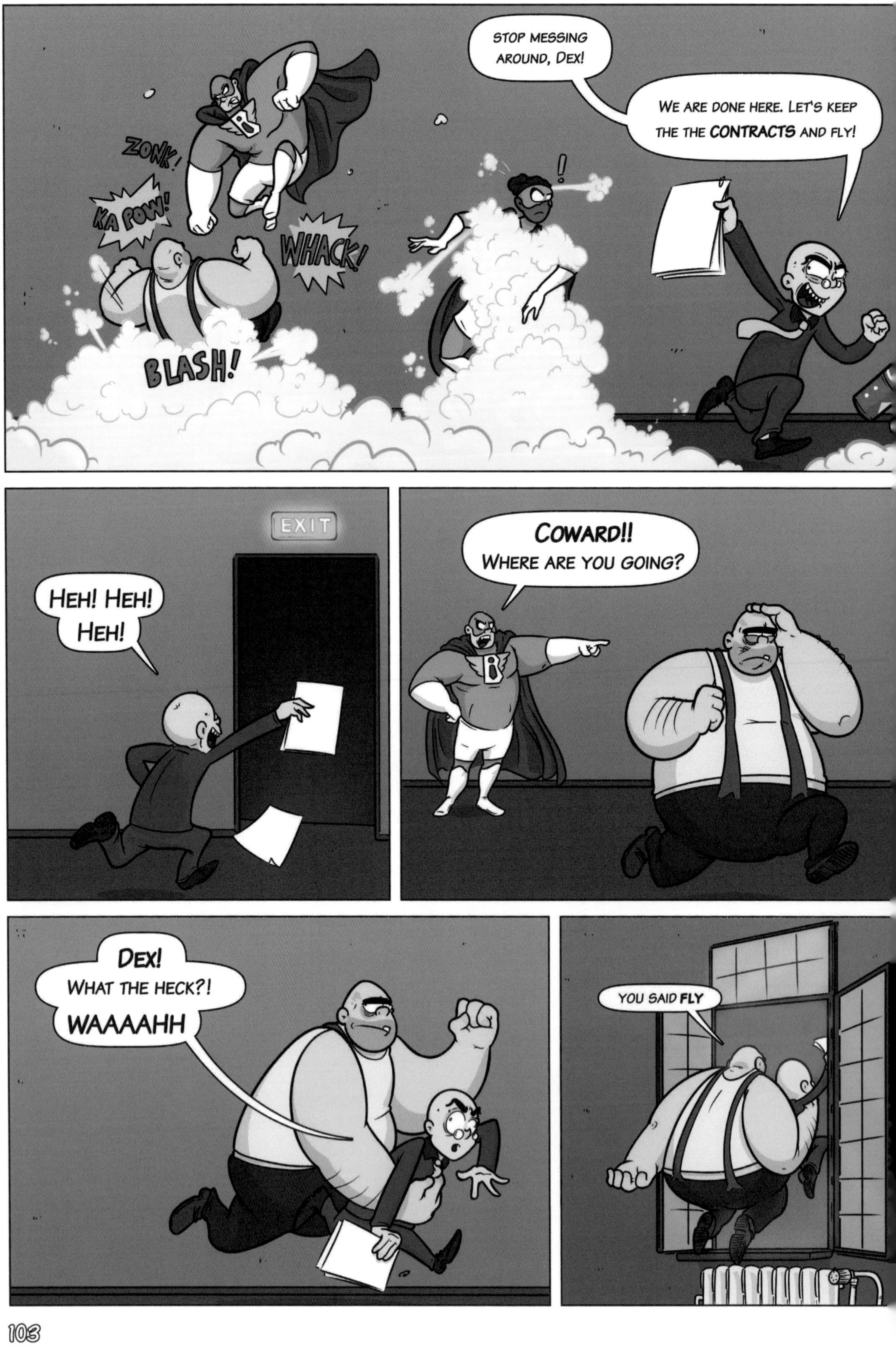
ZONK!
KA POW!
WHACK!
BLASH!
STOP MESSING AROUND, DEX!
!
WE ARE DONE HERE. LET'S KEEP THE THE CONTRACTS AND FLY!
EXIT
HEH! HEH! HEH!
COWARD!! WHERE ARE YOU GOING?
DEX! WHAT THE HECK?! WAAAAHH
YOU SAID FLY

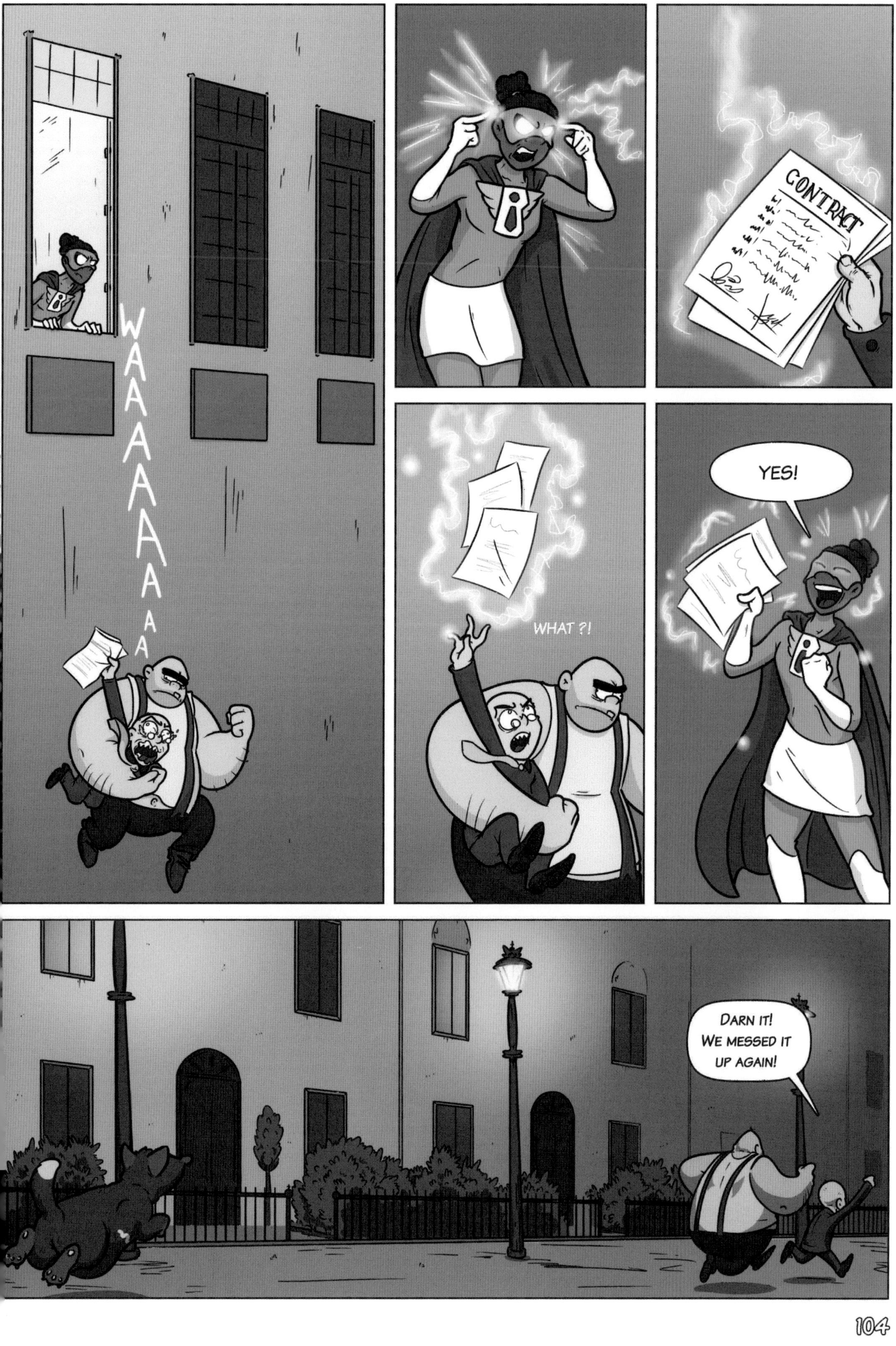
WAAAAAAAAAAA
CONTRACT
WHAT ?!
YES!
DARN IT! WE MESSED IT UP AGAIN!

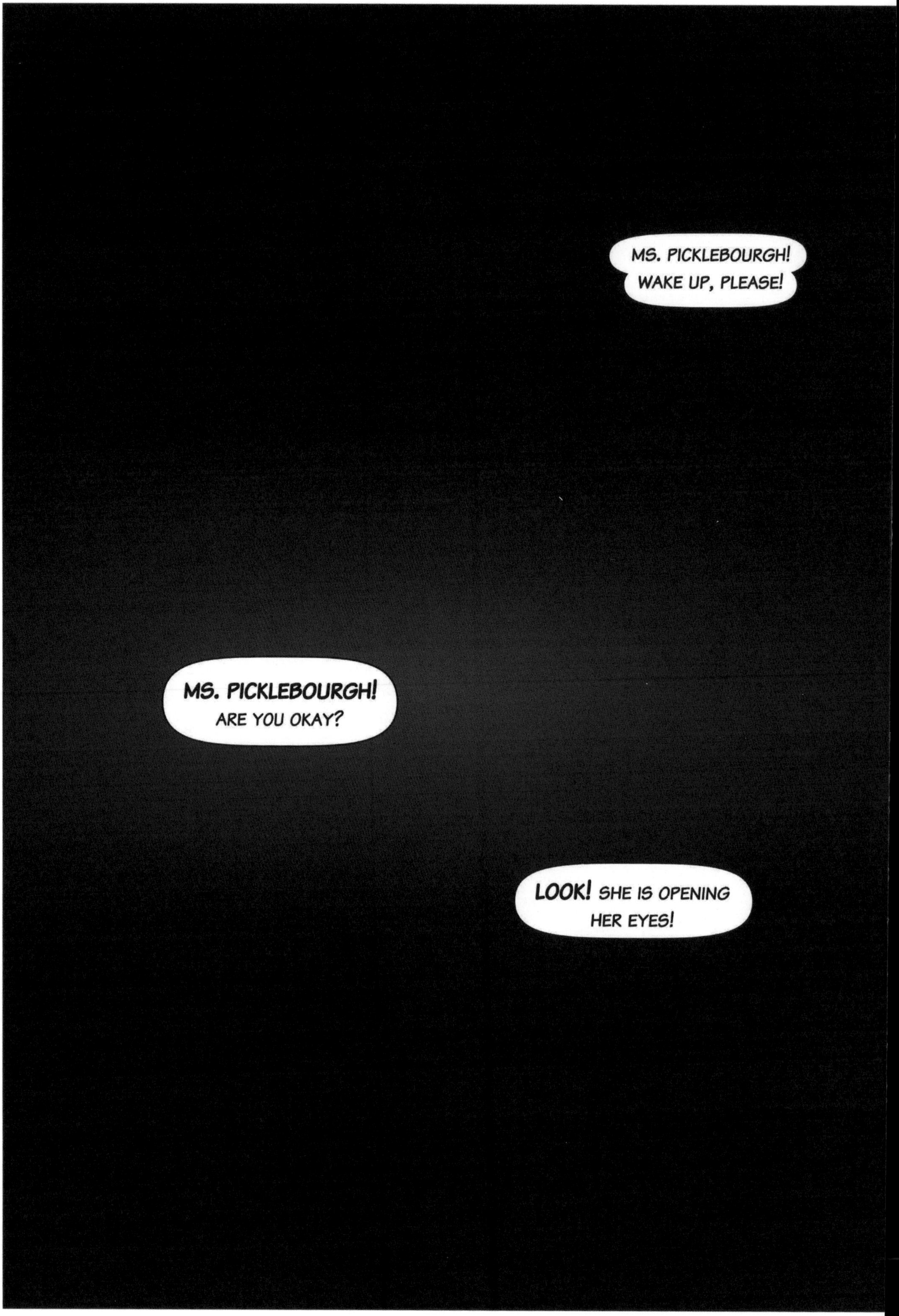
MS. PICKLEBOURGH! WAKE UP, PLEASE!
MS. PICKLEBOURGH! ARE YOU OKAY?
LOOK! SHE IS OPENING HER EYES!

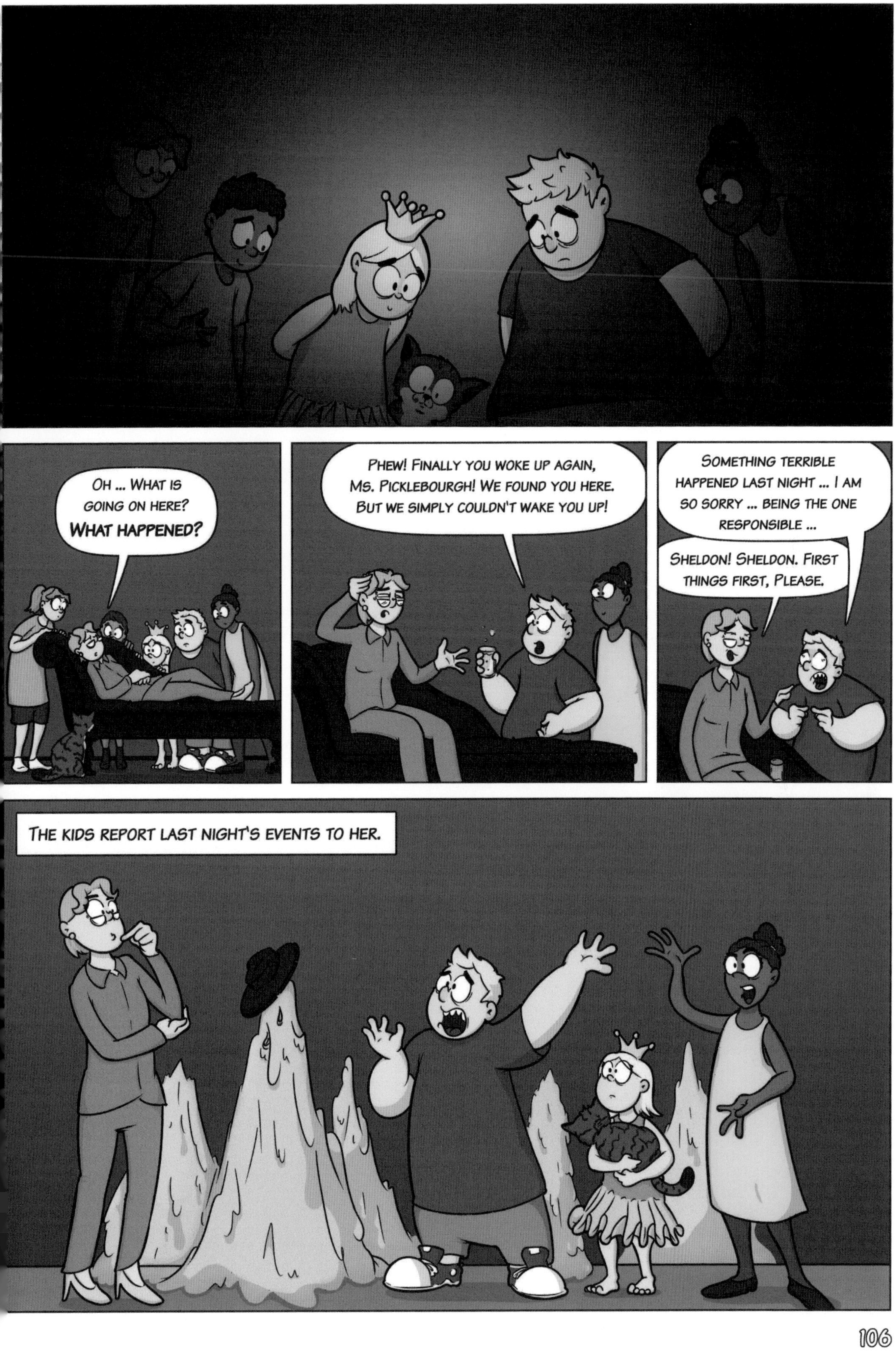

OH ... WHAT IS GOING ON HERE? **WHAT HAPPENED?**
PHEW! FINALLY YOU WOKE UP AGAIN, MS. PICKLEBOURGH! WE FOUND YOU HERE. BUT WE SIMPLY COULDN'T WAKE YOU UP!
SOMETHING TERRIBLE HAPPENED LAST NIGHT ... I AM SO SORRY ... BEING THE ONE RESPONSIBLE ...
SHELDON! SHELDON. FIRST THINGS FIRST, PLEASE.
THE KIDS REPORT LAST NIGHT'S EVENTS TO HER.

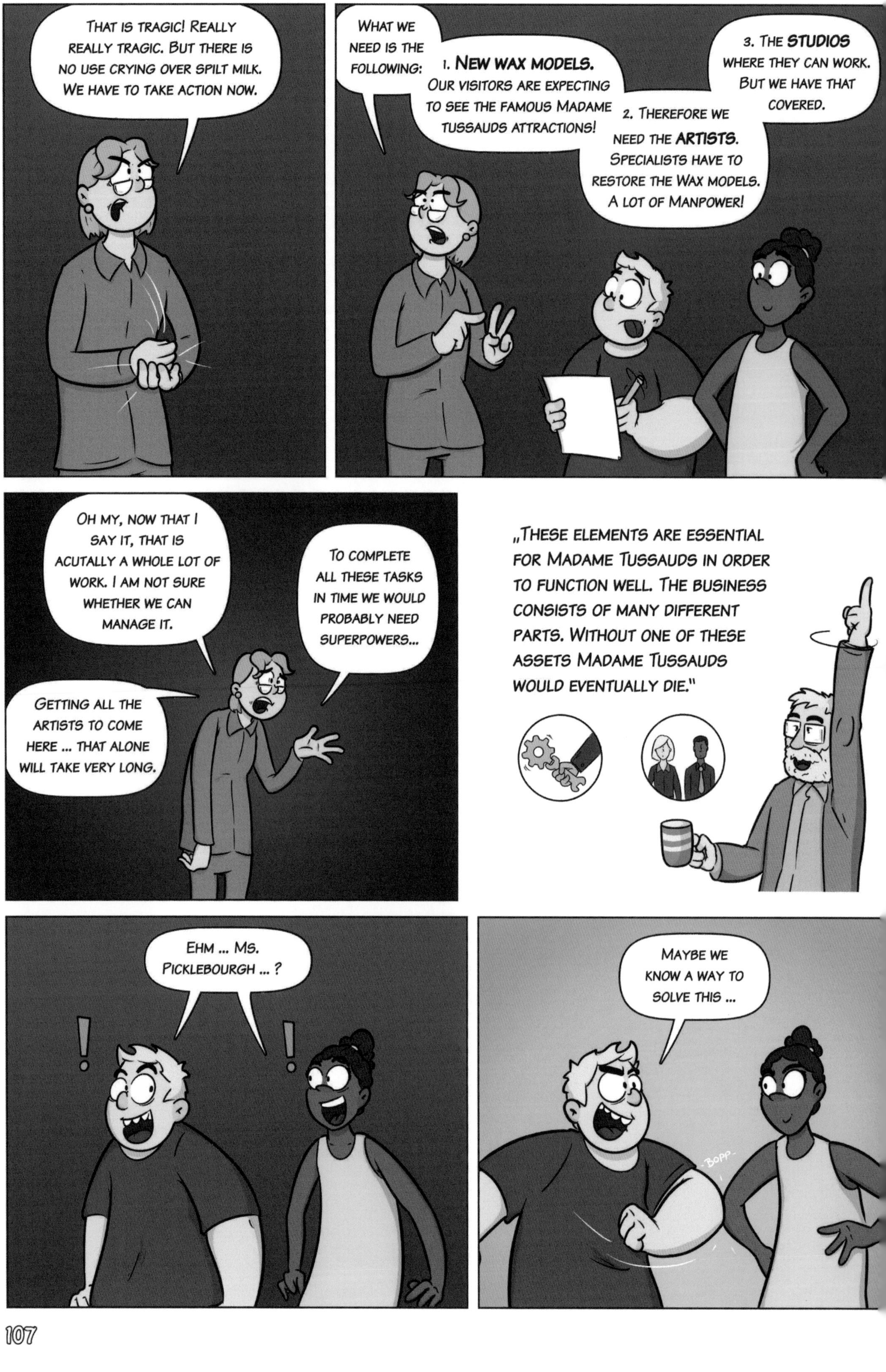
THAT IS TRAGIC! REALLY REALLY TRAGIC. BUT THERE IS NO USE CRYING OVER SPILT MILK. WE HAVE TO TAKE ACTION NOW.
WHAT WE NEED IS THE FOLLOWING:
1. NEW WAX MODELS. OUR VISITORS ARE EXPECTING TO SEE THE FAMOUS MADAME TUSSAUDS ATTRACTIONS!
2. THEREFORE WE NEED THE ARTISTS. SPECIALISTS HAVE TO RESTORE THE WAX MODELS. A LOT OF MANPOWER!
3. THE STUDIOS WHERE THEY CAN WORK. BUT WE HAVE THAT COVERED.
OH MY, NOW THAT I SAY IT, THAT IS ACUTALLY A WHOLE LOT OF WORK. I AM NOT SURE WHETHER WE CAN MANAGE IT.
TO COMPLETE ALL THESE TASKS IN TIME WE WOULD PROBABLY NEED SUPERPOWERS...
GETTING ALL THE ARTISTS TO COME HERE ... THAT ALONE WILL TAKE VERY LONG.
„THESE ELEMENTS ARE ESSENTIAL FOR MADAME TUSSAUDS IN ORDER TO FUNCTION WELL. THE BUSINESS CONSISTS OF MANY DIFFERENT PARTS. WITHOUT ONE OF THESE ASSETS MADAME TUSSAUDS WOULD EVENTUALLY DIE."
EHM ... MS. PICKLEBOURGH ... ?
MAYBE WE KNOW A WAY TO SOLVE THIS ...
-BOPP-

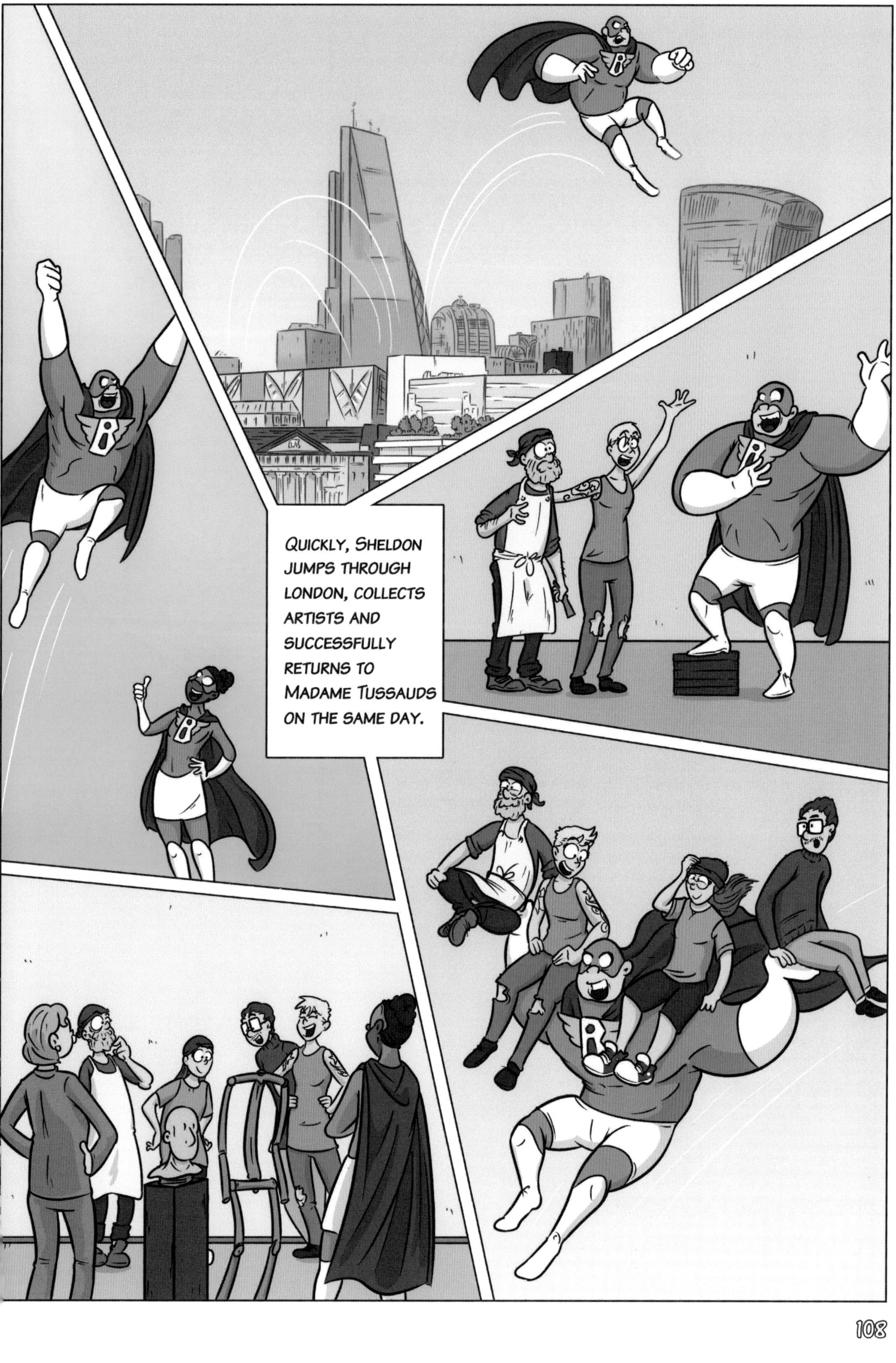
QUICKLY, SHELDON JUMPS THROUGH LONDON, COLLECTS ARTISTS AND SUCCESSFULLY RETURNS TO MADAME TUSSAUDS ON THE SAME DAY.

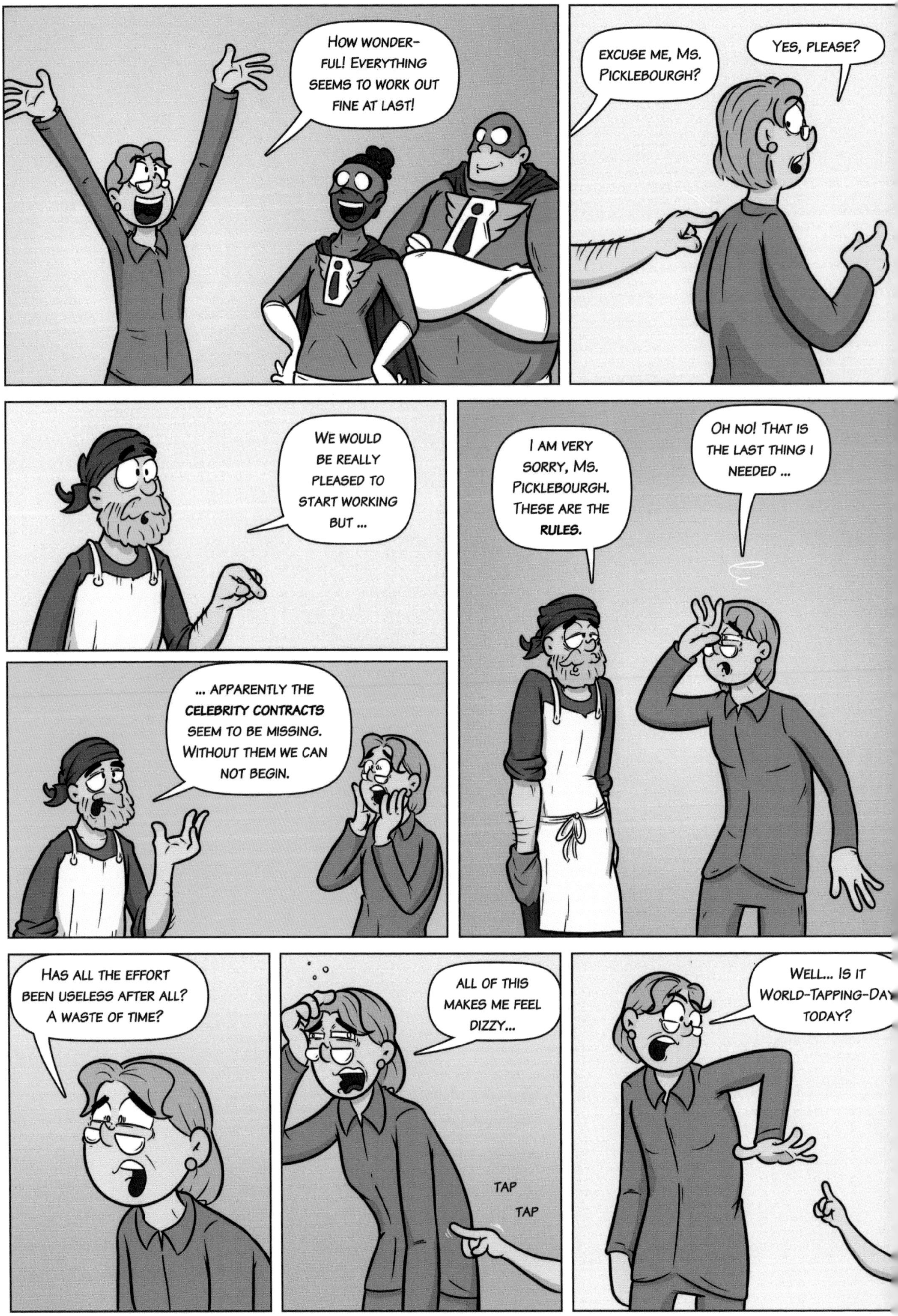
How wonder-ful! Everything seems to work out fine at last!
Excuse me, Ms. Picklebourgh?
Yes, please?
We would be really pleased to start working but ...
... apparently the **celebrity contracts** seem to be missing. Without them we can not begin.
I am very sorry, Ms. Picklebourgh. These are the **rules.**
Oh no! That is the last thing I needed ...
Has all the effort been useless after all? A waste of time?
All of this makes me feel dizzy...
TAP
TAP
Well... Is it World-Tapping-Da
today?

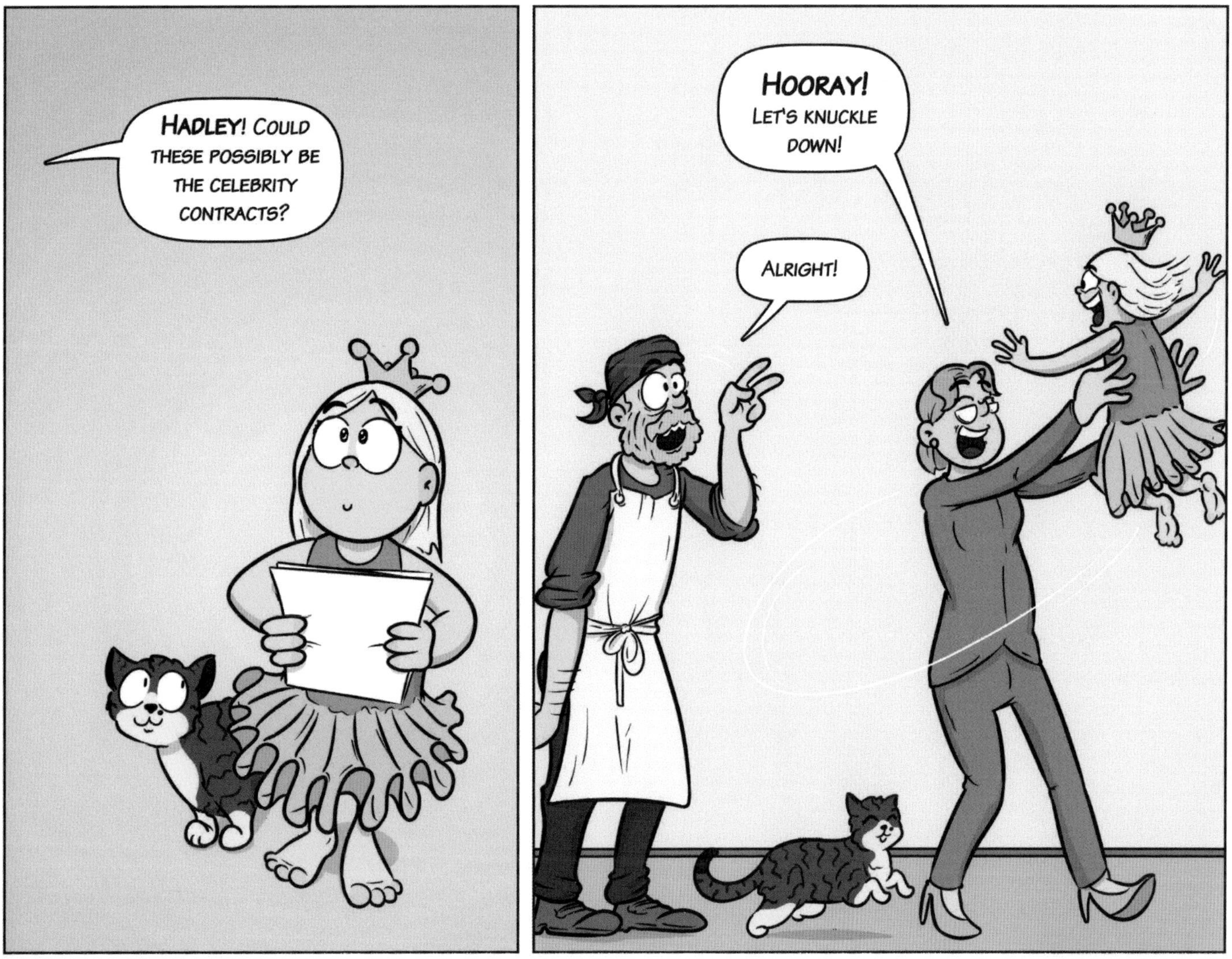
HADLEY! COULD THESE POSSIBLY BE THE CELEBRITY CONTRACTS?
HOORAY! LET'S KNUCKLE DOWN!
ALRIGHT!

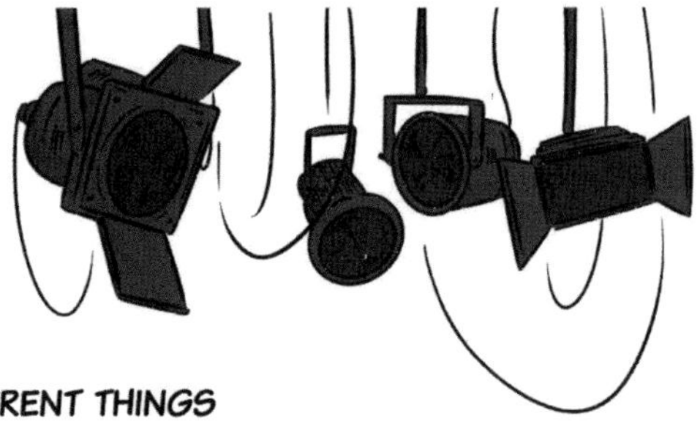

"THERE ARE MANY DIFFERENT THINGS GOING ON BEHIND THE SCENES OF A SUCCESSFUL BUSINESS, LIKE MADAME TUSSAUDS. MANY OF THESE THINGS ARE NOT VISIBLE AT FIRST. THEY HAPPEN ‚BEHIND THE CURTAINS'."

"LET'S TAKE A CLOSER LOOK AT WHAT ASPECTS THERE ARE, WHICH THE VISITORS OF THE WAX ATTRACTION DO NOT SEE."

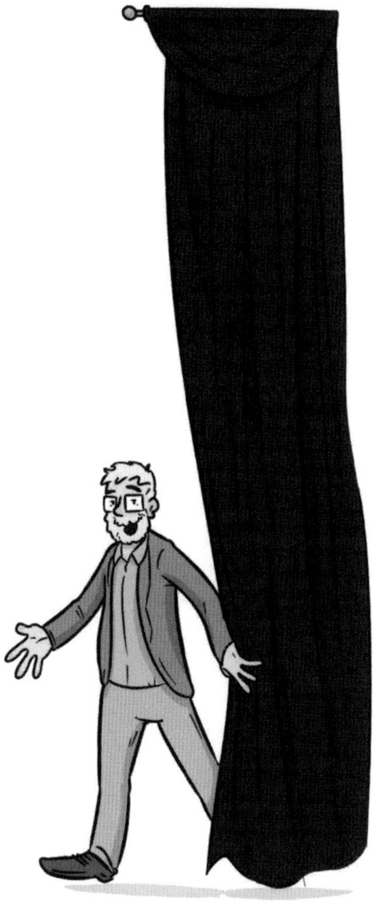

"A VERY **ESSENTIAL** **RESSOURCE** OF MADAME TUSSAUDS ARE ALL THE ARTISTS WHO CREATE THE WAX MODELS. THE ARTISTS, SCULPTORS, PAINTERS, PHOTOGRAPHERS ARE ALL WORLD-CLASS AT THEIR CRAFT AND COLLECTIVELY WORK ON THE WAX FIGURES."

"THEN THERE ARE THE STUDIOS WHERE THESE PEOPLE WORK. THEY NEED WORKSHOPS WITH ALL THE MATERIALS, TOOLS AND EQUIPMENT. MADAME TUSSAUDS HAS TO PROVIDE THAT AS WELL."

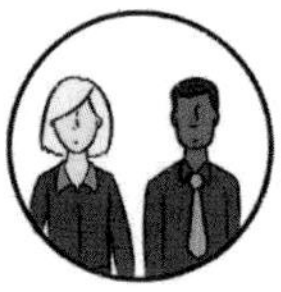

"MADAME TUSSAUDS COOPORATES WITH CELEBRITIES AND MAKES CONTRACTS WITH THEM. THE CELEBRITIES WILL POSE FOR THE ARTISTS, PHOTOGRAPHERS TAKE PICTURES FROM ALL ANGLES AND MEASURE THEIR PROPORTIONS."

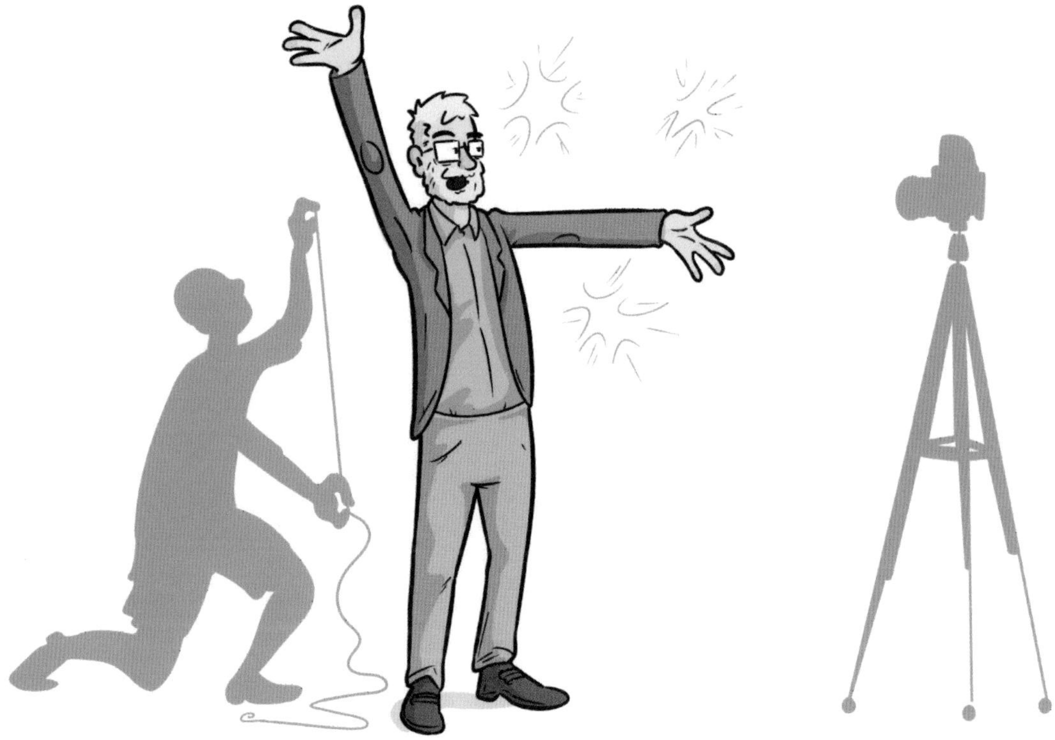

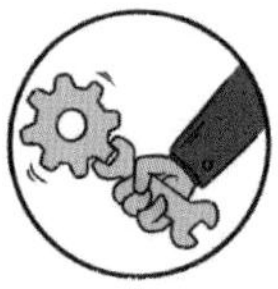

"BECAUSE OF MADAME TUSSAUDS TREMENDOUS SUCCESS THE BUSINESS HAS LOCATIONS WORLDWIDE. PEOPLE CAN VISIT THE WAX ATTRACTIONS IN GREAT CITIES LIKE LONDON, BERLIN OR NEW YORK."

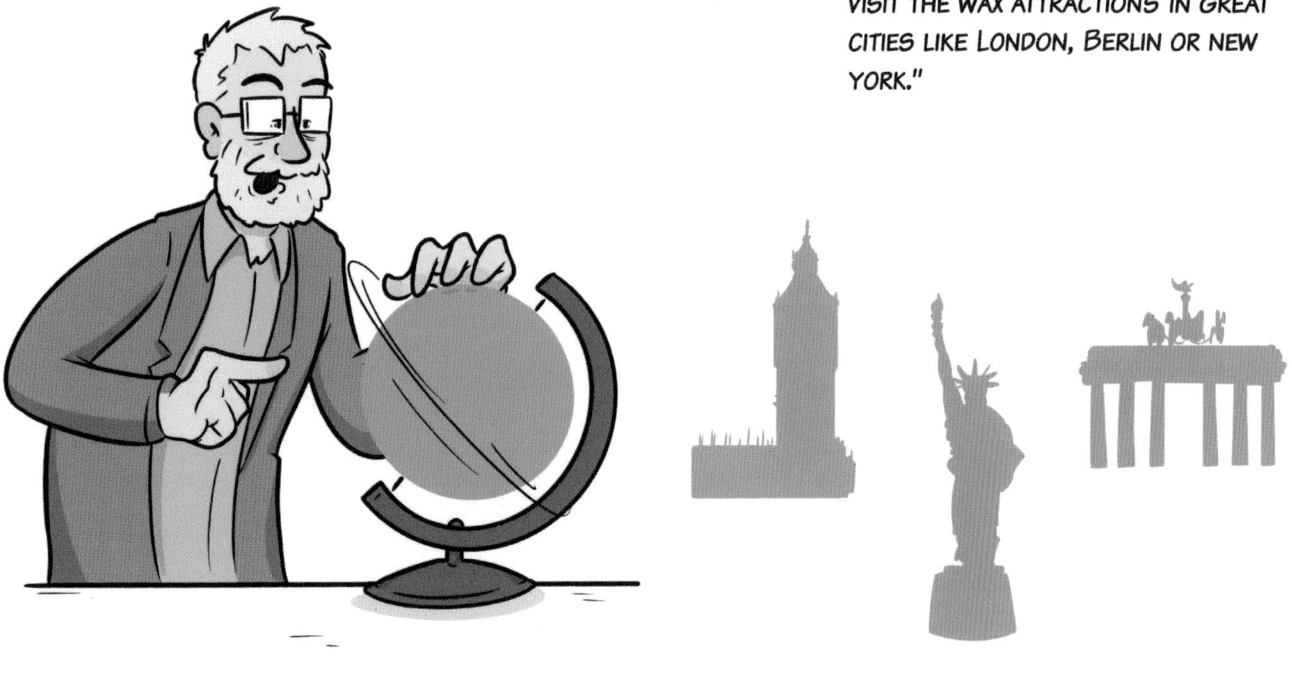

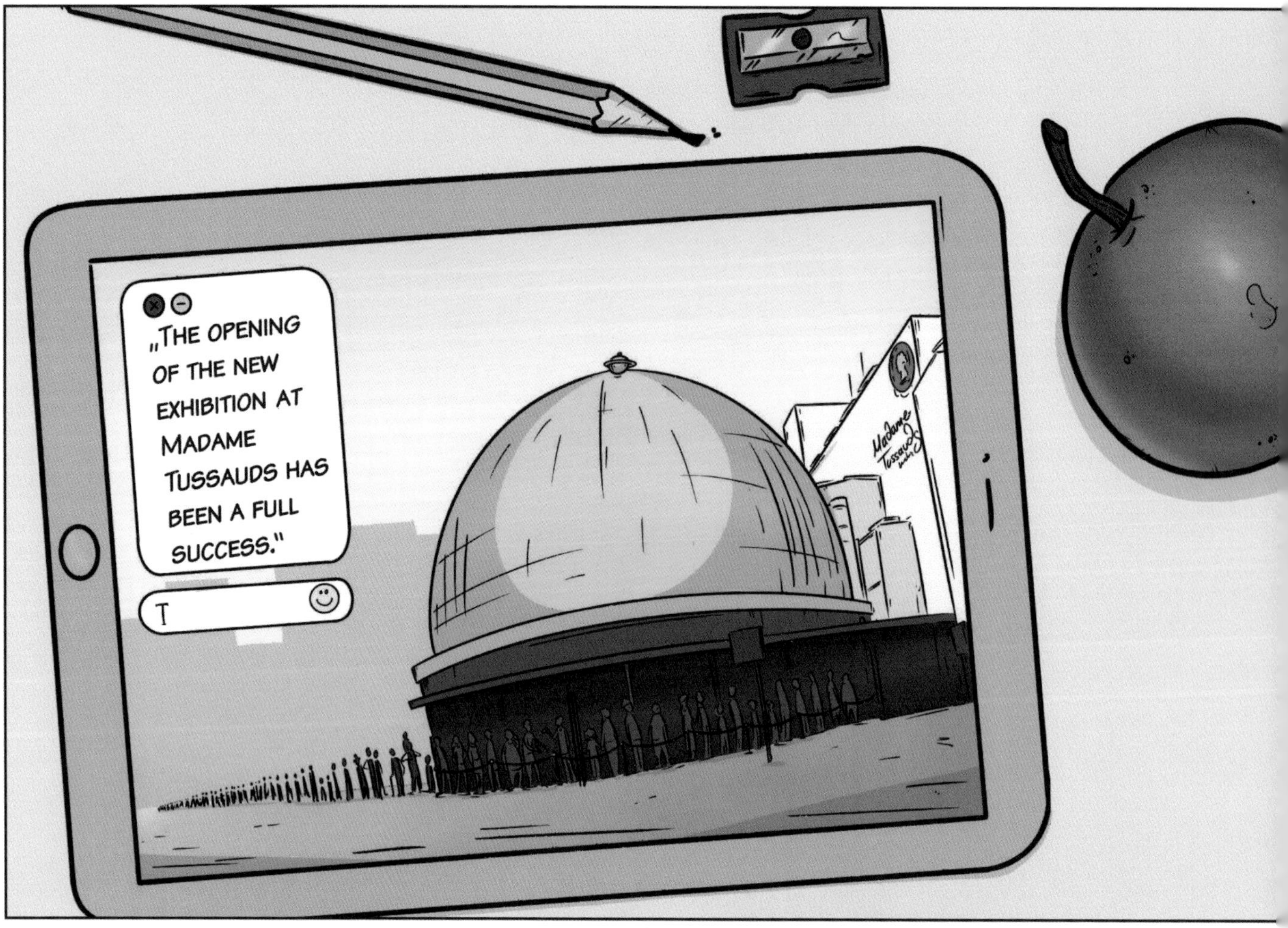
„THE OPENING OF THE NEW EXHIBITION AT MADAME TUSSAUDS HAS BEEN A FULL SUCCESS."
T
Madame Tussauds

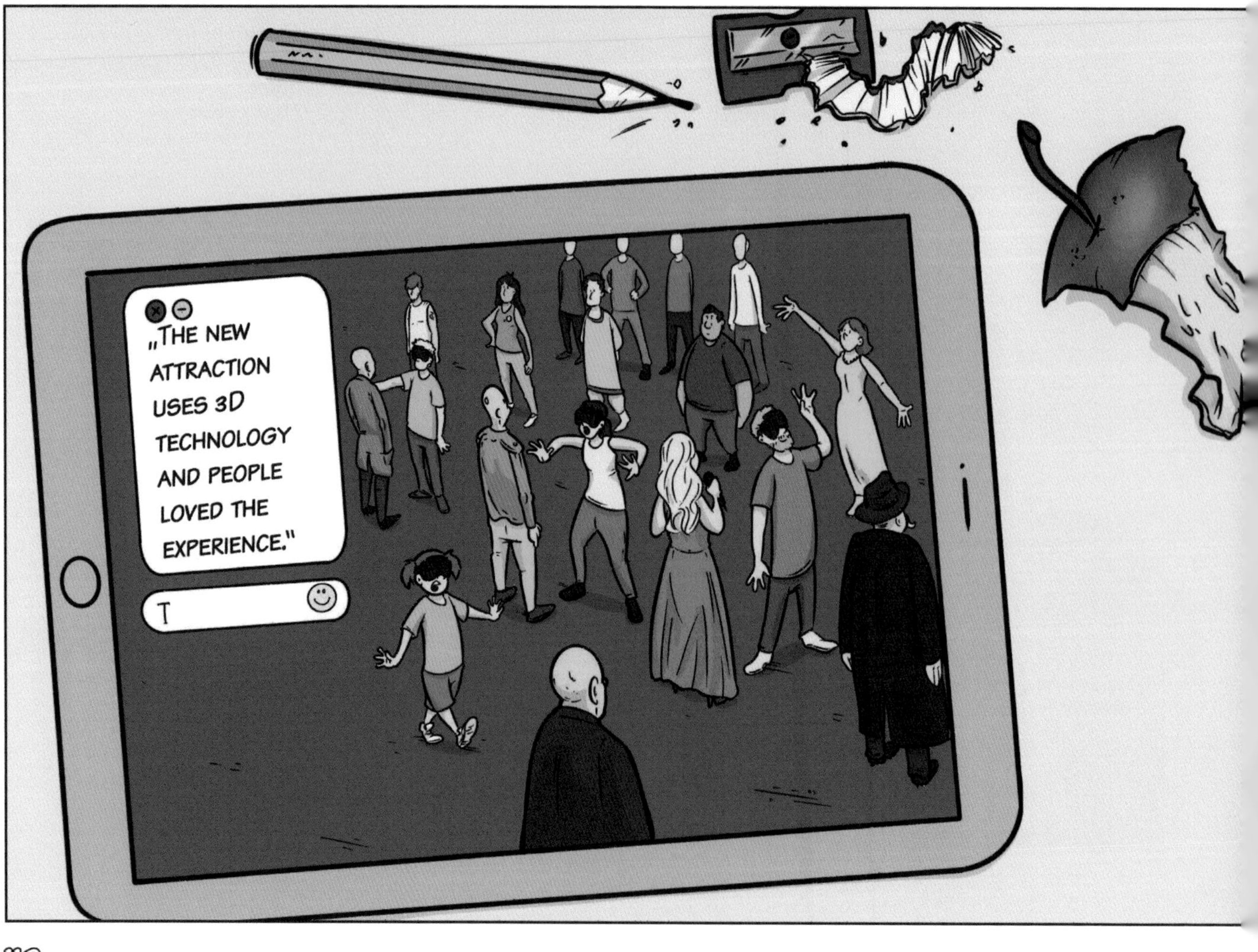
„THE NEW ATTRACTION USES 3D TECHNOLOGY AND PEOPLE LOVED THE EXPERIENCE."
T

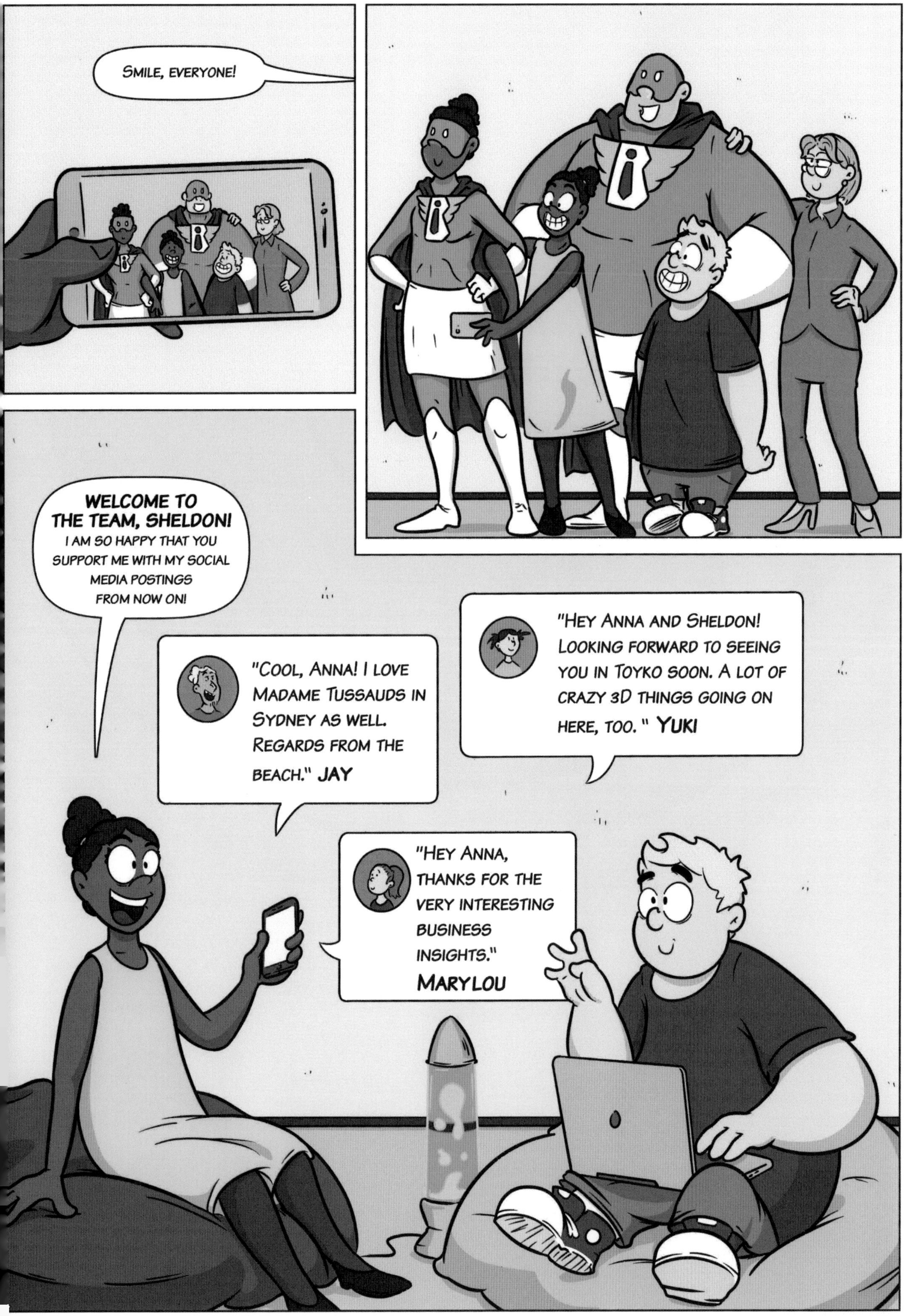

SMILE, EVERYONE!
WELCOME TO THE TEAM, SHELDON! I AM SO HAPPY THAT YOU SUPPORT ME WITH MY SOCIAL MEDIA POSTINGS FROM NOW ON!
"HEY ANNA AND SHELDON! LOOKING FORWARD TO SEEING YOU IN TOYKO SOON. A LOT OF CRAZY 3D THINGS GOING ON HERE, TOO. " YUKI
"COOL, ANNA! I LOVE MADAME TUSSAUDS IN SYDNEY AS WELL. REGARDS FROM THE BEACH." JAY
"HEY ANNA, THANKS FOR THE VERY INTERESTING BUSINESS INSIGHTS." MARYLOU

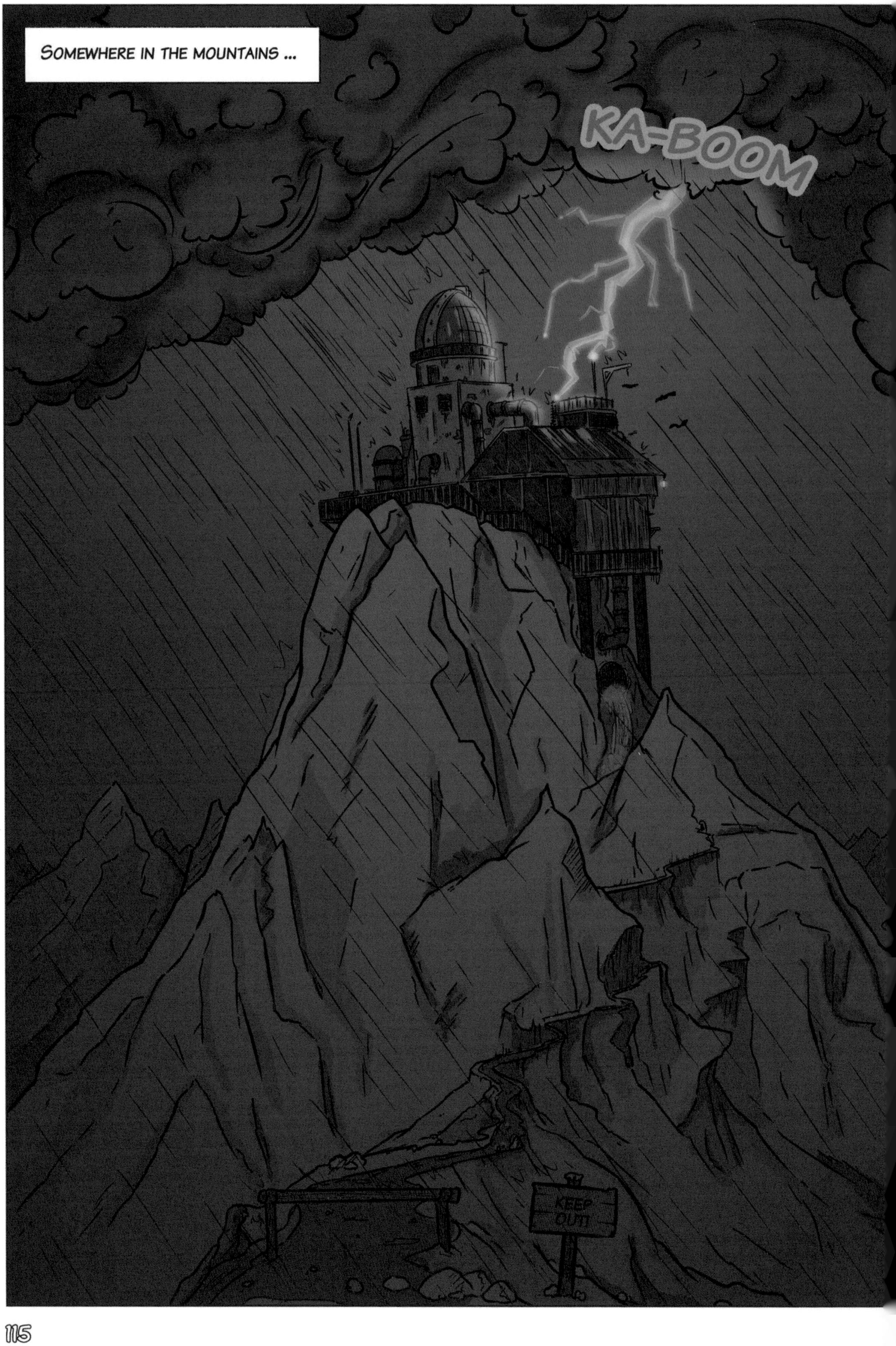
Somewhere in the mountains ...
KA-BOOM
KEEP OUT!

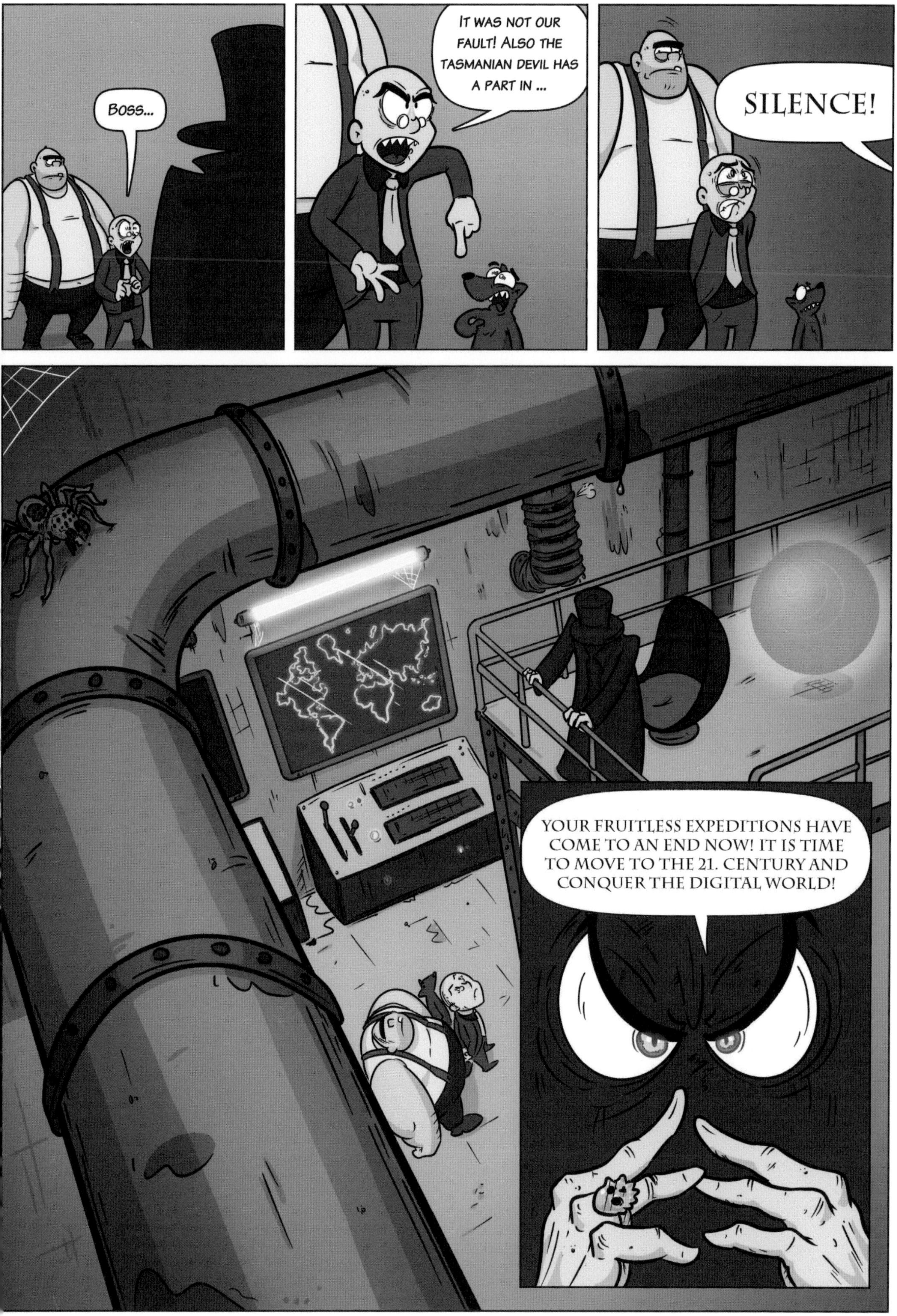
BOSS...
IT WAS NOT OUR FAULT! ALSO THE TASMANIAN DEVIL HAS A PART IN ...
SILENCE!
YOUR FRUITLESS EXPEDITIONS HAVE COME TO AN END NOW! IT IS TIME TO MOVE TO THE 21. CENTURY AND CONQUER THE DIGITAL WORLD!

Biz4Kids

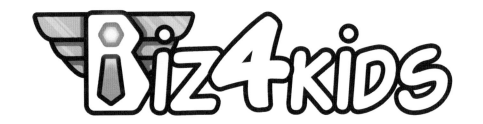

CHAPTER 3: TOKYO

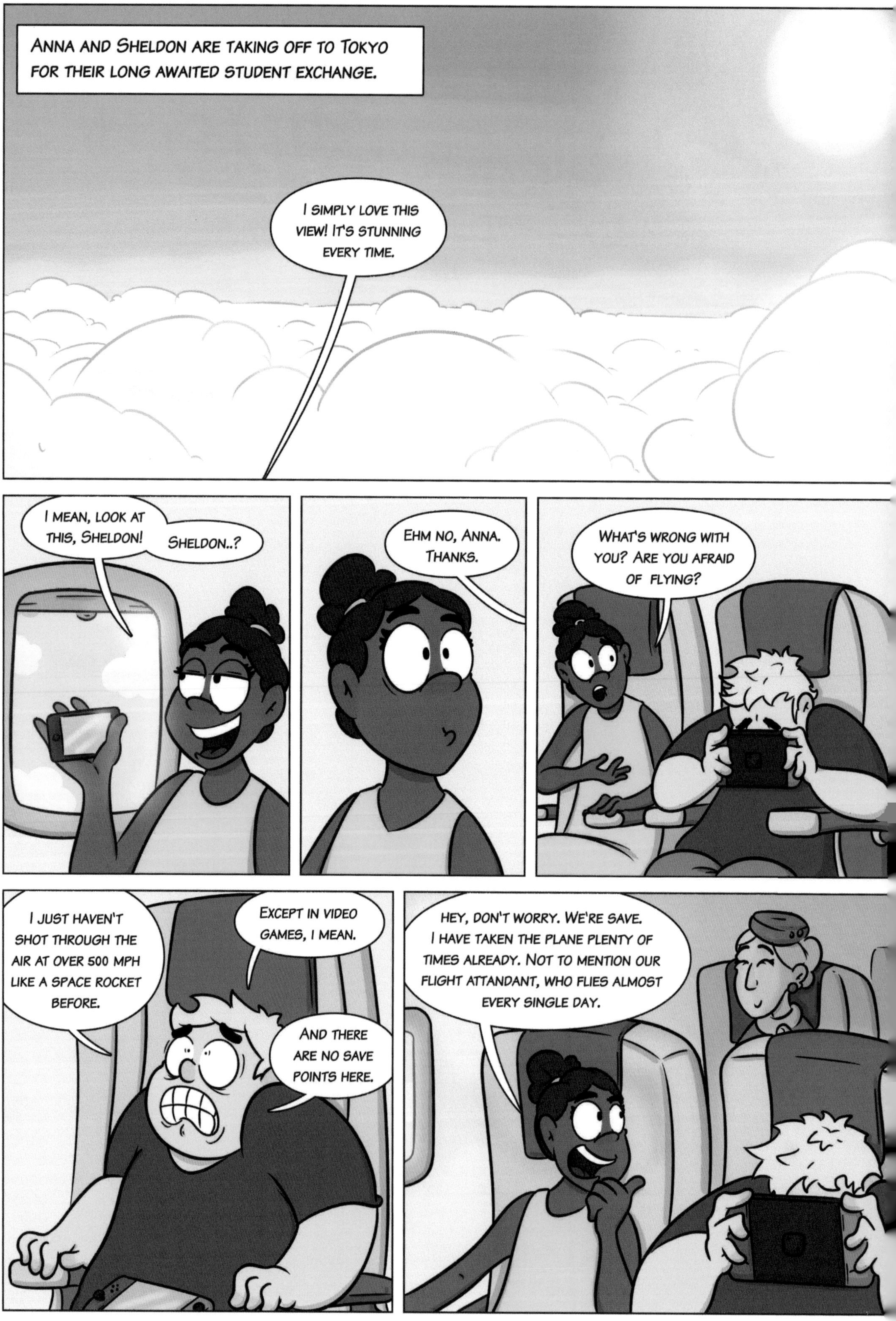

ANNA AND SHELDON ARE TAKING OFF TO TOKYO FOR THEIR LONG AWAITED STUDENT EXCHANGE.
I SIMPLY LOVE THIS VIEW! IT'S STUNNING EVERY TIME.
I MEAN, LOOK AT THIS, SHELDON!
SHELDON..?
EHM NO, ANNA. THANKS.
WHAT'S WRONG WITH YOU? ARE YOU AFRAID OF FLYING?
I JUST HAVEN'T SHOT THROUGH THE AIR AT OVER 500 MPH LIKE A SPACE ROCKET BEFORE.
EXCEPT IN VIDEO GAMES, I MEAN.
AND THERE ARE NO SAVE POINTS HERE.
HEY, DON'T WORRY. WE'RE SAVE. I HAVE TAKEN THE PLANE PLENTY OF TIMES ALREADY. NOT TO MENTION OUR FLIGHT ATTANDANT, WHO FLIES ALMOST EVERY SINGLE DAY.

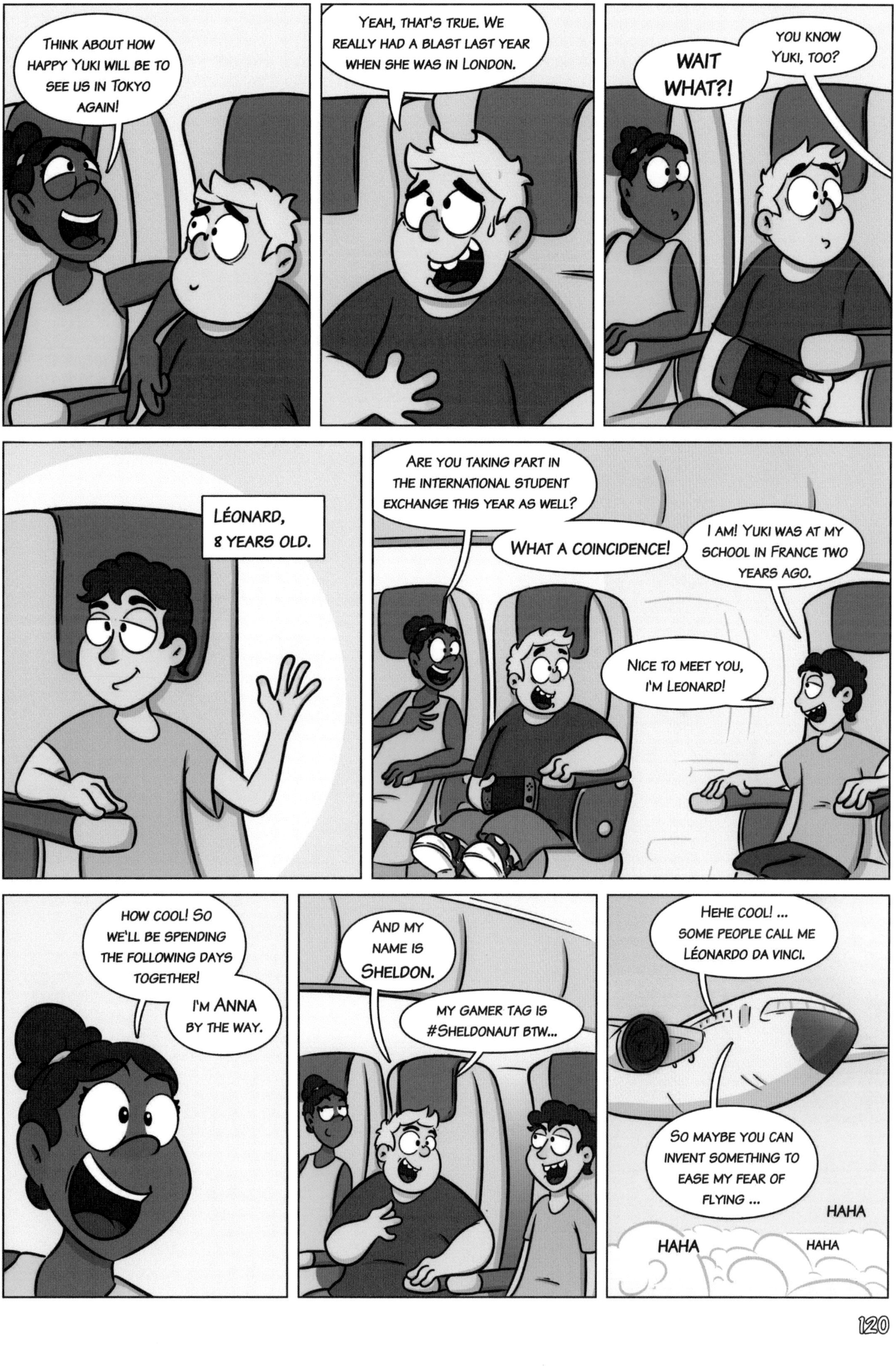
Think about how happy Yuki will be to see us in Tokyo again!
Yeah, that's true. We really had a blast last year when she was in London.
Wait what?!
You know Yuki, too?
Léonard, 8 years old.
Are you taking part in the international student exchange this year as well?
What a coincidence!
I am! Yuki was at my school in France two years ago.
Nice to meet you, I'm Leonard!
How cool! So we'll be spending the following days together!
I'm Anna by the way.
And my name is Sheldon.
My gamer tag is #Sheldonaut btw...
Hehe cool! ... some people call me Léonardo da vinci.
So maybe you can invent something to ease my fear of flying ...
HAHA
HAHA
HAHA

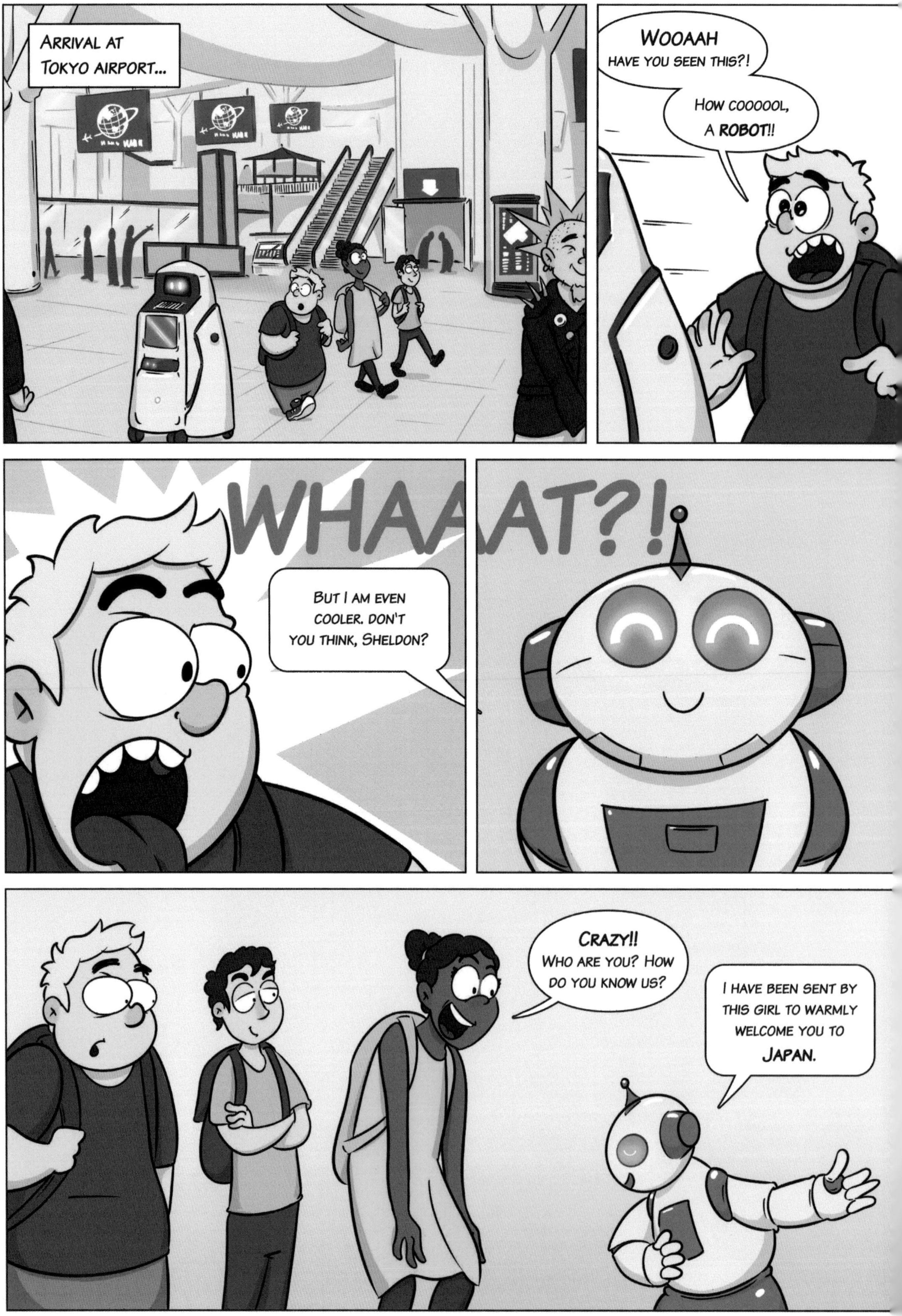

Arrival at Tokyo airport...
Wooaah have you seen this?!
How coooool, a ROBOT!!
WHAAAT?!
But I am even cooler. Don't you think, Sheldon?
Crazy!! Who are you? How do you know us?
I have been sent by this girl to warmly welcome you to Japan.

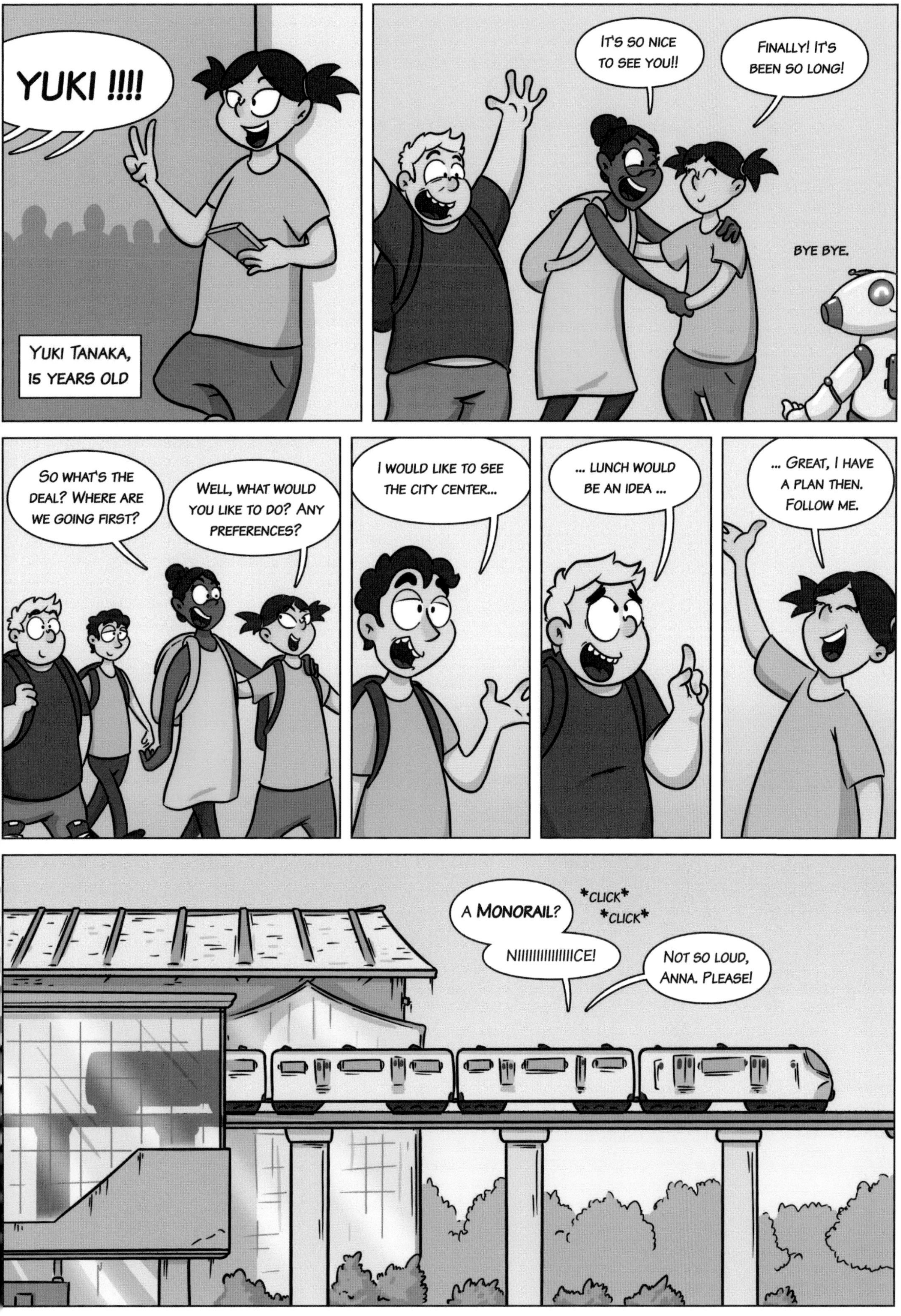
YUKI !!!!
YUKI TANAKA, 15 YEARS OLD
IT'S SO NICE TO SEE YOU!!
FINALLY! IT'S BEEN SO LONG!
BYE BYE.
SO WHAT'S THE DEAL? WHERE ARE WE GOING FIRST?
WELL, WHAT WOULD YOU LIKE TO DO? ANY PREFERENCES?
I WOULD LIKE TO SEE THE CITY CENTER...
... LUNCH WOULD BE AN IDEA ...
... GREAT, I HAVE A PLAN THEN. FOLLOW ME.
A MONORAIL?
CLICK *CLICK*
NIIIIIIIIIIIIIICE!
NOT SO LOUD, ANNA. PLEASE!

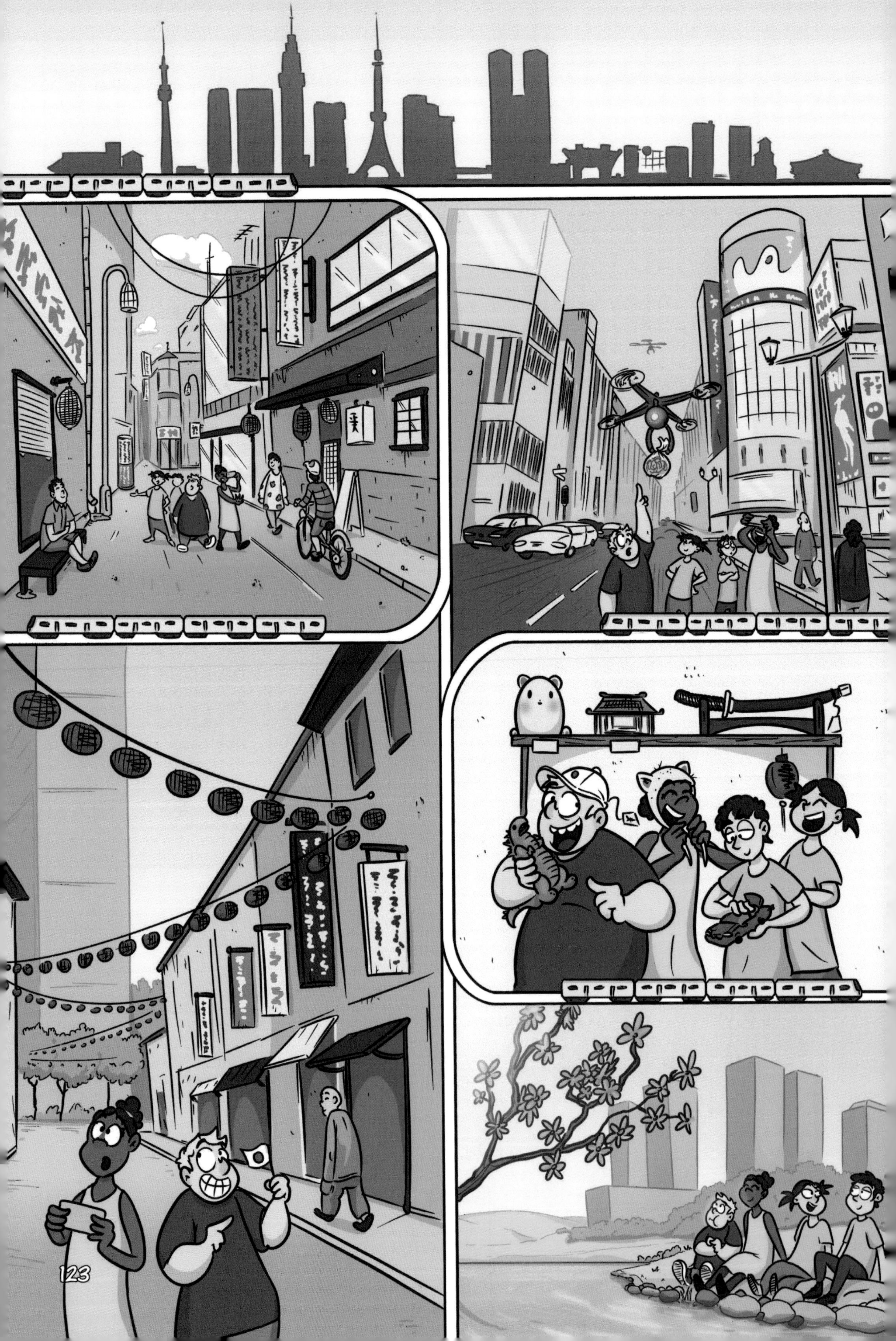

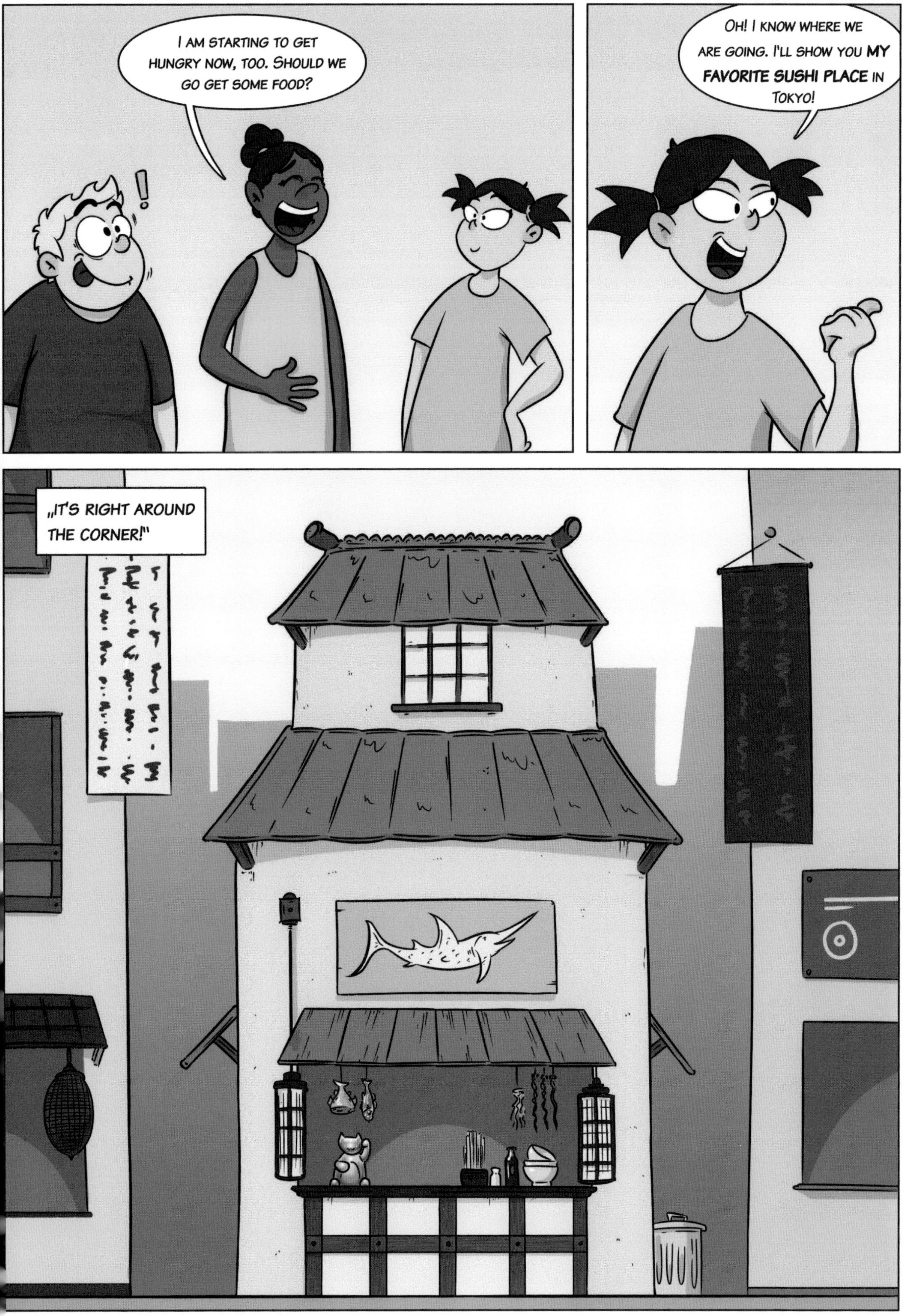

I AM STARTING TO GET HUNGRY NOW, TOO. SHOULD WE GO GET SOME FOOD?
!
OH! I KNOW WHERE WE ARE GOING. I'LL SHOW YOU **MY FAVORITE SUSHI PLACE** IN TOKYO!
„IT'S RIGHT AROUND THE CORNER!"

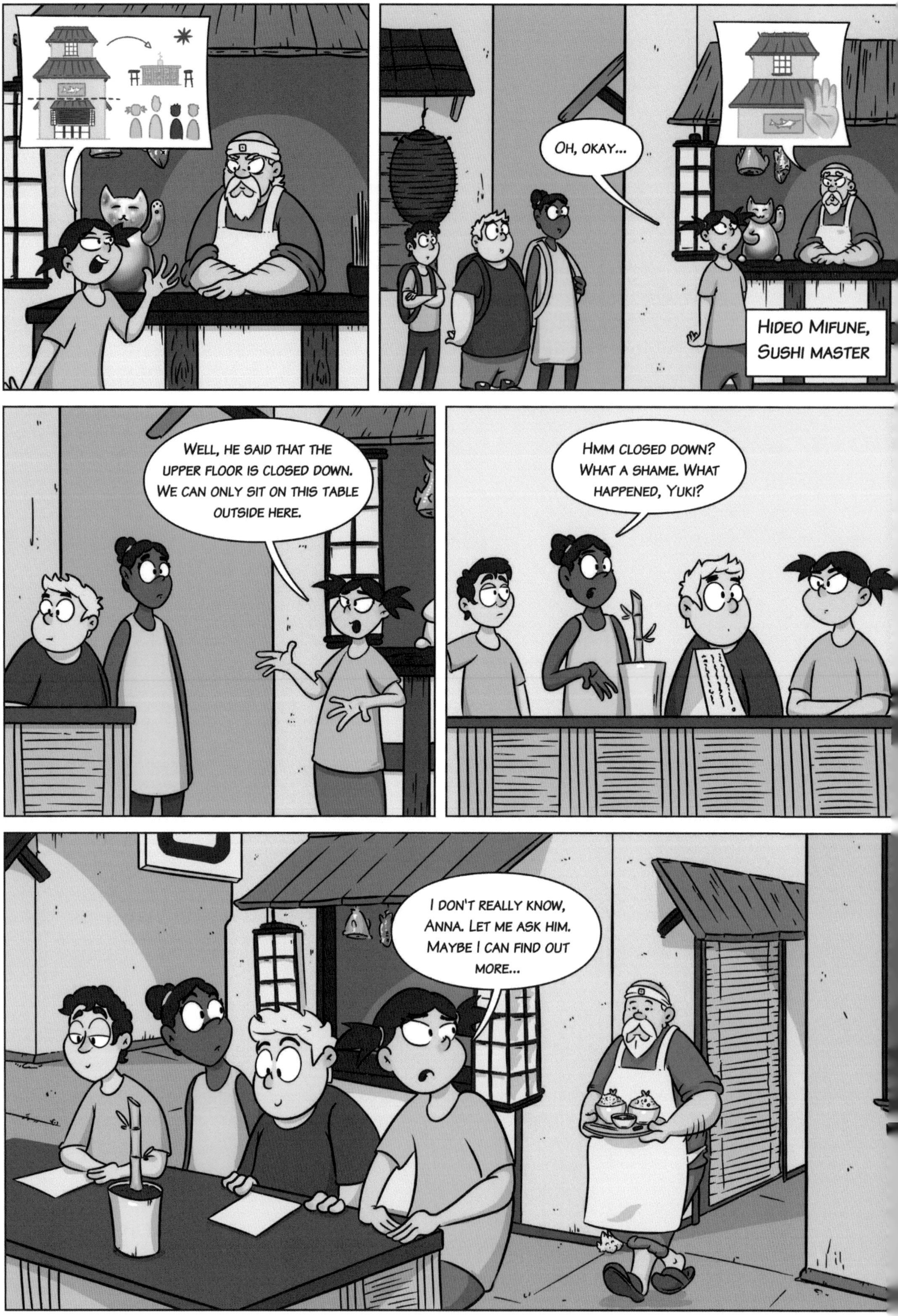
OH, OKAY...
HIDEO MIFUNE, SUSHI MASTER
WELL, HE SAID THAT THE UPPER FLOOR IS CLOSED DOWN. WE CAN ONLY SIT ON THIS TABLE OUTSIDE HERE.
HMM CLOSED DOWN? WHAT A SHAME. WHAT HAPPENED, YUKI?
I DON'T REALLY KNOW, ANNA. LET ME ASK HIM. MAYBE I CAN FIND OUT MORE...

* KONICHIWA, MR. MIFUNE. IS THERE A TABLE AVAILABLE FOR THE FOUR OF US UPSTAIRS, PLEASE? [TRANSLATED FROM JAPANESE]

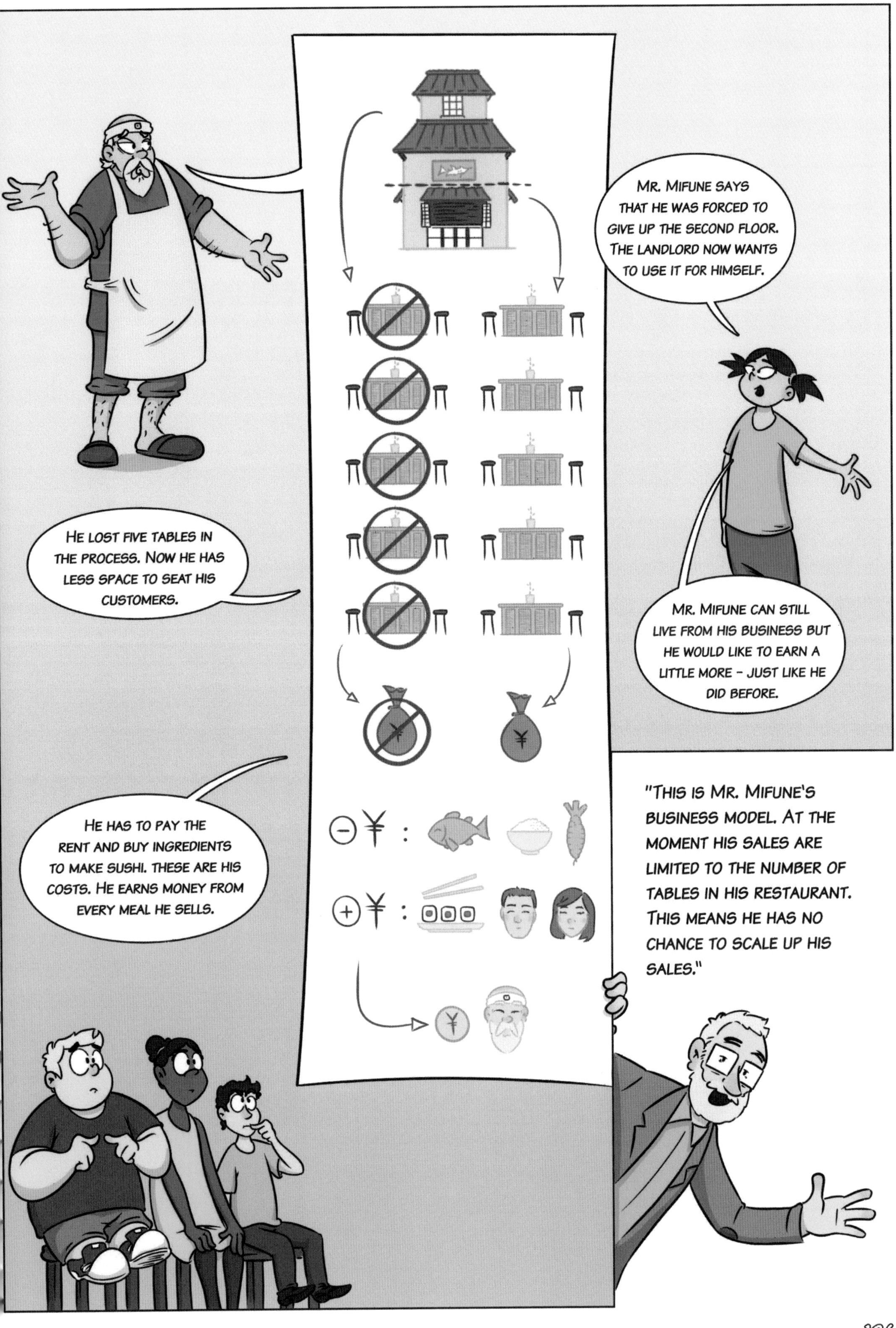

MR. MIFUNE SAYS THAT HE WAS FORCED TO GIVE UP THE SECOND FLOOR. THE LANDLORD NOW WANTS TO USE IT FOR HIMSELF.
HE LOST FIVE TABLES IN THE PROCESS. NOW HE HAS LESS SPACE TO SEAT HIS CUSTOMERS.
MR. MIFUNE CAN STILL LIVE FROM HIS BUSINESS BUT HE WOULD LIKE TO EARN A LITTLE MORE - JUST LIKE HE DID BEFORE.
HE HAS TO PAY THE RENT AND BUY INGREDIENTS TO MAKE SUSHI. THESE ARE HIS COSTS. HE EARNS MONEY FROM EVERY MEAL HE SELLS.
"THIS IS MR. MIFUNE'S BUSINESS MODEL. AT THE MOMENT HIS SALES ARE LIMITED TO THE NUMBER OF TABLES IN HIS RESTAURANT. THIS MEANS HE HAS NO CHANCE TO SCALE UP HIS SALES."

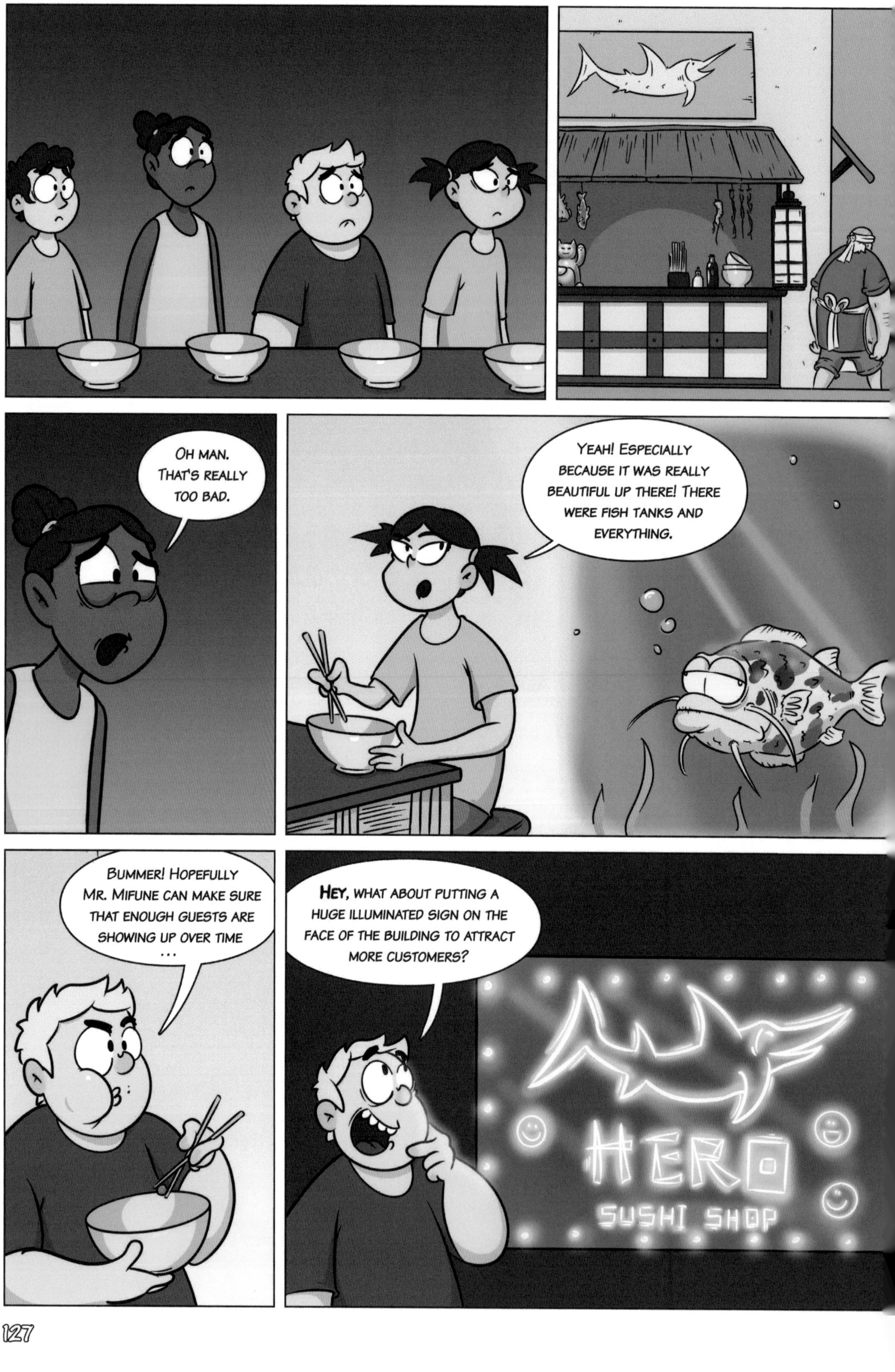

OH MAN. THAT'S REALLY TOO BAD.
YEAH! ESPECIALLY BECAUSE IT WAS REALLY BEAUTIFUL UP THERE! THERE WERE FISH TANKS AND EVERYTHING.
BUMMER! HOPEFULLY MR. MIFUNE CAN MAKE SURE THAT ENOUGH GUESTS ARE SHOWING UP OVER TIME . . .
HEY, WHAT ABOUT PUTTING A HUGE ILLUMINATED SIGN ON THE FACE OF THE BUILDING TO ATTRACT MORE CUSTOMERS?
HERO
SUSHI SHOP

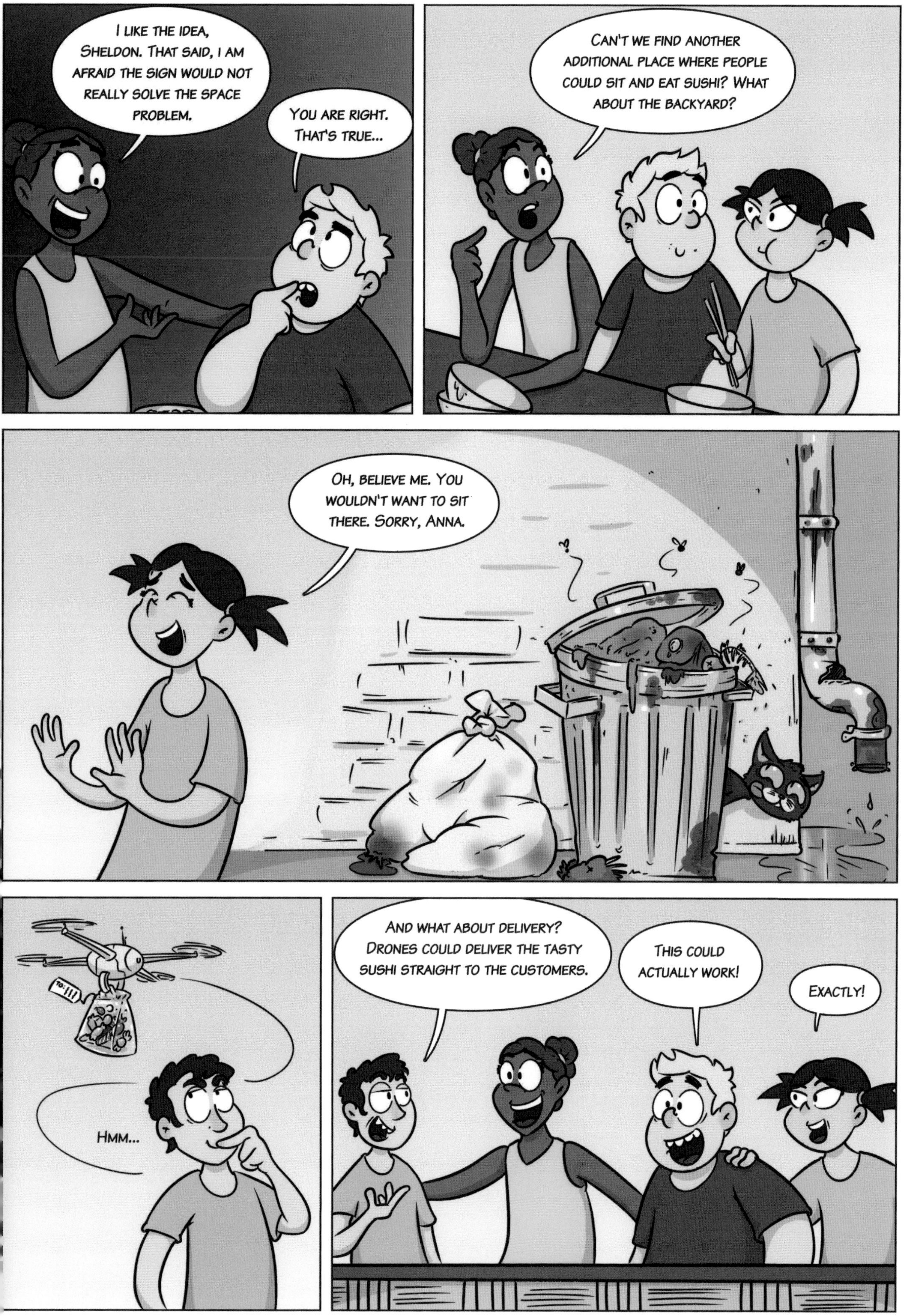
I LIKE THE IDEA, SHELDON. THAT SAID, I AM AFRAID THE SIGN WOULD NOT REALLY SOLVE THE SPACE PROBLEM.
YOU ARE RIGHT. THAT'S TRUE...
CAN'T WE FIND ANOTHER ADDITIONAL PLACE WHERE PEOPLE COULD SIT AND EAT SUSHI? WHAT ABOUT THE BACKYARD?
OH, BELIEVE ME. YOU WOULDN'T WANT TO SIT THERE. SORRY, ANNA.
HMM...
AND WHAT ABOUT DELIVERY? DRONES COULD DELIVER THE TASTY SUSHI STRAIGHT TO THE CUSTOMERS.
THIS COULD ACTUALLY WORK!
EXACTLY!

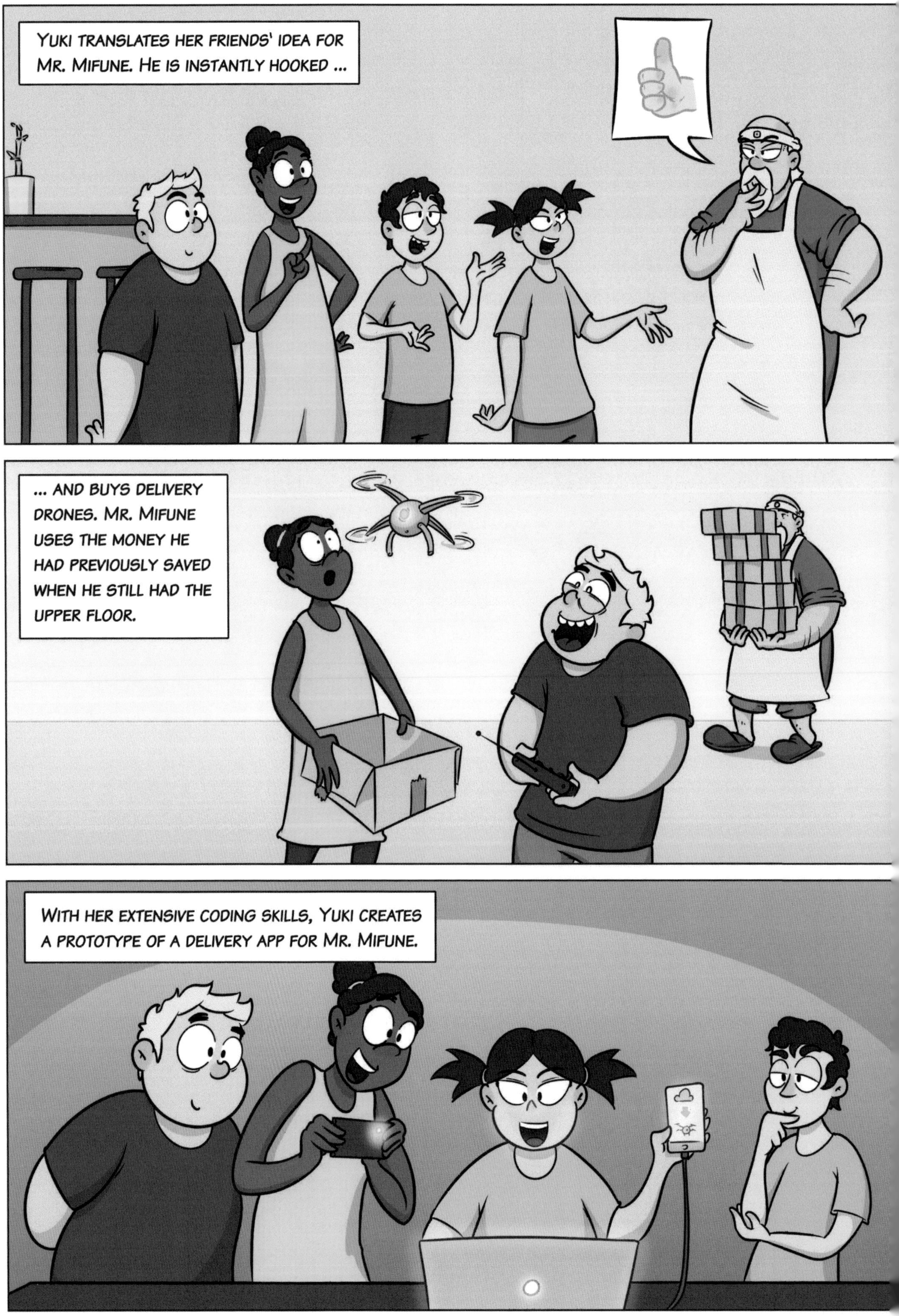
YUKI TRANSLATES HER FRIENDS' IDEA FOR MR. MIFUNE. HE IS INSTANTLY HOOKED ...
... AND BUYS DELIVERY DRONES. MR. MIFUNE USES THE MONEY HE HAD PREVIOUSLY SAVED WHEN HE STILL HAD THE UPPER FLOOR.
WITH HER EXTENSIVE CODING SKILLS, YUKI CREATES A PROTOTYPE OF A DELIVERY APP FOR MR. MIFUNE.

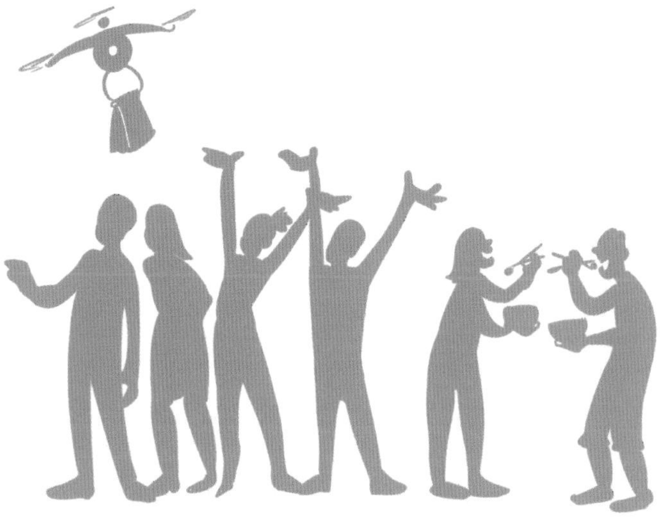

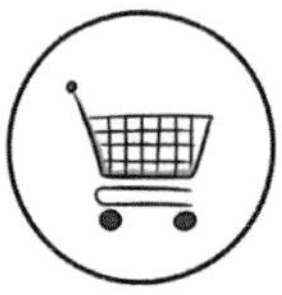

"MR. MIFUNE CHANGES HIS BUSINESS MODEL NOW. INSTEAD OF BEING BOUND TO THE NUMBER OF TABLES IN HIS RESTAURANT, HE CAN NOW SERVE MANY CUSTOMERS REMOTELY."

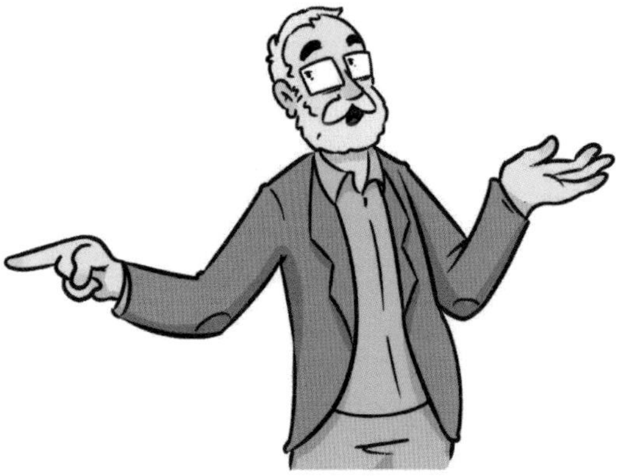

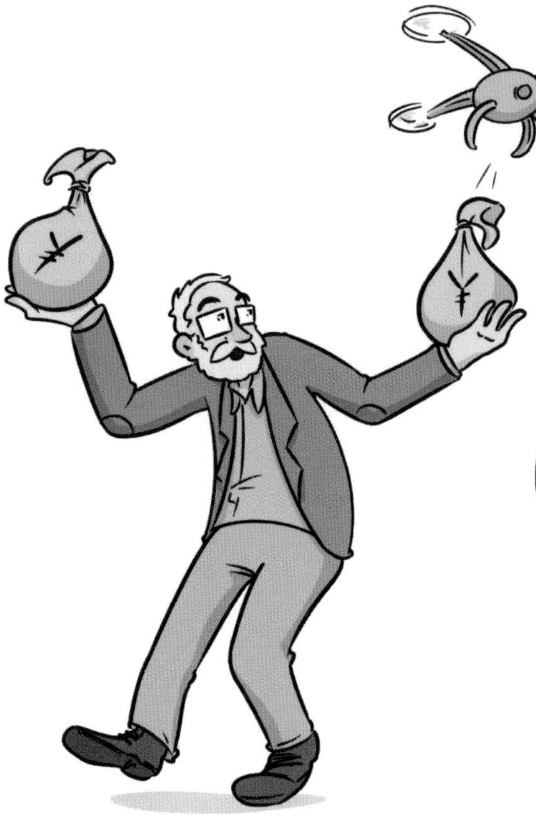

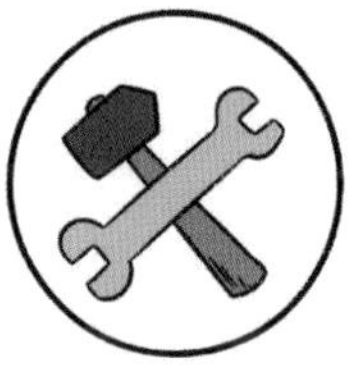

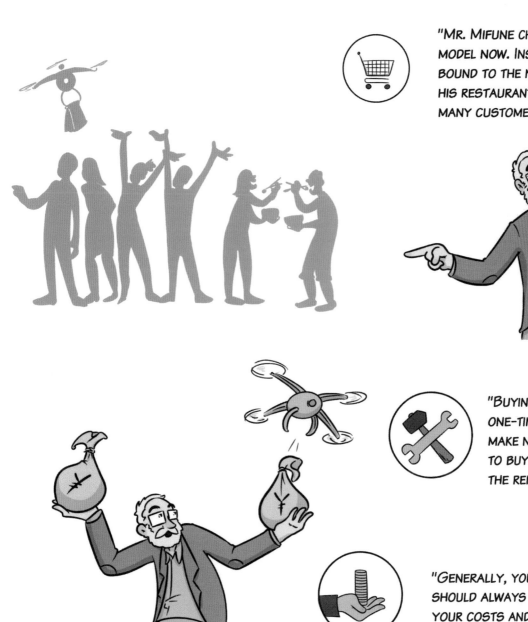

"BUYING DELIVERY DRONES IS A ONE-TIME INVESTMENT HE HAS TO MAKE NOW. ADDITIONALLY, HE HAS TO BUY SUSHI INGREDIENTS, PAY THE RENT AND INVEST HIS TIME."

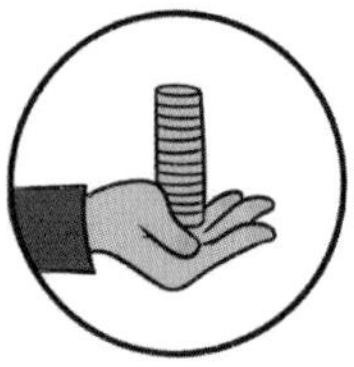

"GENERALLY, YOUR EARNINGS SHOULD ALWAYS BE HIGHER THAN YOUR COSTS AND INVESTMENTS. "

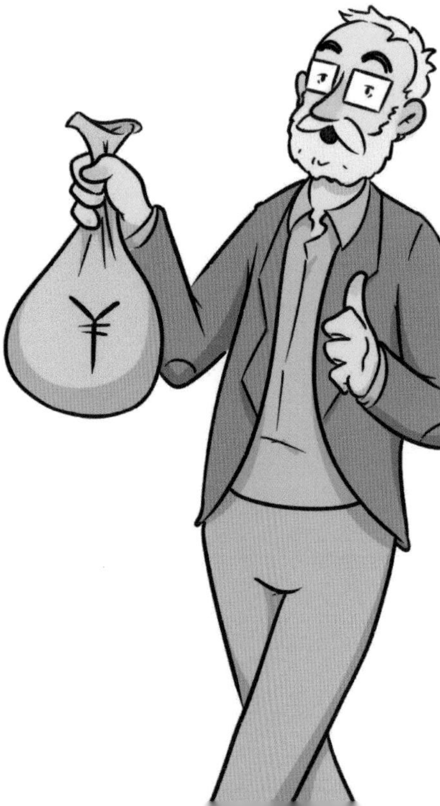

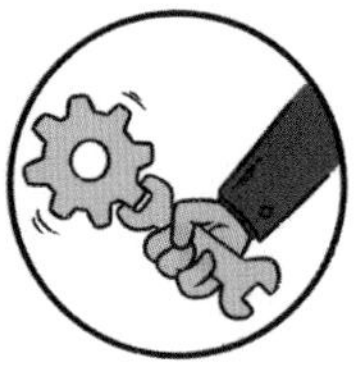

"THE SUSHI BUSINESS IS NOW SCALABLE. THIS MEANS MR. MIFUNE CAN EARN MORE MONEY THAN BEFORE BECAUS MORE PEOPLE CAN BUY SUSHI FROM HIM."

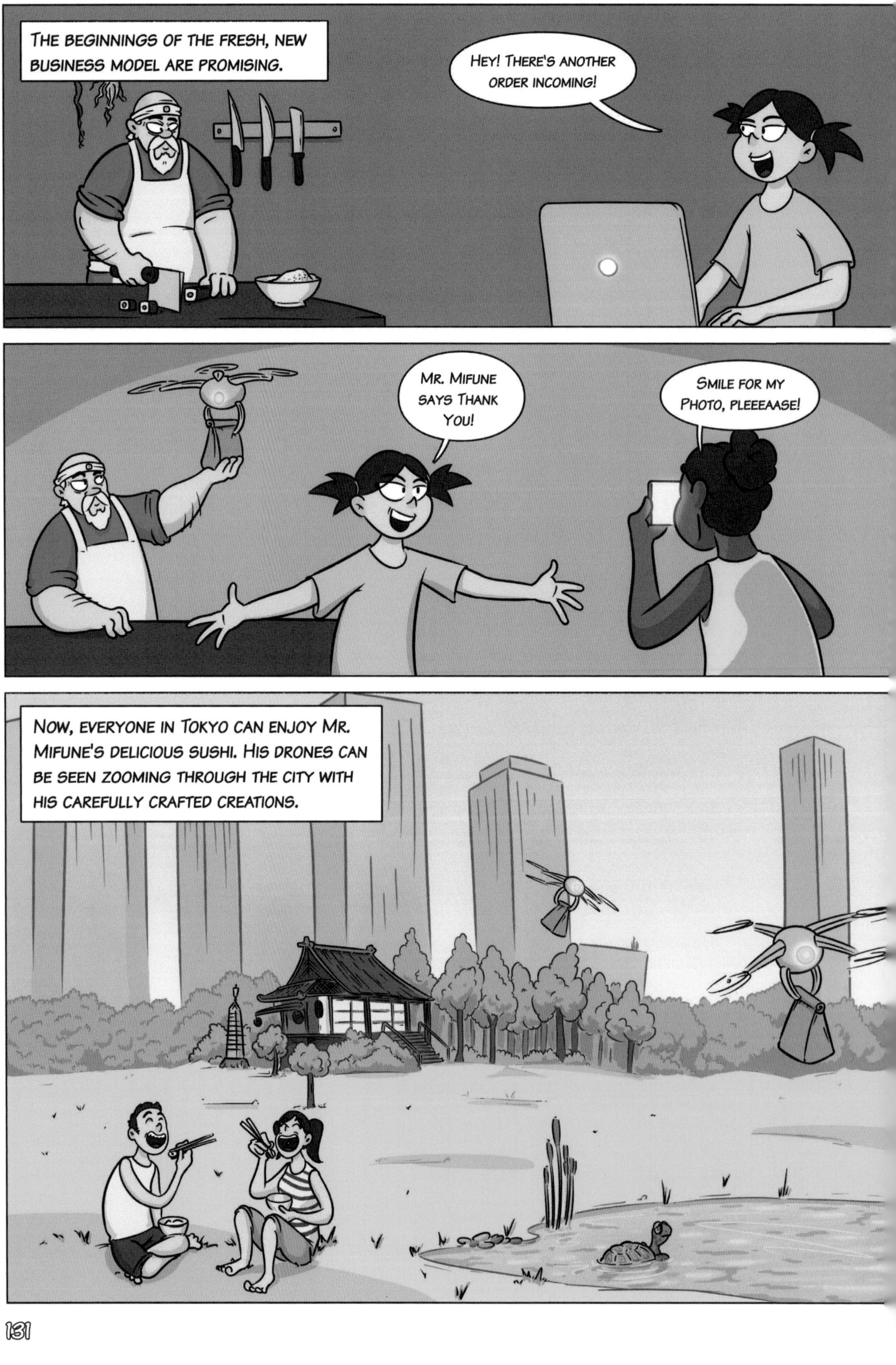

THE BEGINNINGS OF THE FRESH, NEW BUSINESS MODEL ARE PROMISING.
HEY! THERE'S ANOTHER ORDER INCOMING!
MR. MIFUNE SAYS THANK YOU!
SMILE FOR MY PHOTO, PLEEEAASE!
NOW, EVERYONE IN TOKYO CAN ENJOY MR. MIFUNE'S DELICIOUS SUSHI. HIS DRONES CAN BE SEEN ZOOMING THROUGH THE CITY WITH HIS CAREFULLY CRAFTED CREATIONS.

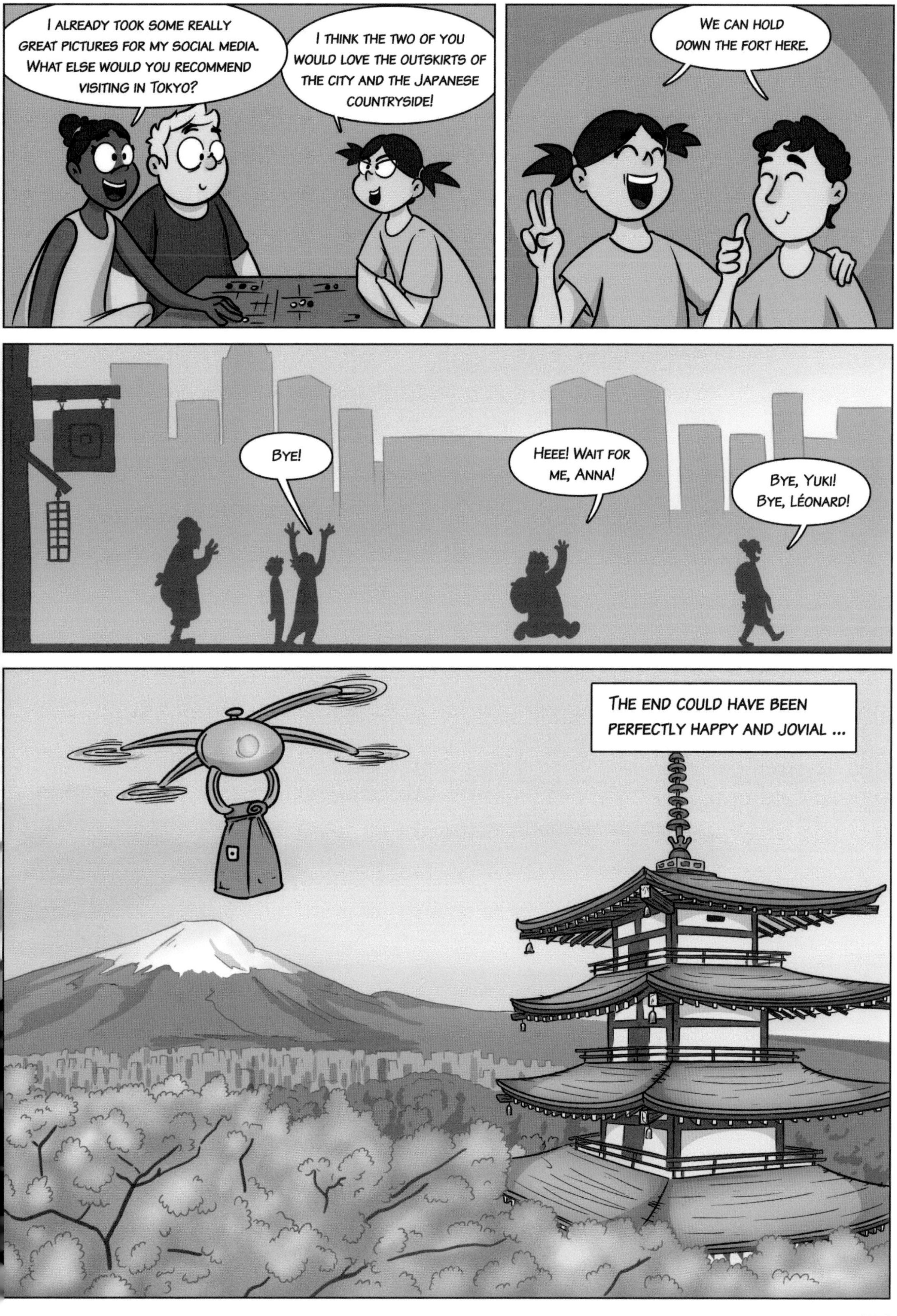
I ALREADY TOOK SOME REALLY GREAT PICTURES FOR MY SOCIAL MEDIA. WHAT ELSE WOULD YOU RECOMMEND VISITING IN TOKYO?
I THINK THE TWO OF YOU WOULD LOVE THE OUTSKIRTS OF THE CITY AND THE JAPANESE COUNTRYSIDE!
WE CAN HOLD DOWN THE FORT HERE.
BYE!
HEEE! WAIT FOR ME, ANNA!
BYE, YUKI! BYE, LÉONARD!
THE END COULD HAVE BEEN PERFECTLY HAPPY AND JOVIAL ...

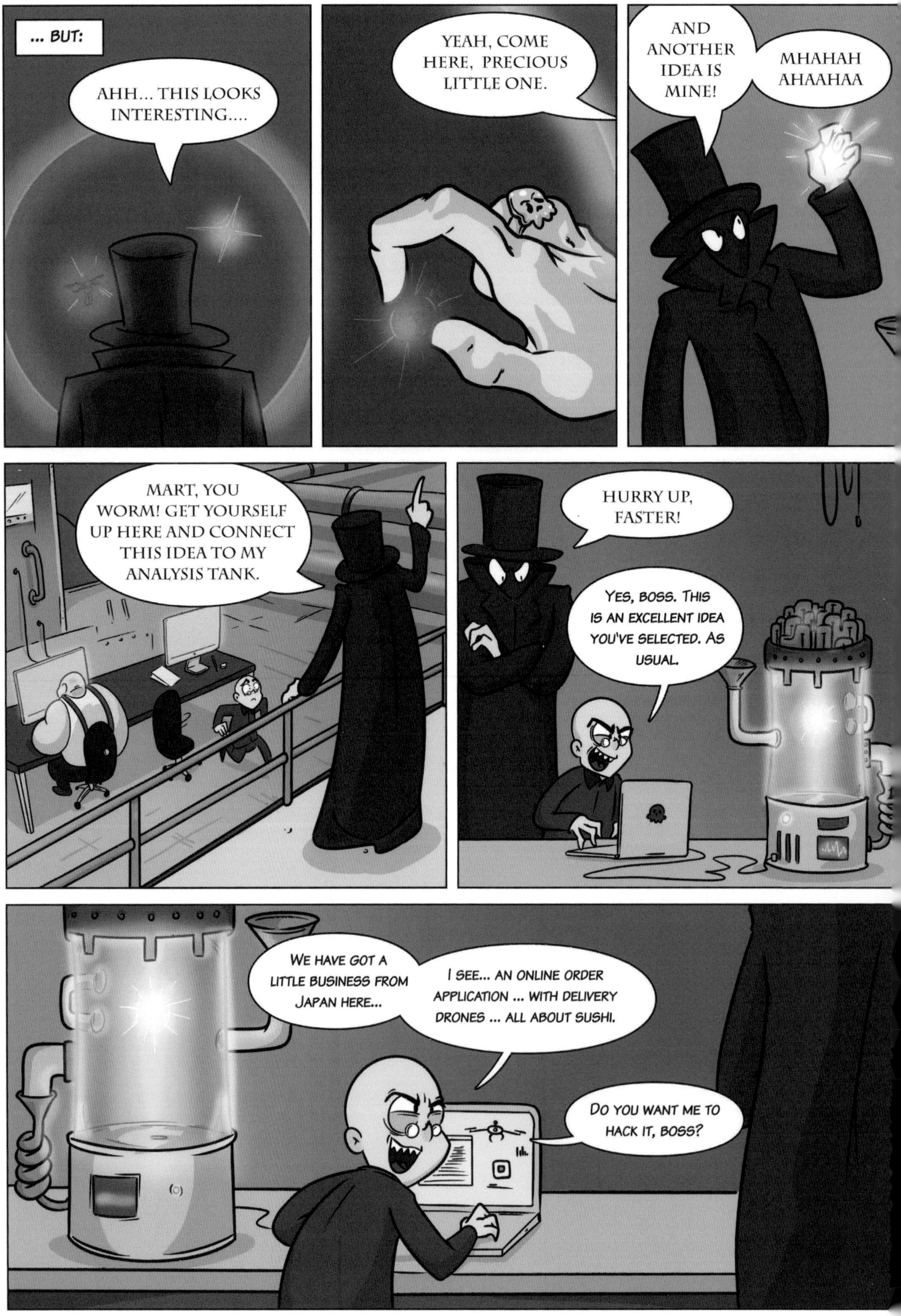
... BUT:
AHH... THIS LOOKS INTERESTING....
YEAH, COME HERE, PRECIOUS LITTLE ONE.
AND ANOTHER IDEA IS MINE!
MHAHAH AHAAHAA
MART, YOU WORM! GET YOURSELF UP HERE AND CONNECT THIS IDEA TO MY ANALYSIS TANK.
HURRY UP, FASTER!
YES, BOSS. THIS IS AN EXCELLENT IDEA YOU'VE SELECTED. AS USUAL.
WE HAVE GOT A LITTLE BUSINESS FROM JAPAN HERE...
I SEE... AN ONLINE ORDER APPLICATION ... WITH DELIVERY DRONES ... ALL ABOUT SUSHI.
DO YOU WANT ME TO HACK IT, BOSS?

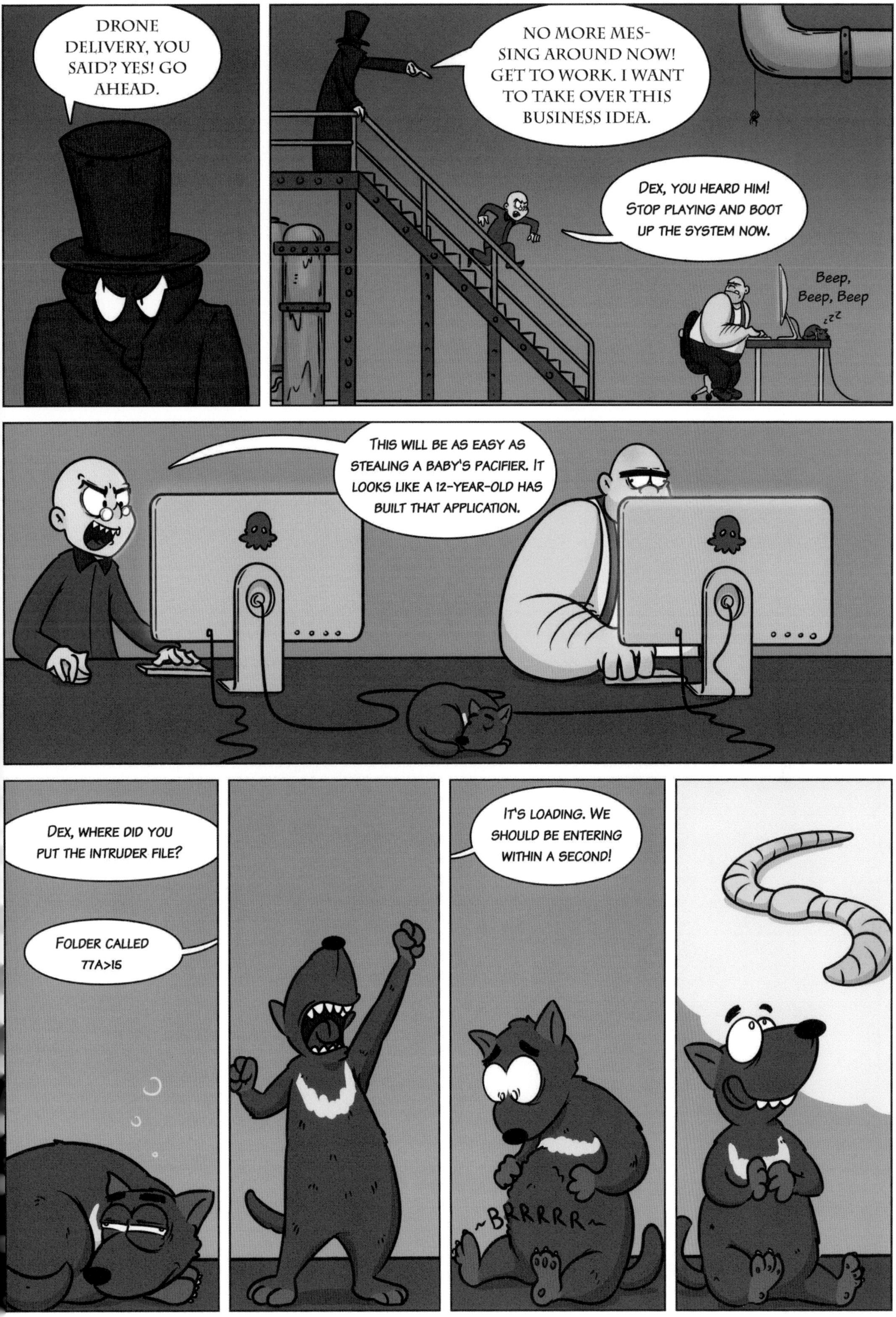
DRONE DELIVERY, YOU SAID? YES! GO AHEAD.
NO MORE MES-SING AROUND NOW! GET TO WORK. I WANT TO TAKE OVER THIS BUSINESS IDEA.
DEX, YOU HEARD HIM! STOP PLAYING AND BOOT UP THE SYSTEM NOW.
Beep, Beep, Beep
zzz
THIS WILL BE AS EASY AS STEALING A BABY'S PACIFIER. IT LOOKS LIKE A 12-YEAR-OLD HAS BUILT THAT APPLICATION.
DEX, WHERE DID YOU PUT THE INTRUDER FILE?
FOLDER CALLED 77A>15
IT'S LOADING. WE SHOULD BE ENTERING WITHIN A SECOND!
~BRRRRR~

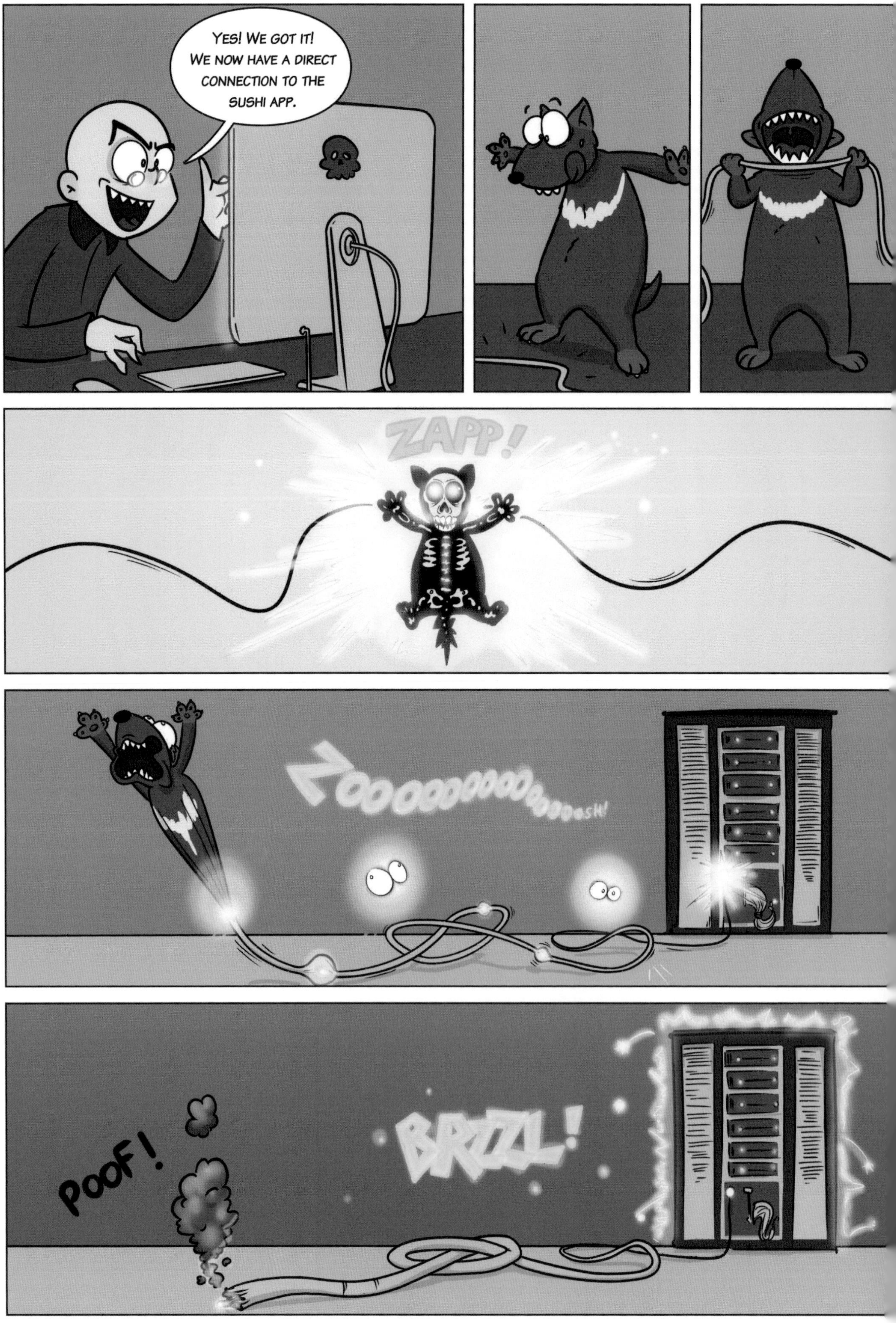

Yes! We got it! We now have a direct connection to the sushi app.
ZAPP!
Zoooooooooooooosh!
POOF!
BRZZL!

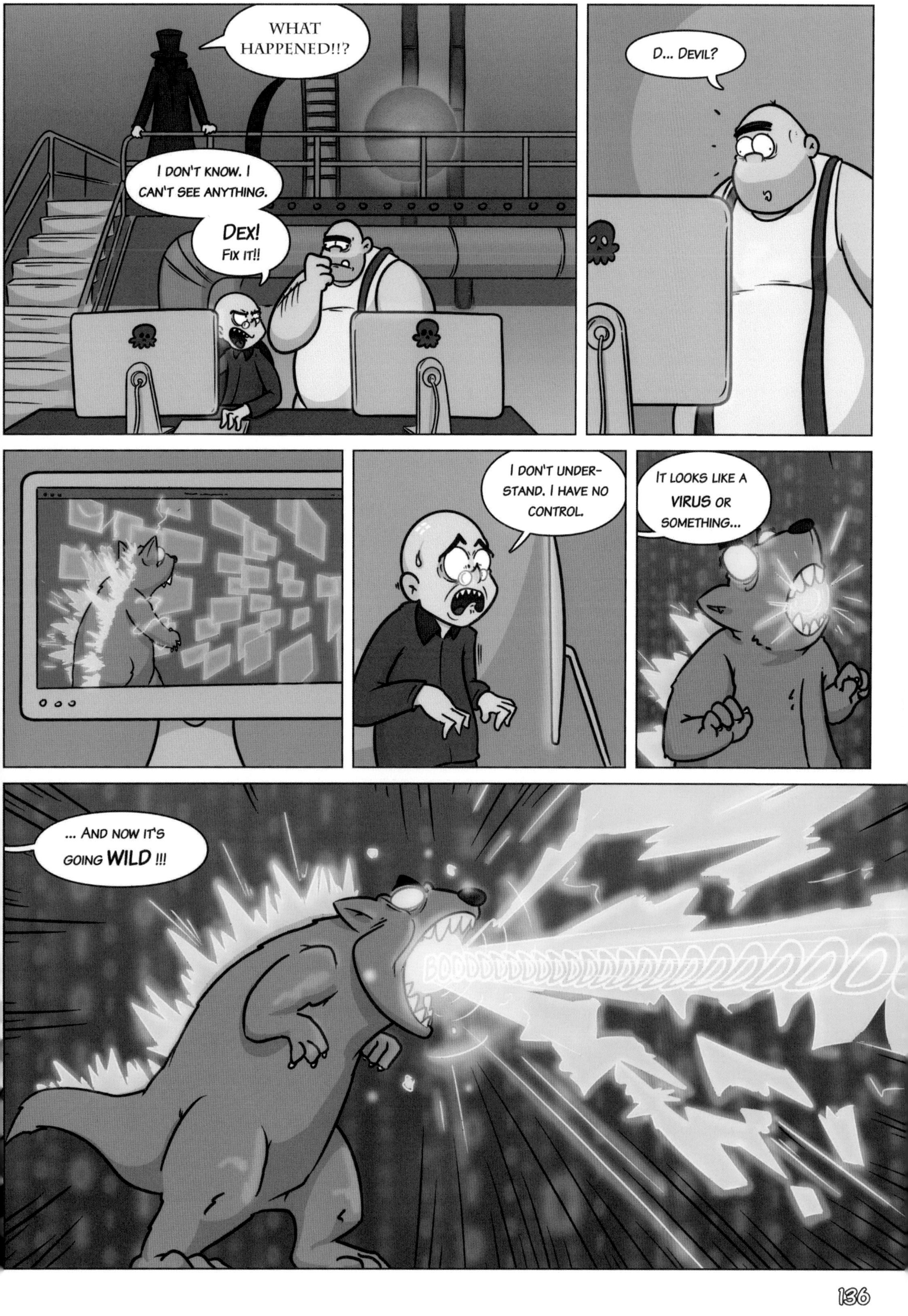

WHAT HAPPENED!!?
I DON'T KNOW. I CAN'T SEE ANYTHING.
DEX! FIX IT!!
D... DEVIL?
I DON'T UNDER-STAND. I HAVE NO CONTROL.
IT LOOKS LIKE A VIRUS OR SOMETHING...
... AND NOW IT'S GOING WILD !!!
BOOOOOOOOOOOOOOOOOOOOOOOO

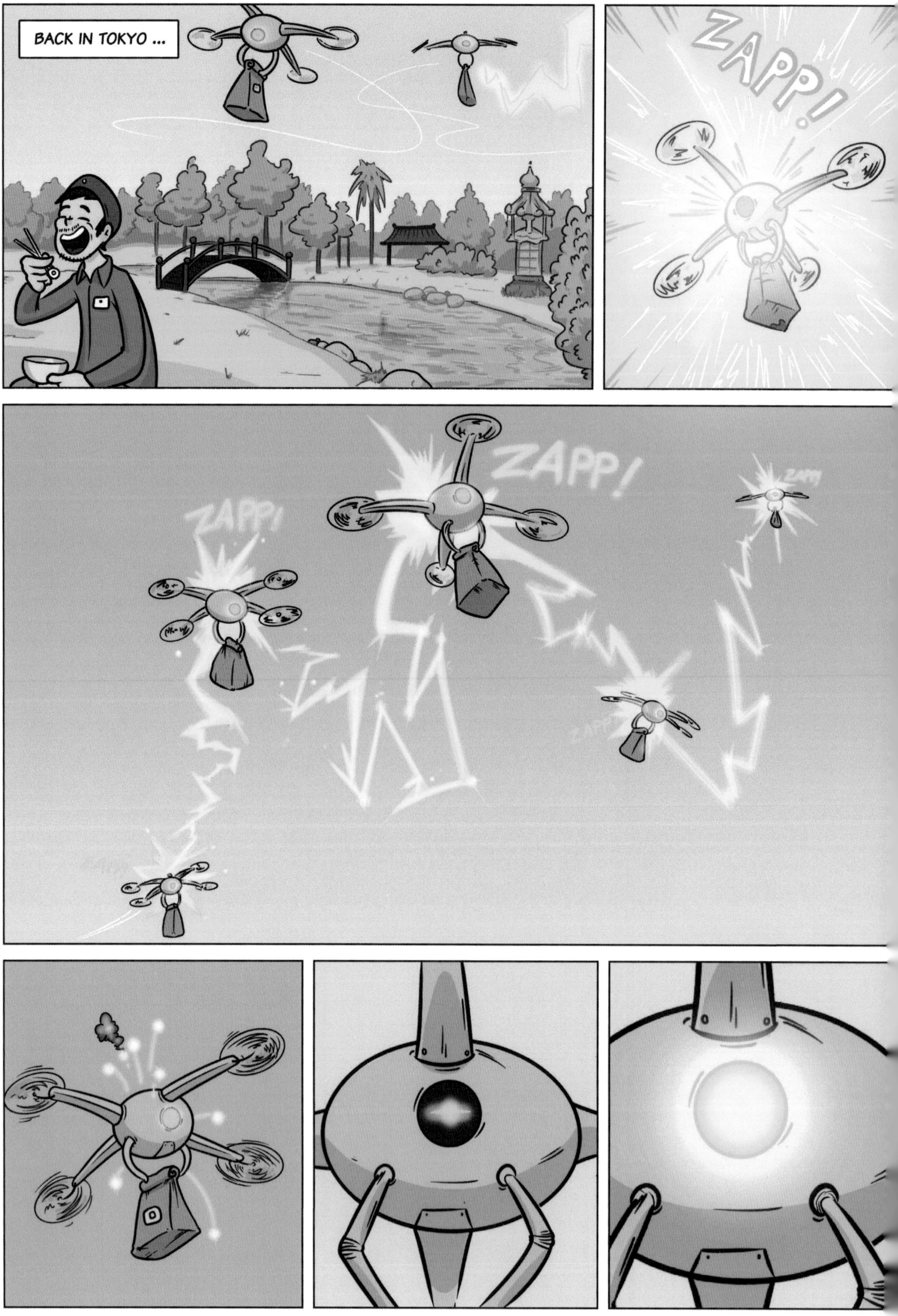
BACK IN TOKYO ...
ZAPP!
ZAPP!
ZAPP!

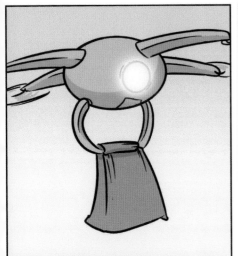

WHAT?!?

SPLASH!

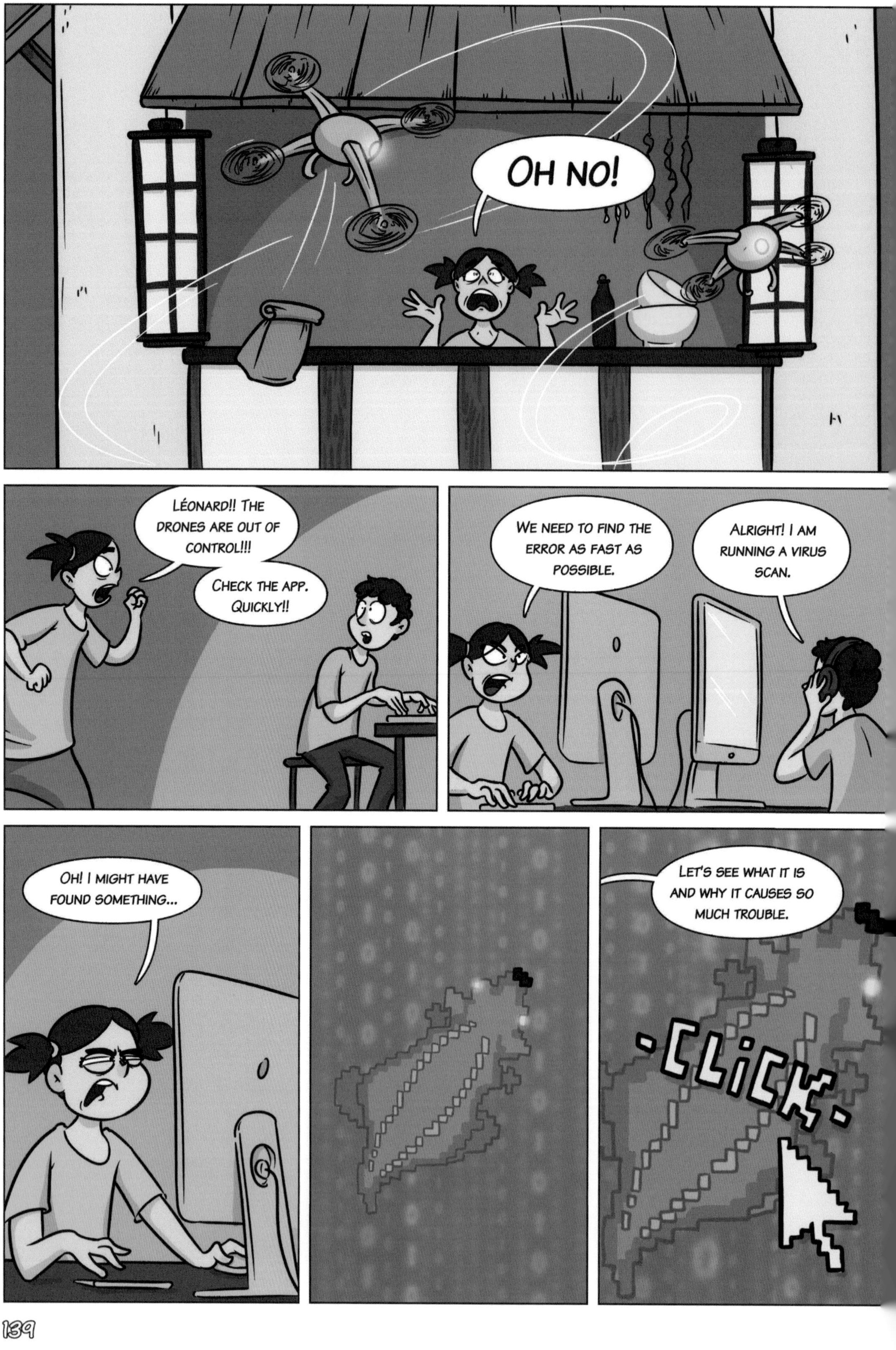
OH NO!
LÉONARD!! THE DRONES ARE OUT OF CONTROL!!!
CHECK THE APP. QUICKLY!!
WE NEED TO FIND THE ERROR AS FAST AS POSSIBLE.
ALRIGHT! I AM RUNNING A VIRUS SCAN.
OH! I MIGHT HAVE FOUND SOMETHING...
LET'S SEE WHAT IT IS AND WHY IT CAUSES SO MUCH TROUBLE.
-CLICK-

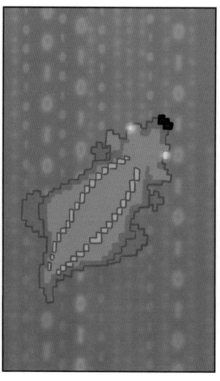

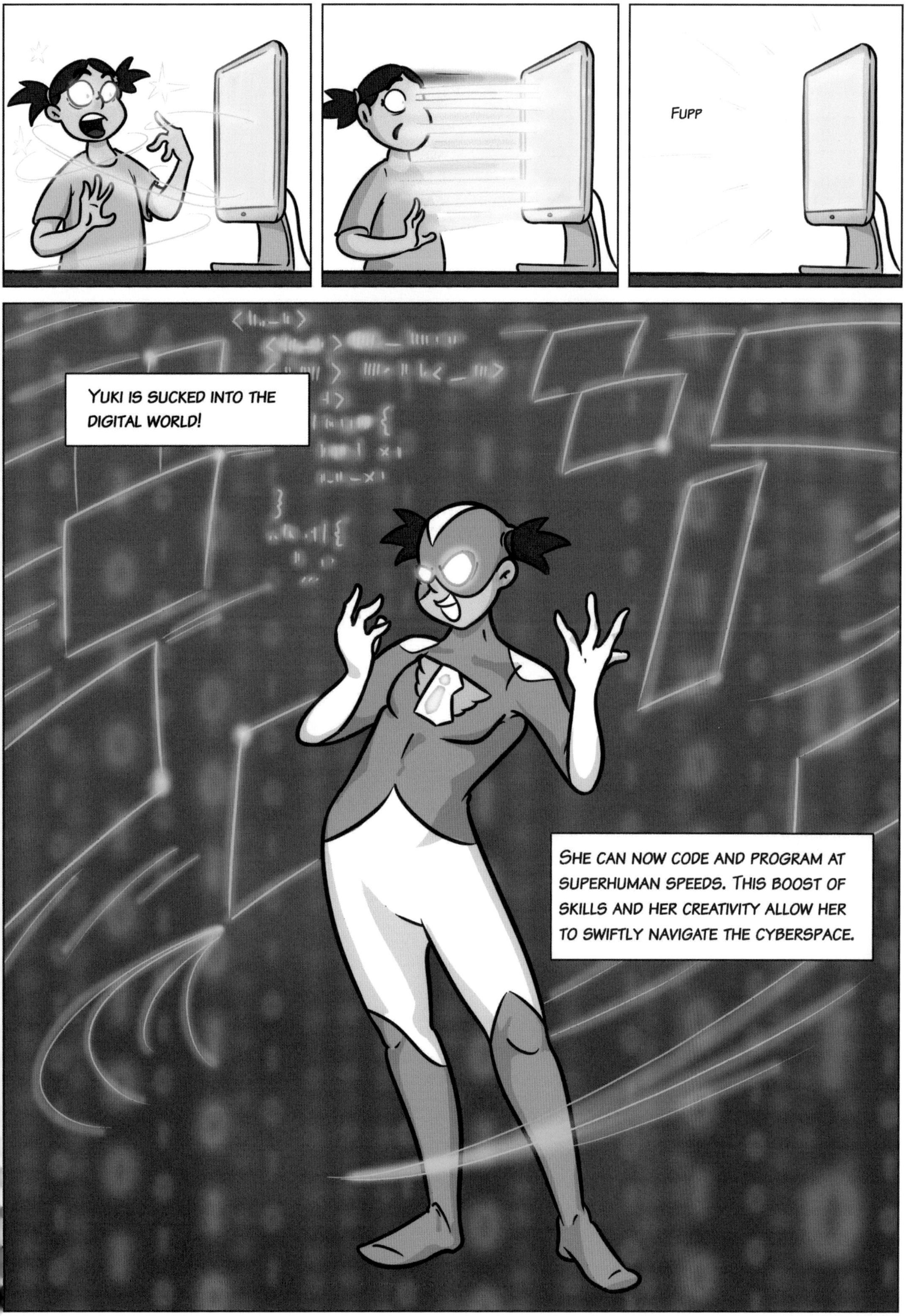
FUPP
YUKI IS SUCKED INTO THE DIGITAL WORLD!
SHE CAN NOW CODE AND PROGRAM AT SUPERHUMAN SPEEDS. THIS BOOST OF SKILLS AND HER CREATIVITY ALLOW HER TO SWIFTLY NAVIGATE THE CYBERSPACE.

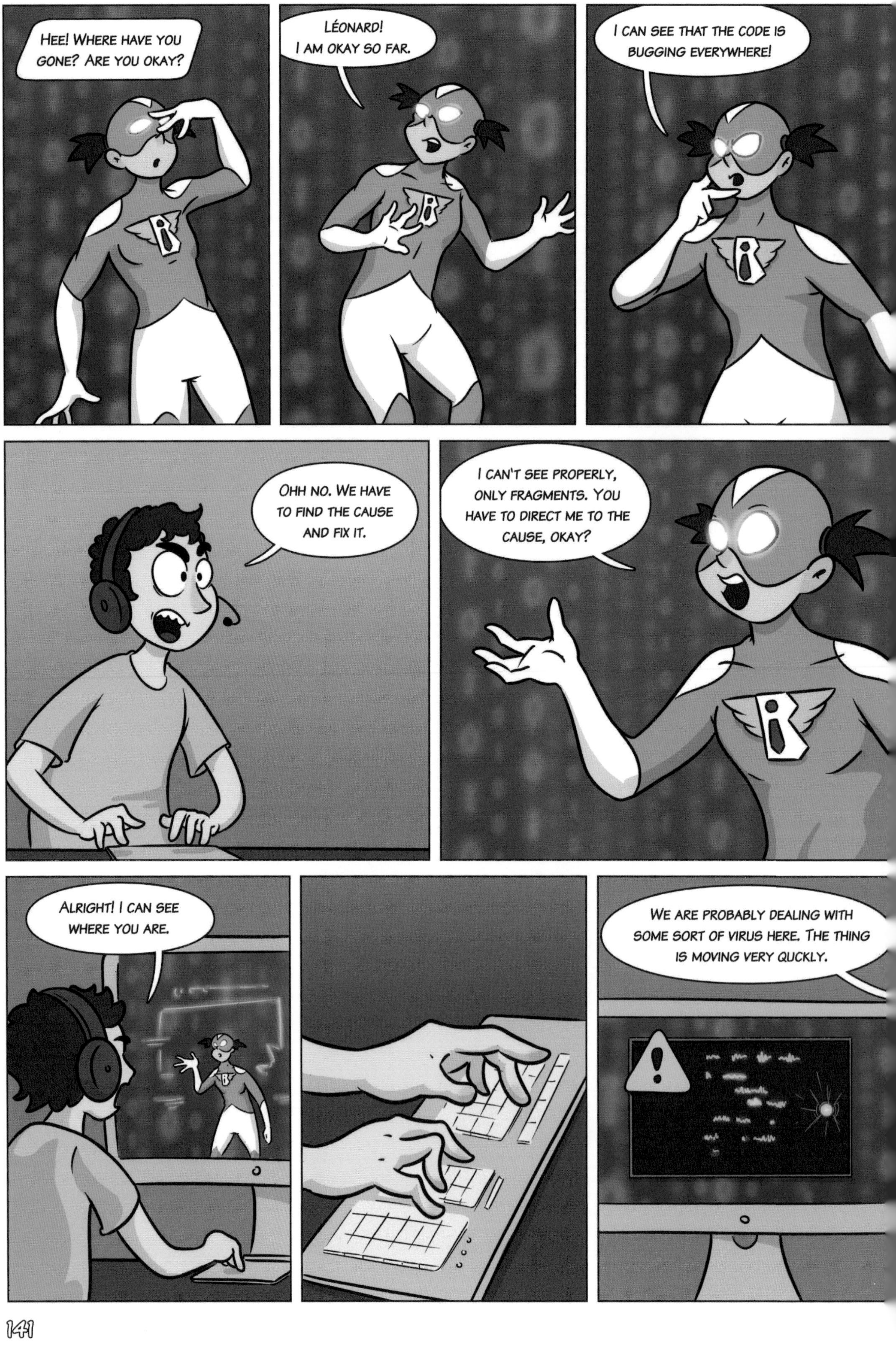
Hee! Where have you gone? Are you okay?
Léonard! I am okay so far.
I can see that the code is bugging everywhere!
Ohh no. We have to find the cause and fix it.
I can't see properly, only fragments. You have to direct me to the cause, okay?
Alright! I can see where you are.
We are probably dealing with some sort of virus here. The thing is moving very quckly.

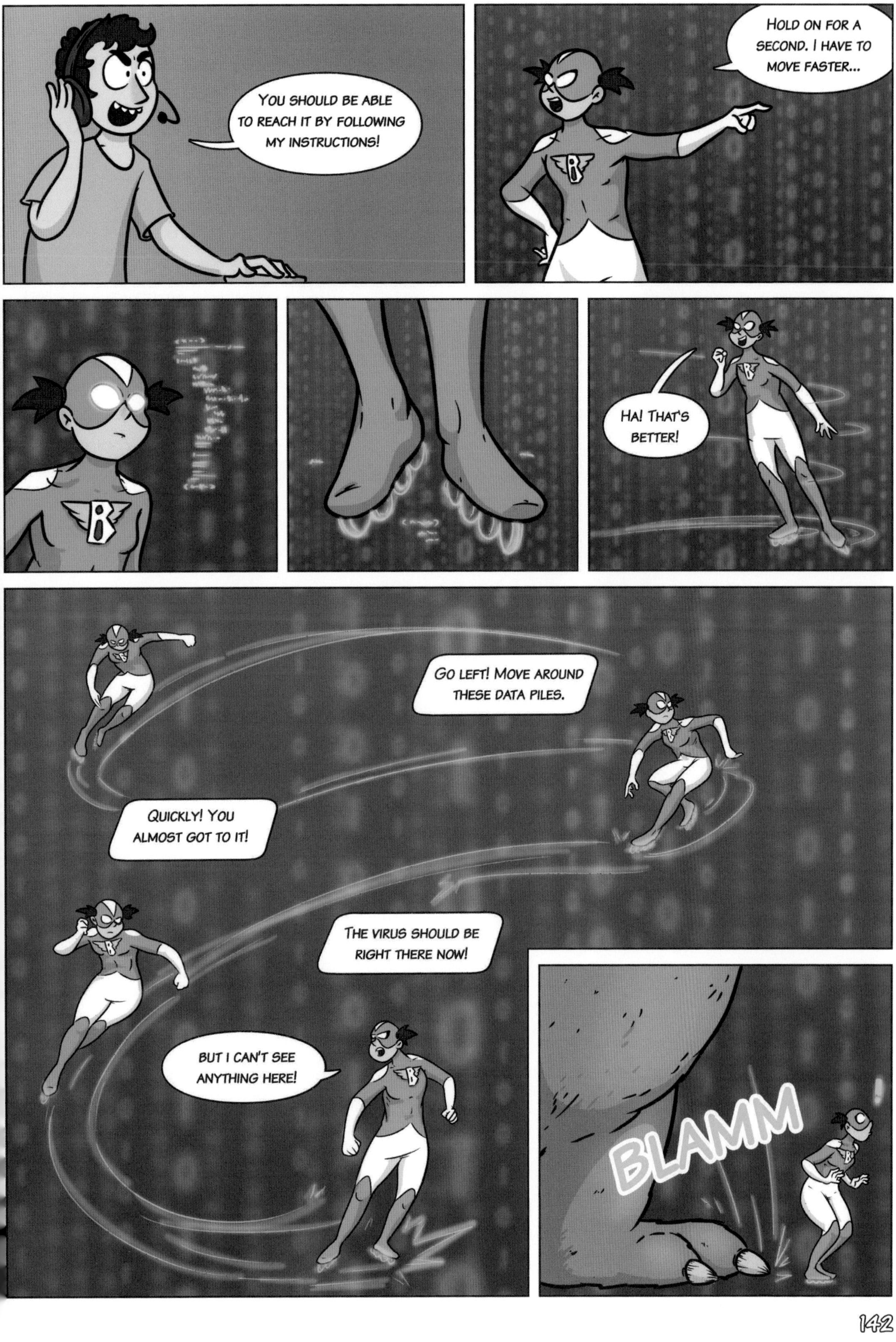
You should be able to reach it by following my instructions!
Hold on for a second. I have to move faster...
Ha! That's better!
Go left! Move around these data piles.
Quickly! You almost got to it!
The virus should be right there now!
But I can't see anything here!
BLAMM

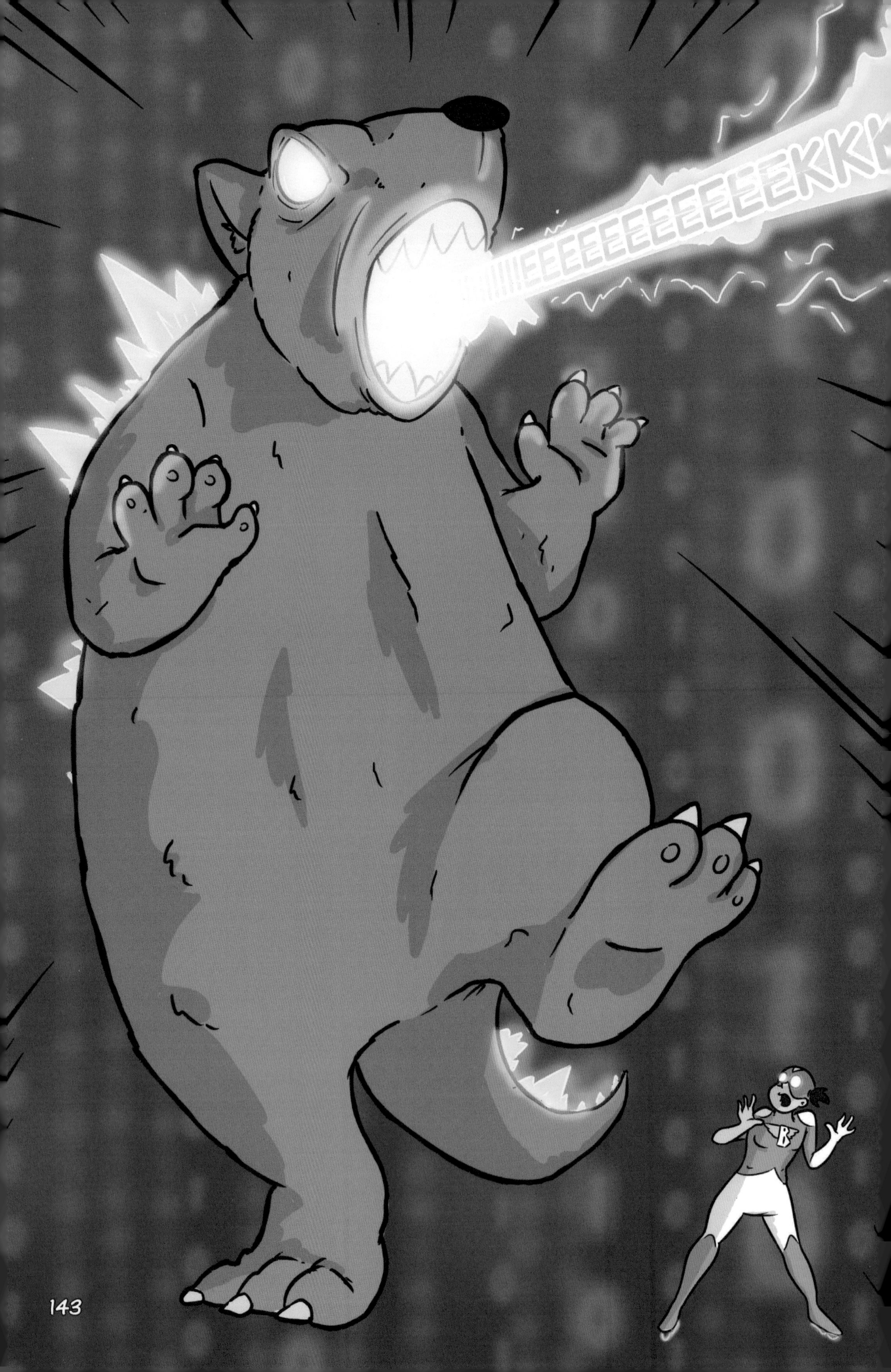
EEEEEEEEEEEKK

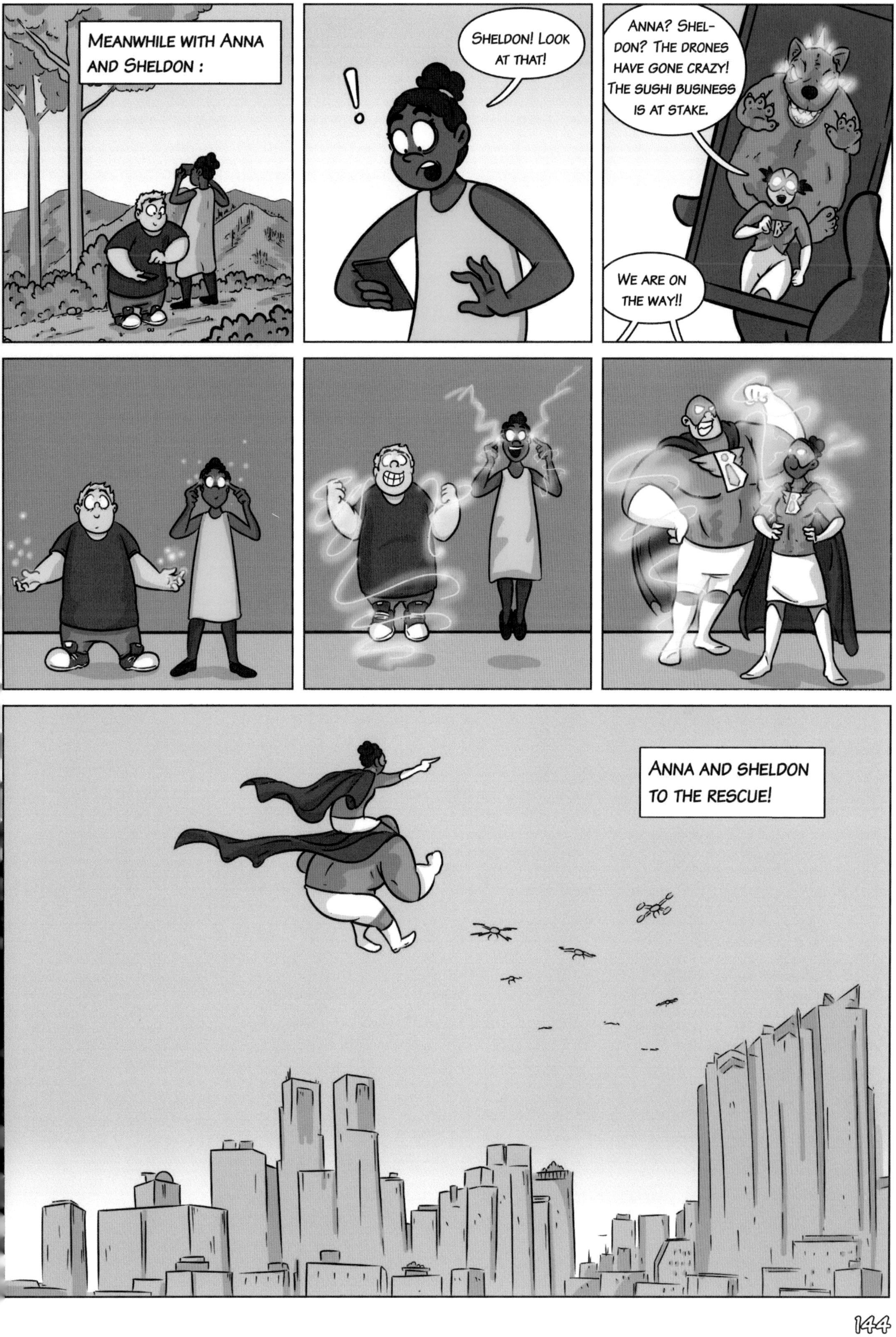

MEANWHILE WITH ANNA AND SHELDON :
SHELDON! LOOK AT THAT!
ANNA? SHEL-DON? THE DRONES HAVE GONE CRAZY! THE SUSHI BUSINESS IS AT STAKE.
WE ARE ON THE WAY!!
ANNA AND SHELDON TO THE RESCUE!

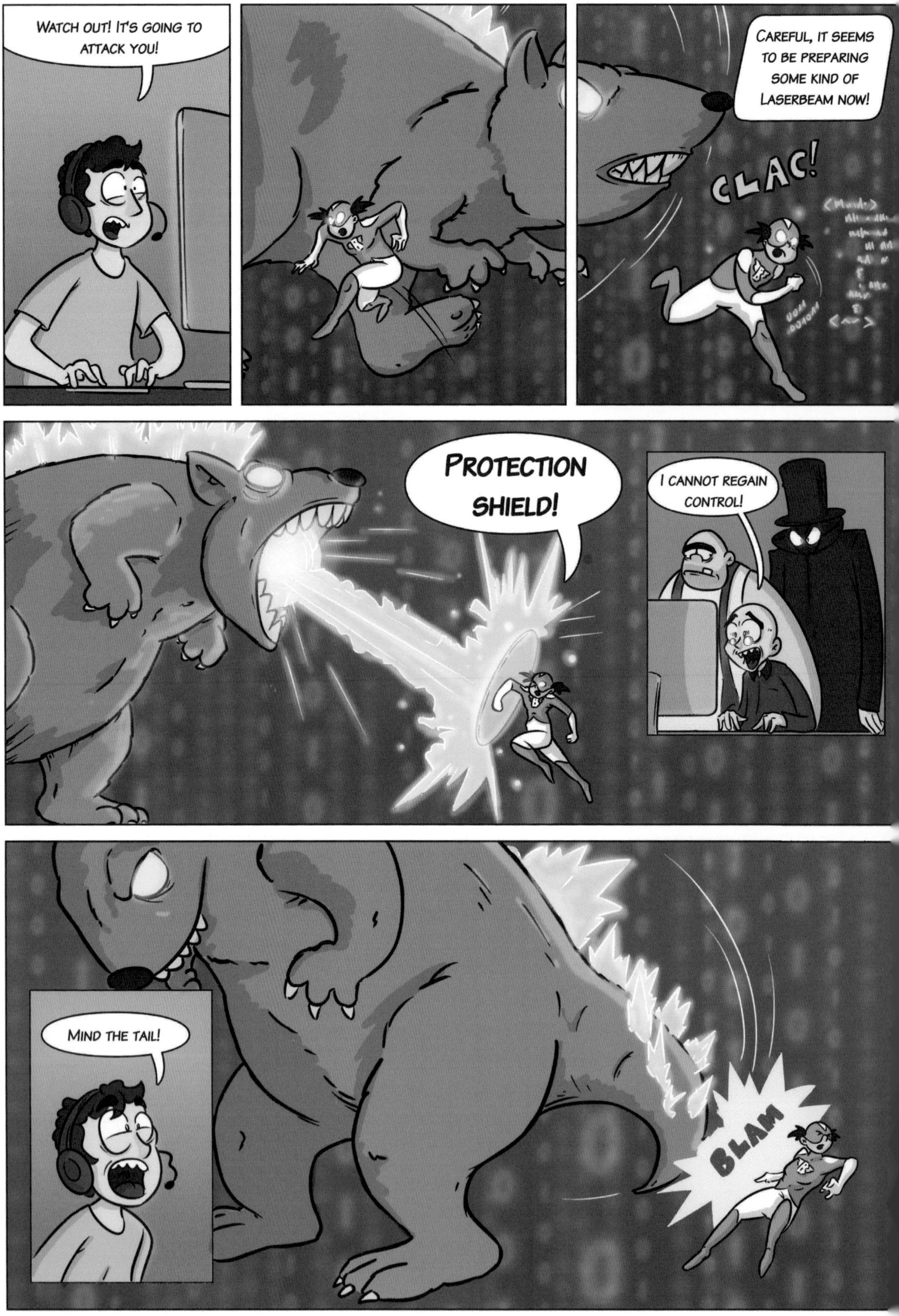
Watch out! It's going to attack you!
Careful, it seems to be preparing some kind of Laserbeam now!
CLAC!
Protection shield!
I cannot regain control!
Mind the tail!
BLAM

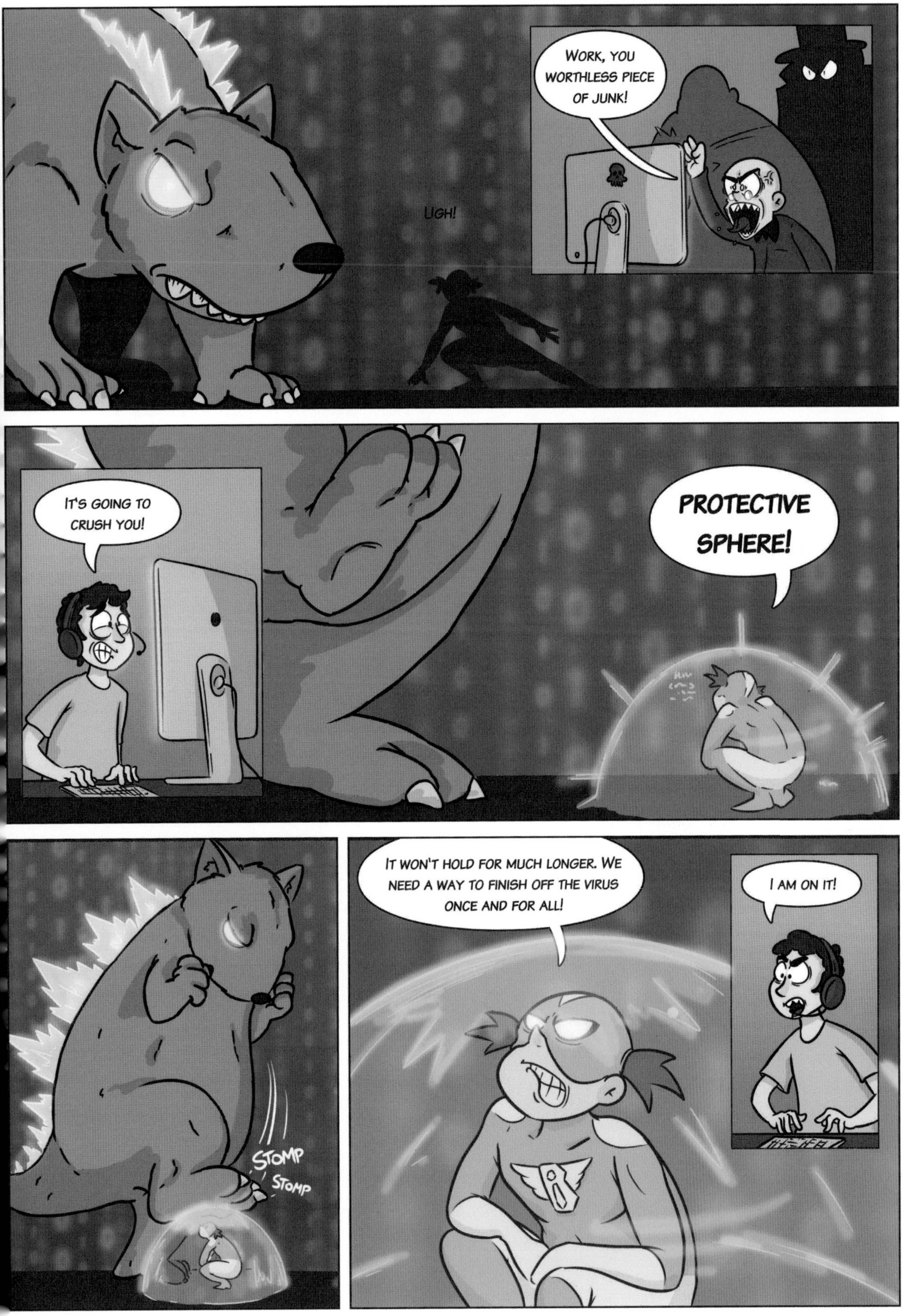
Work, you worthless piece of junk!
Ugh!
It's going to crush you!
PROTECTIVE SPHERE!
Stomp
Stomp
It won't hold for much longer. We need a way to finish off the virus once and for all!
I am on it!

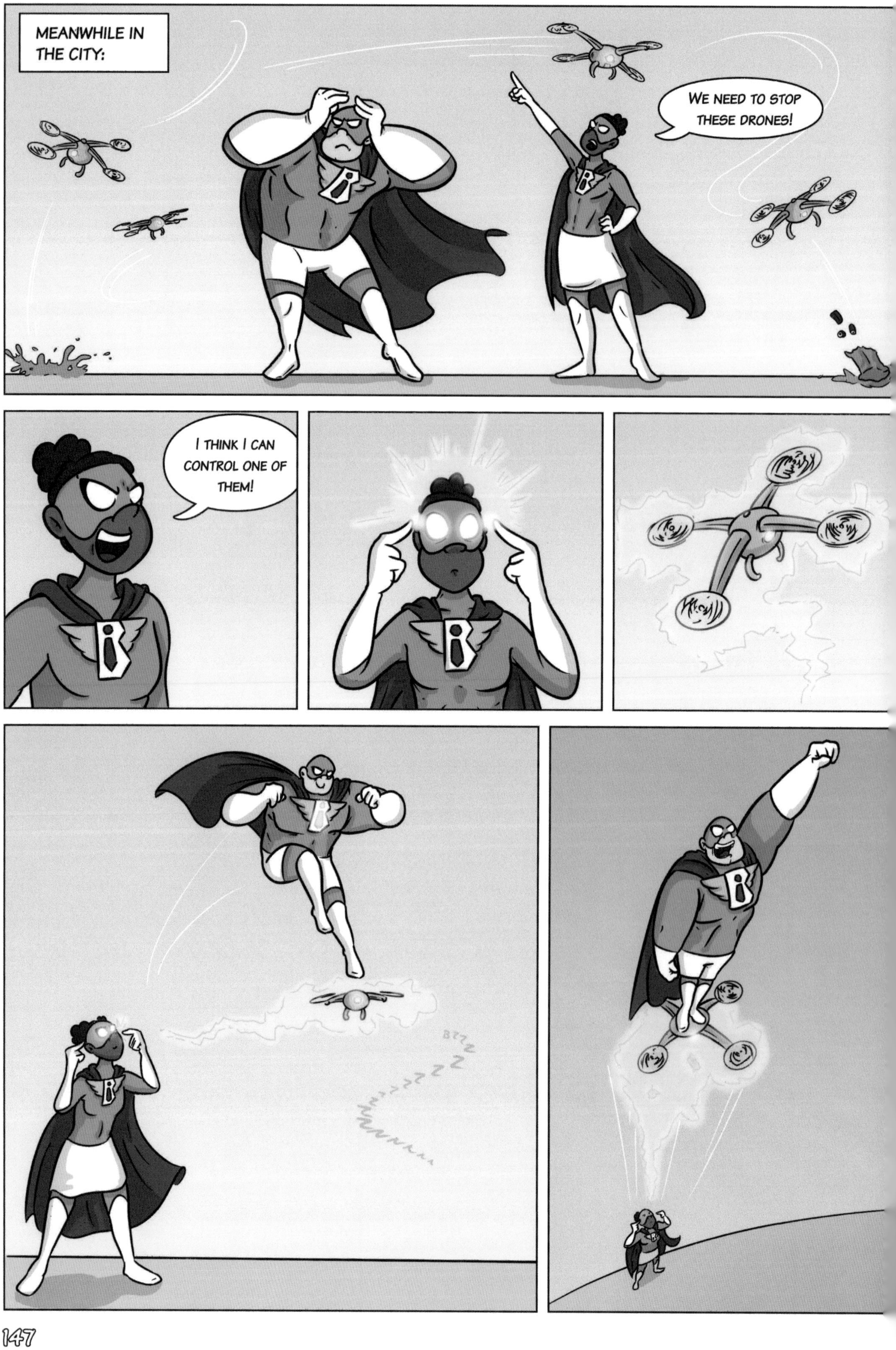
MEANWHILE IN THE CITY:
WE NEED TO STOP THESE DRONES!
I THINK I CAN CONTROL ONE OF THEM!
BZZZ

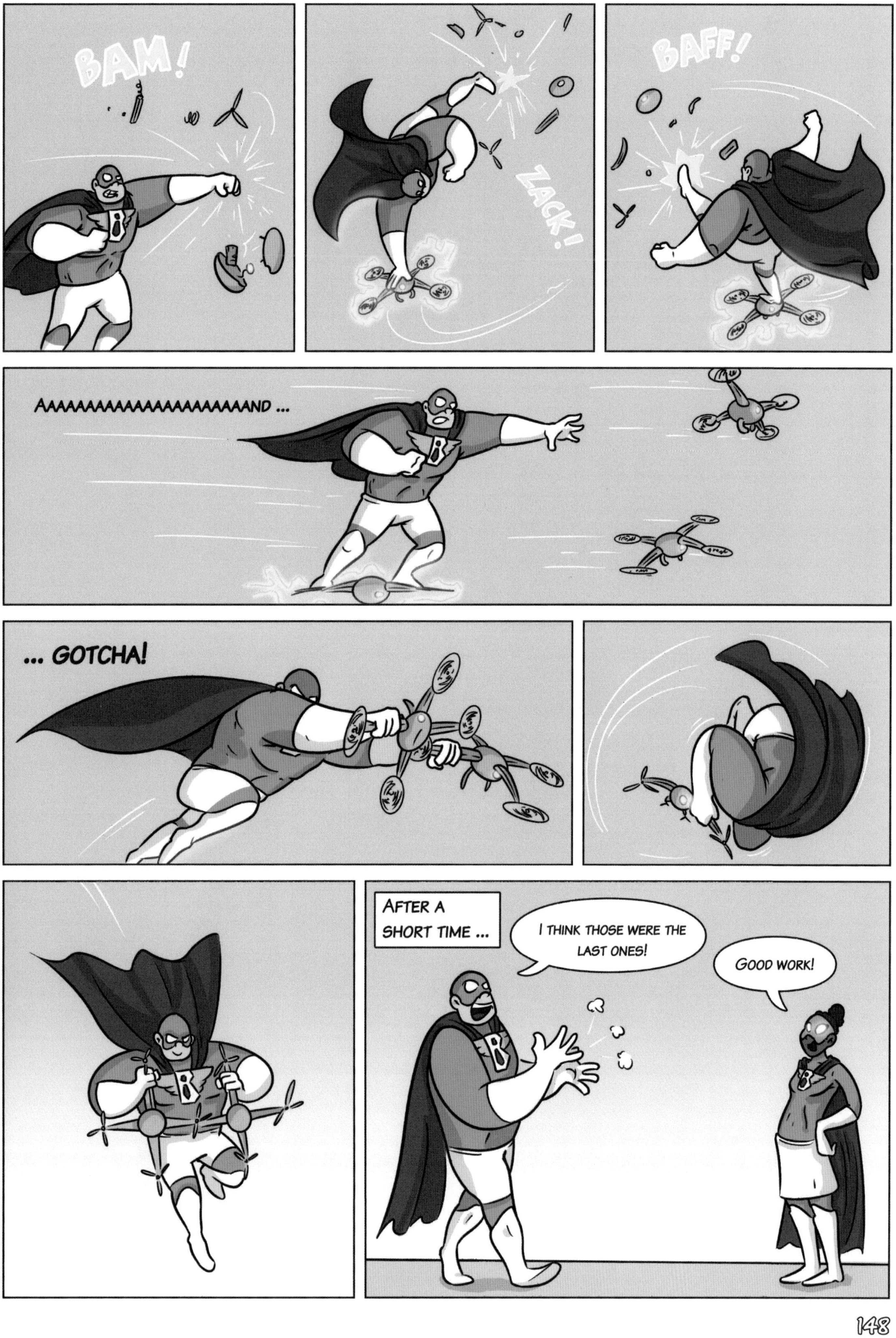
BAM!
ZACK!
BAFF!
AAAAAAAAAAAAAAAAAAAAAAND ...
... GOTCHA!
AFTER A SHORT TIME ...
I THINK THOSE WERE THE LAST ONES!
GOOD WORK!

HURRY UP, LÉONARD! THERE ARE CRACKS IN MY SPEHRE ALREADY!!

SHATTER!

GULP

WAIT! I HAVE JUST FIGURED IT OUT!

TO STOP THE VIRUS...

IT'S GETTING CLOSER!!!

... YOU'LL NEED A ...

FASTER!!!!

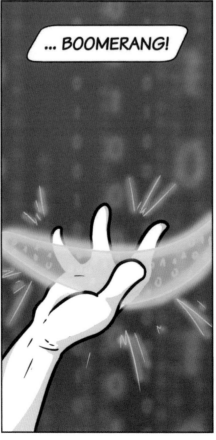

... BOOMERANG!

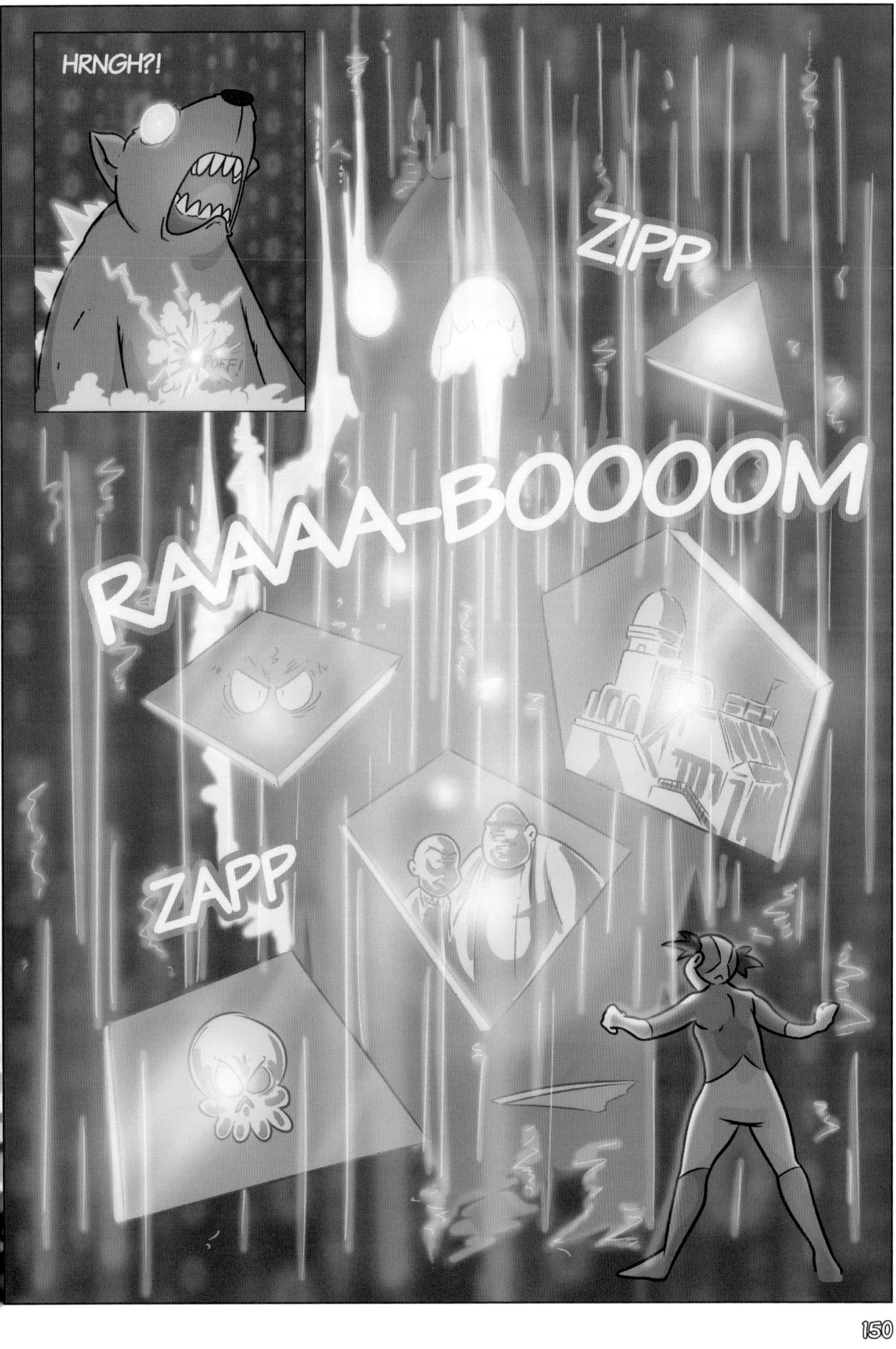
HRNGH?!
POFF!
ZIPP
RAAAA-BOOOOOM
ZAPP

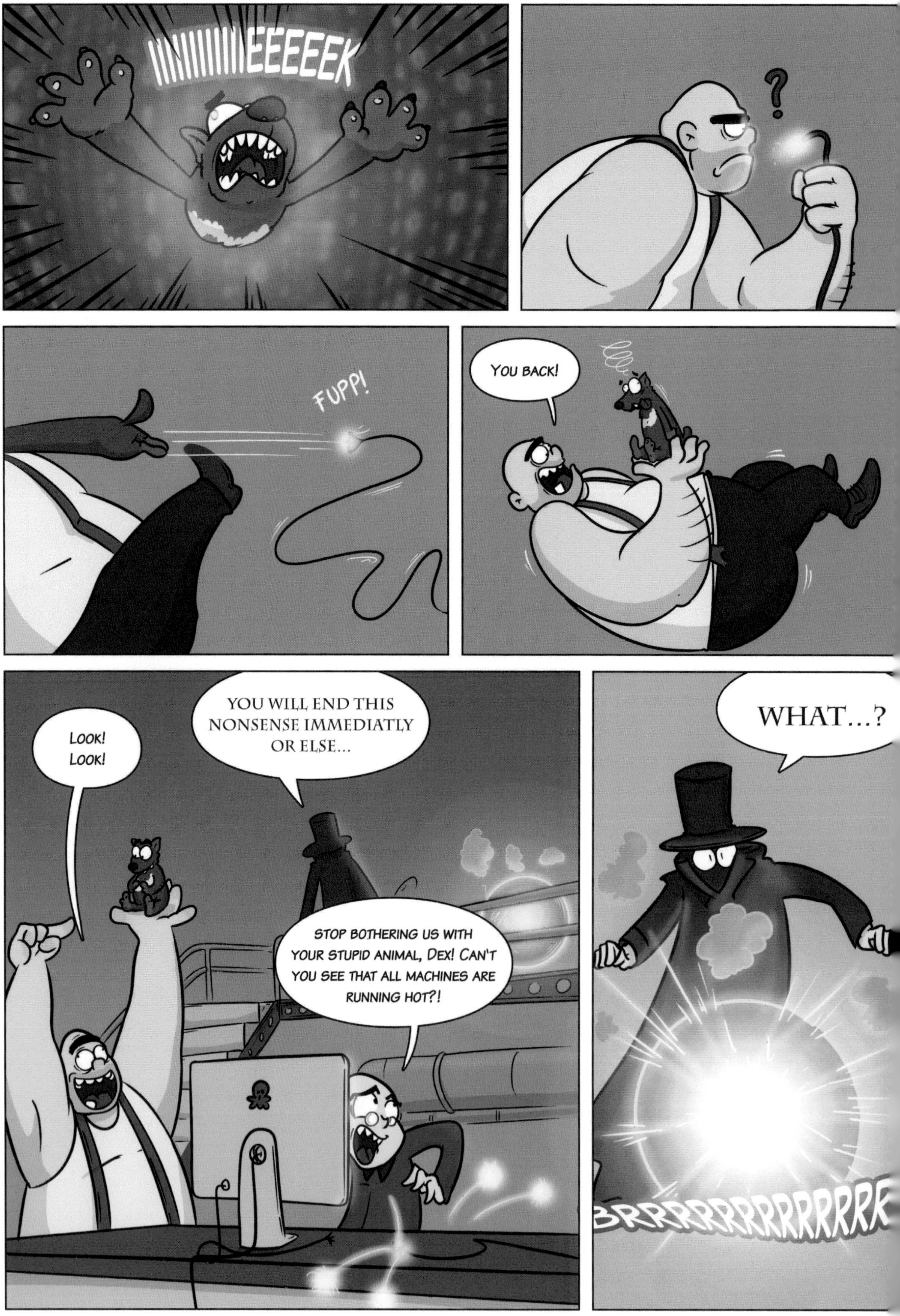
IIIIIIIIIIIIEEEEEK
?
FUPP!
YOU BACK!
LOOK!
LOOK!
YOU WILL END THIS
NONSENSE IMMEDIATLY
OR ELSE...
STOP BOTHERING US WITH
YOUR STUPID ANIMAL, DEX! CAN'T
YOU SEE THAT ALL MACHINES ARE
RUNNING HOT?!
WHAT...?
BRRRRRRRRRRRRRR

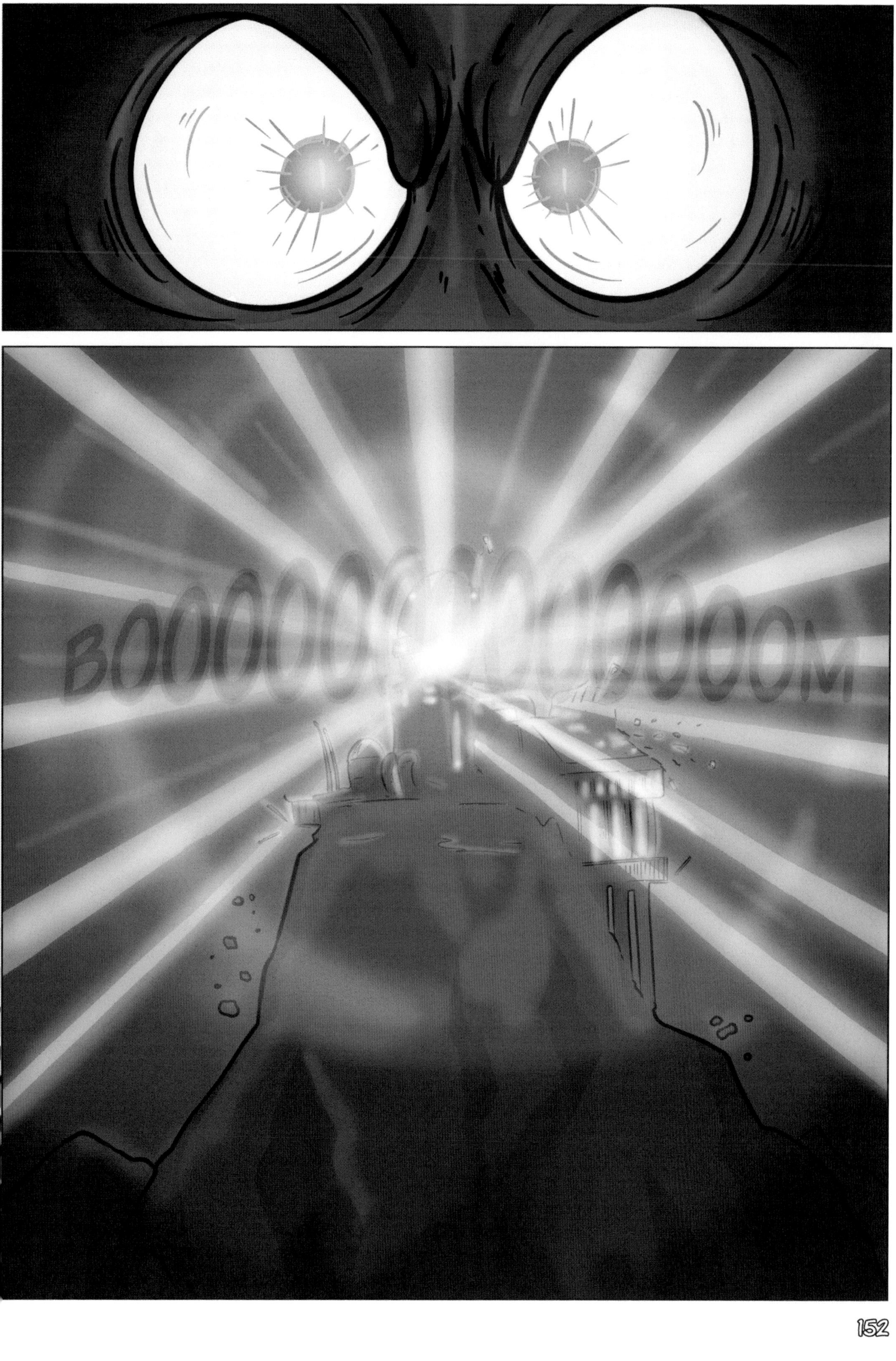
BOOOOOOOOOOOOM

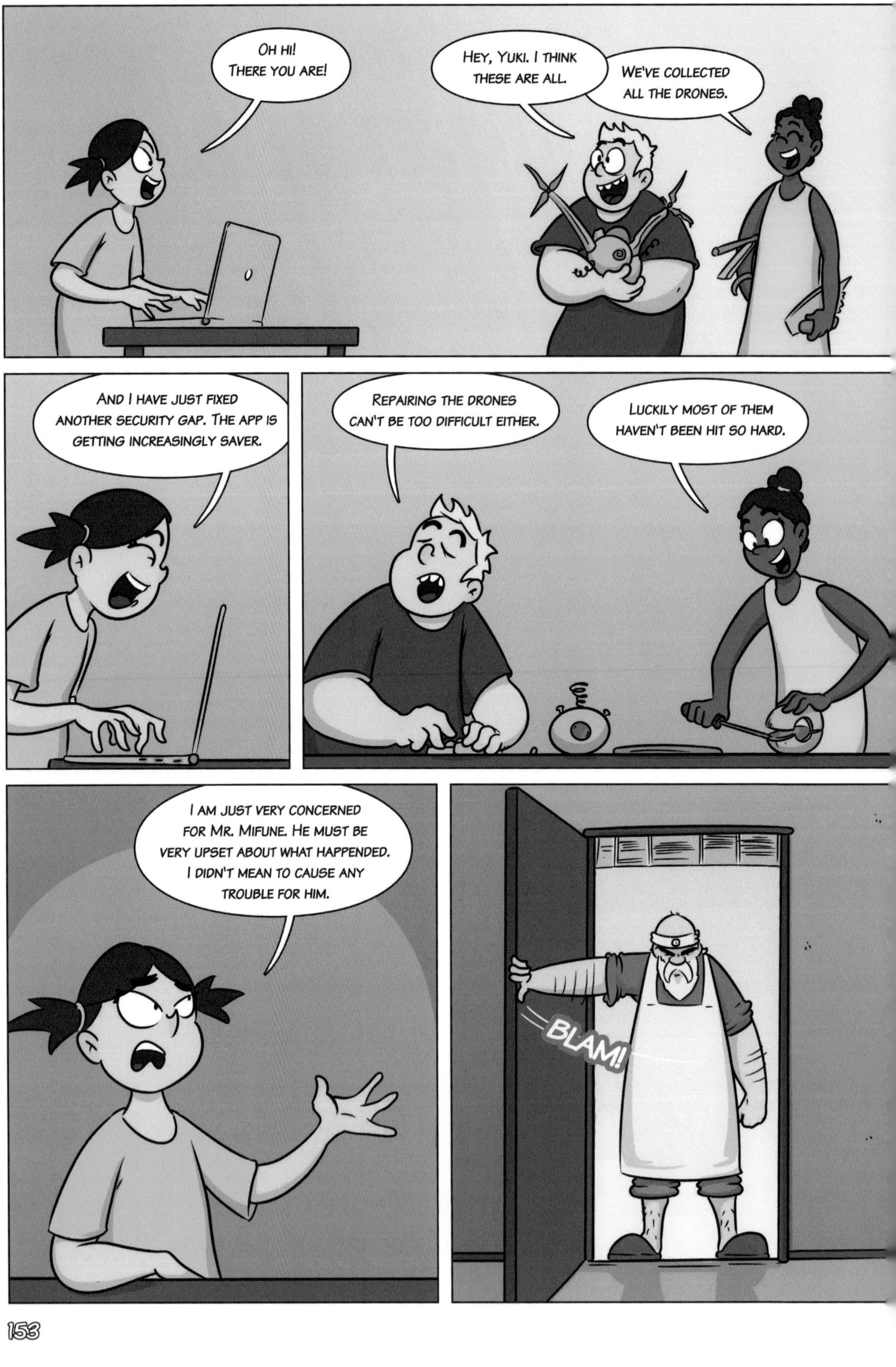
OH HI! THERE YOU ARE!
HEY, YUKI. I THINK THESE ARE ALL.
WE'VE COLLECTED ALL THE DRONES.
AND I HAVE JUST FIXED ANOTHER SECURITY GAP. THE APP IS GETTING INCREASINGLY SAVER.
REPAIRING THE DRONES CAN'T BE TOO DIFFICULT EITHER.
LUCKILY MOST OF THEM HAVEN'T BEEN HIT SO HARD.
I AM JUST VERY CONCERNED FOR MR. MIFUNE. HE MUST BE VERY UPSET ABOUT WHAT HAPPENDED. I DIDN'T MEAN TO CAUSE ANY TROUBLE FOR HIM.
BLAM!

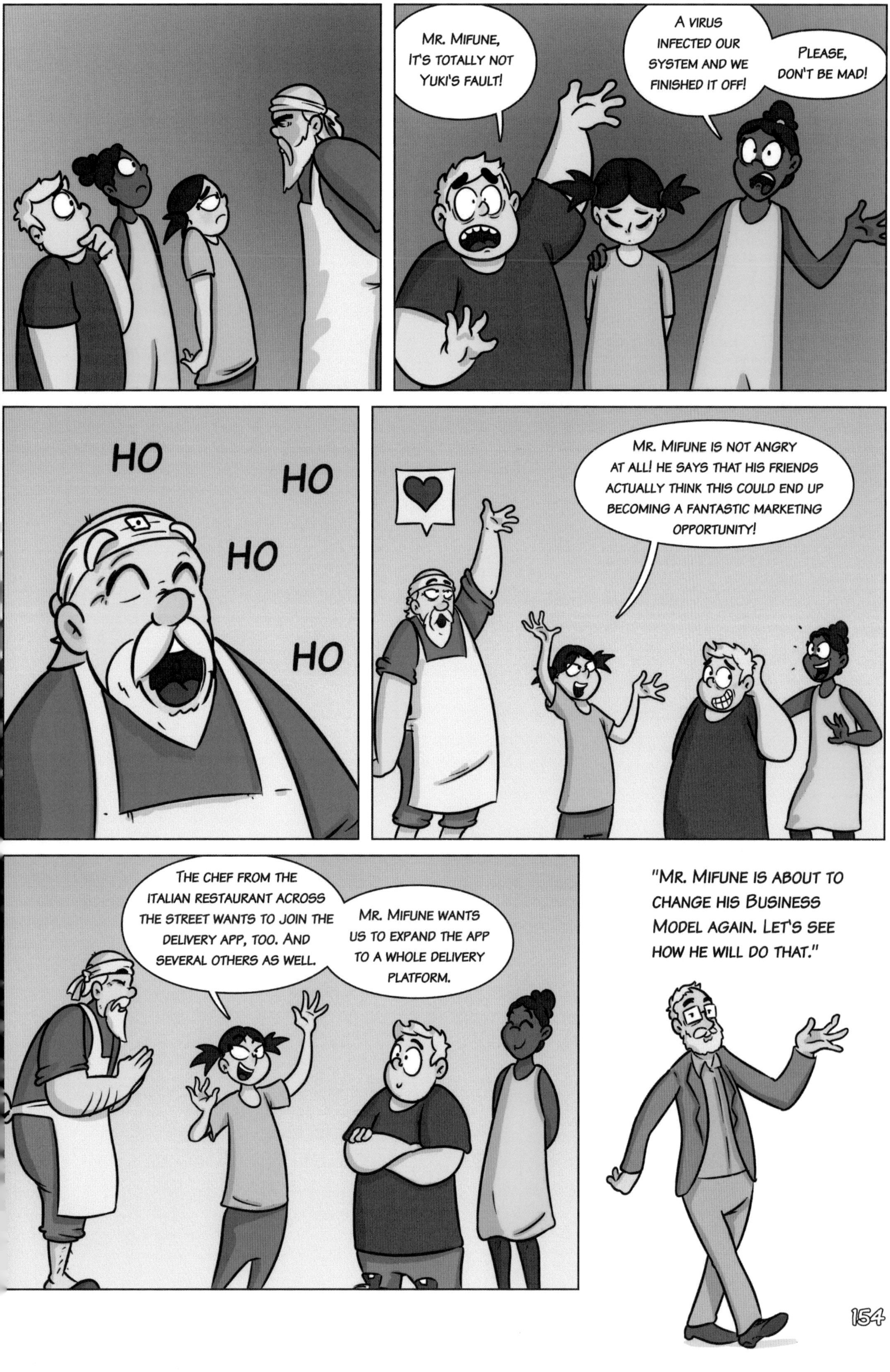
Mr. Mifune, it's totally not Yuki's fault!
A virus infected our system and we finished it off!
Please, don't be mad!
HO
HO
HO
HO
Mr. Mifune is not angry at all! He says that his friends actually think this could end up becoming a fantastic marketing opportunity!
The chef from the Italian restaurant across the street wants to join the delivery app, too. And several others as well.
Mr. Mifune wants us to expand the app to a whole delivery platform.
"Mr. Mifune is about to change his Business Model again. Let's see how he will do that."

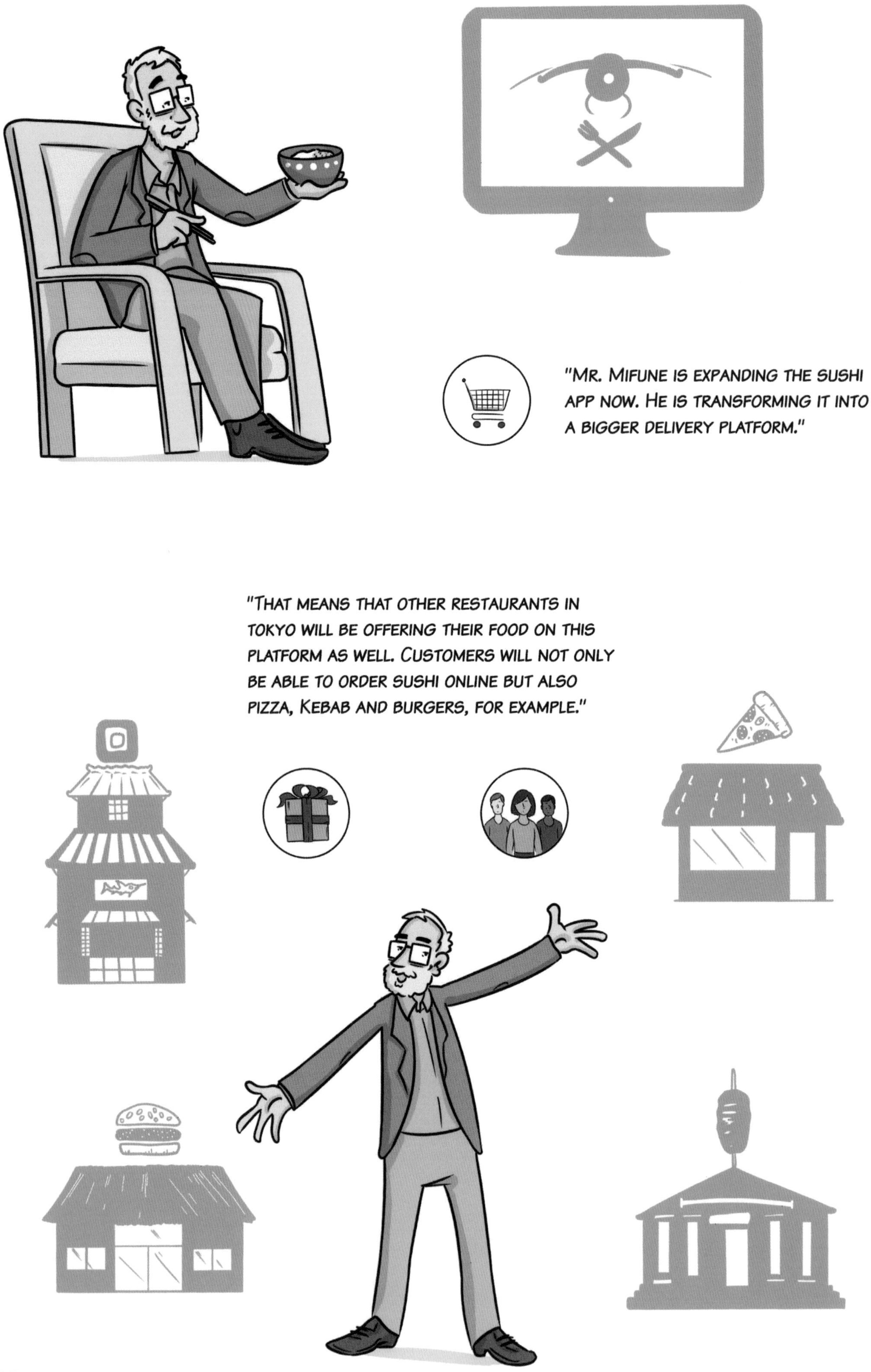
"MR. MIFUNE IS EXPANDING THE SUSHI APP NOW. HE IS TRANSFORMING IT INTO A BIGGER DELIVERY PLATFORM."
"THAT MEANS THAT OTHER RESTAURANTS IN TOKYO WILL BE OFFERING THEIR FOOD ON THIS PLATFORM AS WELL. CUSTOMERS WILL NOT ONLY BE ABLE TO ORDER SUSHI ONLINE BUT ALSO PIZZA, KEBAB AND BURGERS, FOR EXAMPLE."

"MR. MIFUNE GETS A FEE FROM THE OTHER RESTAURANT OWNERS FOR EVERY MEAL THEY SERVE THROUGH HIS PLATFROM."

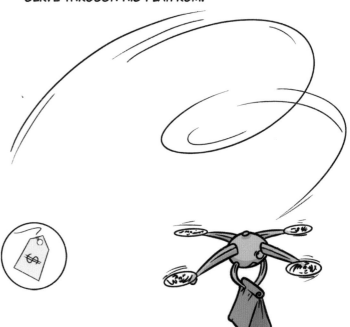

"THIS WAY HE WILL BE ABLE TO EARN MORE MONEY THAN HE DID BEFORE."

"THIS BUSINESS MODEL GENERATES THE MOST PROFIT BECAUSE IT IS VERY SCALEABLE. A HIGH NUMBER OF CUSTOMERS CAN BE SERVED NOW. THERE IS NO LIMIT."

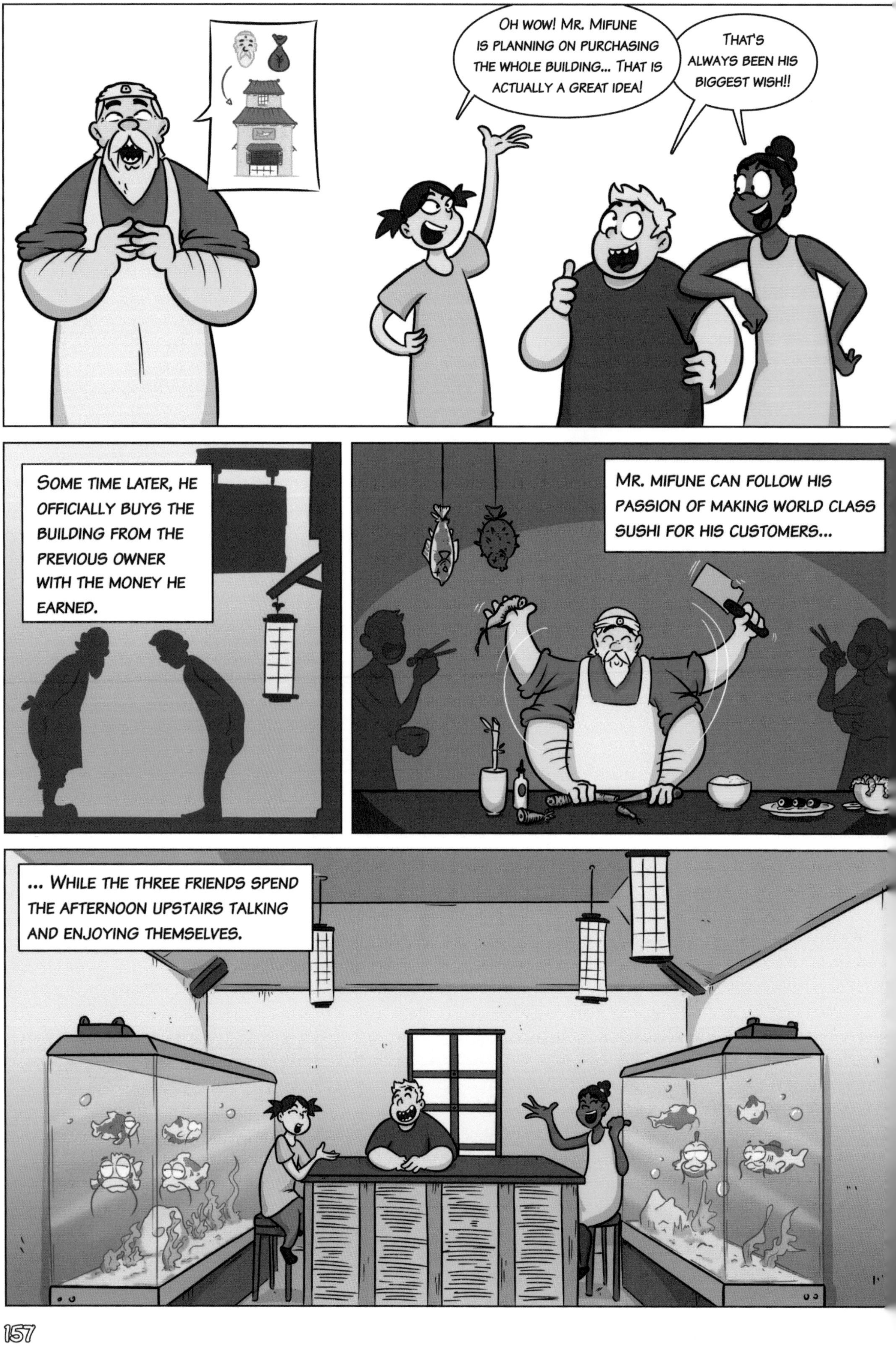
OH WOW! MR. MIFUNE IS PLANNING ON PURCHASING THE WHOLE BUILDING... THAT IS ACTUALLY A GREAT IDEA!
THAT'S ALWAYS BEEN HIS BIGGEST WISH!!
SOME TIME LATER, HE OFFICIALLY BUYS THE BUILDING FROM THE PREVIOUS OWNER WITH THE MONEY HE EARNED.
MR. MIFUNE CAN FOLLOW HIS PASSION OF MAKING WORLD CLASS SUSHI FOR HIS CUSTOMERS...
... WHILE THE THREE FRIENDS SPEND THE AFTERNOON UPSTAIRS TALKING AND ENJOYING THEMSELVES.

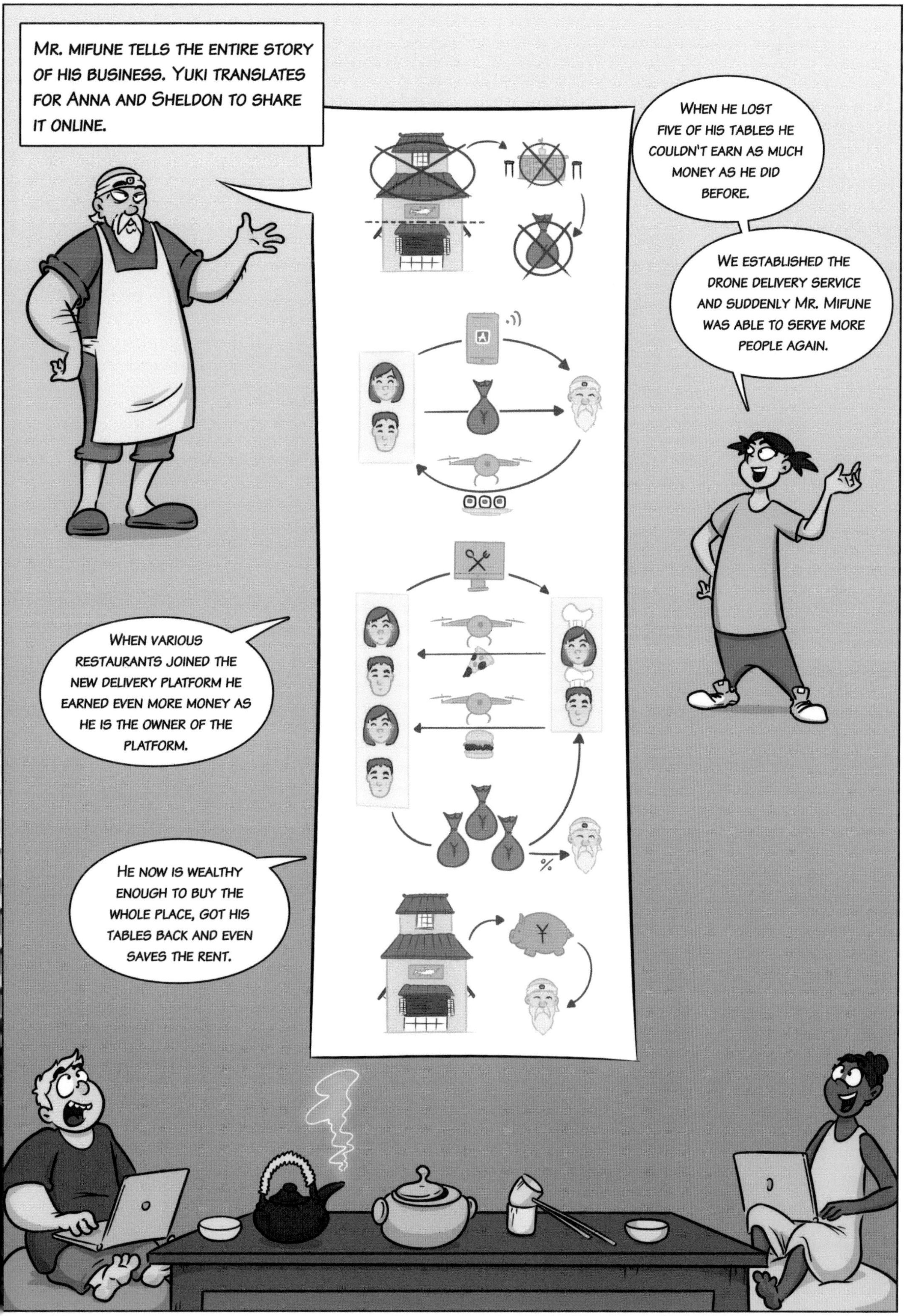
MR. MIFUNE TELLS THE ENTIRE STORY OF HIS BUSINESS. YUKI TRANSLATES FOR ANNA AND SHELDON TO SHARE IT ONLINE.
WHEN HE LOST FIVE OF HIS TABLES HE COULDN'T EARN AS MUCH MONEY AS HE DID BEFORE.
WE ESTABLISHED THE DRONE DELIVERY SERVICE AND SUDDENLY MR. MIFUNE WAS ABLE TO SERVE MORE PEOPLE AGAIN.
WHEN VARIOUS RESTAURANTS JOINED THE NEW DELIVERY PLATFORM HE EARNED EVEN MORE MONEY AS HE IS THE OWNER OF THE PLATFORM.
HE NOW IS WEALTHY ENOUGH TO BUY THE WHOLE PLACE, GOT HIS TABLES BACK AND EVEN SAVES THE RENT.
%

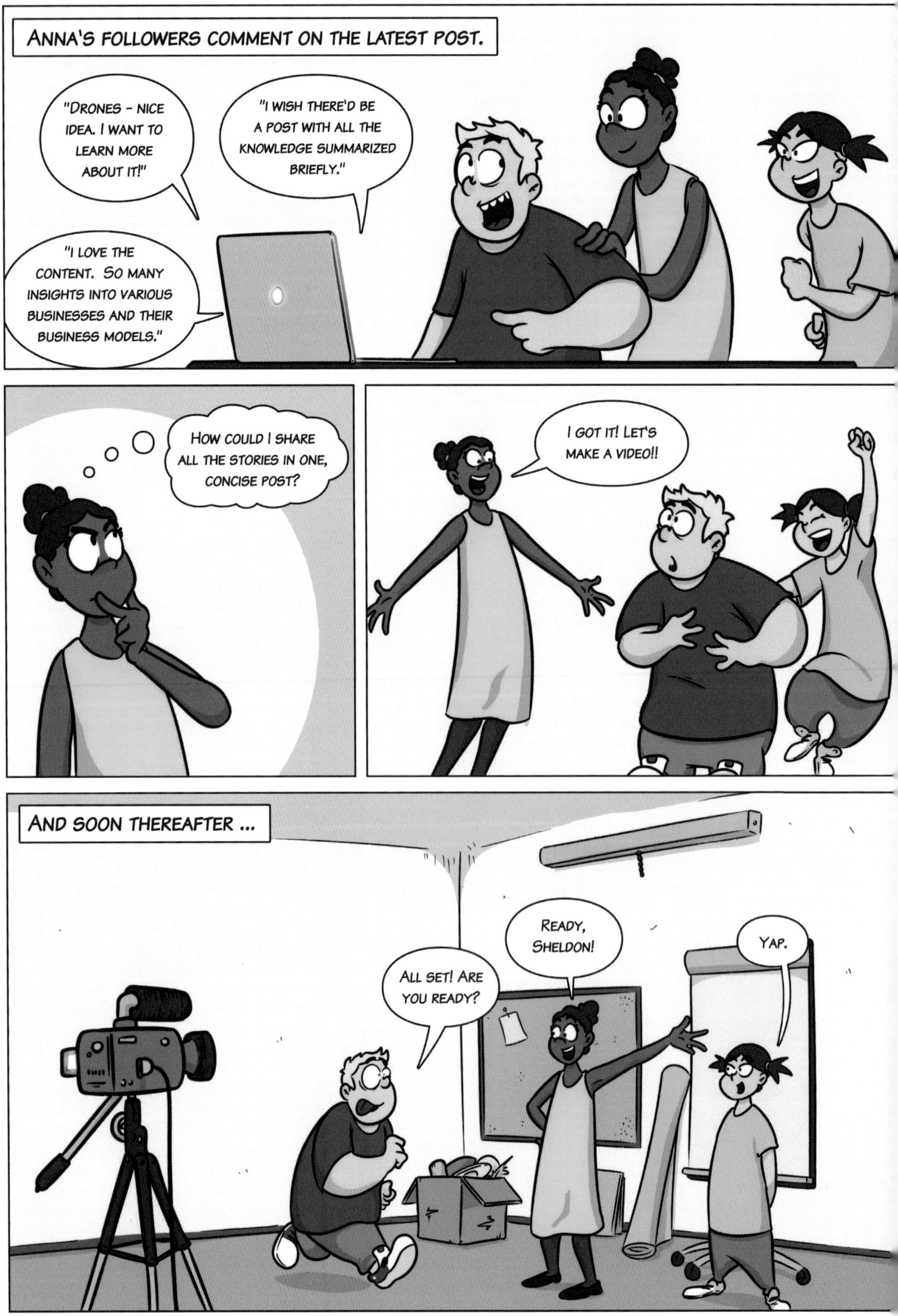
ANNA'S FOLLOWERS COMMENT ON THE LATEST POST.
"DRONES - NICE IDEA. I WANT TO LEARN MORE ABOUT IT!"
"I WISH THERE'D BE A POST WITH ALL THE KNOWLEDGE SUMMARIZED BRIEFLY."
"I LOVE THE CONTENT. SO MANY INSIGHTS INTO VARIOUS BUSINESSES AND THEIR BUSINESS MODELS."
HOW COULD I SHARE ALL THE STORIES IN ONE, CONCISE POST?
I GOT IT! LET'S MAKE A VIDEO!!
AND SOON THEREAFTER ...
ALL SET! ARE YOU READY?
READY, SHELDON!
YAP.

THIS IS THE BUSINESS MODEL CANVAS. IT ALLOWS YOU TO DRAW ANY EXISTING OR IMAGINARY BUSINESS IN THE WORLD WITH THESE NINE BUILDING BLOCKS.

DURING THE SUMMER IN AUSTRALIA I LEARNED A LOT ABOUT CUSTOMERS AND HOW TO INTERACT WITH THEM.

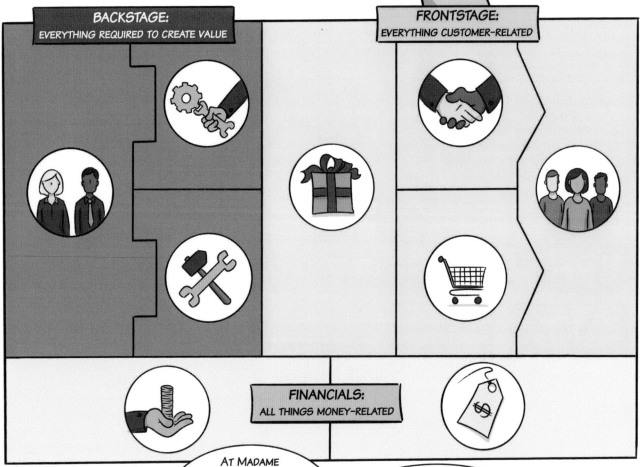

BACKSTAGE: EVERYTHING REQUIRED TO CREATE VALUE

FRONTSTAGE: EVERYTHING CUSTOMER-RELATED

FINANCIALS: ALL THINGS MONEY-RELATED

AT MADAME TUSSAUDS IN LONDON I GAINED SOME INSIGHTS OF THE BACKSTAGE OF A BUSINESS. THERE ARE MANY THINGS GOING ON BEHIND THE SCENES THAT YOU CAN NOT SEE AT FIRST.

IN TOKYO WE ALL LEARNED QUITE A BIT ABOUT ALL THINGS MONEY-RELATED IN A BUSINESS.

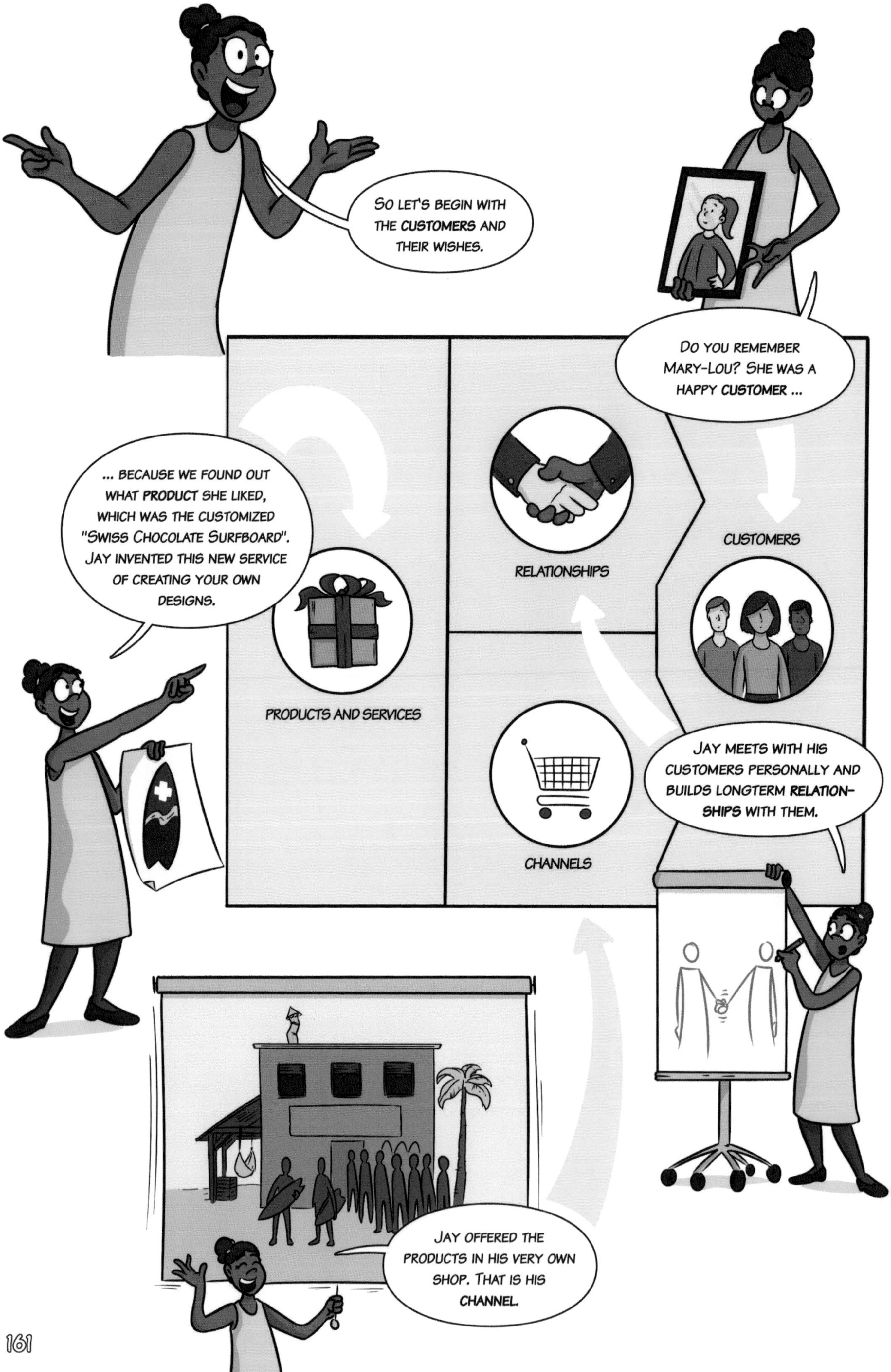
SO LET'S BEGIN WITH THE CUSTOMERS AND THEIR WISHES.
DO YOU REMEMBER MARY-LOU? SHE WAS A HAPPY CUSTOMER ...
... BECAUSE WE FOUND OUT WHAT PRODUCT SHE LIKED, WHICH WAS THE CUSTOMIZED "SWISS CHOCOLATE SURFBOARD". JAY INVENTED THIS NEW SERVICE OF CREATING YOUR OWN DESIGNS.
RELATIONSHIPS
CUSTOMERS
PRODUCTS AND SERVICES
CHANNELS
JAY MEETS WITH HIS CUSTOMERS PERSONALLY AND BUILDS LONGTERM RELATIONSHIPS WITH THEM.
JAY OFFERED THE PRODUCTS IN HIS VERY OWN SHOP. THAT IS HIS CHANNEL.

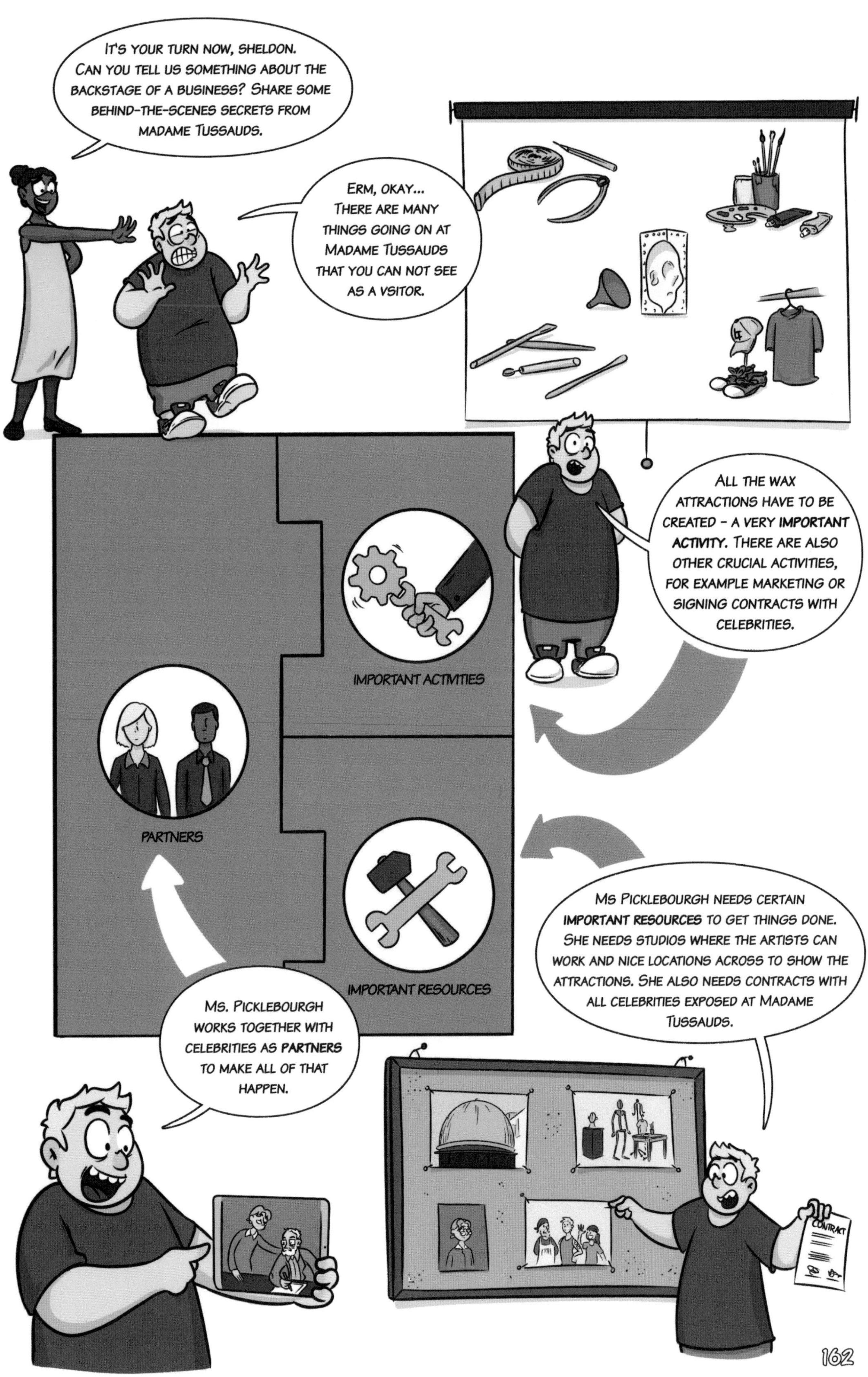
IT'S YOUR TURN NOW, SHELDON. CAN YOU TELL US SOMETHING ABOUT THE BACKSTAGE OF A BUSINESS? SHARE SOME BEHIND-THE-SCENES SECRETS FROM MADAME TUSSAUDS.
ERM, OKAY... THERE ARE MANY THINGS GOING ON AT MADAME TUSSAUDS THAT YOU CAN NOT SEE AS A VSITOR.
ALL THE WAX ATTRACTIONS HAVE TO BE CREATED - A VERY **IMPORTANT ACTIVITY**. THERE ARE ALSO OTHER CRUCIAL ACTIVITIES, FOR EXAMPLE MARKETING OR SIGNING CONTRACTS WITH CELEBRITIES.
IMPORTANT ACTIVITIES
PARTNERS
IMPORTANT RESOURCES
MS PICKLEBOURGH NEEDS CERTAIN **IMPORTANT RESOURCES** TO GET THINGS DONE. SHE NEEDS STUDIOS WHERE THE ARTISTS CAN WORK AND NICE LOCATIONS ACROSS TO SHOW THE ATTRACTIONS. SHE ALSO NEEDS CONTRACTS WITH ALL CELEBRITIES EXPOSED AT MADAME TUSSAUDS.
MS. PICKLEBOURGH WORKS TOGETHER WITH CELEBRITIES AS **PARTNERS** TO MAKE ALL OF THAT HAPPEN.
CONTRACT

THAT'S ALL. YOUR TURN, YUKI.
THANKS, SHELDON.
HERE IN TOKYO MY FRIENDS AND I FOUND OUT HOW YOU DEAL WITH MONEY IN A BUSINESS.
MR MIFUNE EARNS MONEY FROM EVERY DRONE DELIVERY.
HE GETS PAID FOR HIS SUSHI AND HE GETS A FEE FROM THE OTHER RESTAURANT OWNERS FOR EVERY SINGLE DRONE FOOD DELIVERY VIA HIS PLATFORM. THIS IS HIS REVENUE.
PIZZA
COSTS
REVENUES
RUNNING A BUSINESS HAS ITS COSTS. MR MIFUNE PAID ME FOR DEVELOPING THE DELIVERY APP AND PLATFORM. HE ALSO NEEDS TO BUY FOOD FOR SUSHI PREPARATION. THEN HE SPENDS MONEY TO ATTRACT OTHER RESTAURANTS TO HIS DELIVERY APP.
SINCE HE BOUGHT THE BUILDING, HE IS NOW ALSO SAVING MONEY. HE DOESN'T NEED TO PAY THE RENT ANYMORE.
AS LONG AS HE EARNS MORE MONEY THAN HE SPENDS HIS BUSINESS WORKS.

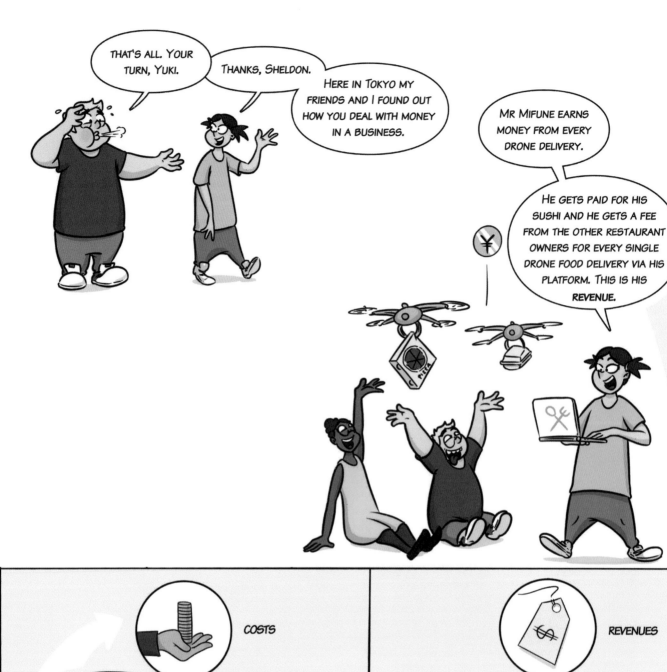

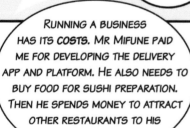

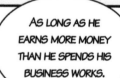

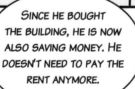

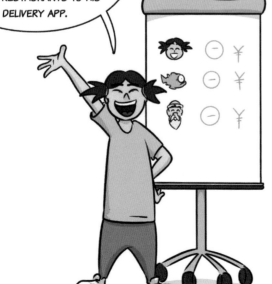

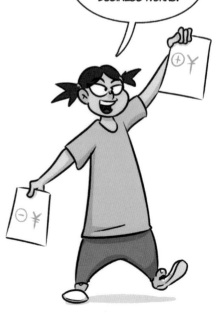

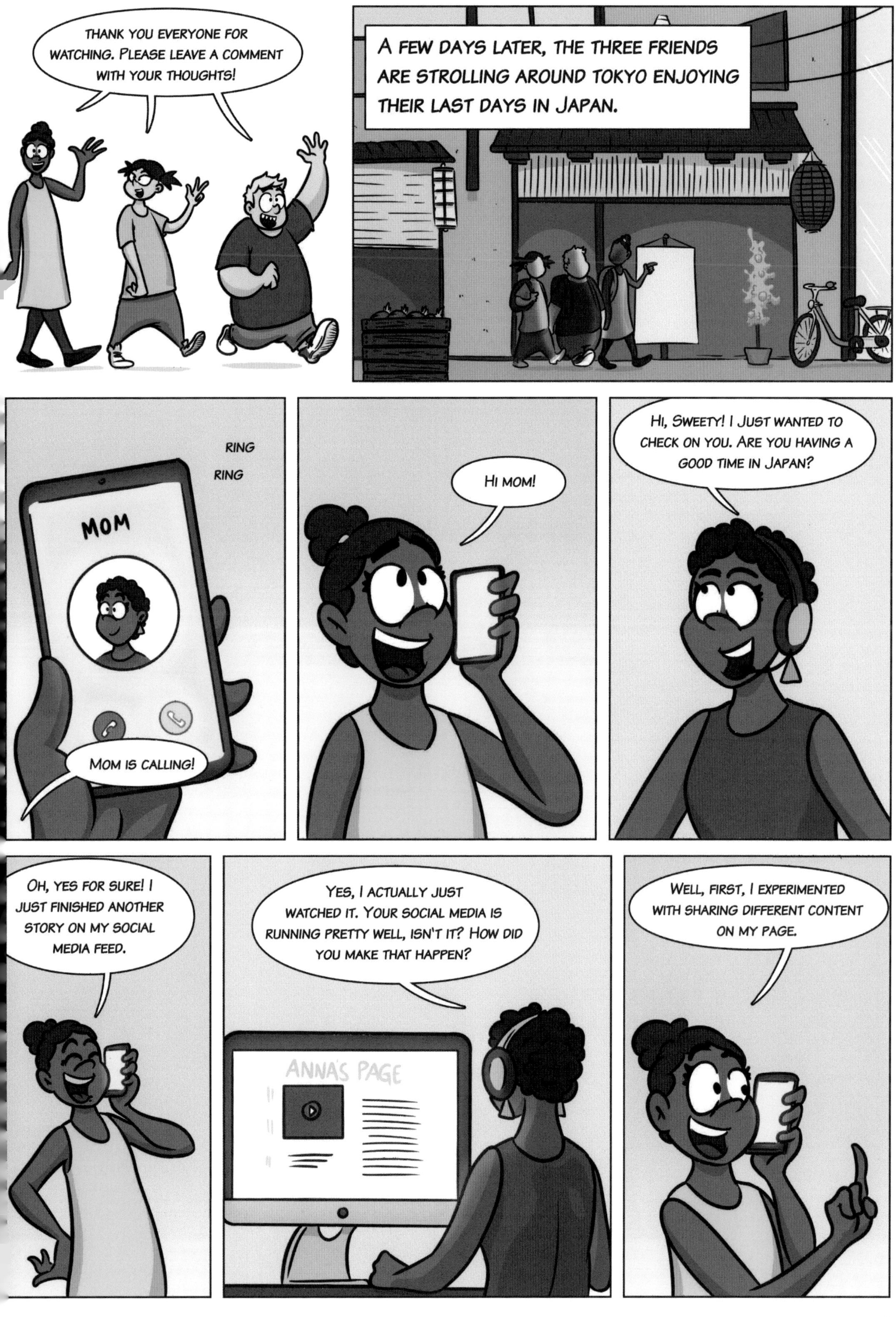
THANK YOU EVERYONE FOR WATCHING. PLEASE LEAVE A COMMENT WITH YOUR THOUGHTS!
A FEW DAYS LATER, THE THREE FRIENDS ARE STROLLING AROUND TOKYO ENJOYING THEIR LAST DAYS IN JAPAN.
RING
RING
MOM
MOM IS CALLING!
HI MOM!
HI, SWEETY! I JUST WANTED TO CHECK ON YOU. ARE YOU HAVING A GOOD TIME IN JAPAN?
OH, YES FOR SURE! I JUST FINISHED ANOTHER STORY ON MY SOCIAL MEDIA FEED.
YES, I ACTUALLY JUST WATCHED IT. YOUR SOCIAL MEDIA IS RUNNING PRETTY WELL, ISN'T IT? HOW DID YOU MAKE THAT HAPPEN?
ANNA'S PAGE
WELL, FIRST, I EXPERIMENTED WITH SHARING DIFFERENT CONTENT ON MY PAGE.

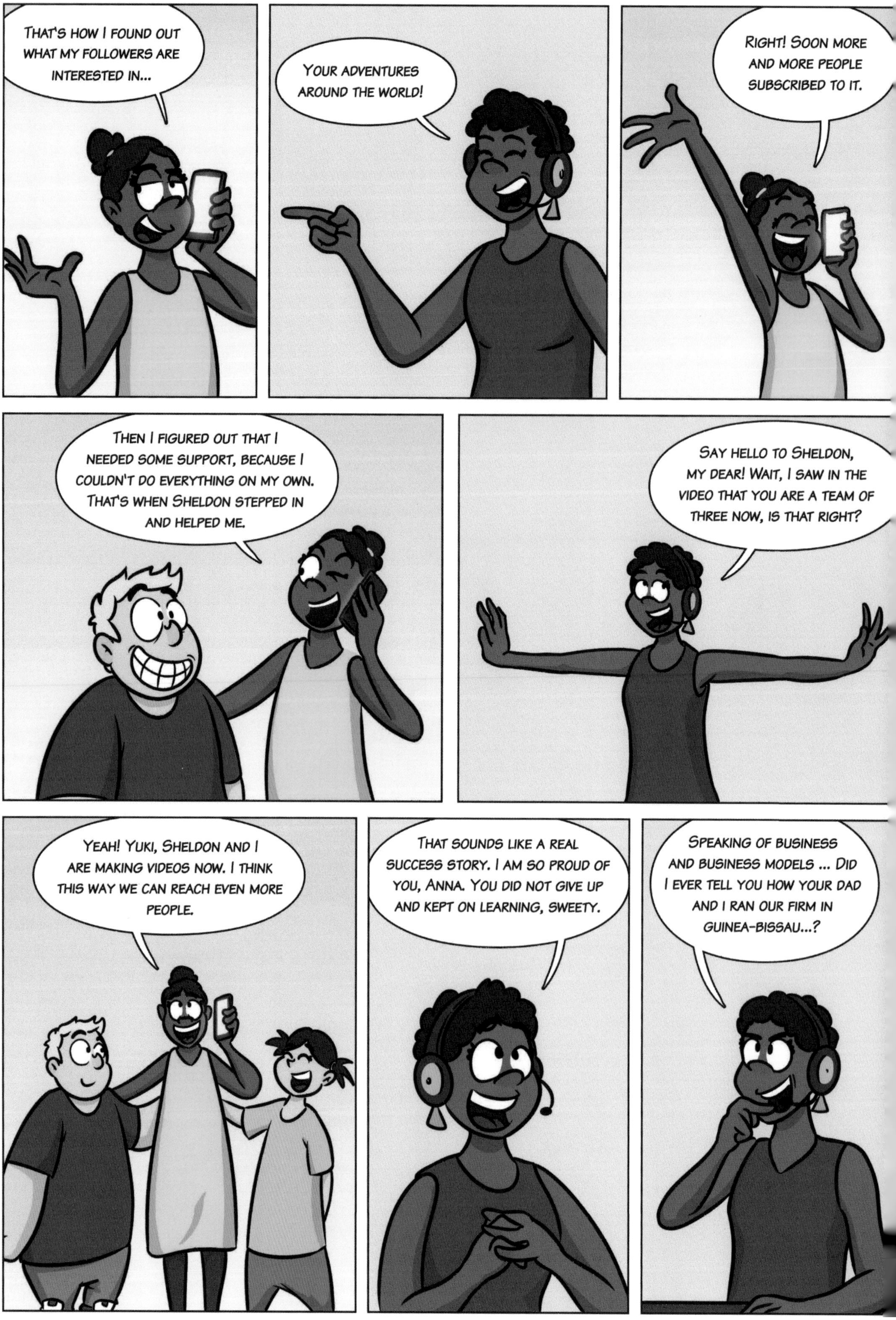
THAT'S HOW I FOUND OUT WHAT MY FOLLOWERS ARE INTERESTED IN...
YOUR ADVENTURES AROUND THE WORLD!
RIGHT! SOON MORE AND MORE PEOPLE SUBSCRIBED TO IT.
THEN I FIGURED OUT THAT I NEEDED SOME SUPPORT, BECAUSE I COULDN'T DO EVERYTHING ON MY OWN. THAT'S WHEN SHELDON STEPPED IN AND HELPED ME.
SAY HELLO TO SHELDON, MY DEAR! WAIT, I SAW IN THE VIDEO THAT YOU ARE A TEAM OF THREE NOW, IS THAT RIGHT?
YEAH! YUKI, SHELDON AND I ARE MAKING VIDEOS NOW. I THINK THIS WAY WE CAN REACH EVEN MORE PEOPLE.
THAT SOUNDS LIKE A REAL SUCCESS STORY. I AM SO PROUD OF YOU, ANNA. YOU DID NOT GIVE UP AND KEPT ON LEARNING, SWEETY.
SPEAKING OF BUSINESS AND BUSINESS MODELS ... DID I EVER TELL YOU HOW YOUR DAD AND I RAN OUR FIRM IN GUINEA-BISSAU...?

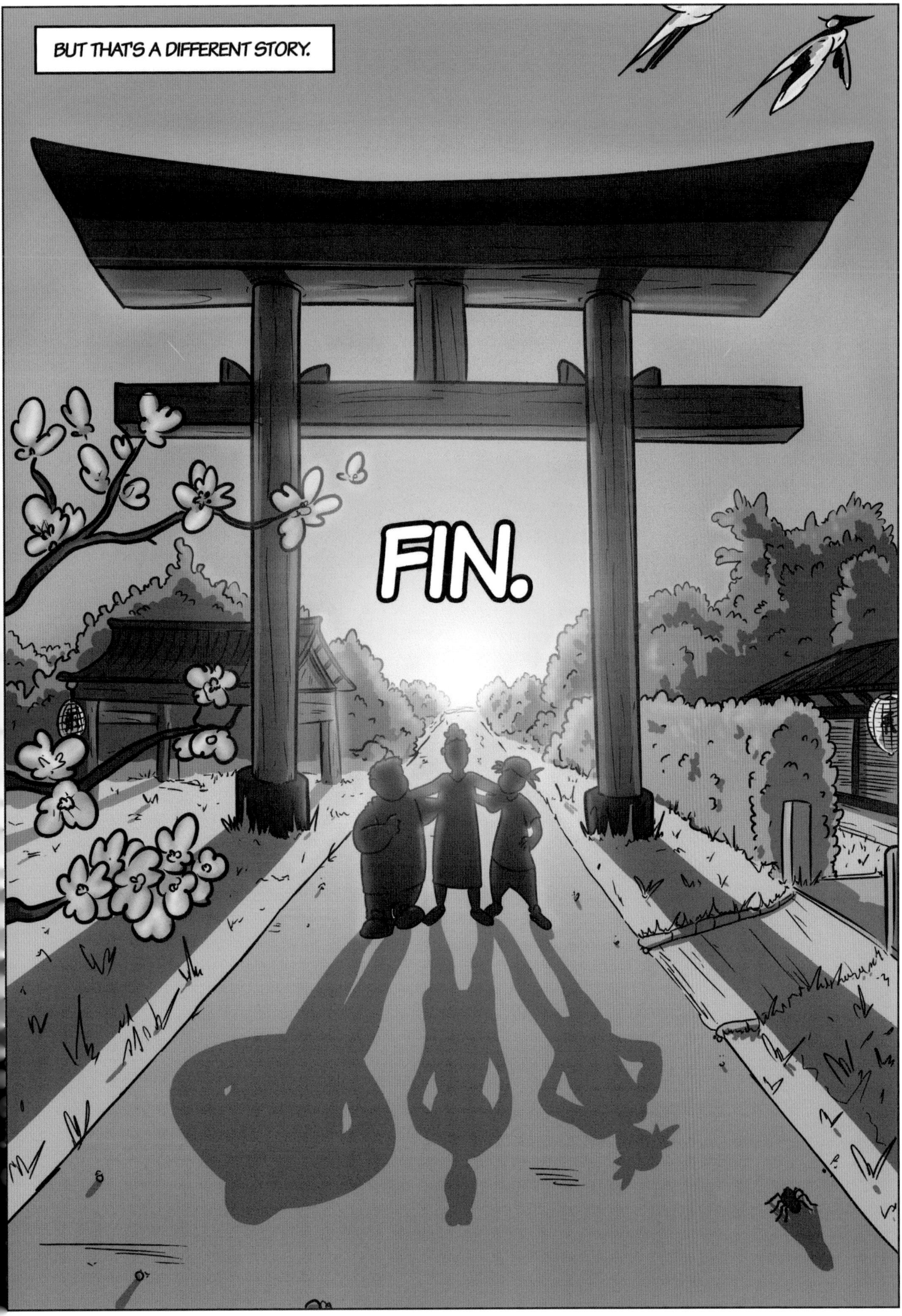
BUT THAT'S A DIFFERENT STORY.
FIN.

"HOW ABOUT CREATING YOUR OWN DREAM BUSINESS BY FILLING OUT THE BUSINESS MODEL CANVAS NOW?
AND DON'T FORGET THAT YOU DON'T HAVE TO GET IT RIGHT IMMEDIATELY. EXPERIMENT WITH YOUR IDEA AND ADAPT IT UNTIL IT WORKS WITH CUSTOMERS AND REVENUES ARE BIGGER THAN COSTS. ENJOY!"

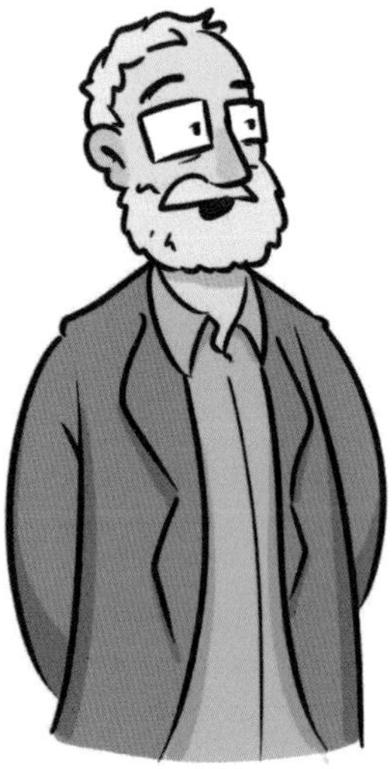

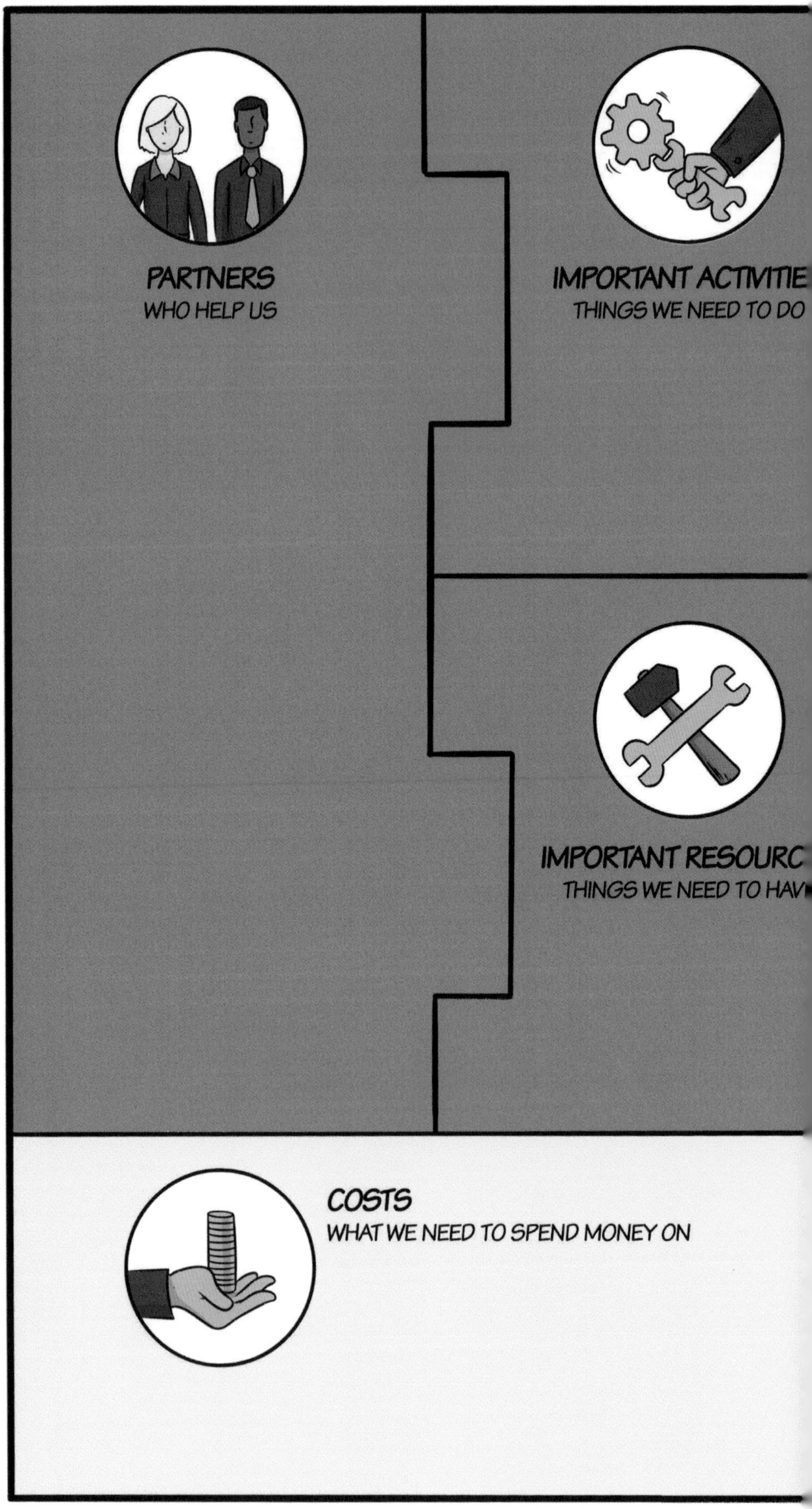
PARTNERS
WHO HELP US
IMPORTANT ACTIVITIE
THINGS WE NEED TO DO
IMPORTANT RESOURC
THINGS WE NEED TO HAV
COSTS
WHAT WE NEED TO SPEND MONEY ON

YOU CAN WRITE ALL THINGS RELATED TO YOUR BUSINESS IDEA ON STICKY NOTES AND PUT THEM INTO THE RELATED BUILDING BLOCKS.

TRY TO HAVE SOMETHING IN EVERY BUILDING BLOCK! THAT WAY YOU START TO SEE THE WHOLE PICTURE OF YOUR BUSINESS.

ODUCTS AND SERVICES
WHAT WE SELL

RELATIONSHIPS
HOW WE INTERACT WITH CUSTOMERS

CUSTOMERS
WHO WE SELL TO

CHANNELS
HOW WE REACH CUSTOMERS

REVENUES
HOW WE EARN MONEY

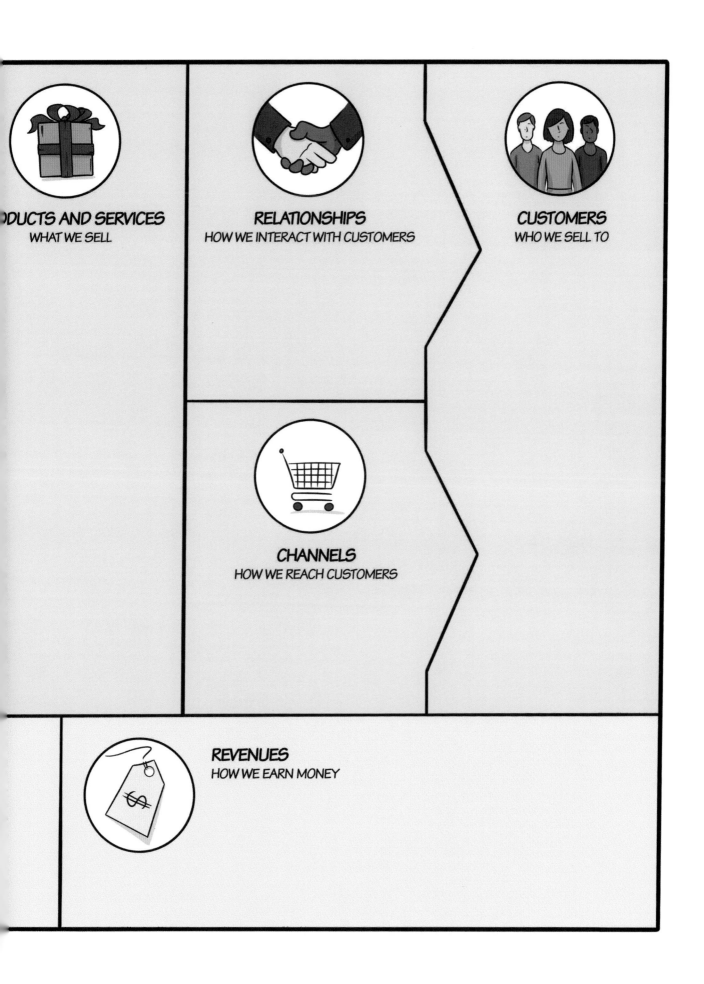

Printed in Great Britain
by Amazon